Lecture Notes in Computer
Edited by G. Goos, J. Hartmanis, and J

Springer

Berlin
Heidelberg
New York
Barcelona
Hong Kong
London
Milan
Paris
Tokyo

Paddy Nixon   Sotirios Terzis (Eds.)

Trust Management

First International Conference, iTrust 2003
Heraklion, Crete, Greece, May 28-30, 2003
Proceedings

 Springer

Series Editors

Gerhard Goos, Karlsruhe University, Germany
Juris Hartmanis, Cornell University, NY, USA
Jan van Leeuwen, Utrecht University, The Netherlands

Volume Editors

Paddy Nixon
Sotirios Terzis
University of Strathclyde
Department of Computer and Information Sciences
Livingstone Tower
26 Richmond Street, Glasgow, G1 1XH, UK
E-mail: {Paddy.Nixon/Sotirios.Terzis}@cis.strath.ac.uk

Cataloging-in-Publication Data applied for

A catalog record for this book is available from the Library of Congress.

Bibliographic information published by Die Deutsche Bibliothek
Die Deutsche Bibliothek lists this publication in the Deutsche Nationalbibliografie;
detailed bibliographic data is available in the Internet at <http://dnb.ddb.de>.

CR Subject Classification (1998): H.4, H.3, H.5.3, C.2.4, I.2.11, K.4.3-4, K.5

ISSN 0302-9743
ISBN 3-540-40224-1 Springer-Verlag Berlin Heidelberg New York

Springer-Verlag Berlin Heidelberg New York
a member of BertelsmannSpringer Science+Business Media GmbH

http://www.springer.de

© Springer-Verlag Berlin Heidelberg 2003
Printed in Germany

Typesetting: Camera-ready by author, data conversion by PTP-Berlin GmbH
Printed on acid-free paper   SPIN: 10927885   06/3142   5 4 3 2 1 0

Preface

iTrust is an Information Society Technologies (IST) working group, which started on 1st of August, 2002. The working group is being funded as a concerted action/ thematic network by the Future and Emerging Technologies (FET) unit of the IST program.

The aim of iTrust is to provide a forum for cross-disciplinary investigation of the application of trust as a means of establishing security and confidence in the global computing infrastructure, recognizing trust as a crucial enabler for meaningful and mutually beneficial interactions.

The proposed forum is intended to bring together researchers with a keen interest in complementary aspects of trust, from technology-oriented disciplines and the fields of law, social sciences, and philosophy. Hence providing the consortium participants (and the research communities associated with them) with the common background necessary for advancing toward an in-depth understanding of the fundamental issues and challenges in the area of trust management in open systems. Broadly the initiative aims to:

- facilitate the cross-disciplinary investigation of fundamental issues underpinning computational trust models by bringing together expertise from technology oriented sciences, law, philosophy, and social sciences
- facilitate the emergence of widely acceptable trust management processes for dynamic open systems and applications
- facilitate the development of new paradigms in the area of dynamic open systems which effectively utilize computational trust models
- help the incorporation of trust management elements in existing standards.

One of the first concerted activities of this forum has been to organize this, the First International Conference on Trust Management, specifically to bring together active researchers interested in trust management in all its forms (technological, legal, or societal). The response to this conference has been excellent. From the 58 submissions, we have brought together in this volume 24 papers by some of the leading world experts. The program also includes three keynote addresses from Stuart Feldman, IBM VP Internet Technology, Bernardo Huberman, HP Fellow and Director Systems Research Center, Hewlett Packard Laboratories, and Theo Papatheodorou, Professor, University of Patras and Chair, Cultural Heritage Digitization Committee, Greek Ministry of Culture.

The running of an international conference requires an immense amount of work from all those people on the program committee and the local organizing committee. We would like to warmly thank them for the exceptional hard work. In particular we would like to thank Professor Christos Nikolaou for being the driving force that started this whole thing.

April 2003   Paddy Nixon and Sotirios Terzis

Organization

The First International Conference on Trust Management was organized by iTrust, a Working Group on Trust Management in Dynamic Open Systems, and the University of Crete and partially funded by the Future and Emerging Technologies (FET) unit of the European IST program.

Executive Committee

Conference Chair:	Christos Nikolaou, U. of Crete, Greece
Program Chair:	Paddy Nixon, U. of Strathclyde, UK
Tutorials:	Theo Dimitrakos, CLRC, UK
Demonstrations:	Dimitris Tsigos, Virtual Trip Ltd, Greece
Panels:	Christian D. Jensen, Trinity College, Ireland and DTU, Denmark

Local Organizing Committee

Eva Michelidaki	U. of Crete, Dissemination
Calliope Anagnostopoulou	U. of Crete, Local accommodation
Yota Spetsidi	U. of Crete, Registration
Shore Shadman	U. of Crete, Registration
Kyriakos Papadakis	U. of Crete, Webmaster
Michalis Klisarchakis	U. of Crete, Webmaster
Vasilis Poursalidis	U. of Crete, Networking Systems
Elias Theoharopoulos	U. of Crete, Networking Systems

Program Committee

Nikos Alivizatos	U. of Athens, Greece
Eliza Bertino	U. of Milan, Italy
Jon Bing	NRCCL, U. of Oslo, Norway
Joan Borrell	Autonomous University of Barcelona, Spain
Sandro Castaldo	Università Bocconi, Italy
Cristiano Castelfranchi	CNR, Italy
Manuel Castells	University of California, Berkeley, USA
Stefano Cerri	University of Montpellier II and CNRS, France
Rosaria Conte	CNR and University of Siena, Italy
Mark Roger Dibben	University of St. Andrews, UK
Theo Dimitrakos	CLRC, UK
George Doukidis	Athens University of Economics and Business, Greece
Rino Falcone	CNR, Italy
Peter Herrmann	U. of Dortmund, Germany
Valerie Issarny	INRIA, France
Keith Jeffery	CLRC, UK
Christian D. Jensen	Trinity College, Ireland and DTU, Denmark
Andrew Jones	King's College, UK
Audun Josang	DSTC, Australia
Graham Klyne	Nine by Nine, UK
Heiko Krumm	U. of Dortmund, Germany
Ninghui Li	Stanford University, USA
Ian Lloyd	University of Strathclyde, UK
Manolis Marazakis	Plefsis, Greece
Erich Neuhold	Darmstadt University of Technology and Fraunhofer IPSI, Germany
Stefan Poslad	Queen Mary College, UK
Dimitris Raptis	Intracom, Greece
Elena Rocco	University of Venice, Italy and University of Michigan, USA
Jakka Sairamesh	IBM Research, USA
Giovanni Sartor	U. of Bologna, Italy
Simon Shiu	Hewlett Packard, UK
Morris Sloman	Imperial College, UK
Bruce Spencer	National Research Council, Canada
Ketil Stoelen	SINTEF, Norway
Yao-Hua Tan	Free University of Amsterdam, Holland
Sotirios Terzis	U. of Strathclyde, UK
Dimitris Tsigos	Virtual Trip Ltd, Greece
Stavroula Tsinorema	U. of Crete, Greece
Emily Weitzenboeck	NRCCL, U. of Oslo, Norway

Table of Contents

First International Conference on Trust Management

Architecture and Algorithms for a Distributed Reputation System

Michael Kinateder* and Kurt Rothermel

University of Stuttgart
Institute of Parallel and Distributed Systems (IPVS)
Breitwiesenstr. 20-22
70565 Stuttgart, Germany
Phone +49-711-7816-{230, 434}
{michael.kinateder, kurt.rothermel}@informatik.uni-stuttgart.de

Abstract. Trust is an essential component of successful interactions in social life as well as in business relationships. In this paper we propose a system that closely reflects real-world trust building in an online environment. We describe the models used to represent trust in entities in various categories, algorithms to calculate and update trust based on experiences of entities with each other and the agent interactions necessary for finding and exchanging trust information.

1 Introduction

The explosive growth of electronic commerce that has come to life over the last decade and has built up what has become known as the New Economy, has finally come to a stagnation. The question has to be answered what the factors are that determine the success or failure of electronic business. Analysts agree (see [1]) that trust is essential for successful business and the ability to build consumer trust is a vital factor of successful B2C electronic commerce. It has furthermore been shown, that the uncertainty of potential buyers about the reputation of online sellers is among the most prominent inhibiting elements. Therefore technology is needed that can be used to convey trust.

1.1 Motivation and Problem Description

As mentioned before it is vital for successful B2C electronic commerce to enable users to build trust into online vendors and their offerings. Trust building in the offline world occurs in various ways, e.g. through repeated good experiences with a product or service, through marketing and branding of a company, through reviews from reputable sources like the "Better Business Bureau" or similar organizations or through hearsay about opinions from friends and acquaintances.

When examining the online environment, some of these elements can already be seen. Obviously there is online marketing and branding at the companies'

---

* This work is funded by Hewlett-Packard Limited.

P. Nixon and S. Terzis (Eds.): Trust Management 2003, LNCS 2692, pp. 1–16, 2003.

websites. Concerning product reviews we note the existence of several more or less well-visited product rating services[1]. Especially when demanding at least a certain degree of privacy there is little online support available for the word-of-mouth area, arguably one could count *www.askme.com* in this category.

What we do not want to do is setting up yet another product review site. The problem that we see is that there is already trust data available from a multitude of different sources and users are simply swamped with finding and rating the quality of this information. We are proposing a completely distributed mechanism that allows entities being in the phase of decision making to *find information* about experiences other entities have in the same area, to *access* this information, to *estimate the trustworthiness* of those information sources, to *condense the information* received and to get a standardized view on the results to *present* to the user.

1.2 Organization

In Section 2 we will present the terms and definitions used in this paper. We proceed in Section 3 to describe basic usage scenarios and use these to derive a set of requirements from the recommender's and requester's side.

Section 4 describes our system from the modeling view by firstly focusing on the system model which is followed by a presentation of the trust model that our work relies heavily upon. We then show briefly the content of the knowledge model which is necessary to understand the system and lastly describe what we understand by a recommendation.

The dynamic interactions between the agents at the different participants are shown in Section 5. Section 6 will provide an overview of related work in the area of trust building and especially in the area of recommendation systems but also trust management issues in general and point out some limitations of the approaches taken so far that we strive to address.

Section 7 describes the open issues and future work and concludes our paper.

1.3 Contributions

The contributions of this paper lie in the identified requirements of the participants of a recommendation system presented in Section 3 and foremost in the fine-grained trust model proposed in Section 4. To the best of our knowledge, the modeling of dependencies of trust categories has not been done before in a recommendation system context. The directed diffusion approach we take in Section 5 in order to send out recommendation requests to is novel in this context as well.

---

[1] *http://www.allexperts.com,*
   http://www.epinions.com

2   Terms and Definitions

2.1   Trust in the Literature

In an informal way, trust in an entity can be explained as the belief that under certain circumstances this entity will perform in a certain way. More formally, Merriam-Webster's Collegiate Dictionary states, that trust is the

> *assured reliance on the character, ability, strength, or truth of someone or something.*

Another definition of trust commonly found is the one of Diego Gambetta in [2] "... trust (or, symmetrically, distrust) is a particular level of the subjective probability with which an agent assesses that another agent or group of agents will perform a particular action...". Lik Mui [3] is adapting this definition slightly in emphasizing the importance of expectation instead of working with probability:"Trust: a subjective expectation an agent has about another's future behavior based on the history of their encounters". We adopt Lik Mui's definition here.

2.2   Reputation

The reputation of entity A in our view is the *average trust* (whatever average means in that context) of *all other entities* towards A. Therefore reputation clearly has a global aspect whereas trust is viewed from a local and subjective angle.

2.3   Experience

Trust of entity A in an entity B in a certain category is built by making experiences with that entity in the category in question. An experience in this context is therefore an observation of A about some behavior of entity B. It is necessary to be able to judge whether an experience has been positive or negative in order to update A's trust in B in the category in question.

2.4   Recommendation

A recommendation in our work is by its nature *subjective* information regarding some aspects like quality, reliability of a target in a target category. Experiences made with an entity are published as a recommendation about the target. The value of a recommendation originating from recommender A for a recipient B depends on the trust of B in A regarding the category of the recommendation in question.

3   Usage Scenarios and Requirements

In the following we will describe the basic usage scenarios of a recommendation system. Starting from these we will point out the requirements of the involved parties and their implications for the recommendation system.

3.1   Usage Scenarios

Two basic usage scenarios can be immediately identified for a recommendation system, namely *publishing recommendations* and *requesting recommendations*.

An entity that is about to create a recommendation has made an experience with a second entity and intends to publish the gained knowledge. Therefore it has to be able to identify the target of the recommendation clearly and include this information in the recommendation so that requesters know without doubt what target is meant.

An entity A that needs advice about a target T will use a recommendation system to formulate a query for recommendations about T. In order to do that, A needs to be able to identify T uniquely and include this target identity in the query. The query is sent to the system and hopefully responses matching the query will be received. The system should be able to condense the data, accumulate the recommendations (if possible, e.g. in cases of numerical ratings) and present the results to A.

3.2   Requirements of the Participants

Requester's Requirements. *Recommendations should fit the query.* As has already been mentioned before, the target of a recommendation has to be uniquely identifiable in order to match a query.

Good quality recommendations. This requirement seems self-explanatory, however it leads directly to three other requirements.

In order to be able to enforce a good quality of recommendations, it is firstly imperative to be able to *provide feedback* to the system about the quality of the recommendation. In case the experience of the requester does not match the one of the recommender, this negative feedback can be used to prevent this requester from receiving further recommendations from the unfitting recommender.

Secondly we need to *link recommendations to their recommenders* in order to identify the recommender and to process the feedback of the requester.

Thirdly to ensure good quality there is the requirement for *timeliness of recommendations*. Especially in highly dynamic areas like for instance recommendations about stock options it is important to receive a new recommendation as quickly as possible after it appeared.

Modeling of real-world trust relationships. As a starting point for the system the requester needs the possibility to include the already existing trust towards colleagues, friends and acquaintances.

Fine-grained trust modeling. An entity might choose to trust another entity only in certain areas whereas doing not so in others. Therefore instead of using just one trust value per entity it is necessary to model a fine-grained set of categories, where this entity can be trusted or not. To our knowledge this requirement is not fulfilled in the related work to the extent presented here.

Recommender's Requirements. *Control over collection of personal data.* To counter the danger of abusing the system for detecting buying habits and generating detailed user profiles (e.g. for direct marketing purposes) we could anonymize the recommendations. However this conflicts with the abovementioned requirement to bind a recommendation to its recommender and the identity is the only place where to attach a it is impossible to build a reputation. We suggest therefore to write recommendations using one or more pseudonyms that do in a way identify the recommender but are not linkable to the real-world identity. In fact we suggest to use one pseudonym for each area of interest of the recommender to complicate breaking the link between real identity and pseudonym.

Control over recommendations. The recommender might want to limit access to sensitive recommendations to a certain group of requesters. Therefore, identity management is needed to handle authentication and authorization tasks. The related work reviewed so far offers no identity management capabilities.

Ensure the authenticity of recommendations. The system has to prevent giving out recommendations in another recommender's name. To solve this issue, the author proposes to add a digital signature to the recommendation. In order not to compromise the privacy issues mentioned above we need a digital certificate that is not bound to the real identity but instead to the pseudonym the recommender is using.

Ease of use. This requirement is aimed at limiting the recommender's disturbance by the recommendation system as much as possible. From the requester's point of view it certainly would be interesting to be able to contact good recommenders with inquiries whereas those popular recommenders most likely would be overwhelmed with the number of requests. The suggested solution for this lies in storing the recommendations and making them accessible for requesters but removing the possibility for requesters to contact recommenders directly.

4 Models for Reputation Systems

In this Section we identify the models necessary for implementing a distributed reputation system, namely the system model, the trust model and the knowledge model in addition to a brief description of the potential content of the communicated information items.

4.1 System Model

The system model we base our work on is closely related to that of a *peer-to-peer* system with distributed *stationary* or *mobile nodes* that have communication capabilities with other nodes. On each of those nodes resides one or more *agents* each in context of a certain *entity* which will be in most cases the end-user of the system. Each user is utilizing different *identities* which might range from the user's real identity to various pseudonyms in order to give or request recommendations up to complete anonymity for requesting recommendations. Each user has his or her own local copy of the *trust-* and *knowledge model.*

As will be described in the following section in more detail we introduce a *neighbourhood* for each entity as overlay over the real network topology for each category that takes into account the developed trust in the various identities (*I1* to *I8* in Fig. 1) in the category in question. There is not necessarily connectivity to all nodes of the neighbourhood at every given point in time. The reachable members of the corresponding neighbourhood are queried first for each recommendation request.

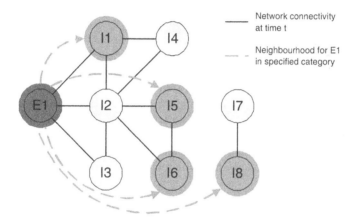

Fig. 1. Neighbourhood in a Certain Category.

Neighbourhood Formation: The set of identities *ONet(category C, entity E, level L)* in the neighbourhood for category *C* that can be "reached" from entity *E* in *L* hops is calculated as follows:

We define *ONet(category C, entity E, 1)* as the set of directly connected identities (in the neighbourhood) to an entity *E* in category *C*. The membership of an identity *I* in this local view or level 1 view of the neighbourhood of an entity *E* is determined by an algorithm described in the following Section that is relying on two inputs: *E's* trust in *I* (stored in its trust model) and *I's* advertised expertise (from *E's* knowledge model entry about *I*).

$$ONet(C, E, L) = \bigcup_{\forall E' \in ONet(C,E,1)} ONet(C, E', L - 1)$$

Example: The level 1 view of entity *E1* on the neighbourhood is initially a tree with height one with root *E1* and leaves *I1, I5, I6* and *I8*. The four entities in the level 1 neighbourhood of *E1* however also build each a height-one tree and therefore form the level 2 neighbourhood for *E1*. Obviously loops are possible in this structure (e.g. *I1* might trust *E1*), therefore we talk about a *directed graph* (with direction from root to leaves) instead of a tree.

Observation: Due to the asymmetry of trust, the neighbourhood observed by *E1* might contain or be contained in the neighbourhood observed by *E2* or might be a completely different "island of trust".

4.2 Trust Model

Content of the Trust Model. Due to the diverse nature of trust, our model consists of a set of *categories* with one *trust value* and one corresponding *confidence vector* for each category.

We define the trust values in the range from 0..1 with 0 indicating either no previous experiences or just bad experiences with that entity in the category and 1 indicating the maximum trust. We assume that having no previous experiences is similar to only bad experiences for the reason that it is relatively simple to switch to a new pseudonym as soon as the old one got a bad reputation. Therefore we set the initial trust in each category to 0 although this can be set manually to a different value for known trusted entities to transfer the real world trust into the system.

The confidence vector stores meta-information used to judge the quality of the trust value and contains the following entries:

- number of direct experiences in that category
- number of indirect experiences (from categories influencing the one in question)
- trail of the last n direct experiences (n depends on the storage capacities of the system the agent is running on) with the associated recommender confidences (see Section 4.4)
- black list flag

20 good experiences have more impact than just one good experience, therefore the total number of experiences in the category and the derived information from other categories are valuable confidence indicators. Keeping track of a certain number of previous experiences with an entity enables the user to better understand a certain trust level and make on-the-fly trust calculations (e.g. by adjusting the parameters of the trust update algorithm). The black list flag is set by the user to prevent recommendations from the selected identity in the category in question to be taken into account at all.

Organization of the Trust Model. We stress the fact, that those trust categories are not strictly independent but they are *influencing* each other in certain ways. What we want to do therefore is modeling *semantic closeness* and other relationships between the categories.

Chen and Singh are considering this effect up to a certain degree in their work [4], as they are organizing trust categories in a hierarchy by using "instance of" relationships with the leaf categories holding the comments (or experiences as we call them) and the trust of the non-leaf categories being calculated from them. We found two drawbacks of this solution: Firstly - as illustrated in the example in Fig. 2 - the hierarchy is not a suitable approach for all sets of categories.

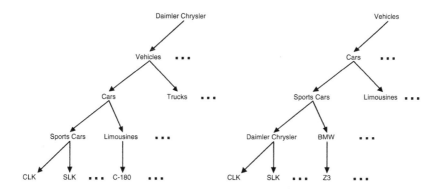

Fig. 2. Problems with a Strict Hierarchy.

The left arrangement in the Fig. makes perfect sense, since persons with expertise in Daimler Chrysler sports cars will most certainly also possess a certain knowledge about other cars of this company. Yet the right side models the fact, that experts in Daimler Chrysler sports cars know something about sports cars in general. Thus a single hierarchy is obviously not enough. Secondly, relationships between categories do not necessarily need to be of the type "instance of", thus modeling trust in such a way would limit the general usability of the model significantly

We introduce therefore a *directed graph of categories* with *weighted vertices* representing the impact of the source category on the target category as presented in Fig. 3. This is an example about how part of such a *dependency graph* may look like with the focus on the category "security books". A good experience with a security book review of recommending identity I will lead to an increase in E's trust in I in the security book category and also (to a much lesser degree with 7% impact as opposed to a direct experience in cryptography) to an increase in trust in cryptography and so on. The weights presented here are example values to illustrate the idea and not validated against reality. In our initial system those weights are set manually by the user, who supposedly knows best the existing relationships between his or her areas of interest. As a later step it might be challenging to investigate, how these relationships can be detected and if this process can be automated.

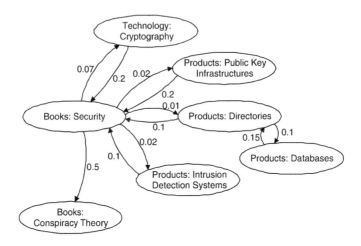

Fig. 3. Dependency Graph of Categories.

4.3 Knowledge Model

What we refer to as knowledge model is a way of creating a local profile at each participant about "who knows what" including each participant's own knowledge. Hence it is used for advertising own expertise areas to other participating entities of the system and keeping track of the expertise of others.

The *own expertise* in a participant's knowledge model consists of a set of category-value pairs with the categories being derived from the trust model and the values denoting the number of recommendations stored in this category. This information is communicated. However for privacy reasons not all categories are communicated by the recommender as such. Instead the content is published in *knowledge parts* with each part being covered by one pseudonym.

For being able to evaluate the *expertise of others*, the number of own recommendation requests is stored for each category in the knowledge model. In addition to that each recipient of a knowledge part stores the provided information under the category and identity in his or her knowledge model and includes a confidence vector (different from the one in the trust model) to each (potential) recommending identity that contains the total number of recommendation responses received via this identity (from other recommenders) and the number of responses with the recommendation being published by this identity (as recommender) in the specified category. This information allows to keep track of the value of the identity as a *hub* (knowing many other recommenders for that category) as well as an *authority* (having stored many recommendations).

4.4   Recommendations or Trusted Information Items

Recommendations in our initial system consist of the three main components *target*, *rating* and a *digital identity* of the recommender. The target information item identifies the recommendation target (another entity, certain product or service, digital content,...) through the recommendation's category in addition to a hierarchical name. Various different types of rating information could be included in the recommendation, like binary ratings ("we recommend the target, or we do not"), percentage values ("the product has a quality of 70%"), multiple attribute-rating pairs, textual reviews or any combination of the former ones.

When discussing the system with colleagues researching in this field we found it to be important to add a *confidence value* to the rating, specifying the recommender's own confidence in the given statement. The confidence influences the impact of this recommendation for the trust update when processing the requester's feedback (see Section 5.5). A recommendation identifier and time of creation is added to facilitate recommendation handling and timeliness checks. In order to prove the authenticity of the recommendation, a digital signature is added under the appropriate pseudonym that the recommender uses for creating recommendations of the category in question.

Instead of focusing on ratings only we could take a more general approach and combine the target and rating to a generic information item. The result is a general reputation system that handles signed (trusted) information items and provides support for judging their quality.

5   System Interactions

In this section we focus on the interactions between the various components and models of the system at the different participants necessary for locating fitting recommendations. Other interactions are necessary for the system to work but are left out due to the limited scope of this paper. The process is divided into the five subtasks of *disseminating* the request, *collecting* responses, *processing* the responses, *organizing* the results and *providing* and *processing feedback* for the system.

5.1   Dissemination of Request

In order to understand the dissemination of the request it is important to keep in mind the recursive structure of the neighbourhood introduced in the previous section. The request message contains the *identity* of the requester, a *request identifier*, the *recommendation target* (target category plus a filter specifying the target more closely), the *trust chain* and a *hop counter*.

The *trust chain* is used to compute the trust of the requester in the recommender and is built during the request dissemination. It contains at *intermediate identity* I_i a list of intermediate identities I_j $(1 \leq j \leq i)$ including the trust T_j of I_{j-1} in I_j with I_0 being the requester.

Once the request message is built by the agent at the requester it is sent to the agents of the reachable members of the level 1 neighbourhood for the corresponding category. Each recipient I_i then processes the *algorithm* described in Fig. 4.

```
calculate trust of Req. in Ii via the current trust chain
if not((request already processed) AND (with higher trust)) {
    if (suitable recommendation available) {
        create recommendation response
        send recommendation response back to Req.
    }
    decrease hopcounter
    if (hopcounter > 0) {
        foreach (member Ij of ONet-1 of Ii) {
            (* create set of new requests *)
            create copy of received request
            insert digitally signed trust statement:
            {
                trust of Ii in Ij
                (pseudonymous) identity of Ii
            }
            send request to Ij
        }
    }
}
```

Fig. 4. Directed Dissemination Algorithm.

5.2 Collection of Recommendations

Each identity $I's$ agent capable of fulfilling the recommendation request (therefore with one or more fitting recommendations in store) is creating a *recommendation response message* that contains a request identifier, the stored and digitally signed (by the recommender that is not necessarily I) recommendation and the trust chain whose last link is the trust of I in the recommender. This recommendation response is sent back directly to the requester.

5.3 Processing Each Received Recommendation

A recommendation is generally not only available at the recommender's agent but can instead be stored at any interested participant's agent. Furthermore those recommendations are not necessarily all up-to-date e.g. due to network partitioning. The reader should note that the same recommendation (same recommender, identifier and version) can be received via completely different paths through the neighbourhoods of the intermediate recommenders leading to different trust chains. What needs to be done here is to *evaluate* the different trust chains from requester to recommender and produce *one* trust value that can be attached to each received recommendation.

One simple option to determine the resulting trust T from a single trust chain (with T_1 denoting the trust of the requester in identity I_1 and T_n denoting the trust in the recommender) is taking the product of all trust values. In an optimistic approach, the strongest trust chain determines the resulting trust that is attached. In the case of direct trust of the requester in the recommender, this direct trust takes precedence over the strongest chain if the number of experiences with the recommender in the trust model is sufficiently high, that is if there is a sufficient amount of certainty in the direct trust. For every kept recommendation the number of responses from this identity is increased in the knowledge model.

$$T = \prod_{i=1}^{n} T_i$$

A second and advanced option is to take into account the *strength of the links* in the trust chains, therefore including into the trust chain the number of direct and indirect experiences in addition to the trust in the next intermediate recommender.

After the trust in the recommender has been computed, all outdated recommendations (same recommender, recommendation identifier but older version) are discarded and just the most current version of each recommendation is kept. For every kept recommendation response and for every identity in the trust chains the number of recommendation responses in the knowledge model of the corresponding identity is increased.

5.4   Organizing the Results

The organization of the results depends on the type of rating information in the recommendation in question. Recommendations with textual reviews or multiple rated attributes are organized by their trust value and highly trusted recommendations are presented first in order to the requester. For the same trust value recommendations with a higher recommender confidence are presented first. Binary ratings of the same value can be accumulated in discrete groups depending on the trust value. For percentage ratings not only the recommendations but also the ratings themselves are categorized in that manner and presented to the requester as a matrix.

5.5   Feedback Handling

The step of handling feedback can be divided in the three sub-steps of *collecting the user feedback, updating trust* and *updating the neighbourhood.*

Collecting User Feedback. The requester has to state what recommendation was fitting in his or her view and which one was not. For binary ratings it is sufficient to specify the "right" answer whereas for percentage values the "correct" range has to be defined. For textual reviews or multiple attribute ratings the process of collecting user feedback cannot be automated and every single recommendation has to be rated.

With this rating the requester has made an *experience* with a recommending identity which is either a *good* or *bad* one. For each identity the experience and the recommender confidence are added to the trust model and the number of direct experiences is increased in the appropriate category.

Updating Trust. The new trust T_{new} in each category is calculated from the old trust T_{old} and the new experience E and is influenced by an aging factor a, the recommender's own confidence in the recommendation c and a distance factor d depending on the distance of the category in question from the original category of the recommendation in the dependency graph.

$$T_{new} = (1 - (a \cdot c \cdot d)) \cdot T_{old} + (a \cdot c \cdot d) \cdot E$$

The aging factor in the range of $]0..1[$ is specific to each category and influences how fast new experiences of the requester change the trust compared to previous experiences. The confidence factor influences the impact of a certain recommendation on the trust update and is under recommender's control. The distance factor handles the influence of an experience in the original category on related categories in the dependency graph. d is the maximum of the products of weights for all paths in the dependency graph from the original category to the category in question. Every trust update in a related category leads to an increase in its number of indirect experiences in the trust model. For efficiency reasons it is necessary to impose a certain limit to the trust update of dependency categories for long distances (reflected in a small d.

This trust update formula does not yet increase the *emphasize of negative experiences* as opposed to positive experiences. Future work will provide different update algorithms and an thorough investigation of their features.

Updating the Neighbourhood. After the trust values have been updated it is necessary to update the identities in the level 1 neighbourhood as well. A certain number of each of three types of identities are chosen (not disjunctive): *reputable identities* (high trust), *confirmedly experienced identities* (high knowledge) and *random* identities.

The decision which reputable recommenders to choose could be made by taking the n recommenders with the most direct experiences and trust over a certain threshold. Concerning the confirmedly experienced identities it might be wise to choose half of those with most recommendations received via themselves and half of those where most recommendations originated from. A certain proportion of identities randomly chosen from all the remaining ones with advertised knowledge in the category is necessary to allow identities not yet popular (since trust is initialized with 0) to be queried and gain a reputation.

6   Related Work

Our approach is related to the *trust management* work of Matt Blaze, Joan Feigenbaum and Jack Lacy. They describe in [5] their trust management system Policymaker. The follow-up work called KeyNote has been published as an Internet RFC in [6]. What they are doing mainly is specifying and interpreting security policies, credentials and relationships in order to allow their system to handle direct authorization of actions instead of the traditional approach of dividing the authorization task in authentication and access control.

Work has been published that is dealing with *trust modeling*, and we will not put our focus on the centralized trust modeling issues but instead consider the *distributed* trust modeling approaches that have been taken so far. Jonker and Treur [7] are proposing a formal framework for the notion of trust within distributed agent systems. They are mainly investigating trust developed through experiences and define properties of what they call trust evolution and trust update functions. Our proposed models and algorithms fit into their framework.

Rahman et al. are working in the area of *trust development* based on *experiences* and describe in [8] a trust model and several algorithms about how trust can be created, distributed and combined. The trustworthiness of an agent is determined based on direct experiences of an agent and recommendations from other agents. The rather ad-hoc nature of some of these algorithms has to be further clarified. Lik Mui et al. are also working in this field and have shown in [3] a computational model of trust and reputation. Neither Rahman's nor Mui's work however gives insights about context respectively categories of reputation.

The area of *recommendation systems* can be categorized in the *centralized* and *distributed* approaches and furthermore in *commercial* applications and *research* work.

The first category being *centralized commercial recommendation systems* is filled by the mechanisms used for example at the Internet auction site eBay, where buyer and seller of an auction can rate each other after a transaction has taken place with a binary value. Although the rating is quite simplistic, having only the possibilities of positive, neutral or negative feedback plus a single line of text describing the reason for the rating, several surveys have shown, that this rating system contributes significantly to the success of eBay, even is vital to the functioning of this auction site. Besides eBay, there are other sites like Amazon, where users can give product ratings and write textual reviews.

The *scientific work* in *centralized recommendation systems* includes among others the work of a group around Konstan and Riedl on Grouplens [9], a collaborative filtering system used for rating Usenet News in order to help people find articles they will like. The term recommendation system in this context has a dual meaning, since it is not only the users recommending articles but also the system recommending suitable articles to its users. The category of algorithms dealing with this problem is known as collaborative filtering. The MIT media lab and Patty Maes have been very active in researching reputation mechanisms. Sporas and Histos are to be named as being the most renowned systems they developed (see [10]) so far.

There is still comparably little *commercial work* in *distributed recommendation systems*. Noteworthy is the Poblano project (see [11]), SUNs work on reputation in their JXTA peer-to-peer architecture. Poblano introduces a decentralized trust model with trust relationships not only between peers but also between peers and content (what they refer to as "codat", code or data). "Trust" in a peer is calculated here based on the content this peer has stored in addition to its performance and reliability.

Scientific work in *distributed recommendation systems* is also still relatively rare. The trust modeling work of Rahman et al can be implemented in a distributed fashion as Karl Aberer and Zoran Despotovic mention in [12]. They are furthermore proposing a model where they focus completely on negative recommendations (complaints) to derive trust in an agent and describe distributed storage issues and trust calculation algorithms for their model.

To summarize the related work here it can be concluded that there are reputation systems out there, but they are either depending on a single merchant or specific product category or under control of one company. The recently published work on distributed recommendation systems shows that this is a promising area worthwhile to pursue further.

7   Conclusions and Future Work

In this paper we have presented models and algorithms for a distributed reputation system with fine-grained trust modeling taking the dependencies of trust categories into account. It allows trust building in other entities while at the same time protecting its participant's privacy. More privacy and identity management aspects of this system can be found in [13].

Currently we have started with the development of a prototype of the proposed system. As soon as that is finished, we will work on a test setup with volunteers to use the system. From the test setup we hope to gain insights on the soundness of the algorithms and a feeling on how to adjust the parameters.

We are going to work further on trust update algorithms that take into account the dynamics of trust, that is the fact that *trust is hard to build* and *easy to destroy*. Furthermore we will investigate how to take into account the strengths of the links in the trust chain evaluation algorithm. Another real challenge for future research is to analyze the possibilities of automatic dependency handling in the trust model.

References

1. Cheskin Research: Trust in the Wired Americas (2000)
   Available via *http://www.cheskin.com/*.
2. Gambetta, D.: Can We Trust Trust? In: Trust: Making and Breaking Cooperative Relations, Department of Sociology, University of Oxford (2000) 213–237
   Available via *http://www.sociology.ox.ac.uk/papers/gambetta213-237.pdf*.
3. Mui, L., Mohtashemi, M., Halberstadt, A.: A Computational Model of Trust and Reputation. In: Proc. of the 35th Hawaii International Conference on System Sciences, Big Island, Hawaii, IEEE (2002)

4. Chen, M., Singh, J.P.: Computing and Using Reputations for Internet Ratings. In: Proc. of the 3rd ACM conference on Electronic Commerce, Tampa, USA (2001) 154–162

5. Blaze, M., Feigenbaum, J., Lacy, J.: Decentralized Trust Management. In: Proc. of the 17th IEEE Symposium on Security and Privacy, Oakland (1996) 164–173

6. Blaze, M., Feigenbaum, J., Ioannidis, J., Keromytis, A.D.: The KeyNote Trust-Management System. RFC 2704, Network Working Group, IETF (1999)

7. Jonker, C., Treur, J.: Formal Analysis of Models for the Dynamics of Trust Based on Experiences. In: Proc. of the 9th European Workshop on Modelling Autonomous Agents in a Multi-Agent World. Volume 1647 of LNAI., Valencia, Springer-Verlag (1999)

8. Abdul-Rahman, A., Hailes, S.: Supporting Trust in Virtual Communities. In: Proc. of the 33rd Hawaii International Conference on System Sciences, Maui Hawaii (2000)

9. Sarwar, B.M., Konstan, J.A., Borchers, A., Herlocker, J.L., Miller, B.N., Riedl, J.: Using Filtering Agents to Improve Prediction Quality in the Grouplens Research Collaborative Filtering System. In: Proc. of the 1998 ACM Conference on Computer Supported Cooperative Work (CSCVO), Seattle (1998) 345–354

10. Zacharia, G., Moukas, A., Maes, P.: Collaborative Reputation Mechanisms in Electronic Marketplaces. In: Proc. of the 32nd Hawaii International Conference on System Sciences, Maui Hawaii (1999)

11. Chen, R., Yeager, W.: Poblano – A Distributed Trust Model for Peer-to-Peer Networks. Technical report, Sun Microsystems, Inc. (2001) Available via *http://www.jxta.org/project/www/docs/trust.pdf.*

12. Aberer, K., Despotovic, Z.: Managing Trust in a Peer-2-Peer Information System. In: Proc. of the 9th International Conference on Information and Knowledge Management (CIKM 2001), Atlanta (2001)

13. Kinateder, M., Pearson, S.: A Privacy-Enhanced Peer-to-Peer Reputation System. (Submitted for Publication.)

Regularity-Based Trust in Cyberspace

Naftaly H. Minsky*

Rutgers University, New Bruswick NJ 08903, USA,
minsky@cs.rutgers.edu,
http:www.cs.rutgers.edu/~minsky/

Abstract. One can distinguish between two kinds of trust that may be placed in a given entity e (a person or a thing), which we call: *familiarity-based* trust and *regularity-based* trust. A familiarity-based trust in e is a trust based on personal familiarity with e, or on testimonial by somebody who is familiar, directly or indirectly, with e; or even on some measure of the general reputation of e. A regularity-based trust is based on the recognition that e belongs to a class, or a community, that is known to exhibits a certain regularity—that is, it is known that *all* members of this class satisfy a certain property, or that their behavior conforms to a certain law. These two types of trust play important, and complementary, roles in out treatment of the physical world. But, as we shall see, the role of regularity-based trust in out treatment of the cyberspace has been limited so far because of dif c ulties in establishing such trust it in this context. It is this latter kind of trust, which is the focus of this paper.

We will describe a mechanism for establishing a wide range of regularity-based trusts, and will demonstrate the effectiveness of this mechanism, by showing how it can enhance the trustworthiness of a certain type of commercial client-server interactions over the internet.

1 Introduction

One can distinguish between two kinds of trust that may be placed in a given entity e (a person or a thing), which we call: *familiarity-based* trust and *regularity-based* trust—or, for short, "F-trust" and "R-trust", respectively. A familiarity-based trust in e is a trust based on personal familiarity with e, or on testimonial by somebody who is familiar with e, directly or indirectly, or even on some measure of the general reputation of e [9]. A regularity-based trust, on the other hand, is based on the recognition that e belongs to a class, or a community, that is known to exhibits a certain regularity—that is, it is known that *all* members of this class satisfy a certain property, or that their behavior conforms to a certain law. Both types of trust play important, and complementary, roles in the physical world. But, as we shall see, the role of regularity-based trust in cyberspace has been limited so far, because of difficulties in establishing it in this context. It is this latter kind of trust, which is the focus of this paper.

To illustrate the nature of regularity-based trust, and its importance, we now consider three familiar examples of regularities (or, approximate regularities, to be exact) in the physical world, and we will discuss the trust they engender:

---

* Work supported in part by NSF grant No. CCR-98-03698

R1: *Everything that goes up must come down.*
R2: *Dollar bills are not forged.*
R3: *Drivers stop at an intersection when they see a red light.*

Although none of these regularities is absolute, they all generate degrees of trust which makes the world we live in simpler and more manageable. The trust engendered by R1 contributes to the predictability of the natural world; this, in spite of the fact that R1 is not satisfied by objects whose speed relative to Earth exceeds the *escape velocity*. The trust engendered by R2 simplifies commerce, in spite of the fact that dollar bills are sometime forged. The occasional violations of R2 does have an effect on the degree of trust emanating from it, as is evident from the fact that while one usually excepts individual dollar bills at their face value, one is likely to check $100 bills more carefully. Finally, it is hard to imagine vehicular traffic without the trust engendered by R3, which allows one to drive through a green light without slowing down. The unfortunately limited validity of R3 is the reason that careful drivers tend to take a quick look at their left and right before crossing an intersection at a green light.

The remarkable usefulness of regularity-based trust is due to the fact that it allows one to deal with a whole class of entities in a uniform manner, without having to be familiar with the individual member at hand—once an entity is recognized as a member. For example, we usually know nothing about the driver we encounter at an intersection, beyond the fact that he or she is driving a car on the road—and thus assumed to satisfy R3. This advantage of R-trust is not shared by familiarity-based trust, which deals with individuals. It is true that *public-key infrastructures* (PKIs), provides for massive and scalable authentication of the identity and roles of principals [19,8] via distribution of certificates; but each such certificate require a degree of familiarity, by somebody, with the individual being certified. The advantage of F-trust, on the other hand, is that it can provide one with comprehensive information about a given individual; while R-trust provides just the common denominator of a class of entities, and thus cannot be very specific. For example, R3 tells us nothing about where would a given driver go after stopping at a red light, which we might know if we are familiar with him, or with her.

It is also important to note that R-trust often relies on certain F-trust, so that these two types of trusts are not quite independent. For example, our trust in R1 is based, for the non-physicists among us, on familiarity with our physics teachers, who told us about Newton's laws, and on the reputation of the physics textbooks we read. And our trust in R2 relies on the reputation of the bank in charge of printing money. We will see additional example of this phenomenon later.

Now, how are regularities established, and what are the reasons for trusting them? In the physical world, one can distinguish between two kinds of regularities: *natural regularities*, like R1 above, which are due to the laws of nature; and *artificial regularities*, like R2 and R3, induced by societal laws, policies and customs. Of course, passing a social law, or declaring an organizational policy, does not, by itself, generate a regularity. One needs some means for ensuring that this law or policy is actually obeyed. Such means include, self interest, social mechanism of enforcement, and physical constraints. For example, the main reason that traffic laws like R3 are generally complied with, is the personal danger in violating them—dangers from other cars, and from the police. And the reasons that money is generally not being forged is due to the physical difficulty of forging money bills (which is becoming easier lately, due to the improving printing technology), together with the fear of being caught in violating the social laws prohibiting forging.

The problem we are facing in establishing R-trust in cyberspace, is that many of the factors that support regularities in the physical world—like physical constraints, and the fear of being caught violating a law—do not exist, or are less effective, over the internet. Nevertheless, certain types of trust-generating regularities do exist in cyberspace, playing critical roles in it. The most important of these is the natural regularity of *complexity of computation*. That is, the universal difficulty of solving certain computational problems. This regularity gives rise to *cryptography* [20], which is, in turn, the foundation on which much of the current trust-management [4,13] technology rests. But in spite of its critical importance for generating trust, the range of regularities that can be *directly* established via cryptography is rather limited. For example, although it is possible to represent money via digital certificates, cryptography alone cannot stop such certificates from being duplicated—which means that *physical cash* cannot be directly represented cryptographically. (We will return to this point later in this paper.)

It is also possible to establish *artificial regularities* in cyberspace, simply by means of *voluntary compliance* with declared policies. This is how important regularities such as the use of HTML for writing web pages, and the use of IP for communication, have been established all over the internet. But the effectiveness of voluntary compliance as a means for establishing regularities is severely limited. Indeed, for voluntary compliance with a given policy P to be reliable, the following two conditions need to be satisfied: (a) it must be the vested interest of everybody to comply with P; and (b) a failure to comply with P, by somebody, or somewhere, should not cause any serious harm to anybody else. If condition (a) is not satisfied (as under R2) then there is little chance for P to be observed everywhere, even if it is declared as a standard. And if condition (b) is not satisfied (as it is under R3) than one has to worry about someone not observing P, perhaps inadvertently, and thus causing harm to others.

Clearly, the only way to ensure conformance with a policy that does not satisfy conditions (a) or (b) above, is to *enforce* it. If the community subject to this policy is small enough, then such enforcement can sometimes be carried out by employing a *trusted third party* (TTP) to function as a kind of *reference monitor* [1], which mediates all the interactions subject to it. This has been done by several projects [3,12], mostly in the context of distributed enterprise systems. But if the community is large, as is often the case over the internet, then the use of a single reference monitor is inherently unscalable, since it constitute a dangerous single point of failure, and could become a bottleneck if the system is large enough. This difficulty can be alleviated when dealing with static (stateless) policies, simply by replicating the reference monitor—as has been done recently in [14].

But replication is very problematic for *dynamic* (or, *stateful*) policies, which are sensitive to the history, or state, of the interactions being regulated. This is because every state change sensed by one replica needs to be propagated, synchronously, to all other replicas of the reference monitor. Such synchronous update of all replica could be very expensive, and is quite unscalable. And dynamic policies are very important for many trust-related applications. In particular, things like *separation of duties* [7,10], the so called Chinese Wall (CW) policy [5], and the effects of the expiration or revocation of a certificate on the power of an agent holding it [2], are all dynamic. Dynamic policies are particularly important for fostering regularity-based trust in electronic commerce, as we will illustrate via an example in the following section. All such dynamic policies would be very hard to enforce scalably via centralized reference monitors, whether replicated or not.

It is the purpose of this paper to show that it is possible to establish a wide range of regularity-based trusts, dynamic and otherwise, by employing a genuinely decentralized approach to policy enforcement, which is based on the following principles:

1. *Policies are to be formulated* locally, *so that the ruling of the policy regarding operations by a given subject depends dynamically only on the history of its own interactions with the rest of the community.*
2. *The enforcement of a policy over a given community is to be carried out by a* set of trusted-third-parties, *one per member of the community, acting as reference monitors, all interpreting the same policy.*

In Section 3 we will outline a mechanism called *law-governed interaction* (LGI), which has been designed according to these principles, and whose current prototype implementation has already been applied to a wide range of distributed and dynamic policies. In Section 4 we present a case study that shows how the this mechanism can be used to support trustworthy e-commerce, by enforcing the example policies introduced in Section 2. We conclude in Section 5, with an examination of the complementary interrelationship between familiarity-based trust and regularity-based trust.

2   Towards Regularity-Based Trust in E-commerce – An Example

The purpose of this section is to demonstrate the potential usefulness of R-trust in cyberspace, and the difficulty of establishing such trust via conventional techniques. For this purpose, we will postulate a certain form of commercial client-server interaction. And we will propose a couple of highly dynamic policies which should ease this interaction, making it more trustworthy—provided that they are enforced, and thus made into regularities.

Consider a large and open community C, distributed over the internet, whose members provide each other with *prepaid* services. Let the standard service request in this community be a message of a form order(specs,fee), where specs specifies the nature of the requested service, and fee is the payment for the service requested, which can be very small—few cents, say. To ease the interaction between clients and servers, making it more efficient and more trustworthy, we introduce here two policies: (a) a policy regarding the treatment of e-cash, used as payment for services, and (b) a policy regarding the response by the server to an order. These policies are described informally, and motivated, below; they would be formalized via an LGI law in Section 4.

The Cash Handling (CH) Policy: Given the possibly small size of payments for services, the use of traditional kind of e-cash certificates is not practical. Because, as has been pointed out by Glassman et. al. [11], each such certificate would have to be validated by the issuing bank, whenever used, for fear of duplication. This is far too expensive for small payments. We would like, therefore, payments to be carried out just like cash payment in the physical world. This should be possible if the following cash handling (CH) policy is established as a regularity among all clients and servers.

1. *Each member of the community must be able to withdraw cash from an account he/she/it has in some bank, storing it in its own* electronic wallet. *(Banks used for this purpose must be authenticated by a specified CA).*
2. *The payment included in an order sent by agent x must be taken from the electronic wallet of x, just as physical cash is taken from one's physical wallet.*
3. *When a payment is obtained by server y, it is to be added to its electronic wallet; and can then be used by orders made by y, or for depositing in y's bank account.*

This policy, if enforced, would be an improvement over the Millicent protocol devised by Glassman et. al. [11] for a similar purpose. Under the Millicent protocol clients use vendor-signed *scrips* for payments. Such scrips are copyable, and thus needs to be validated by the vendor, for every query, which requires a centralized database of valid scrips. Moreover, the vendor has to send a new scrip to the client, as his change. All this involves substantial overhead, and is not very scalable because of the centralized database that it employs. Under our CH policy, however, none of this overhead would be necessary—provided that individual agents in community C can be trusted to observe this highly dynamic policy.

A Policy Regarding Server's Response (SR): Clients generally cannot predict the time it would take the server to carry out his order, in particular because the server may have a backlog of prior orders. Moreover, suppose that the server may end up declining the order, because it is too busy, or because it is unable or unwilling to carry it out for some other reasons. This situation presents the following difficulties for clients: First, once an order is sent, the client may be stuck, waiting indefinitely for the service to be performed, with his money tied up in an order that may eventually be declined. Second, the client has no certainty that if the order is declined his money will be ever returned.

To alleviate these difficulties, we would like to provide clients with the assurance that the following (SR) policy regarding response to service orders is satisfied for all their orders:

> *Once a client* x *sends a message* order(specs,fee) *to a server* y, *he is guaranteed to receive one of the following two responses within a* bounded delay D, *which is independent of (and generally much smaller than) the time it takes to carry out the requested service itself:*
> 1. *The message* accept(specs,fee), *which signifies that the server agrees to carry out the service, for the specified fee.*
> 2. *The message* decline(spec,fee), *which is signifies that the server declines the service order,* returning, *in this message, the* fee *sent by the client.*

Note that SR has nothing to say about the time it should take to carry out the requested service, nor does it provide any assurances that the service will be carried out properly, or at all. Yet, if this policy can be established as a regularity, for any order, sent to any server in community C, it would provide the following advantages:

- An accept(specs,fee) message from a server y can be viewed as a commitment by y to carry out this service for the specified fee. If this message can be authenticated as coming from y, then it can be used by the client, *in a court of law*, as a proof of this commitment. (Authentication of such messages cab be accomplished via cryptography; the proof in a court of law is not a technical matter, of course.)
- The assurance, provided by SR, that every order will be either accepted or declined within D seconds, with the money returned in the latter case, allows a client to plan a "shopping expedition" — by trying out a sequence of servers, one each D seconds, until somebody accept the order.

3   The Concept of Law-Governed Interaction (LGI) – An Overview

Broadly speaking, LGI is a message-exchange mechanism that allows an *open* group of distributed agents to engage in a mode of interaction *governed* by an explicitly specified and strictly enforced policy, called the *interaction-law* (or simply the "law") of the group. The messages thus exchanged under a given law $\mathcal{L}$ are called $\mathcal{L}$-messages, and the group of agents interacting via $\mathcal{L}$-messages is called an $\mathcal{L}$-community $\mathcal{C_L}$ (or, simply, a *community* C.)

We refer to members of an $\mathcal{L}$-community as *agents*[1], by which we mean autonomous actors that can interact with each other, and with their environment. An agent might be an encapsulated software entity, with its own state and thread of control, or a human that interacts with the system via some interface. Both the *subjects* and the *objects* of the traditional security terminology are viewed here as agents. A community under LGI is *open* in the following sense: (a) its membership can change dynamically, and can be very large; and (b) its members can be heterogeneous. For more details about LGI, and about its implementation, than provided by this overview the the reader is referred to [18], and to [23] for more recent results.

3.1   On the Nature of LGI Laws, and Their Decentralized Enforcement

The function of an LGI law $\mathcal{L}$ is to regulate the exchange of $\mathcal{L}$-messages between members of a community $\mathcal{C_L}$. Such regulation may involve (a) restriction of the kind of messages that can be exchanged between various members of $\mathcal{C_L}$, which is the traditional function of access-control policies; (b) transformation of certain messages, possibly rerouting them to different destinations; and (c) causing certain messages to be emitted spontaneously, under specified circumstances, via a mechanism we call obligations.

---

[1] Given the currently popular usage of the term "agent", it is important to point out that we do not imply either "intelligence" nor mobility by this term, although we do not rule out either of these.

A crucial feature of LGI is that its laws can be *stateful*. That is, a law $\mathcal{L}$ can be sensitive to the dynamically changing *state* of the interaction among members of $C_\mathcal{L}$. Where by "state" we mean some function of the history of this interaction, called the *control-state* (CS) of the community. The dependency of this control-state on the history of interaction is defined by the law $\mathcal{L}$ itself.

But the most salient and unconventional aspects of LGI laws are their strictly local formulation, and the decentralized nature of their enforcement. To motivate these aspects of LGI we start with an outline of a centralized treatment of interaction-laws in distributed systems. Finding this treatment unscalable, we will show how it can be decentralized.

On a Centralized Enforcement Interaction Laws: Suppose that the exchange of $\mathcal{L}$-messages between the members of a given community $C_\mathcal{L}$ is mediated by a reference monitor $\mathcal{T}$, which is trusted by all of them. Let $\mathcal{T}$ consist of the following three part: (a) the law $\mathcal{L}$ of this community, written in a given language for writing laws; (b) a generic *law enforcer* $\mathcal{E}$, built to interpret any well formed law written in the given law-language, and to carry out its rulings; and (c) the control-state ($\mathcal{CS}$) of community $C_\mathcal{L}$ (see Figure 1(a)). The structure of the control-state, and its effect on the exchange of messages between members of $C_\mathcal{L}$ are both determined by law $\mathcal{L}$. .

This straightforward mechanism provides for very expressive laws. The central reference monitor $\mathcal{T}$ has access to the entire history of interaction within the community in question. And a law can be written to maintain any function of this history as the control-state of the community, which may have any desired effect on the interaction between community members. Unfortunately, this mechanism is inherently unscalable, as it can become a bottleneck, when serving a large community, and a dangerous single point of failure.

Moreover, when dealing with stateful policies, these drawbacks of centralization cannot be easily alleviated by replicating the reference monitor $\mathcal{T}$, as it is done in the Tivoli system [14], for example. The problem, in a nutshell, is that if there are several replicas of $\mathcal{T}$, then any change in $\mathcal{CS}$ would have to be carried out *synchronously* at all the replicas; otherwise x may be able to get information from other companies in set s, via different replicas. Such maintenance of consistency between replicas is very time consuming,and is quite unscalable with respect to the number of replicas of $\mathcal{T}$.

Fortunately, as we shall see below, law enforcement can be genuinely *decentralized*, and carried out by a distributed set $\{\mathcal{T}_x \mid x \mathrm{in} C\}$ of, what we call, *controllers*, one for each members of community C (see Figure 1(b)). Unlike the central reference monitor $\mathcal{T}$ above, which carries the CS of the entire community, controller $\mathcal{T}_x$ carries only the *local control-state* $\mathcal{CS}_x$ of x—where $\mathcal{CS}_x$ is some function, defined by law $\mathcal{L}$, of the history of communication between x and the rest of the $\mathcal{L}$-community. In other words, changes of $\mathcal{CS}_x$ are strictly local, not having to be correlated with the control-states of other members of the $\mathcal{L}$-community, However, such decentralization of enforcement requires the laws themselves to be *local*, in a sense to be defined next.

The Local Nature of LGI Laws: An LGI law is defined over a certain types of events occurring at members of a community C subject to it, mandating the effect that any such

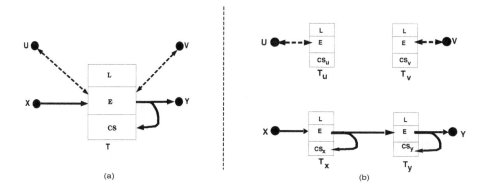

Fig. 1. Law Enforcement: (a) centralized version; (b) decentralized law enforcement under LGI

event should have. Such a mandate is called the *ruling* of the law for the given event. The events subject to laws, called *regulated events*, include (among others): the *sending* and the *arrival* of an $\mathcal{L}$-message; the occurrence of an *exception*; and the coming due of an *obligation*. The operations that can be included in the ruling for a given regulated event, called *primitive operations*, are all local with respect to the agent in which the event occurred (called, the "home agent"). They include, operations on the control-state of the home agent; operations on messages, such as `forward` and `deliver`; and the imposition of an obligation on the home agent. To summarize, an LGI law must satisfy the following locality properties:

- a law can regulate explicitly only *local events* at individual agents;
- the ruling for an event e at agent x can depend only on e itself, and on the *local control-state* $\mathcal{CS}_x$; and
- the ruling for an event that occurs at x can mandate only *local operations* to be carried out at x.

Decentralization of Law-Enforcement: As has been pointed out, we replace the central reference monitor $\mathcal{T}$ with a distributed set $\{\mathcal{T}_x \mid x \text{ in } \mathcal{C}\}$ of controllers, one for each members of community $\mathcal{C}$. Structurally, all these controllers are generic, with the same law-enforcer $\mathcal{E}$, and all must be trusted to interpret correctly any law they might operate under. When serving members of community $\mathcal{C}_\mathcal{L}$, however, they all carry the *same law* $\mathcal{L}$. And each controller $\mathcal{T}_x$ associated with an agent x of this community carries only the *local control-state* $\mathcal{CS}_x$ of x (see Figure 1(b)).

Due to the local nature of LGI laws, each controller $\mathcal{T}_x$ can handle events that occur at its client x strictly locally, with no explicit dependency on anything that might be happening with other members in the community. It should also be pointed out that controller $\mathcal{T}_x$ handles the events at x strictly sequentially, in the order of their occurrence, and atomically. This, and the locality of laws, greatly simplifies the structure of the controllers, making them easier to use as our *trusted computing base* (TCB).

Note that an LGI law cannot deal *directly* with an exchange of messages between agents. But it can regulate such an exchange, indirectly, by regulating the local events of the sending of a message, and of its arrival, at two different agents. Indeed, as we can see in Figure 1(b), every $\mathcal{L}$-message exchanged between a pair of agents x and y, passes through a pair of controllers: $\mathcal{T}_x$ and $\mathcal{T}_y$. This may seem to be less efficient than using a single central controller $\mathcal{T}$, when $\mathcal{T}$ is not congested. But as has been shown in [18], the decentralized mechanism is actually more efficient in a wide range of its applicability.

Finally, we point out that the LGI model is silent on the placement of controllers *vis-a-vis* the agents they serve, and it allows for the sharing of a single controller by several agents. This provides us with welcome flexibilities, which can be used to minimize the overhead of LGI under various conditions. A preliminary study [18] of such an optimization produced very positive results. The sharing of single controller by several agents, in particular, allows one to optimize law enforcement by devising various sharing strategies, including the use of a single centralized controller to mediate all message exchange among the members of a given community—where such centralized enforcement happen to be optimal.

3.2   A Concept of Enforceable Obligation

Obligations, along with permissions and prohibitions, are widely considered essential for the specification of policies for financial enterprises [15]. The concept of obligation being employed for this purpose is usually based on conventional *deontic logic* [16], designed for the specification of normative systems, or on some elaborations of this logic, such as taking into account interacting agents [6]. These types of obligations allows one to reason about what an agent must do, but they provide no means for ensuring that what needs to be done will actually be done [21]. LGI, on the other hand, features a concept of obligation that can be enforced.

Informally speaking, an obligation under LGI is a kind of *motive force*. Once an obligation is imposed on an agent—which can be done as part of the ruling of the law for some event at it—it ensures that a certain action (called *sanction*) is carried out at this agent, at a specified time in the future, when the obligation is said to *come due*—provided that certain conditions on the control state of the agent are satisfied at that time. The circumstances under which an agent may incur an obligation, the treatment of pending obligations, and the nature of the sanctions, are all governed by the law of the community. For a detailed discussion of obligations the reader is referred to [18].

3.3   The Deployment of LGI

All one needs for the deployment of LGI is the availability of a set of trustworthy controllers, and a way for a prospective client to locate an available controller. This can be accomplished via one or more *controller-services*, each of which maintains a set of controllers, and one or more certification authorities that certifies the correctness of controllers. A prototype of such a controller service has been implemented, and is fully operational at Rutgers University—it is expected to be released by the end of the summer of 1993. This prototype can serve as the basis for the deployment of LGI within an enterprise. However, for effective deployment over the internet, the controller services need to be provided by some reliable commercial or governmental institutions.

Now, for an agent x to engage in LGI communication under a law $\mathcal{L}$, it needs to locate a controller, via a controller-service, and supply this controller with the law $\mathcal{L}$ it wants to employ. Once x is operating under law $\mathcal{L}$ it may need to distinguish itself as playing a certain role, or having a certain unique name, which would provide it with some distinct privileges under law $\mathcal{L}$. One can do this by presenting certain digital certificates to the controller, as we will see in our case study.

3.4   The Language for Formulating Laws

Abstractly speaking, the law of a community is a function that returns a *ruling* for any possible regulated event that might occur at any one of its members. The ruling returned by the law is a possibly empty sequence of primitive operations, which is to be carried out locally at the *home* of the event. (By default, an empty ruling implies that the event in question has no consequences—such an event is effectively ignored.) Such a function can be expressed in many languages. We are currently using two languages for writing our laws, which are restricted versions of Prolog and of Java. In the rest of this paper we employ the Prolog-based langauge for writing LGI-laws.

3.5   The Basis for Trust between Members of a Community

Note that we do not propose to coerce any agent to exchange $\mathcal{L}$-messages under any given law $\mathcal{L}$. The role of enforcement here is merely to ensure that *any exchange of $\mathcal{L}$-messages, once undertaken, conforms to law $\mathcal{L}$*. In particular, our enforcement mechanism needs to ensure that a message received under law $\mathcal{L}$ has been sent under the same law; i.e., that it is not possible to forge $\mathcal{L}$-messages). For this one needs the following assurances: (a) that the exchange of $\mathcal{L}$-messages is mediated by correctly implemented controllers; (b) that these controllers are interpreting the *same law* $\mathcal{L}$; and (c) that $\mathcal{L}$-messages are securely transmitted over the network. This architectural idea has been later adopted by Stefik in his "trusted systems" work [22]—although Stefik's work may have been done without any knowledge of the previous (1991) work of this author [17]. But Stefik applied this idea only in the limited context of *right management*.

Broadly speaking, these assurances are provided as follows. controllers used for mediating the exchange of $\mathcal{L}$-messages authenticate themselves to each other via certificates signed by a certification authority specified by the clause cAuthority of law $\mathcal{L}$ (as will be illustrated by the case study in the following section). Note that different laws may, thus, require different certification levels for the controllers used for its enforcement. Messages sent across the network must be digitally signed by the sending controller, and the signature must be verified by the receiving controller. To ensure that a message forwarded by a controller $\mathcal{T}_x$ under law $\mathcal{L}$ would be handled by another controller $\mathcal{T}_y$ operating under the *same* law, $\mathcal{T}_x$ appends a one-way hash [20] H of law $\mathcal{L}$ to the message it forwards to $\mathcal{T}_y$. $\mathcal{T}_y$ would accept this as a valid $\mathcal{L}$-message under $\mathcal{L}$ if and only if H is identical to the hash of its own law.

Finally, note that although we do not compel anybody to operate under any particular law, or to use LGI, for that matter, one may be *effectively compelled* to exchange $\mathcal{L}$-messages, if one needs to use services provided only under this law. For instance, if servers, in our case study in Section 4, are accept service-orders only via $\mathcal{SL}$-messages, then the clients will be compelled to send their orders via $\mathcal{SL}$-messages as well. Conversely, once clients commit themselves to using $\mathcal{SL}$-messages for their orders, servers would be effectively compelled to accept these commands only in this manner. Similarly, if a bank wants to serve agents in the $\mathcal{SL}$-community, it will have to do operate under this community itself. This is probably the best one can do in the distributed context, where it is impossible to ensure that all relevant messages are mediated by a reference monitor, or by any set of such monitors.

4 Establishing Trustworthy Client-Server Interaction – A Case Study

In this Section we introduce an LGI law called $\mathcal{SL}$ (for service law), which enforces the cash handling policy (CH) and the server's response policy (SR), introduced in Section 2—thus establishing them as regularities over the community that uses this law. We will also examine, in Section 4.1, the relationship between R-trust and F-trust, as both of these are employed in this example.

Law $\mathcal{SL}$, displayed in Figures 2 and 3, has two parts: *preamble* and *body*. The preamble of this law contains the following clauses: First there is the cAuthority(pk1) clause that identify the public key of the certification authority (CA) to be used for the authentication of the controllers that are to mediate $\mathcal{SL}$-messages. This CA is an important element of the trust between the agents that exchange such messages. Second, there is an authority clause, which provide the public key of the CA that would be acceptable under the this law for certifying banks; this CA is given a local name— "bankingCA," in this case—to be used within this law. Third, the initialCS clause specifies the initial control-state of all members in this community, which are to have the term cash(0), signifying that each member of this community starts with zero balance in it electronic wallet (represented by the term cash).

The body of this law is a list of all its rules, each followed by a comment (in italic), which, together with the following discussion, should be understandable, at least roughly, even for a reader not well versed in our language for writing laws. These rules can be partitioned into three groups, dealing with different aspects of the law: (a) rules $\mathcal{R}1$ through $\mathcal{R}5$, which govern banking; (b) rules $\mathcal{R}6$ and $\mathcal{R}7$, which deals with the making of service orders; and (c) rules $\mathcal{R}8$ through $\mathcal{R}12$, which govern server's responses to orders. These three aspects of the law are now discussed in this order.

Banking: By Rule $\mathcal{R}1$, an agent can claim the role of a bank, and thus get the term role(bank) into its control-state—by presenting an appropriate certificate issued by bankingCA. By Rule $\mathcal{R}2$, such a bank—i.e., any agent that has the term role(bank) in its control-state—can send messages of the form giveMoney(D) to anybody in this community. When this message arrives at its destination y, then, by Rule $\mathcal{R}3$, the value of the cash term in the control-state of y will be incremented by D, and the message would be delivered to y itself, to notify him of this event. In this way a bank can provide arbitrary amount cash to any community member.

Symmetrically, by Rules $\mathcal{R}4$ and $\mathcal{R}5$ anybody can send any part of his cash balance for deposit in a bank. (It should be pointed out, though, that if a deposit message is sent

Preamble:
    cAuthority(pk1).
    authority(bankingCA, pk2).
    initialCS([cash(0)]).

$\mathcal{R}1.$
    `certified([issuer(bankingCA),subject(X),`
        `attributes([role(bank)])) :- do(+role(bank))).`
    an agent may claim the role of a bank by presenting an appropriate certificate issued by ca).

$\mathcal{R}2.$
    `sent(B,giveMoney(D),X) :- role(bank)@CS, do(forward).`
    A `giveMoney` *message can be sent by a bank to anybody*

$\mathcal{R}3.$
    `arrived(B,giveMoney(D),X) :- do(incr(cash(Bal1),D), do(deliver).`
    A `giveMoney(D)` *message arriving at any agent* X *would increment the cash of* X *by D.*

$\mathcal{R}4.$
    `sent(X,deposit(D),B) :- cash(Bal)@CS, ( D =< Bal),`
        `do(decr(cash(Bal),D)), do(forward).`
    A message `deposit(D)` *would be forwarded to its destination if the sender has more than* D *of cash, after his cash balance is reduced by D.*

$\mathcal{R}5.$
    `arrived(X, deposit(D),B) :- role(bank)@CS,`
        `do(deliver).`
    If the reciepient of a `deposit` *message is a bank, the message would be delivered to it without further ado; otherwise it would be blocked (see comment in the text of the paper).*

$\mathcal{R}6.$
    `sent(C,order(Specs,Fee),S) :- cash(Bal)@CS, ( Fee =< Bal),`
        `do(decr(cash(Bal),Fee)), do(forward).`
    A message `order(_,Fee)` *can be send only by one whose cash balance is larger than* `Fee`. *This balance is decremented by the sending.*

$\mathcal{R}7.$
    `arrived(C,order(Specs,Fee),S) :- do(incr(escrow(Bal),Fee)),`
        `do(impose_obligation(respond(C,Specs,Fee),60)),`
        `do(deliver).`
    When an order arrives, its `Fee` *is added to the cash of the reciepient, the order is delivered to him, and an obligation is imposed to respond to the order in 60 seconds (see Rule* $\mathcal{R}12$).*

Fig. 2. The Service Law ($\mathcal{SL}$)—Part I

to a non-bank, the money in it would be lost. Such loss can be easily prevented, at the cost of a slight complication of these rules).

A point of clarification is in order here: this law does not deal with the withdrawal requests sent to the bank, which presumably prompt the bank to send cash—such requests are left unregulated here, so they can be communicated in arbitrary ways, such as via e-mail.

making Service Orders: The sending of service order of the form order(specs,fee) is governed by Rule $\mathcal{R}6$, which allows this message to be sent only if the cash balance of the sender is at least as large as `fee`. If the order is sent, then the cash balance of the sender is decremented by `fee`. By Rule $\mathcal{R}7$, the arrival of this order at a server S causes the following operations to be carried out: (a) the escrow account of s is incremented by `fee`; (b) an obligation `respond(c,specs,fee)` is imposed on s, to become due in 60 seconds (used here as an example); and (c) the order is delivered to s itself. As we shall see below, the money deposited into escrow will be withdrawn from it when a response to the order in question is given. Note that this money cannot be used by s to make his own orders, because, by Rule $\mathcal{R}6$, orders can utilize only money defined as cash.

$\mathcal{R}8.$

```
sent(S,accept(Specs),C) :- obligation(respond(C,Specs,Fee),T)@CS,
        do(decr(escrow(Bal),Fee)), do(incr(cash(Bal),Fee)),
        do(repeal_obligation(respond(C,Specs,Fee),_)),
        do(forward).
```

An agent can send an `accept` *message only if it has a matching obligation to* `respond`; *this obligation is automatically repealed by this responce.*

$\mathcal{R}9.$

```
sent(S,decline(Specs,Fee),C)
    :- obligation(respond(C,Specs,Fee),T)@CS,
        do(decr(escrow(Bal),Fee)),
        do(repeal_obligation(respond(C,Specs,Fee),_))),
        do(forward).
```

Similar to the previous rule, except that the `decline` *message carries with it the* Fee *found in the obligation to respond, after removing it from the balance.*

$\mathcal{R}10.$

```
arrived(S,accept(Specs,Fee),C) :-
        do(+receipt(accept(Specs,Fee),Time)), do(deliver).
```

Upon its arrival, an `accept` *message is recorded in the CS of agent* C, *and delivered to its agent.*

$\mathcal{R}11.$

```
arrived(S,decline(Specs,Fee),C) :-
        do(incr(cash(Bal),Fee)), do(deliver).
```

Get the money and deliver the message

$\mathcal{R}12.$

```
obligationDue(respond(C,Specs,Fee)) :- do(decr(escrow(Bal),Fee)),
        do(forward(decline(Specs,Fee),C,Self)).
```

The sanction consists of (a) decrementing the balance, to allow for the money to be returned, and (b) forwarding the `decline` *message to the original client, which has the same effect as the* `decline` *message sent voluntarily under Rule* $\mathcal{R}11.$

Fig. 3. The Service Law ($\mathcal{SL}$)—Part II

Responses to Orders: As long as the obligation `respond(c,specs,fee)` is pending, s can respond voluntarily to the order he received from c, either by accepting or be declining it, as follows:

– To *accept* an order(specs,fee) received from c, the server s sends a message accept(specs,fee) to it. This message is governed by Rules $\mathcal{R}8$ and $\mathcal{R}10$. By Rule $\mathcal{R}8$, the sending of an accept message causes the following operations to be carried out: (a) fee dollars are removed from the escrow and added to the cash value of s, thus making this money usable by s for making its own orders; (b) the relevant respond(...) obligation is repealed, since it is obviously not needed any longer; and (c) the accept message is forwarded to c.

By Rule $\mathcal{R}10$, the arrival of a message accept(specs,fee) causes the term

  receipt(accept(specs,fee),Time)

to be added to the CS of the receiver c, which can serve as a time-stamped record of the promise of the server to carry out the service. Note that the parameter fee in this message does *not* cause any transfer of cash.

– To *decline* an order(specs,fee) received from c, the server s sends a message decline(specs,fee) to it. This message is governed by Rules $\mathcal{R}9$ and $\mathcal{R}11$. By Rule $\mathcal{R}9$, the sending of an decline message causes fee dollars to be removed from the escrow, and to be transferred in the message forwarded to c; the respond(...) obligation is then repealed, as in the previous case, and the declined message is forwarded. By Rule $\mathcal{R}11$, the arrival of a message decline(specs,fee) at c, causes fee dollars to be added to the cash of c, thus returning to it the money it send with the request hereby declined.

If server s did not respond to order(specs,fee) from c in time, then obligation respond(c,specs,fee) (imposed by the arrival of this order) would come due, triggers the sanction defined by Rule $\mathcal{R}12$.

This sanction is as follows: (a) fee dollars are withdrawn from the escrow of s; (b) a decline message is forwarded to client c, with precisely the same effect that a voluntary decline would have. The promise of bounded delay of the response, made by the policy SR in Section 2, is based on fairly standard, even if not entirely reliable, assumptions of reliable communication, bounded message-transition time, and bounded difference between the rate of clocks.

4.1   On the Relationship between R-Trust and F-Trust

We conclude this section with an examination of the complementary interrelationship between familiarity-based trust (F-trust) and regularity-based trust (R-trust), as it is reflected in the case study of this paper. Basically, we will show that the two types of trust support and enhance each other, albeit in different ways.

We start by showing that R-trust, as implemented via LGI laws, is based on some F-trust. Indeed the basis for trusting law $\mathcal{SL}$—that is, for trusting that interaction via $\mathcal{SL}$ messages satisfies policies CH and SR formalized by this law—is the correctness of the controllers that mediate this interaction. And the reason to trust the controllers in this case is the F-trust we have in the CA (identified here by its public key pk1), which certifies these controllers. And the reason that this CA certifies controllers is, presumably, that it has an F-trust in their correctness.

Moreover, we note that the trust in law $\mathcal{SL}$ does not, by itself, have much practical meaning, without an assurance that the money one is offered as a fee for service originates from a trustworthy bank, and that this money can be deposited in one's bank account. Under law $\mathcal{SL}$ such assurances depends on the trustworthiness of the CA pk2, used here to authenticate banks. So, the R-trust established by law $\mathcal{SL}$ depends on the F-trust in CA pk2, and on the F-trust that this CA has in the banks it certifies.

On the other hand, the effectiveness of F-trust could be enhanced by an appropriate R-trust. In our case, the F-trust one has in the banks certifies by the CA pk2 allows members of the $\mathcal{SL}$-community to trust funds obtained from any other members, without having to worry about the origin of these funds. That is, the fee one gets in a service-order under this law, taken from the cash balance of the client, may be the result of direct or indirect contributions of several banks. But one does not need to know the identity of these banks for trusting the validity of the currency. This is the consequence of one's R-trust in the validity of the cash handling policy CH generated by law $\mathcal{SL}$. This is similar to the trust we have in cash in the physical world, which is due to the trust we have that dollar bills are not forged, regardless of the bank that issued them (this is regularity R2, of the introduction.)

5   Conclusion

The type of trust identified in this paper as *regularity-based trust*, is a critical factor in the comprehensibility and manageability of the physical world—in both the natural and artificial aspects of it. But the role of such trust in cyberspace has been limited so far, because of difficulties in establishing sufficiently wide range of useful regularities in this context.

We have demonstrated in this paper that the use of middleware such as LGI can help enhance the role of regularity-based trust in cybersapce, making it a significant factor in activities such as e-commerce. We also discussed the relationship between this kind of trust, and what we have called familiarity-based trust, which is currently more commonly employed in cyberspace.

References

1. J.P. Anderson. Computer security technology planning study. Technical Report TR-73-51, Air Force Electronic System Division., 1972.
2. X. Ao, N. Minsky, and V. Ungureanu. Formal treatment of certificate revocation under communal access control. In *Proc. of the 2001 IEEE Symposium on Security and Privacy, May 2001, Oakland California*, May 2001.
   (available from http://www.cs.rutgers.edu/~minsky/pubs.html).
3. J. Barkley, K. Beznosov, and J. Uppal. Supporting relationships in access control using role based access control. In *Proceedings of the Fourth ACM Workshop on Role-Based Access Control*, pages 55–65, October 1999.
4. M. Blaze, J. Feigenbaum, J. Ioannidis, and A. Keromytis. The role of trust management in distributed systems security. *Secure Internet Programming: Issues in Distributed and Mobile Object Systems*, 1603, 1999.
5. D. Brewer and M. Nash. The Chinese Wall security policy. In *Proceedings of the IEEE Symposium in Security and Privacy*. IEEE Computer Society, 1989.

6. M. Brown. Agents with changing and conflicting commitments: a preliminary study. In *Proc. of Fourth International Conference on Deontic Logic in Computer Science (DEON'98)*, January 1998.

7. D.D. Clark and D.R. Wilson. A comparison of commercial and military computer security policies. In *Proceedings of the IEEE Symposium in Security and Privacy*, pages 184–194. IEEE Computer Society, 1987.

8. C. Ellison. The nature of a usable pki. *Computer Networks*, (31):823–830, November 1999.

9. C English, P. Nixon, and S. terzis. Dynamic trust models for ubiquitous computing environemnt. In *Proceedings of the Ubicom 2002 Security Workshop*, 2002.

10. S. Foley. The specification and implementation of 'commercial' security requirements including dynamic segregation of duties. In *Proceedings of the 4th ACM Conference on Computer and Communications Security*, April 1997.

11. S. Glassman, M. Manasse, M. Abadi, P. Gauthier, and P. Sobalvarro. The Millicent protocol for inexpensive electronic commerce. In *Fourth International World Wide Web Conference Proceedings*, pages 603–618, December 1995.

12. R.J. Hayton, J.M. Bacon, and K. Moody. Access control in an open distributed enviroment. In *Proceedings of the 1998 IEEE Symposium on Security and Privacy*, 1998.

13. A. Herzberg, Y. Mass, J. Mihaeli, D. Naor, and Y. Ravid. Access control meets public key infrastructure, or: Assigning roles to strangers. In *Proceedings of the 2000 IEEE Symposium on Security and Privacy*, 2000.

14. G. Karjoth. The authorization service of tivoli policy director. In *Proc. of the 17th Annual Computer Security Applications Conference (ACSAC 2001)*, December 2001. (to appear).

15. P.F. Linington. Options for expressing ODP enterprise communities and their policies by using UML. In *Proceedings of the Third Internantional Enterprise Distributed Object Computing (EDOC99) Conference*. IEEE, September 1999.

16. J. J. Ch. Meyer, R. J. Wieringa, and Dignum F.P.M. The role of deontic logic in the specification of information systems. In J. Chomicki and G. Saake, editors, *Logic for Databases and Information Systems*. Kluwer, 1998.

17. N.H. Minsky. The imposition of protocols over open distributed systems. *IEEE Transactions on Software Engineering*, February 1991.

18. N.H. Minsky and V. Ungureanu. Law-governed interaction: a coordination and control mechanism for heterogeneous distributed systems. *TOSEM, ACM Transactions on Software Engineering and Methodology*, 9(3):273–305, July 2000. (available from `http://www.cs.rutgers.edu/~minsky/pubs.html`).

19. R. Rivest and B. Lampson. SDSI-a simple distributed security infrastructure. Technical report, MIT, 1996. http://theory.lcs.mit.edu/~rivest/sdsi.ps.

20. B. Schneier. *Applied Cryptography*. John Wiley and Sons, 1996.

21. M. Sloman. Policy driven management for distributed systems. *Journal of Network and Systems Management*, 1994.

22. Mark Stefik. *The Internet Edge*. MIT Press, 1999.

23. V. Ungureanu and N.H. Minsky. Establishing business rules for inter-enterprise electronic commerce. In *Proc. of the 14th International Symposium on DIStributed Computing (DISC 2000); Toledo, Spain; LNCS 1914*, pages 179–193, October 2000.

A Trust Matrix Model for Electronic Commerce

Yao-Hua Tan

Free University Amsterdam
Department of Economics and Business Administration
De Boelelaan 1105, 1081 HV Amsterdam, Netherlands
ytan@feweb.vu.nl

Abstract. We propose a so-called trust matrix model to build trust for conducting first trade transactions in electronic commerce; i.e. transactions in an electronic commerce environment between two parties that have never conducted trade transactions between them before. The trust matrix model is based on the idea that for business-to-business electronic commerce a balance has to be found between anonymous procedural trust, i.e. procedural solutions for trust building, and personal trust based on positive past experiences within an existing business relation. Procedural trust building solutions are important for first trade situations, because of the lack of experience in these situations. The procedural trust solutions are related to the notion of institution-based trust, because the trust in the procedural solutions depends on the trust one has in the institutions that issued or enforces the procedure. The trust matrix model can be used as a tool to analyze and develop trust-building services to help organizations conduct first-trade electronic commerce transactions.

1 First Trade Transactions in Electronic Commerce

In this paper we focus on building online trust in electronic commerce between partners that have never traded with each other before (i.e. in a *first trade* situation). Most trust building theories and mechanisms put the emphasis on trust via a history of exchanges between partners. See for example [Keen et al, 00], [Lewicki & Bunker, 95] and [Nooteboom, Klos & Jorna, 01]. This type of experience is probably the best way to build trust, but is simply not always available. Still, there are many trade opportunities where companies could make a good deal with another company that is unknown to them. In electronic commerce, particularly, with all the emphasis on globalization and opportunities to meet new international partners, trust building in a first trade situation becomes more prominent and needs special investigation.

International e-trade is more complicated than traditional off-line domestic trade in two respects. First, import and export in international e-trade require a wide variety of trade documents ranging from customs declarations to other kinds of documents like country of origin declarations and health certificates. Moreover, there are fewer shared norms and business practices due to the international character,. To compensate this, people demand more safeguards. A typical example of such a safeguard is a *Letter of Credit*. It is typically used by a seller in international trade to

P. Nixon and S. Terzis (Eds.): Trust Management 2003, LNCS 2692, pp. 33–45, 2003.
© Springer-Verlag Berlin Heidelberg 2003

get payment from a buyer with whom he has perhaps never traded before and to whom he has shipped the goods. Letters of Credit are rarely used in domestic trade.

Second, in addition to the inherent complexity of international trade, there are complexities due to the electronic character: It is more difficult on the Internet than in the off-line world to discover how solid an on-line business partner is, i.e. "on the Internet nobody knows you are a dog." Another complexity is the unclear legal environment of the Internet. Currently, for most of the international trade documents it is unclear if the electronic version has the same status as the paper version. Also, digital signatures that can be used to sign electronic documents do not have a clear legal status yet. Another legal issue is how to apply existing privacy and consumer protection laws to Internet trade-transactions. These laws vary enormously from country to country. Should one apply the laws from where the transaction server is located, or where the good is consumed, or produced? Does a US based company run the risk of violating European privacy laws, that tend to be stricter than US ones, if they sell goods to European customers via the Internet? Bewildered by the complexities, the average company and especially small and medium size enterprises (SME) are reluctant to step into international e-trade.

An ultimate challenge of the first trade problem in electronic commerce is to develop online services that can help companies build trust among each other without any previous experience. In [Bons, Lee & Wagenaar, 99] and [Lee & Bons, 96] one specific way to build this first trade trust is described, namely through electronic trade-procedures. In particular, they focused their research on the procedures related to an electronic version of Letter of Credit.

In this article we present a model to analyze and develop this type of trust-building services for first trade situations. One could interpret these services as a generalization of the services of a trusted third party (TTP) in public key infrastructures (PKI) to secure electronic communication with digital certificates. However, our perspective is broader. Trust-building services in international e-trade are not only related to secure communication of the trade documents, but also to creating trust and understanding in the legal content of these documents, and creating trust in the business reliability of the on-line trade-partner. [Tan & Thoen, 00] and [Tan & Thoen, 02] presented a generic trust model for first trade situations mentioned before. The basic idea of the model is that an individual party or agent only engages in a transaction if his level of trust exceeds his personal threshold; see [Castelfranchi and Falcone, 98]. This threshold depends on the type of the transaction involved. For example, it could be high if the value of the transaction is high, and it could be low if the agent is a risk seeker. Fig. 1 gives a graphical representation of the model. In the center is the trustor's transaction trust; i.e. a mental state that determines whether he has sufficient trust to engage in a transaction. The determinants of the trustor's trust threshold are represented in the lower half. The potential profit for the agent, the risk involved, the agent's attitude or propensity towards risk, are examples of such determinants. The upper half of Fig. 1 represents the so-called *trust sources*, i.e. the entity that creates the trust. These can be the counter party of the transaction, or a control mechanism. Control mechanisms are procedures and protocols, e.g. based on trade documents, that monitor and control the successful performance of a transaction. They are usually provided by a TTP.

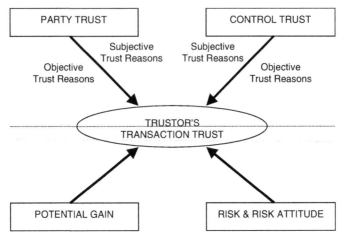

Fig. 1. Generic Trust Model

It has been argued that trust and control are parallel concepts that supplement each other, see e.g. [Das & Teng, 98]. Tan and Thoen defined transaction trust as party trust supplemented with control trust:

Party Trust + Control Trust = Transaction Trust

The strength of control trust depends not only on the control mechanisms used, but is also influenced by how much trust a party has in the TTP responsible for the control mechanisms. The more trust the party has in the TTP, the stronger is the control trust effected by the TTP and its control mechanisms. For example: Control trust effected on a party by the use of a Letter of Credit as a control mechanism may be zero if the party does not trust the issuing bank at all, and may be very strong if the party trusts the issuing bank completely. Hence, trust is not created by just having a counter party or a control procedure, but a trustor should also be convinced of the quality of the sources. Tan and Thoen distinguished several reasons by which a trustor can be convinced by a trust source:

Party Trust

Objective Trust Reasons:
- Social signs; e.g. you trust someone's medical advice, because he wears a doctor's uniform.

Subjective Trust Reasons:
- Personal experience; e.g. you trust a person based on a history of positive previous interactions.

- Understanding; e.g. you trust a person, because you understand his goals, capabilities and plans, and hence know what to expect from him.

- Communality; e.g. you trust the opinion of somebody, because other members of your community trust him too.

Control Trust

Objective Trust Reasons:
- Social signs; e.g. you trust a control procedure because it is certified by an organization. For example, you trust the electronic payment procedure of a web site, because this site carries the VISA logo.

Subjective Trust Reasons:
- Personal experience; e.g. you trust a control procedure based on a history of positive previous interactions. In none of these interactions the procedure failed.

- Understanding; e.g. you trust a control system (e.g. the SET protocol for electronic credit card transactions), because you understand how it works, and your assessment of its effectiveness was positive.

- Communality; e.g. you assume that a control system protects you against fraud, because other members of your community rely on it too.

These trust sources and reasons have some interesting links with the theory on trust developed in [Castelfranchi & Falcone, 98]. For example, our trust reasons Social Signs, Personal Experience, Understanding and Communality have much in common with the belief sources in their theory; namely Categorization, Personal Experience, Reasoning and Reputation, respectively. However, there are also differences between our generic trust model and their theory. In particular, in the generic trust model it is assumed that risk perception and attitude directly influences the transaction trust of the agent, whereas in the theory of Castelfranchi and Falcone this influence is mediated via a decision process. It is interesting to test these differences in empirical research that we plan to do in future research.

Although this generic trust model can be used to analyze certain developments in electronic commerce (for instance, it was applied to analyze electronic payment systems in [Tan & Thoen, 00]), it does not address trust issues in electronic commerce specifically. In the remainder of this paper, we add elements to the model that are relevant for specific trust issues in electronic commerce.

2   Trade Transaction Layers and Related Trust Issues

[Bons, 97] distinguished communication and business levels for inter-organizational trade procedures. Communication level addresses the underlying communication infrastructure, i.e. the physical transfer of information. Business level identifies the business risks associated with inter-organizational trade transactions in general. This level can be further investigated as comprising two components: the relationship between the parties doing business, and the exchange of business information (contained mainly in trade documents) and related regulation. In summary, there are three layers involved: communication layer, trade documents exchange and regulation layer, and business relationship layer. All three layers have to be trustworthy enough for parties to conduct a trade transaction. Let us look at the issues that may affect their trustworthiness, especially in the context of international electronic commerce.

Layer I: Communication
In a traditional trade environment, we would like to confirm the identity of the other party. We have probably met the other party in person or spoken to him over the telephone and we are able to identify the other party by his look or his voice. Then we would like to establish a common language with the other party, so that we can understand each other. After having established the identity and found a common language, the transfer of information can begin and we will expect the integrity of the information sent and received. Take for example the situation of a telephone conversation. Here both parties should be able to assume that the content of the message they receive from the other party is genuine, because tampering with a real-time conversation over the telephone or in person is uncommon.

In an electronic environment, the processes involved are similar. However, they are less easily performed. First, in an electronic environment we cannot easily identify the other party. For example, identifying by his look or voice is generally excluded. Second, we often do not have a real tangible communication, but use electronic messages. These are often not considered as trustworthy as the traditional equivalents. E.g. in a phone conversation one can actually hear the other's voice and when using paper documents one can actually touch the documents and examine the paper used, the signatures on the documents, the date stamp on the envelope etc.

In summary, communication needs to be trustworthy. Important issues concerning this, especially in electronic commerce, are (see for example [Bons, 97] and [Keen et al, 00]):

- *Authentication*: Verification that information received is from the identified partner.

- *Information integrity*: Verification that information received is not altered in anyway.

- *Confidentiality*: Protecting the content of information exchanged from disclosure to parties other than those approved.

- *Non-repudiation*: Irrefutable evidence of a message's or transaction's existence, binding the messenger party to the message or transaction.

- *Time-stamping*: Evidence of the time and date when a message was sent and received.

In some cases authors combine privacy policy issues with communication security issues. Where with privacy policy is meant the policy how companies deal with sensitive data of the customer that is obtained during the online business relationship; e.g. whether these data are used for cross-selling, or sold to third parties. We prefer to separate these issues, and consider privacy policy issues as a specific type of business partner reliability that is part of Layer III.

Layer II: Trade Documents and Regulation

Having established a trustworthy layer for communicating information between trade parties, the important thing is the content and use of this information, which is mainly in the form of trade documents (see for an overview of these issues [Lee & Bons, 96], [Das & Teng, 98]). There are many specific documents in use, especially in international trade as mentioned before. It is essential for trade parties to know which documents to use, what these mean, and when and how to use them. The legal value of the trade documents plays an important role too. Most of the control mechanisms dealing with opportunistic behaviors are based on the legal enforcement of the performance by the trustee to the trustor of the promised action (like delivery or payment of goods) as stated in the documents. If, because the legal status of the trade documents is not clear, we do not trust the available measures to deal with possible opportunistic behaviors, it is not likely that we will engage in the transaction. In summary, the most important issues for this layer in electronic commerce are:

- *Document use*: When to use which documents and how?

- *Document interpretation*: What do the documents mean?

- *Legal status*: What is the legal status of the trade documents and attributes (like electronic signatures, confirmations etc.)?

- *Governance*: Knowledge of country-specific rules (like tax-rates, import/export restrictions etc.)

Layer III: Business Relationship

When the first two layers are trustworthy enough and work well, the success of a trade transaction still depends on how the parties involved act and relate to each other. It is important to be assured that our business partner is reliable, that he has the capacity and intention to deliver the goods that he has promised (or pay for the goods that we have delivered) on time, and so on (for an overview of these issues see [Doney & Cannon, 97], [Jap & Ganesan, 99] and [Dwyer, Schurr & Oh, 87]).

In an electronic trade environment, the trustworthiness of our business partner may even be more important than in a traditional environment. This is because business relationship layer can compensate for the other layers. For example, if we do not entirely trust the used trade documents and legal mechanisms to enforce fulfillment of the contract, enough trust in the reliability of our business partner could, up to a point, compensate for this lack of trust in the trade documents. Also, if something went wrong in the communication layer such that we received a particular piece of information incorrectly or our business partner did not receive the information we had sent, things can be corrected in an uncomplicated manner (for example, by just sending the information again) if the relationship between us and our business partner is solid. The most important issues for the business relationship layer, also in electronic commerce, are:

- *Transaction history*: Information on how a potential business partner behaved in former similar transactions (were the deliveries or payment on time, did the products meet the agreed qualifications, etc.).

- *Financial reliability*: Is the ordering party reliable enough to live up to the financial part of the agreement?

- *Production capability*: Is the delivering party capable enough to make and deliver the products on time for the agreed price?

- *Business partner reliability*: All other information concerning the trustworthiness of potential business partners.

3 Trust Matrix for First Trade Transactions in Electronic Commerce

It has been argued that trust is needed only in risky situations and that to trust essentially means to take risks and leave one vulnerable to the actions of trusted others; see [Hosmer, 95] and [Nooteboom, 99]. Electronic commerce environment is a risky one. It brings more or new uncertainties in all layers of trade transaction. Trust related issues and problems are even magnified because parties reach out beyond their familiar trade environment; see [Castelfranchi & Tan, 01]. Control mechanisms, provided by a TTP, may prove valuable to provide more trust that is necessary to conduct electronic commerce transactions. Their role may even be bigger in providing or building trust for a first trade transaction in open electronic commerce. It would be fruitful if we could have a tool to analyze and develop trust services that a TTP (could) provide to parties who need to engage in such a transaction.

As discussed before, the generic trust model only addresses the problem of a first trade transaction in a generic way. Combining the generic model with the trade transaction layers described before results in a tool called a trust matrix, for analyzing and developing trust services. When each of the trade transaction layers is extended with the specific trust issues in electronic commerce, we get a trust matrix for electronic commerce shown in Figure 2. We can use this trust matrix to analyze and develop the trust services that a TTP can offer to help organizations conduct a first trade transaction in open electronic commerce.

The trust reasons in the matrix can be seen as the different techniques a TTP can use to provide organizations or parties who want to engage in a trade transaction with the services designed to build more trust in a trade transaction layer. The trust built can be either in the other party (i.e. party trust) or in the control mechanisms (i.e. control trust). For example, a TTP (the organization behind the trust service) may explain that it uses the authentication protocols chosen by VISA. In this case the TTP is using a Social Sign trust reason to create Control Trust in the Communication Layer.

Trust Barrier		Social Signs		Personal Experience		Understanding		Communality	
		Party Trust	Control Trust	Party Trust	Control Trust	Party Trust	Control Trust	Party Trust	Control Trust
Communication	Authentication								
	Information Integrity								
	Confidentiality								
	Non-Repudiation								
	Time-Stamping								
Trade Document & Regulation	Document Use								
	Document Interpretation								
	Legal Status								
	Governance								
Business Relationship	Transaction History								
	Financial Reliability								
	Production Capability								
	Business Partner Reliability								

Fig. 2. Trust matrix for first trade transaction in electronic commerce

4 Application of Trust Matrix to Trusted Third Parties

Several prominent organizations that act as third parties on the Internet have been analyzed based on the services they provide for enabling electronic commerce. These organizations can be divided into two categories:

- Traditional organizations, which already existed before the Internet and use it as a distribution channel for their existing services: World Trade Organization (http://www.wto.org/index.htm), International Chamber of Commerce (http://www.iccwbo.org/index.asp), Dun & Bradstreet (http://www.dnb.com).
- 'Virtual' organizations, which have arisen along with the Internet and whose services are based upon the global existence and use of information technology for international trade: Bolero (http://www.bolero.net), Identrus (http://www.identrus.com) , TradeCard (http://www.tradecard.com).

In the following, the analyses and application of the trust matrix are demonstrated for Dun & Bradstreet and Bolero. We have selected on purpose two rather extreme opposite cases to illustrate that the trust matrix model can bring out fundamental distinctions between various trust services that are provided.

4.1 Dun & Bradstreet Example

Dun & Bradstreet (D&B) is a provider of business information for credit, marketing, purchasing, and receivables management decisions worldwide. On the D&B web site a description of the company is given. The emphasis lies on communality, age (159 years), and the reputation of business partners. D&B also provides extensive information on the services they offer, including their 'most comprehensive global database of its kind' with information on more than 60 million companies in more than 200 countries around the world. It also provides information on the accuracy and completeness of the database and the sophistication of the data collection procedures and tools. The primary business of D&B is providing company information. Its database with company information allows them to perform and provide business analyses, which are D&B's main products, and reports. Most of the information in the reports and business analyses is about the financial aspects of an organization. There is also the possibility to get additional information like the antecedents of the principal owner or manager of a company and important legal information. D&B does not have any authority over their customers. Its services are not tied to a special line of business and anybody can become a member and buy business reports. The amount of its member clients (over 100.000) is of importance.

Trust Matrix of Dun & Bradstreet
The services and products of D&B apply to the business relationship layer. The trust in D&B as a TTP, is created through its long history and reputation, and the enormous size of its user base (i.e. huge international community of companies). The trust matrix in Fig. 3 helps distinguish the different ways in which trust is created. All the services of D&B web site are focused on the Business Relationship layer.

A more detailed analysis of these services reveals subtle distinctions. D&B is a kind of certification institute that applies certain analysis models to assess the trustworthiness of companies. This is an example of control trust creation with the analysis models as the control mechanisms. The recommendations of D&B are only trustworthy to the extent that one is convinced that their models provide the right analyses of companies. D&B uses Understanding and Communality as trust reasons to create trust in the quality of its recommendations. From the perspective of Understanding it is the quality of the D&B database and data collection tools that are emphasized. Understanding how scientifically the data are collected creates trust in the recommendations of D&B. From the perspective of Communality it is emphasized how many companies are using the D&B information. You can trust D&B's recommendations, because all your colleagues trust them. Clearly, Understanding and Communality are two complete different ways to create trust in the control mechanisms of D&B.

4.2 Bolero Example

Bolero's aim is to provide a technical and administrative infrastructure that enables electronic trade document exchange over the Internet among members of its community, without the need for a bilateral electronic data interchange agreement. Bolero first focused on the Bill of Lading. This market was too small so it decided to expand its efforts and is now working on developing new electronic trade document standards. Through its 'electronic trade documents', 'core messaging system', 'title registry application', and 'specially designed contracts and agreements' (like its legal 'Rulebook') Bolero provides a global digital marketplace. The platform is primarily designed to support exchange of electronic trade-documents, electronic registration of ownership of goods, and electronic messaging. Bolero currently accounts for over 12,500 freight forwarders, container fleet carriers, port authorities, and financial institutions from all over the world. For all these members Bolero mainly functions as a TTP and therefore has a great authority over its members. Bolero rules, guidelines, decisions, etc. only apply to members of its community. However, the legal framework (created by Bolero) in which the transactions are done is widely accepted by law.

Trust Barrier		Social Signs		Personal Experience		Understanding		Communality	
		Party Trust	Control Trust	Party Trust	Control Trust	Party Trust	Control Trust	Party Trust	Control Trust
Commu-nication	Authentication								
	Information Integrity								
	Confidentiality								
	Non-Repudiation								
	Time-Stamping								
Trade Document & Regulation	Document Use								
	Document Interpretation								
	Legal Status								
	Governance								
Business Relation-ship	Transaction History	Reputation of D&B and partners				Payment Score	Explanation of D&B's database	Size of community	
	Financial Reliability	Idem				D&B Rating	Idem	Idem	
	Production Capability	Idem				Company Information	Idem	Idem	
	Business Partner Reliability	Idem				Principal Antecedents	Idem	Idem	

Fig. 3. Trust matrix applied to Dun & Bradstreet

Trust Matrix of Bolero
The services provided by Bolero address the first two layers. The third layer, i.e. business relationship layer, is not addressed to: there are no indices, history of business behavior, financial reliability or any other information available to establish the reliability of a potential business partner. The trust matrix as applied to Bolero is shown in Figure 4.

Trade Transaction Layer I: Communication
The Bolero architecture provides services for all five issues of this layer. The trust in the core messaging system of Bolero is created on one hand through an extensive explanation of the systems and procedures, hence Understanding. On the other hand, the trust is created by referring to the reputation and size of Bolero's partners and the world wide inter bank payment organization SWIFT. They would not have partnered with Bolero if the quality of the core messaging system was not appropriate.

Trade Transaction Layer II: Trade Documents and Regulation
The explanation of the use and interpretation of standardized electronic trade documents that are exchanged via the core messaging system, partners' support, and an impressive list of members are the main trust-production factors. Bolero also provides a so-called 'Rulebook', which defines the legal status of electronic trade documents; e.g. it stipulates which electronic messages are considered legal documents, time-stamping of message exchange via the log files of the core messaging system, title registry etc. The explanation of the legal framework and the acceptation of this framework by legal courts create trust in the use of these standardized electronic documents.

For the Bolero case the Trade Transaction Layer III is empty. The main reason for this is that Bolero explicitly disclaims to provide any information about the business relationship. They want to make very clear to their customers that they only guarantee the secure exchange of electronic trade documents as well as the legal status of these documents, but they have no insights in the business quality or reliability of the companies that send these documents. One might argue that this secure electronic document service of Bolero is itself a business service that requires business relationship trust of the customers in Bolero as company, but this aspect is already covered by the reputation of the partners that are backing up Bolero and Swift that is positioned at the intersection of Layer I Communication and social signs.

5 Conclusions

We addressed a specific problem in electronic commerce, namely how to build online trust between trading partners that have never traded before, the so-called first trade situation. Most trust building mechanisms and theories on trust are based on the assumption that trust is built through experience between partners, but experience is not always available. Still there are many unique trade opportunities where people can make very good trades. In electronic commerce, the first trade situation problem is even more prominent and needs a special investigation. We extended the generic trust model that was introduced by Tan and Thoen with specific electronic commerce elements. This resulted in a trust matrix for analyzing trust services for first trade in electronic commerce. Its usefulness was demonstrated in analyses of the services of Dun & Bradstreet and Bolero. The result of these analyses was that the services by these two TTPs are more or less complementary. Our analysis suggests the hypothesis that a complete service for online trust building should be the right combination of the services comparable to those of Dun & Bradstreet and Bolero.

Trust Barrier		Social Signs		Personal Experience		Understanding		Communality	
		Party Trust	Control Trust	Party Trust	Control Trust	Party Trust	Control Trust	Party Trust	Control Trust
Commu-nication	Authentica-tion		Reputation of partners and SWIFT				Explanation of digital signatures and encryption		Size of community and reputation of members
	Information Integrity		idem				Explanation of guaranteed document originality		idem
	Confi-dentiality		idem				Explanation of encryption and ensured privacy		idem
	Non-Repudiation		idem				Explanation of guaranteed delivery and logging procedures		idem
	Time-Stamping		idem				Explanation of logging system and title registry		idem
Trade Document & Regulation	Document Use		Reputation of Partners				Explanation of title registry system and standardized trade documents		idem
	Document Interpretation		idem				Explanation of core messaging system and standardized trade documents		idem
	Legal Status		Standards accepted by courts				Explanation of legal framework (Bolero's Legal Rulebook)		idem
	Governance								
Business Relation-ship	Transaction History								
	Financial Reliability								
	Production Capability								
	Business Partner Reliability								

Fig. 4. Trust matrix applied to Bolero

The Dun & Bradstreet and Bolero cases are two rather extreme opposite cases that we have selected on purpose to illustrate that the trust matrix model can bring out fundamental distinctions between various trust services that are provided. However, a serious limitation of the trust matrix model is that it is purely qualitative. Hence, applying the matrix model can be difficult when it comes to case descriptions that are less clear cut as the ones we presented here. Therefore, we plan to develop in future research more quantitative measurements for the parameters for the matrix model.

Acknowledgements. I would like to thank Samuel Santosa and Edwin Stam for their earlier contributions to this research.

References

Bons, R.W.H. (1997). *Designing Trustworthy Trade Procedures for Open Electronic Commerce,* Ph.D. Dissertation, EURIDIS and Department of Business Administration, Erasmus University, Rotterdam.

Bons, R.W.H, Lee, R.M and Wagenaar, R.W. (1999). Computer-aided Auditing of Inter-organizational Trade Procedures, *International Journal of Intelligent Systems in Accounting, Finance & Management*, Vol. 8, pp. 25–44.

Castelfranchi, C. and Tan, Y.H. (2001). The Role of Trust and Deception in Virtual Societies, *Proceedings of the 34th Hawaii International Conference on System Sciences (HICSS'01)*, IEEE Computer Society Press, Los Alamitos, CA.

Castelfranchi, C. and Falcone, R. (1998). Principles of Trust for Multi-Agent Systems: Cognitive Anatomy, Social Importance, and Quantification, *Proceedings of the International Conferences on MAS - ICMAS'98*, Paris, 2–8 July, AAAI-MIT Press.

Das, T.K. and Teng, B. S. (1998). Between Trust and Control: Developing Confidence in Partner Cooperation in Alliances, *Academy of Management Review*, Vol. 23, No. 3, pp. 491–512.

Doney, P.M. and J.P. Cannon (1997), An Examination of the Nature of Trust in Buyer-Seller Relationships, *Journal of Marketing*, 61 (1), 35–51.

Dwyer, F.R, P.J. Schurr, and S Oh (1987), Developing Buyer-Seller Relationships, *Journal of Marketing*, 52 (1), 21–34.

Hosmer, L.T. (1995). Trust: The Connection Link between Organizational Theory and Philosophical Ethics, *Academy of Management Review*, Vol. 20, No. 3, pp. 213–237.

Jap, S.D. and S. Ganesan (1999), Control Mechanisms and the Relationship Life-Cycle, *Journal of Marketing Research*, 37, 227–45.

Lee, R.M. and Bons, R.W.H. (1996). Soft-Coded Trade Procedures for Open-EDI, *International Journal of Electronic Commerce,* Fall, Vol. 1, No. 1, pp. 27–49.

Lewicki, R.J. and Bunker, B.B. (1995). Trust in Relationships: A Model of Development and Decline, *Conflict, Cooperation and Justice*, Bunker, B.B. and Rubin, J.Z. (eds.), Jossey-Bass, San Francisco.

Keen, P., Ballance, C., Chan, S. and Schrump, S. (2000). *Electronic Commerce Relationships: Trust by Design*, Prentice Hall PTR, Upper Saddle River, New Jersey.

Nooteboom, B. (1999). Trust as a Governance Device, *Inter-Firm Alliances: Analysis & Design*, Routledge, London.

Nooteboom, B., Klos, T. and Jorna, R. (2001). Adaptive Trust and Co-Operation: An Agent-Based Simulation Approach, *Fraud, Deception, and Trust in Agent Societies*, Falcone, R., Singh, M. and Tan, Y.H. (eds.), *Lecture Notes in Computer Science (LNCS/LNAI)*, Springer Verlag

Tan, Y.H. and Thoen, W. (2000). A generic model of trust in electronic commerce, *International Journal of Electronic Commerce*, Vol. 5(2), 61–74.

Tan, Y.H. and Thoen, W. (2002). A formal analysis of a generic model of trust for electronic commerce, *Journal of Decision Support Systems*, Vol 33, 233–246.

Hardware Security Appliances for Trust

Adrian Baldwin and Simon Shiu

Trusted Systems Laboratory, Hewlett Packard Labs, Bristol, UK
{Adrian.Baldwin, Simon.Shiu}@hp.com

Abstract. This paper looks at the trust relationships that exist within an outsourcing scenario finding that whilst some of the trust relationships are clear other implicit trust relationships need exposing. These implicit trust relationships are often a result of information supplied for the main explicit task for which an entity is being trusted. The use of hardware security appliance based services is proposed allowing trust to be dissipated over multiple parties whilst retaining efficient execution. Such an approach helps mitigate these implicit trust relationships by increasing the control and transparency given to the trustor.

1   Introduction

Trust is seen as a key enabler for e-business [1]. However, trust is also recognised as a complex phenomenon with technological, behavioural, social and organizational aspects [2] [3]. It is, therefore, not surprising that trust in electronic records and transactions is confused – oftentimes the trusted parties and the main tasks for which they are trusted may be clear, but there are often residual trust relationships that in many cases remain implicit and unnoticed.

Trust is viewed here as a subjective belief about a system or entity within a particular context. Further, a trust relationship takes the form 'A trusts B for C' and this paper concentrates on 'C', i.e. the reasons or tasks for which 'A' is trusting 'B'. This is similar to other work that seeks to categorize the *aspects* or *dimensions* of trust [4] [5]. Such categorizations reflect that we trust a car mechanic to service a car, but not to give medical advice. Most such relationships carry additional implicit trust relationships, for example, in trusting a mechanic to service my car I trust him with my keys and address – which can be copied and retained similarly the doctor is privy to much personal information. In both cases there is potential to copy, and misuse this information long after the main task is complete.

Making such relationships explicit is important since it reveals the extent to which an individual or organisation is actually exposed, and is therefore an important aspect in calculating a trust decision. Moreover, this paper shows that through the application of secure hardware, there are ways of reducing the need to put blind faith into a single entity, and that these implicit aspects can even be dealt with by separately trusted entities, i.e. a 3rd party to manage your car keys, or your medical data.

P. Nixon and S. Terzis (Eds.): Trust Management 2003, LNCS 2692, pp. 46–58, 2003.

This paper contributes in two ways; firstly, issues around implicit trust relationships are brought out using in an example outsourcing scenario. Secondly, it is shown how hardware security appliances can be used to mitigate these problems changing the trust relationships in a system whilst retaining efficiency.

After discussing related work on trust management this paper discusses the trust relationships that exist in outsourcing. The next two sections describe hardware security appliances (HSA) [6] and their application in an outsourcing scenario showing a resultant increased in control and transparency. The next section demonstrates how the resulting trust relationships, particularly those implicit ones relating to information retention, have been changed. With section 7 relating the approach back to the trust management and summarising its current status of the research.

2   Related Work

This work builds on the large existing volume of work on trust and commerce. Bailey [7] describes how philosophers' right back to Plato grappled with what it means to trust distinguishing reliance from trust as when the trustor believes the trustee has a good disposition towards the trustor. For this work the intension of the trustee is not considered important rather significance is placed on the need to trust as a belief, without direct control or likely retribution, and how an understanding and adaptation of this need to trust can lead to an improved trust model. It has been observed [1,3] that trust is a crucial block for e-commerce, particularly as it widens to e-health and e-government. This paper is concerned with ensuring that the trust relationships are fully understood and describes a technique for dissipating this trust over multiple parties.

O'Neill [8] discusses trust in terms of ensuring transparency thereby ensuring that entities can be held to account; however, this is contrasted with the costs of observation. In some ways transparency and data collection is easier to achieve electronically, as it requires little extra effort. The work described here introduces third party observers gathering, certifying storing and evidence thereby enabling transparency as well as adding limited third party control, both are achieved using HSA technology to ensure the associated costs are minimised.

Grandisone & Sloman [5] and Abdul-Rahman & Hailes [4] categorise aspects of trust in terms what entities are trusted for, and the level to which they should be trusted. Jong Kim *et-al* [2] distinguishes technology, product, institutions, and transaction as different dimensions of trust. They also include information content, but focus on the reliability of web content, rather than trust placed to hold, manage and delete information as appropriate. These approaches try to understand holistically the determinants of trust; this paper tries to identify and separate various concerns so that they can be addressed.

Also highly related is the significant body of work done on trust management following the model of KeyNote and PolicyMaker [9]. This work defines trust management as "a unified approach to specifying and interpreting security policies, credentials, relationships which allow direct authorisation of security critical actions", a major contribution being to bind the policy with the public key (as opposed to just identities). This binding and its strong enforcement is a major concern in the HSA work described [6].

Josang [10] defines trust management slightly more generally as "the activity of collecting, codifying, analysing and presenting security relevant evidence with the purpose of making assessments and decisions regarding e-commerce transactions". The paper observes that "the evidence should include, in addition to belief and expectation of intent, proof of competence and correct behaviours". In pushing transparency via HSA based third party observers this work aims to expose this correct behaviour by competent parties.

Also in the field of trust management Grandisone & Sloman [5] describes the SULTAN toolkit, which incorporates an expressive language for specifying and analysing trust relationships. Such languages and toolkits are essential in ensuring trust relationships can be discovered, expressed and reasoned about. It is important to ensure that these tool kits support reasoning about the implied trust relationships and residual information as well as the major trust issues.

3   Trust in Outsourcing

The intent of this section is to describe a scenario of a small or medium sized merchant outsourcing their online presence. They should have a large range of trust concerns although typically, only a few will be explicit and many will be implicit in

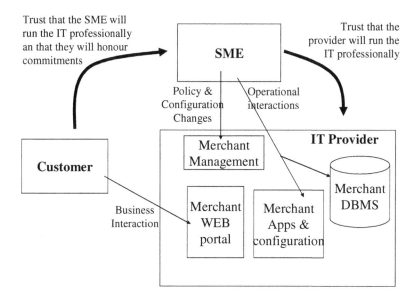

Fig. 1. Operational and Trust Relationships between an SME and it's IT Service Provider

the normal IT operations. The model shown in Fig 1 shows three parties and basic trust relationships between them; the customer trusts the SME who in turn trusts the outsourcer – but it is important to break the trust relationship down into a set of simpler task orientated relationships of the form of 'A trusts B for C'.

Trust is, of course, strongest where there is the least evidence that C is or will be achieved. Trust here is often based on reputation; brand and certification (e.g. operate using best practice). This section describes some of the implicit and explicit trust relationships in this outsourcing scenario with later sections addressing how the trust model can be changed using HSAs.

Consider the case of an average small to medium enterprise (SME) wishing to trade electronically. They may already have some IT infrastructure but may consider the extra web and security skills not core and therefore outsource these functions. On the surface the trust relationships are quite straightforward, the use of an IT provider is transparent to the SME's customers, and the SME trusts the provider to run the IT to the specified standard so that the customer has a good experience of dealing with "them", see fig1.

To be cost effective and to gain economies of scale the IT provider will manage similar infrastructures for many clients. They will ensure that there data centre is run to best practice; that appropriate security measures are in place; that hardware is maintained; disaster recovery policies exist; and that there is sufficient redundancy in their systems to meet the contract and SLAs. Where possible they will use shared infrastructure between clients – for example, storage may be on a SAN, and there may be a single management server. An extreme is the utility data centre [11] where machines are dynamically re-provisioned as needed by customers.

The IT provider is therefore being trusted with commercially sensitive data, processes, cryptographic keys and therefore the identity of a number of, potentially competing, SMEs. These SMEs are also trusting that this data is correctly managed within the data centre; that there is no interference between the various customers and that information will be destroyed on termination of the relationship.

3.1   Identity

The simplest example of this is the identity problem. As fig 1 shows, customers directly interact with the IT Provider, and yet are intended to believe they are interacting directly with the merchant. This means the provider must hold the ability to masquerade as the merchant[1]. Grounding this example in current technology, identity will likely be based on a public key infrastructure (PKI) with the private key being associated with the SME. The private key will be invoked to prove to a customer that they are interacting with the SME (eg using SSL), and potentially to sign/authorize significant transactions (for example, quotes, dispatches, or payments).

Certification Authorities (CAs) are an example of a trusted 3rd party that resolves some of the trust problem by binding the public private key pair to an entity (in this case the SME), see Fig 2. But this is separate from trusting the IT provider with custodianship (and control) of the private key. Fig 2 shows these relationships more explicitly.

---

[1] It is assumed to be inefficient to pass all authentication requests back to the SME itself.

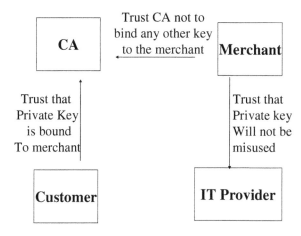

Fig. 2. Trust Relationships for Identity and PKI

The IT provider will of course follow best practice in protecting such keys – for example using hardware security modules (HSMs) to stop accidental disclosure. Such systems provide some protection but they are still under the control of the IT provider, or a hacker gaining access to their systems. That is although the private key is unlikely to leak from the hardware the IT provider can request its use for any operations they wish.

3.2   Information Management

The SME trusts the IT provider with their data both to hold it, and to ensure it is correctly used. The SME needs to retain control over the data and decisions made to change it (eg prices or credit privileges). There are a number of trust relationships that exist here:

1. *Data will be kept confidential.* The SME will not want sensitive data disclosing to outsiders but should also be concerned about disclosures within the IT providers systems for example to a rogue administrator or to one of the other hosted parties.
2. *Data is held with integrity.* The SMEs business processes will be dependant on the data (including business rules) held. The SME trusts that the IT provider provides the necessary security such that only the SME can change the data. Data is vulnerable to change from other parties with access to the IT infrastructure (eg administrators, other SMEs through to hackers).
3. *Processes are run with integrity.* This is at the heart of the outsourcing; the SME wants a third party with IT expertise to run their IT system. Hence the SME trusts that the IT outsourcer will do this correctly – but they will have issues over validating that SLAs are achieved [10].
4. *SME remains in control of the data.* The SME needs to know that changes they make to their data (e.g. a price change) will occur as specified and that the IT provider has accepted their changes. Audit systems may help here but electronic information is easily created and faked.

3.3   Summary

This section has described a scenario and expanded on some of the trust relationships that exist within the IT infrastructure. Clearly these trust relationships could be further refined and are highly interdependent; however, there is sufficient detail here to look at how the trust relationships can be changed using hardware security appliances. The trust relationships have been examined from the external merchants perspective – clearly the IT provider would need a different analysis that would also include its internal trust relationships with their administrators, operators etc. The next two sections describe the HSA concept and how it can be applied in this situation to change some of the trust relationships.

4   Hardware Security Appliances

The example above requires a merchant to place considerable trust in many aspects of the outsourced IT provider, their systems and staff. This paper is concerned with changing the trust model by introducing further parties who are trusted for particular elements in the overall process – thus enhancing the overall trust. Such services may help build trust by controlling certain operations or by ensuring there is a non-repudiable evidence trail of actions. Such services could not take the form of conventional web based trust services [12] which would involve considerable network traffic and inefficiencies. Instead, it is proposed, that a set of simple services running on trusted hardware within the IT outsourcers infrastructure provides an efficient mechanism for adding additional trust anchors into the system.

A hardware security appliance (HSA) is a trusted environment where such services can be run. As well as providing physical security for keys (as in hardware security modules *HSMs*) the HSA model retains control over them ensuring that processes authorising the use of keys are also protected with in the secure hardware. The service aspect suggests that a third party will load a service on a HSA; certify its operation and in doing so give that service instance an identity (and associated private key). Relying parties can now check this certification – they need to trust that the service running in the hardware is secure and that the hardware will prevent observation and tampering.

The HSA is a protected piece of hardware capable of running a simple service such as binding policy checking with the use of cryptographic keys (e.g. controlling signing). The HSA includes a general-purpose processor (e.g. ARM or Pentium) along with supporting RAM and flash memory for service code. It also includes protected memory for storing secrets, counters, and cryptographic keys along with the private key and associated certificate identifying the service instance. The hardware has a protected shell (for example as specified in FIPS 140- level 4 [13]) which would prevent tampering with processes and keys with the contents of protected memory being destroyed on tampering. HSM hardware with a high level of protection exists [Att02] although the HSA usage model is different. These devices can be integrated into existing IT infrastructure as either PCI or LAN devices.

5   Using HSAs

The HSA provides a way that a service provider can run a simple service that remains under their control even when part of an alternative infrastructure. Other parties can interact securely with these services using the service's identity and therefore can have confidence in the role that these services play within the overall system. This section briefly looks at the way HSA based services can be used within the outsourcing example to change the trust model with the introduction of additional, and remote, third parties (the HSA service providers).

5.1   Order Processing

One of the critical operations with in an outsourced e-commerce site is the production of quotes or prices for the end customer. This example considers the production of a signed quote as should happen in more complex e-business processes where documentation is retained; for example, insurance or maintenance agreements or where web services are composed to form more complex purchase solutions (eg booking travel).

The quotation processing system responds to a request made by the customer and takes information from the product, price and customer database. This information is then combined according to a set of, potentially complex, business rules into a quotation, which is then signed and sent back to the customer. These rules may include discounts for packages of products, or for certain customers, types of customers etc. Errors or mistakes in this process could lead to quotations that are too cheap (reducing profit) or too expensive thus leading to a loss of contracts. A greater misuse of the signing identity could allow the outsourcer (or a hacker gaining control) to have the ability to make arbitrary offers, quotations or contracts on behalf of the merchant. Typically, the merchant needs to put a great deal of trust in the outsourcer their systems and staff – as discussed in section 3.

An alternative solution, Fig 3, uses an HSA (labelled HSA1) to control the merchants signing identity by taking the raw quotation generated by the business rules, validating the form of the quotation and that it meets certain policy constraints. In doing so the HSA based signing service ensures that the merchant's identity can only be used within a set of constrained operations making identity theft or misuse much harder.

The quotation must be in a structured machine-readable form, say some form of XML or ASN.1 such that the signing service can first parse and check the form of the quotation. A number of simple constraints can then be validated against a set of policy constraints that the merchant has issued for the signing service ensuring they are tightly tied to the identity. For example, in producing a quote for medical insurance the policies may check that the liability limits are within certain bounds; that certain contractual clauses are present and that there is a reference to a health statement from a patient. The signing HSA will only sign the quotation after these checks have been correctly completed.

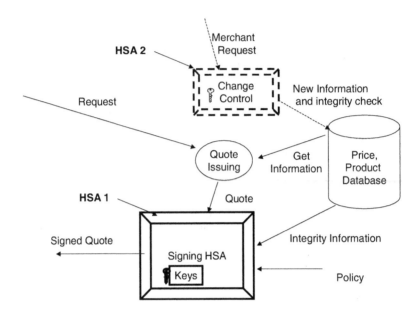

Fig. 3. The Quotation Signing Process

Figure 3 shows this basic process, however, an extra complication is how the signing service can trust the integrity of the price/product database. The simple answer is that there should be cryptographic integrity checks (signatures or message authentication codes) attached to the data. The next question is why this extra signing process should be trusted. The suggested solution in figure 3 is to use a change control HSA (in dotted lines labeled HSA 2). This device receives merchant requests to change information in the product database, authenticates the request, and only then signs meta-data to allow independent authentication of the changed data. Validation policies can now be more dynamic so that rather than checking values are with in certain ranges checks on the integrity of the source can be made. For example, it is possible to check that the price and discount offered are derived from legitimate values from the database.

5.2   Receipting and Audit

One of the key areas of trust between the merchant and the outsourcer is in ensuring that management actions such as price changes are properly handled. The merchant is using the outsourcer in the belief that they are more capable of correctly carrying out changes – this relationship can be supported by providing signed evidence that actions have been carried out. Such evidence could come from the HSA based services within the IT providers system – for example, the signing service issues signed acknowledgements for changes in the quote validation policies.

Another useful HSA based service is a receipting service that contains an identity associated with the IT provider but also with the receipting service providers such that the service will produce timestamped receipts acknowledging requested management actions. The merchant can then be sent the receipts and they can be kept as proof that changes were requested, received and should have been acted upon. A receipting service running within an HSA guarantees that requests cannot be backdated to correct errors. The merchant must still retain receipts so a more convenient solution would use a more sophisticated audit service with HSA based notarisation and allowing the merchant access to their audit records.

5.3   Storage

One of the concerns in section 3 was over the confidentiality of data in both reducing backdoors to the merchant's data and ensuring a strong separation of data between co-hosted merchants. An encrypted SAN system using a HSA based key manager and corresponding HSA enhanced host bus adaptors (SHBA) for bulk encryption is proposed by Baldwin and Shiu [6]. The key manager can run as a unique entity holding and managing secrets that are associated with policies concerning which machines or SHBAs can access which encryption keys and therefore data. Keys are always kept within the secure hardware thereby preventing future leaks. The SHBA can be more tightly integrated into systems above the storage layer providing further confidentiality guarantees.

5.4   Properties

In each of the above examples, simple services are run within an HSA each of which has its own identity and its own domain of control. Each service can be thought of as being independent but they function as an integral part of the IT infrastructure hence bringing a separation of tasks and control whilst retaining execution efficiency.

6   Transformed Trust Model

Section 3 discussed a number of trust relationships that existed with in the outsourcing scenario – the use of HSAs (described above) has significantly changed these relationships. This section looks in more detail at how the trust relationships, in the quotation process, have been modified using these HSA based services.

The identity relationship has been transformed from trusting the IT provider with the identity to trusting the IT provider with a set of tasks they can perform with the identity and trusting the signing HSA to maintain and enforce this task set (Fig 4 (a)). The signing service has an identity allowing the merchant to send it encrypted messages (such as its private key) and allowing a signed audit trail to be created.

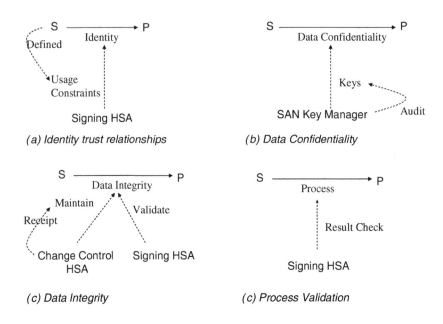

Fig. 4. The changing trust relationships

On the information management side four major aspects were discussed:
1. *Confidentiality.* Even with the course grained SAN encryption scheme referred to above the trust relationship is changed (Fig 4 (b)). A third party holds and allocates keys to decrypt data thereby reducing the possibilities of its inadvertent release. Additionally, a strong audit log of when machines had access to disks –combined with other audit information, helps provides evidence as to the correct handling of data.
2. *Integrity.* The IT provider still holds the basic information and must ensure it does not change but now the integrity checks are securely added and checked as part of the signing process (Fig 4 (c)). Here the IT provider can still change data but the chances of unauthorised changes are reduced by auditing and receipting
3. *Process.* The merchant should trust the IT provider to run the applications correctly and therefore their processes. The trust relationship is modified in that additional checks are made before the SMEs identity is placed on the result (Fig 4 (d)).
4. *Control.* The change control HSA authenticates requests coming from the merchant and only then issues appropriate integrity checks, hence allowing changes to be made (Fig 4 (c)). More importantly, the SME will be sent a secure receipt making the required change non-repudiable – providing evidence of the request.

From the above discussion it is clear that adding HSA based services into the IT provider's infrastructure changes the trust model from one where the IT provider is more or less completely trusted to one with many more controls in place. These changes in the trust relationships are enforced by a mixture of controlling and checking elements in the processes and by enhancing transparency in the system by having strong audit trails. These audit trails should act as a control in that the IT provider's actions are placed on record – however, this is only really a control if these audit trails are easily accessible and meaningful.

The HSA model does not necessarily reduce the trust that the merchant must place in the overall system but it does dissipate it by spreading it over multiple parties. For example, the merchant is still delegating complete control over its digital identity but now the control is spread over multiple parties who are assumed not to collude. The overall effect of this dissipation should allow the merchant to have considerably more confidence in the solution.

The use of the HSA hardware both makes the use of multiple parties possible and also involves a remote trusted entity that has no direct access over its service – thus making collusion hard. The HSA model does rely heavily on device security and trust in its ability to prevent intruders altering or observing the services.

7   Discussion and Current Status

The outsourcing scenario showed that in a rich (and typical) relationship there are explicit and implicit trust relationships each taking the form 'A' trusts 'B' for 'C'. The merchant explicitly trusts the IT provider to run their IT processes but other trust relationships involve trusting them with their digital identity; and with the correct handling of their digital assets (information and processes). This leads to two problems: firstly, how to analyse a relationship to ensure all trust implications become explicit and secondly how these relationships can be expressed and reasoned about. Tools supporting this type of analysis begin to address the rich set of trust issues in any relationship and in doing so remove blocks to such relationships.

Section 2 identified that there is a lot of good current work in this area, however, it is not clear that the tools and methodologies described are sufficiently rich to reason over the range of levels (from abstract descriptions to implementation detail) required for security and trust analysis. Further more, ideally such tools would be driven by those forming the business decisions rather than requiring skilled IT personnel or expensive consultants. Such a problem could be compared to the policy refinement problem [15] where a combination of security and business knowledge is required.

There is also a great deal of work on expressivity or how to describe identified trust relationships. Common within the relationships discussed here has been the notion of duty of care of information necessarily passed to perform an action. For example, the keys that can be used to sign on behalf of the merchant or the commercially sensitive data held within databases. Typically, trust notations allow you to specify the trustor (A), the trustee (B), an action set or collection of resources to be accessed (C), a level of trust, and perhaps a constraint set. Nevertheless, in our case, the action set may be to sign or run a process with constraints being policies on valid quotes that can be signed, or the need to manage information used in processes correctly and not to use it elsewhere. Such constraints can be hard to capture and reason over, especially when they include much longer timescales than those intended for the trust relationships.

A further problem with trust management is concerning how polices are enforced. When expressing policies the ability to enforce those policies becomes an essential part of assessing the trust relationship. This is one of the motivations behind the HSA approach. It is ensuring that policies are strongly enforced within the IT systems. This changes the trust model in the sense that more control and transparency can be given to the trustor, which reduce the amount of trust they have to place before committing to a relationship.

This paper has talked relatively loosely about the problem of producing HSA's and the services that run on them. Currently a few specific software simulations of HSA services have been created. They show they can improve the security of various architectures and a number of patterns for their use are being developed. The next steps in terms of complex business relationships and showing that HSA's can be an enabler, is to deploy a real example service in a trial situation where real trustors and trustees could be involved in discussing the trust issues and hopefully become convinced of the value of the approach.

8   Conclusions

This paper treats a trust relationship, as being of the form 'A' trusts 'B' for 'C'. The focus has been on the form 'C', i.e. that for which 'B' is trusted. The example showed that there are many implicit and yet extremely significant trust relationships. In the electronic world, a large set of these relationships concern residual information that is necessarily shared as part of the overall relationship.

It has been demonstrated that secure hardware, in the guise of HSA's, can be used to increase the control and transparency given to the trustor relating to these types of implicit trust relationships. This in turn changes the trust model and makes them a significant and useful tool for trust management.

References

1. Castelfranchi, C.& Yao-Hua Tan: Why Trust and Deception are Essential for Virtual Societies. In Castelfranchi C. & Yao-Hua Tan (Eds): Introduction to Trust and Deception in Virtual Societies. Kluwer Academic Publishers 2001.
2. Jong Kim, Y.Il Song, D.,, Braynov, S.B., Raghav Rao, H.: A B-to-C Trust Model for On-line Exchange. In Americas Conference on Information Systems, pp 784-787 Boston 2001
3. EC: Open Access to Electronic Commerce for European Small and Medium Size Companies. Memorandum of Understanding, European Commission, DG-XIII-B, 1999
4. Abdul-Rahman A., Hailes S.: A Distributed Trust Model. In Proceedings of the 1997 New Security Paradigms Workshop. Pages 48-60
5. Grandison, T., & Sloman, M.: *SULTAN – A Language of Trust Specification and Analysis*. 8th Workshop of the HP Openview University association. 2001 http://www.hpovua.org
6. Baldwin, A., Shiu, S.: Encryption and Key Management in a SAN, In Proceedings First IEEE International Security in Storage Workshop, Maryland, December 2002
7. Bailey, T.: The Philosophy of Trust (response to 2002 Reith Lecture) http://www.open2.net/trust/on_trust/on_trust1.htm

8.   O'Neill O,: Question of Trust: BBC Reith Lectures 2002. Cambridge University Press 2002 http://www.bbc.co.uk/radio4/reith2002/
9.   Blaze, M., Feigenbaum, J., Lacy J.: Decentralized Trust Management. In Proceedings of IEEE Conference on Security and Privacy 1996.
     http://www.crypto.com/papers/policymaker.pdf
10. Josang, A., Tran, N.: Trust Management for E-Commerce. In Proceedings Virtual Banking 2000. http://195.13.121.137/virtualbanking2000/index.htm
11. Turner, V. Utility Data Center: HPs first proof point for service centric computing. 2001 http://www.hp.com/solutions1/infrastructure/ infolibrary/idcwhitepaper.pdf
12. Baldwin, A., Shiu, S., Casassa Mont, M.: Trust Services: A Framework for Service based Solutions, In proceedings of the 26th IEEE Computer Software and Applications Conference (COMPSAC), Oxford UK, 2002
13. Fips: Security Requirements for cryptographic modules. Fips 140-2 2001
     http://csrc.ncsl.nist.gov/publications/fips/fips140-1/fips1402.pdf
14. Attalla: Atalla Security Products (HP) http://atalla.inet.cpqcorp.net
15. Casassa Mont, M,, Baldwin, A., Goh., C.: Power Prototype: Towards integrated policy based management. In Hong, J., Weihmayer R. (eds): Proceedings of the IEEE/IFIP Network Operations and Management Symposium (NOMS 2000), Hawaii May 2000, pp 789-802

Managing Trust and Reputation in the XenoServer Open Platform

Boris Dragovic, Steven Hand, Tim Harris, Evangelos Kotsovinos, and
Andrew Twigg

University of Cambridge Computer Laboratory, Cambridge, UK
{firstname.lastname}@cl.cam.ac.uk

Abstract. Participants in public distributed computing do not find it
easy to trust each other. The massive number of parties involved, their
heterogeneous backgrounds, disparate goals and independent nature are
not a good basis for the development of relationships through purely
social mechanisms. This paper discusses the trust management issues
that arise in the context of the XenoServer Open Platform: a public infrastructure for wide-area computing, capable of hosting tasks that span
the full spectrum of distributed paradigms. We examine the meaning
and necessity of trust in our platform, and present our trust management architecture, named XenoTrust. Our system allows participants
of our platform to express their beliefs and advertise them, by submitting them to the system. It provides aggregate information about other
participants' beliefs, by supporting the deployment of rule-sets, defining
how beliefs can be combined. XenoTrust follows the same design principles that we are using throughout the XenoServer project: it provides
a flexible platform over which many of the interesting distributed trust
management algorithms presented in the literature can be evaluated in
a large-scale wide-area setting.

1 Introduction

The XenoServer project [9] is developing a public infrastructure for wide-area distributed computing, creating a world in which XenoServer execution platforms
are scattered across the globe and available to any member of the public. Users
of our platform are able to run programs at points throughout the network in order to reduce communication latencies, avoid network bottlenecks and minimize
long-haul network charges. They can also use it to deploy large-scale experimental services, and to provide a network presence for transiently-connected mobile
devices. Resource accounting is an integral part of the XenoServer Open Platform, with clients paying for the resources used by their programs and server
operators being paid for running the programs that they host.

The public and open nature of the platform imposes a need for a trust management system. In the real world, servers and clients operate autonomously.
Servers may be unreliable; they may try to overcharge clients, may not run programs faithfully, or may even try to extract client secrets. Clients may attempt to

P. Nixon and S. Terzis (Eds.): Trust Management 2003, LNCS 2692, pp. 59–74, 2003.

abuse the platform; they may try to avoid paying their bills, or to run programs with nefarious, anti-social or illegal goals.

This paper covers the trust and reputation management architecture that is used in the XenoServer Open Platform. In Sect. 2 we introduce the context in which we are doing this work and then in Sect. 3 we identify the threat model within which XenoTrust is designed to operate. Sect. 4 presents the XenoTrust architecture and the notions of trust and reputation it manages. In Sect. 5 we discuss the implementation choices and trade-offs that exist. Sect. 6 describes related work and Sect. 7 concludes.

1.1   Contributions

This paper makes two primary contributions:

- Firstly, as we shall see in Sect. 2, the architecture of the XenoServer platform sets it apart from those within which existing distributed trust management systems operate. Unlike simple peer-to-peer recommendation services, we are concerned with running real tasks on real servers for real money within a federated system whose constituent parts may have different notions of "correct" behaviour.
- Secondly, within this setting, the XenoTrust architecture provides a trust management system which accommodates flexible policies for allowing its participants to derive their own context-dependent notions of one anothers' reputations. This is again in contrast to existing systems which assume either that reputation is a global property or that the way in which it is assessed is fixed.

2   XenoPlatform Overview

Fig. 1 illustrates the high-level architecture of the XenoServer Open Platform, distinguishing the various rôles and interfaces involved. On the left hand side we see a XenoServer, on the right hand side a client, and at the top an entity called XenoCorp. XenoServers host tasks that are submitted by clients and XenoCorp acts as a trusted third party. For exposition, it is easiest to assume a single XenoCorp. However our architecture is designed to support multiple competing entities, providing that they follow the same basic interfaces. This is analogous to the way in which the commercial world supports many distinct and competing institutions and currencies.

To set the general scene, it is important to realize the separation between a XenoCorp and the organizations running XenoServers. The former provides authentication, auditing, charging and payment, and has contractual relationships with clients and with XenoServer operators – much as VISA or MasterCard act as intermediaries between credit card holders and the merchants from which they make purchases. It is the third party trusted by both clients and servers.

The XenoServers themselves may be run by disparate organizations, akin to the way in which server hosting facilities currently operate. XenoServers function

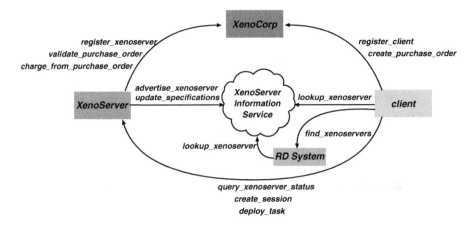

Fig. 1. The XenoServer Open Platform

on a commercial basis using well-maintained machines with long-term network presence – not in "spare cycles" on users' desktop systems. This, along with the existence of XenoCorps, is an important distinction between our system and "peer-to-peer" distributed computing projects.

In the center of Fig. 1 we see the XenoServer Information Service. This acts as an intermediary between XenoServers, who advertise information within it, and clients, who perform queries on the service. There are no architectural conventions requiring that there be only one XIS although we envisage that this situation will develop naturally since it makes sense for XenoServers to advertise as widely as possible, and for clients to draw on the largest possible information base when performing lookups.

The information held in the XIS takes the form of low-level information about particular XenoServers – for instance their location and an indication of the facilities that they offer. Queries take simple forms such as "Which servers claim to be in the UK?" or "Which servers support IA-64 tasks?". The timescales over which XIS updates are made and the currency which queries should enjoy follows much the same model as the existing Domain Name Service (DNS). That is, we expect that XenoServer's advertisements within the XIS will be updated on the order of hours or days and that it is acceptable to use aggressive caching within the XIS. Of course, this model raises some of the same problems that occur with the DNS – for instance, who should operate and fund it. As we shall see, these same questions also arise for XenoTrust and we shall return to them in Sect. 5.

The initial XIS implementation is a distributed storage service optimized under the assumptions that (i) writes are always total rewrites, (ii) XenoServers arrange that there is only ever one writer for each piece of data, (iii) reads of stale data are always either safe or can be verified and (iv) information held in the XIS is for use by tools rather than humans. Self-certifying names [10] are used to ensure the authenticity of retrieved information and to allow clients to complain to the XenoServer's XenoCorp about inaccurate advertisements.

Although there is nothing to stop clients from using the XIS directly to select appropriate XenoServers, or indeed from contacting prospective servers directly without introduction, we anticipate that most will make use of one of a number of Resource Discovery (RD) systems. These perform a matchmaking process between clients and XenoServers, receiving specifications of clients' requirements and using a search algorithm to identify a number of suitable servers. As with the XIS, the information returned is based on the advertisements received; clients then query the suggested XenoServers directly to obtain up-to-date resource availability and a spot price. However, unlike the XIS, the queries are at a much higher level, for instance corresponding to "Find a XenoServer for a networked game of Quake that is suitable for clients A, B and C".

There may be multiple such RD Systems, either for simple competition (as exists between online search engines) or for specialisation to particular kinds of client, XenoServer or task. The algorithm with which the mapping is performed is entirely dependent on the RD mechanism.

In companion papers we introduce this high-level architecture in more detail [11] and describe our prototype XenoServer platform [3].

3   Threat Model

We assume that some out-of-band mechanism is available to provide assurance of XenoCorp's identity; for instance, our first XenoCorp will interact over *https* connections with a suitably signed certificate. In turn, one of XenoCorp's rôles is to authenticate XenoServers and clients to its satisfaction; in our prototype deployment this will be evinced by signed credentials that can be tied to the issuing XenoCorp.

This means that both XenoServers and clients have a way of mapping one another back to a real-world identity, either directly or through a XenoCorp. This capability ultimately provides a way in which they can carry complaints through to non-technical solutions in the judicial system. What, then, is the rôle of XenoTrust? In answering this question, and identifying the requirements of XenoTrust, we shall consider the major kinds of threat which exist to the participants in platform.

Threats to XenoServers. XenoServers face the clearest threats. Disreputable clients may try to place tasks on them but then not pay. They may also try to run tasks that use XenoServers as the source of some nefarious activity on the network, perhaps to try to conceal the actual originator. Server operators must therefore take care over both the jobs that they accept, and their management of auditing information for investigating any problems reported. If security flaws are discovered in the XenoServer software then clients may try to exploit those.

Threats to Clients. Clients may find that the jobs they submit to a particular XenoServer are not executed faithfully. A malicious server operator may overcharge for resource consumption. Others operators may simply have been unlucky and bought unreliable machines to use as XenoServers. In either case, technical solutions are not present; to date, software mechanisms such as proof carrying code have focussed on ensuring the safety properties of clients, rather than of servers. Although "trusted computing" schemes such as TCPA [15] provide mechanisms for ensuring tamper-proof execution of core system components, they cannot prevent software errors, or faults in the underlying hardware. In any case, such schemes do not fit with our goal of allowing the XenoServer platform to host code written in a broad range of existing distribution formats which may not be supported on the trusted platforms that arise.

Threats to XenoCorps. If there are many XenoCorps then disreputable clients or server operators may try to register with each in succession if they continue to be ejected from the platform.

Where these threats involve an identifiable component misbehaving, either a XenoServer or a task running on a XenoServer, then it is of course possible for the other parties involved to complain to their common XenoCorp. Problems can arise, however, in a number of ways. Firstly, it is quite unrealistic to expect all of the participants to agree on common standards of behaviour – even if a single "acceptable use policy" could be enforced by XenoCorp then it would most likely be written in a natural language. Secondly, the volume of complaints may be large and the distinction between trivial and important ones unclear. Finally, issuing a complaint is difficult when the source of misbehavior is not straightforward to determine.

Consider, for example, a situation where a client is running a POSIX application on a XenoServer – perhaps within the XenoLinux environment that forms part of our initial deployment. Monitoring suggests that the XenoLinux environment in question starts requiring more network bandwidth than initially specified when the job was started. There are several possible explanations:

- The client's application is misbehaving as part of its normal operation, perhaps acting as a server subject to an unexpectedly high level of demand.
- Perhaps the client's estimate of the resources necessary is simply inaccurate. The XenoServer will be multiplexing its physical resources between a range of tasks and predicting context switch overheads or the effects of contention in caches and shared buffers is difficult. Similarly, there will be subtle differences between the performance of processors or execution engines even if they accept the same execution formats (for instance between a Pentium-3 and Pentium-4 processor, or between a JVM from Sun and a JVM from IBM).
- Perhaps the client's application has been compromised and is thus being caused to misbehave.
- The XenoServer itself could have been compromised and be misbehaving.

One can also envisage more intricate causes of problems. For instance, it would be naïve to assume that the XenoServer software will not exhibit the kinds of fault that occur in mainstream operating systems. One task could exploit such a fault and plant code to cause latent problems for subsequent jobs, to extract data from them, to consume their resources, to masquerade as their owner or simply to cause them to fail. Such problems can often only be tracked down after the fact, once forensic evidence of such an exploit has been gathered.

In a setting like this it is very difficult to identify which of these explanations is the actual cause of the higher resource demands. Any naïve decision making policy at this stage would open numerous possibilities for misuse and deception by sophisticated attackers.

4   XenoTrust Design

Fundamental to all of these concerns is a notion of *trust*. Should a XenoServer trust a prospective client to submit reasonable code for execution? Should a client trust that a XenoServer it is considering will execute its code correctly? Should a XenoCorp trust that a prospective XenoServer operator or client is going to be a trouble-free participant? As is usually observed, these questions are all subjective and context dependent.

We take a two-level approach to managing trust in the XenoServer Open Platform by distinguishing *authoritative* and *reputation-based* trust:

- *Authoritative trust.* This boolean property is established between a Xeno-Corp and the clients and servers that register with it. It is evinced by the credentials issued by the XenoCorp. These can be validated by any of that XenoCorp's other clients and servers.
- *Reputation-based trust.* This is a continuous property which quantifies, in a particular setting, the trustworthiness that one component ascribes to another.

We discuss these aspects of our trust management architecture in Sections 4.1 and 4.2 respectively.

4.1   Authoritative Trust

As was illustrated in Fig. 1, each XenoCorp acts as an authority which is responsible for registering the clients and servers that wish to participate. The XenoCorp has ultimate authority for registering and ejecting participants and for establishing authoritative trust between them and itself.

It issues credentials to correctly-validated participants and can rescind these credentials should the participant de-register from the system or be ejected from it. Note that the validation step indicated in Fig. 1 and performed between a XenoServer and XenoCorp before starting a session provides an opportunity to detect rescinded credentials.

This "authoritative trust" underpins the XenoServer Open Platform because it confirms that a XenoCorp is aware of a "real-world" identity bound to the participant. This enables recourse through the courts should it be necessary and – so long as new real-world identities cannot be created trivially – makes it harder for a participant to re-register once ejected.

An analogy with the real world is that an individual may decide to be law-abiding and socially responsible, or they may decide to behave objectionably and thereby risk prosecution by a globally acceptable authority – the judicial system. In important transactions, interaction is often underpinned by the examination of identification documents or checks for criminal records and so on – that is, by evidence of authoritative trust between the state and the parties involved.

XenoCorps will differ in exactly what information is required at registration time – in a commercial setting this may be a credit card number registered to the participant, or physical evidence of a passport or picture-ID enabling charges to be traced.

4.2 Reputation-Based Trust

Observing the same analogy as presented above, people in the real world, whether offenders or not, have a reputation which influences their relationships with other members of society. In an extreme case, someone might be believed to be an offender, but not yet be convicted. This notion of reputation is subjective, as listeners attach different significance to what they hear. Mrs Smith's reputation for always being ten minutes late may be of little consequence to her friends and family (who, knowing this fact, may already incorporate it into their own timekeeping arrangements), but be of great importance to a potential employer. These observations carry over to how interactions are managed in the XenoServer Open Platform and the way in which clients and XenoServers form opinions about one another.

The second layer of the XenoTrust model is this form of "reputation-based trust". Compared to the authoritative trust relationship, this second-level is established on a point-to-point and highly dynamic basis between individual XenoServers and clients. Unlike registration with XenoCorp, it is entirely up to participants to choose whether or not to use the system – as in the real world, some participants may choose to bear what others believe to be an unacceptable risk or to rely on other sources of information.

Conceptually, each component forms a *reputation vector*, which stores values about different aspects of the reputation of other components in the platform. Ordinarily, individual clients and servers will build up this information locally as they interact with others. Their views will be subjective, perhaps with some clients favouring one aspect of a server's behaviour (say, factually correct price advertisements) and others favouring other aspects (say, a reliable service with low jitter during network transmission). It is the participant's responsibility to decide how to interpret the scores in its reputation vector, e.g. to decide at what point a counterpart is deemed unworthy of further interaction.

Participants will also tell others about their observations. Again, it is up to participants to decide how to deal with the reports that they hear. However, the community as a whole may benefit from participants exchanging reputation information with one other, each using that information to influence their own reputation vector. For instance, when a new member arrives in the XenoServer Open Platform, and is looking to co-operate with other components, it is useful to give it access to existing participants' reputation information.

Of course, a direct implementation of such a scheme would not be practical an any large setting. Broadcasting information from every participant is unfeasible. In the XenoServer platform many participants will interact with only a small subset of others and will only need to form trust judgements about them. Instead, we will present the operation of XenoTrust first of all at the level of the operations that it exposes to participants and we will then discuss, in Sect. 5, some of the implementation and deployment options that exist.

Our model involves three steps; *statement advertisement* in which one participant provides XenoTrust with information about another, *rule-set deployment* in which a participant describes how to compute its reputation vector and then *reputation retrieval* in which entries from its reputation vector are actually evaluated and delivered to the participant.

Statement Advertisement. We define a *statement* as the unit of reputation information that components advertise to others. A statement is a tuple, including the advertiser's identity, the subject component's identity, a token representing the aspect of the subject's reputation that is being considered and a series of values which indicate the extent of this reputation. The tuple is signed using the advertiser's authoritative credentials to prevent forgery.

The interpretation of these tokens and values is a matter for convention between the components that are using XenoTrust. For exposition, we may consider statements such as $(C, X, \text{payment}, 1, 50)$ giving component C's view on how X scores in terms of making payments. The scores 1, 50 may indicate a maximum value of 1 on a $[0 \ldots 1]$ scale based on an experience of 50 interactions. In other statements, C may report $(C, X, \text{belief}, 0.8)$ meaning that C attaches a weight of 0.8 to what they hear from X. Again, the interpretation of these is a matter of convention by C.

Self-certifying names are used to prevent forged statements. However, beyond that, XenoTrust does nothing beyond this to ensure that statements are in any sense valid: as with real-world advertisements, users are under no compulsion to believe what they see or to pay any attention to it.

Rule-set Deployment. Components are welcome to search XenoTrust directly for statements that have been made. For instance, before hosting a job from a particular client, a XenoServer may query the XenoTrust system for any statements that have previously been made about the client. Again, these would be simple queries of the form "return all the statements naming participant A". However, this scheme is far from scalable and – unless very extensive queries are made – it will only take into account direct statements made about the component in question.

Instead, the approach that we take is to move the computation of reputation vectors from the participants involved into XenoTrust itself. This allows the

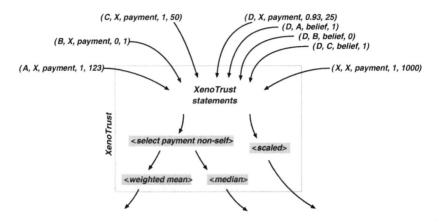

Fig. 2. Aggregation of statements by XenoTrust

aggregation of information to take place within XenoTrust and, crucially, allows it to be updated incrementally as new statements are received. It also allows the results of this computation to be shared between participants who are using the same rulesets to derive their reputation vectors. Some examples of the kind of rules we anticipate are given within the example scenario considered in Sect. 4.3.

Reputation Retrieval. The final step in using XenoTrust is for one component to query the rule-sets that it has deployed in order to retrieve elements from its reputation vector.

4.3 Example

Fig. 2 provides an overview of how these stages of XenoTrust may be used. This example shows statements issued by five components – four servers (A, B, C, D) which have been hosting jobs on behalf of a client X. All of these statements are held in the XenoTrust system, available for public view.

Statements labeled "payment" refer to the server's view of whether the client is reputable when it comes to settling their bills, indicating how likely they believe an interaction with X is to proceed without problems in this regard (a value between 0 and 1) and how many times they have interacted with X (an integer). For instance, A has interacted with X 123 times and assigns X the maximum score. In contrast, B has interacted with X just once and assigns the lowest possible score. Furthermore, D has made additional statements indicating the value it places on statements made by each of the other three servers, again as a value from 0 to 1. In this case the client X has also made a statement about itself, claiming to have interacted a great many times and always successfully – other users of XenoTrust would be wise to attach little credence to this statement.

Various users of XenoTrust have installed different rule-sets for quantifying their trust in clients on the basis of the statements that have been made.

In this case D is using a rule set "<scaled>" which combines the "payment" statements according to D's own "belief" statements. For instance B and X's statements would not influence D, but A and C's would. Other rule-sets select statements made by other parties (i.e. discarding X's self-referential statement) before combining them according to various averages.

4.4   Users of XenoTrust

The service provided by XenoTrust is valuable across the XenoServer platform in ways beyond its direct use by clients and by XenoServer operators:

Resource Discovery. As we saw in Sect. 2 we anticipate that many clients will take advantage of search facilities provided by resource discovery systems. These RD services may use XenoTrust to determine the "trustworthiness" of a XenoServer as one of the axes along which a resource search may be performed. If an RD service specializes in a particular category of task – such as networked games – then this would influence the kinds of rule-set that it would deploy.

XenoCorps. To make valid decisions over when to consider ejecting a participant, a XenoCorp can use information gathered through XenoTrust. This creates a link between the authoritative trust level and the reputation-based trust level, whereby the former is influenced and ultimately modeled by the latter.

From the point of view of the XenoTrust service there is no distinction between XenoCorp and any other component in the system. Rule-sets used by XenoCorp and the algorithms employed for deciding whether a component should be ejected are implementation are policy specific and outside the scope of this paper. The level of sophistication at a XenoCorp can be expected to be proportional to the financial, commercial etc. sensitivity inherent in a particular setting; for example, the amount of anti-fraud insurance cover obtained should be proportional to the incentive to commit fraud.

The outlined inter-layer links ensure that misbehaving components, whether faulty or malicious, will eventually be penalized platform-wide by XenoCorp. An interesting aspect of the approach is that optional reputation-based trust is projected onto a mandatory authoritative trust level. The effect of this should be an incentive for components to participate fully within the XenoTrust model. Furthermore, if an inter-XenoCorp trust information sharing agreement is in place, offending components may suffer global consequences for misbehaving.

4.5   Discussion

Most widely spread attacks on reputation systems are from the family of so-called *Sybil attacks* [8]. Sybil attacks assume that a single hostile or faulty entity can present multiple indentities, and by using those, substantially influence the behavior of the overall system. As argued in [8], these attacks are prevalent in systems in which it is easy to come by fresh identities. However, we argue that Sybil attacks are not feasible in the XenoServer platform for two main reasons:

1. XenoCorp acts as a centralized, trusted, certification agency that validates all identities used in the platform. For an entity to fraudulently register multiple identities it would be neccessary to present XenoCorp with the same number of real world, unlinkable, legal identities. The nature of credentials required by XenoCorp depends on the level of security required against Sybil attacks; we can expect a balance to be drawn between the cost of validating credentials and the cost of a successful Sybil attack.

2. As participation in XenoTrust is optional and as the way in which each component uses reputation data obtained from XenoTrust is implementation-specific, it would be difficult for a hostile entity to accurately estimate the impact of an attack. In effect, an attacker would not be able to balance the costs of obtaining multiple identities against its financial gain. Furthermore, as the platform is expected to be dynamic in terms of participants, even analysis of historical behavior of the system would not gain an attacker deep insight into the future on which it could base its gain estimates.

A further possible kind of attack on XenoTrust is *shilling*; providing a financial incentive to real world entities for providing fake reputation data about a set of components to XenoTrust. The problem of uncertainty for the attacker, as described earlier, further influenced by the number of components in the system, would provide a strong disincentive for this type of attack.

5   Deploying XenoTrust

The previous section discussed the core architecture of XenoTrust. We will now turn to a number of more practical questions, implementation considerations and further issues.

5.1   XenoTrust Implementation

There are several options that one could consider in terms of where XenoTrust will be hosted, how statements are advertised, and how rulesets are deployed and evaluated. XenoTrust statements could be stored centrally in each XenoCorp, or in a specialized component, or, indeed, it may be that XenoTrust would be implemented over the XIS (XenoServer Information Service). In this case, statements advertised are stored in XIS, and rule-set deployment and reputation retrieval are performed on XIS.

With XenoTrust one can imagine some people wanting to run storage nodes for themselves holding their statements, rather than casting them into the "best effort" XIS cloud. One possibility is for a XenoCorp to provide such a store and make it mandatory for its clients and servers to feed information back. Alternatively a "Which?"-style consumer magazine or a "Slashdot"-style online community could run one from which to promulgate its recommendations.

In the case of our prototype deployment, we anticipate that the same people who run the first XenoCorp would also run the first XIS and XenoTrust systems, providing the latter two as an incentive to encourage business on the former – much as existing DNS servers are run as a convenience to the Internet community without explicit transaction-based charging.

5.2 Funding XenoTrust

An interesting aspect of the operation of XenoTrust is how the system's operation will be funded in the XenoServer Open Platform. Resources in our platform need to be paid for in order to make the system economically practical.

One option would be to use a subscription-based system, where components would have to sign up for using the XenoTrust in advance and pay for it. A problem with this model is that all components are charged the same, which can be unfair for ones that use the system less.

Another possibility is to charge components whenever they advertise a statement. The disadvantage here is that participants that advertise a lot of – potentially valuable – information are discouraged from doing so, while components that overuse the query mechanisms for obtaining that information are not charged at all. Participants can also be charged in a per-query basis, but this model does not encourage components to advertise information. Another difficulty is that queries can vary from very simple to fairly complex, so figuring out the price of each query according to the deployed rule-sets may be difficult and/or costly.

Rewarding advertisement is in general rather difficult since there is no easy way to distinguish between credible statements and ones advertised simply for gaining credit. Using the "belief" component of the reputation of an advertiser may offer possibilities here.

5.3 Rule-Set Selection

The selection of a suitable set of rules or the language for defining them needs to take into account the computational cost of applying them, the possibility for sharing of this computation between users with similar rules and (perhaps) the possibility of XenoTrust forming a covert-channel communication mechanism.

In terms of concrete rule-sets that may be used, a promising direction is to use XenoTrust to support the evaluation of some of the policies being developed by the SECURE project [16]. This uses a lattice to represent trust values and allows principals to provide expressions that define their rules for delegation. For instance one principal might specify:

$$Pol(t_g, p) = (p = \text{Tim})?0.5 : (t_g(\text{Alice})(p) \sqcap t_g(\text{Bob})(p))$$

In this case t_g is the *global trust space*, conceptually the combination of all of the principals' current trust values and p is the principal about whom a trust decision is being evaluated. In this case if p is the principal "Tim" then a value of 0.5 is returned directly, otherwise the least-upper-bound of the trust values believed by Alice and Bob is returned. The use of a functional language should allow evaluation work to be shared between users whose policies co-incide.

Of course, we can do other things with this, but it provides an effective framework whilst still not requiring, on a global basis, a specific method of computation or set of trust values.

5.4 Load Balancing

The XenoTrust system can also be used to facilitate load balancing within the network. Highly loaded servers will disobey QoS agreements more often than less loaded ones, as the resources on those servers will become more congested.

Thus, under the XenoTrust model, this will lead to more negative statements being issued about them, and, therefore, to a reduction of the tasks that will be submitted to them for deployment. This will help reduce their load, as the reputation of fresh and less loaded servers will increase for as long as they provide good service. This also provides an incentive for XenoServer owners not to over-estimate what work their machines can do – brief overloading could lead to long-term underloading, or to their having to lower their prices.

This is an intriguing use of a reputation system, although it throws up a large number of further issues. We hope to investigate these further in the future.

6 Related Work

Over the last ten years, several researchers have developed trust models and implementations based on them. Josang provides definitions and categorization of several kinds of trust [12]. One of the first trust models and formal definitions of trust in electronic communities was introduced by Marsh [13]. His model, based on social and psychological properties, is considered rather complex, essentially theoretical and possibly impractical. Beth et al. suggest a theoretical model and methodology to represent and derive trust relationships [4].

Real-world paradigms that incorporate trust management subsystems include on-line auctions and retailers, like eBay and the `amazon.co.uk` marketplace. In such systems, buyers and sellers can rate each other after each transaction. The reputation of each participant is computed as the average of the scores reported over a specific amount of time – e.g. the last six months – and stored in a centralized repository. Kasbah [7] introduces the use of designated "regulator agents" that roam the marketplace to ensure that participant agents do not misbehave.

Systems like Kasbah and the on-line auctions and retailers have very limited expressiveness, as they assume that all participants agree on the criteria on which such reputations are based, and that they attach equal credence to everyone's statements. Moreover, reputation in those systems is usually single-dimensional, and their scalability is restricted, as the central repository or agent that stores the reputation information is a single point of failure, and has to grow in proportion to the number of participants.

Another research avenue relates to peer-to-peer systems. In the model suggested by Rahman and Hailes, each participant uses an agent to decide both which participants to trust, and which other agents' opinions to trust [1]. Even though implementation issues are not discussed in detail in that paper, reputation statements advertised are somehow broadcast or multicast between the participants and are then stored in each peer independently. This is inefficient in terms of network traffic as well as information redundancy; in the XenoServer system, many participants will never interact with one another and need not know one another's reputation, while statements are stored in XenoTrust rather than in the participants themselves. Yu and Singh [17] propose a social mechanism of reputation management relying on agents that exchange and assess reputation information on behalf of the users. The model proposed by Aberer and Despotovic is the one that is closest to ours [2]. Our approach is fundamentally different from all the above, as in the XenoServer Open Platform all entities are associated with a real or legal identity, and operate in a pseudonymous rather than totally anonymous manner.

Approaches like the PGP system, the X.509 framework, PolicyMaker [6] and KeyNote [5] use a different notion of trust, as they focus on techniques to formulate security policies and credentials, determining whether particular sets of credentials satisfy the relevant policies and deferring trust to third parties. Maurer proposes a probabilistic alternative to the above models [14]; trust management in that context is tightly coupled with hard security and the mapping between keys and identities. In such systems, identity-based certificates create an artificial layer of indirection between the information that is certified (which answers the question "who is the holder of this public key") and the question that a secure application must answer ("can we trust this public key for this purpose?"). Hard security approaches help establish that the party one is dealing with is authenticated and authorized to take some particular actions, but do not ensure that that party is doing what is expected and delivering good service.

Our system differs fundamentally from these in that it combines hard security trust and soft, reputation-based trust, while maintaining a flexible and scalable architecture.

7   Conclusion

The XenoServer Open Platform allows users to deploy and run computations on a large number of globally dispersed XenoServers, while performing accurate accounting and charging for the resources consumed. In such an environment, it is crucial to have a model of trust which allows individual components to decide whether to interact with each other. We have presented XenoTrust, a two-layer model which combines authoritative and reputation-based trust: the former prevents the Sybil attacks that most peer-to-peer and other ad-hoc open platforms are defenseless against; the latter avoids the notion of a global interpretation of "trust" and "risk". This is crucial in a large-scale computing platform with users and suppliers from many cultures and jurisdictions. It gives individuals the flexibility to make whatever game-theoretic trade-offs they wish.

The design is simple and should lead to a straightforward implementation. However the ultimate test will take place when we make our initial public deployment of the XenoServer Open Platform. Please contact us if you would like to be involved.

References

1. ABDUL-RAHMAN, A., AND HAILES, S. Supporting Trust in Virtual Communities. In *Proceedings of the Hawaii International Conference on System Sciences 33, Maui, Hawaii (HICSS)* (January 2000).
2. ABERER, K., AND DESPOTOVIC, Z. Managing Trust in a Peer-2-Peer Information System. In *CIKM* (2001), pp. 310–317.
3. BARHAM, P. R., DRAGOVIC, B., FRASER, K. A., HAND, S. M., HARRIS, T. L., HO, A. C., KOTSOVINOS, E., MADHAVAPEDDY, A. V., NEUGEBAUER, R., PRATT, I. A., AND WARFIELD, A. K. Xen 2002. Tech. Rep. UCAM-CL-TR-553, University of Cambridge, Computer Laboratory, Jan. 2003.
4. BETH, T., BORCHERDING, M., AND KLEIN, B. Valuation of Trust in Open Networks. In *Proceedings of the 3rd European Symposium on Research in Computer Security – ESORICS '94* (1994), pp. 3–18.
5. BLAZE, M., FEIGENBAUM, J., AND KEROMYTIS, A. D. KeyNote: Trust Management for Public-Key Infrastructures (Position Paper). *Lecture Notes in Computer Science 1550* (1999), 59–63.
6. BLAZE, M., FEIGENBAUM, J., AND LACY, J. Decentralized Trust Management. In *Proceedings of the 1996 IEEE Symposium on Security and Privacy* (May 1996), pp. 164–173.
7. CHAVEZ, A., AND MAES, P. Kasbah: An agent marketplace for buying and selling goods. In *Proceedings of the First International Conference on the Practical Application of Intelligent Agents and Multi-Agent Technology (PAAM'96)* (London, UK, 1996), Practical Application Company, pp. 75–90.
8. DOUCEUR, J. R. The Sybil Attack. In *Proceedings of the 1st International Workshop on Peer-to-Peer Systems, Boston, MA* (March 2002).
9. FRASER, K. A., HAND, S. M., HARRIS, T. L., LESLIE, I. M., AND PRATT, I. A. The Xenoserver computing infrastructure. Tech. Rep. UCAM-CL-TR-552, University of Cambridge, Computer Laboratory, Jan. 2003.
10. FU, K., KAASHOEK, M. F., AND MAZIERES, D. Fast and secure distributed read-only file system. *Computer Systems 20*, 1 (2000), 1–24.
11. HAND, S., HARRIS, T., KOTSOVINOS, E., AND PRATT, I. Controlling the XenoServer Open Platform, November 2002. To appear in the Proceedings of the 6th International Conference on Open Architectures and Network Programming (OPENARCH), April, 2003.
12. JOSANG, A. The right type of trust for distributed systems. In *Proceedings of the 1996 New Security Paradigms Workshop.* (1996), C. Meadows, Ed., ACM.
13. MARSH, S. *Formalising Trust as a Computational Concept.* PhD thesis, Department of Mathematics and Computer Science, University of Stirling, 1994.
14. MAURER, U. Modelling a Public-Key Infrastructure. In *ESORICS: European Symposium on Research in Computer Security* (1996), LNCS, Springer-Verlag.

15. Trusted Computing Platform Alliance (TCPA): Main Specification, Version 1.1b, 2002. TCPA Specifciation, available at
    http://www.trustedcomputing.org/docs/main\%20v1_1b.pdf.
16. TWIGG, A. SECURE project overview.
    http://www.cl.cam.ac.uk/Research/SRG/opera/projects/index.html.
17. YU, B., AND SINGH, M. P. A Social Mechanism of Reputation Management in Electronic Communities. In *Cooperative Information Agents* (2000), pp. 154–165.

Trust-Based Protection of Software Component Users and Designers

Peter Herrmann

University of Dortmund, Computer Science Department,
44221 Dortmund, Germany,
Peter.Herrmann@udo.edu

Abstract. Software component technology supports the cost-effective design of applications suited to the particular needs of the application owners. This design method, however, causes two new security risks. At first, a malicious component may attack the application incorporating it. At second, an application owner may incriminate a component designer falsely for any damage in his application which in reality was caused by somebody else. The first risk is addressed by security wrappers controlling the behavior at the component interface at runtime and enforcing certain security policies in order to protect the other components of the application against attacks from the monitored component. Moreover, we use trust management to reduce the significant performance overhead of the security wrappers. Here, the kind and intensity of monitoring a component is adjusted according to the experience of other users with this component. Therefore a so-called trust information service collects positive and negative experience reports of the component from various users. Based on the reports, special trust values are computed which represent the belief or disbelief of all users in a component resp. the uncertainty about it. The wrappers adjust the intensity of monitoring a component dependent on its current trust value.
In this paper, we focus on the second security risk. To prevent that a component user sends wrong reports resulting in a bad trust value of the component, which therefore would be wrongly incriminated, the trust information service stores also trust values of the component users. The trust values are based on valuations resulting from validity checks of the experience reports sent by the component users. Therefore an experience report is tested for consistency with a log of the component interface behavior which is supplied by the component user together with the report. Moreover, the log is checked for being correct as well. By application of Jøsang's subjective logic we make the degree, to which the experience reports of a component user are considered to compute the trust value of a component, conditional upon the user's own trust value. Thus, users with a bad reputation cannot influence the trust value of a component since their experience reports are discounted.

1 Introduction

Component-structured software gets more and more popular since applications can be cost-effectively composed from components which are developed indepen-

P. Nixon and S. Terzis (Eds.): Trust Management 2003, LNCS 2692, pp. 75–90, 2003.

dently from each other and are separately offered on an open market (cf. [1]). Suitable components are selected according to the particular needs of the desired user and are coupled to an application. The components are either executed locally on the application's host or run on a remote server and are integrated by means of a special telecommunication service.

The composition process, however, is aggravated by the heterogeneity of the component interfaces. Here, component contracts, which are ideally legally binding, prove helpful. They can be used to adapt the interfaces in order to fit to each other since the context dependencies of a component have to be explicitly stated in its contract. According to Beugnard et al. [2] a contract consists of four parts modeling the structure of a component interface (i.e., the methods with input and output parameters, events, exceptions), constraints about the interface behavior demanded from the component and its environment, synchronization aspects, and quantitative quality-of-service properties. Moreover, reflection and introspection [3] facilitate the coupling of components by providing special methods enabling the exploration of component properties, methods, and interfaces at runtime. These methods are utilized by visual application builder tools (e.g., [4]) making the component composition easier. Well-established platforms for component-structured software are Java Beans [3] and, in particular, Enterprise Java Beans [5], Microsoft's COM/DCOM [6], and the CORBA component model [7]. Each platform provides notations to describe component types, parameter types, and interfaces. Furthermore, means to introspect components and special composition support are provided as well.

The heterogeneity of the components also results in a new class of security risks. Compared with ordinary monolithic applications in component-structured software new principals and roles are introduced. Besides of application owners and users we have to consider also a number of different component designers as well as application builders and component service providers. On the one hand, these principals introduce their own security objectives which have to be fulfilled. On the other hand, each principal is also a potential threat to the application, its components, and the other principals. A taxonomy of security risks for components is introduced in [8] and an extended list is published in [9].

Here, we concentrate on two main security risks:

1. A malicious component must not be able to distort components of its environment and, in consequence, spoil the whole application incorporating it.
2. A component and its designer must not be incriminated falsely for damage in a component-structured application which in reality was caused by another principal.

In [10,11] we introduce an approach addressing the first risk. It is based on the component contracts which are extended by models specifying security-relevant behavior to be fulfilled by a component and its behavior. We assume that malicious or compromised components behave in a way which diverges from the contract models. Therefore we use so-called security wrappers observing the interface behavior of the component at runtime. Security wrappers are specialized software wrappers (cf. [12]) which are pieces of code extending a component. A security wrapper is inserted at the interface between a component and its environment. It temporarily blocks an event passing the interface and checks it for compliance with the behavior models in the contract which are simulated. If the event complies with all models, it may pass. Otherwise, the wrapper seals the component temporarily in order to prevent harm for the component environment and notifies the application administrator.

Since the security wrappers cause a significant performance overhead of 5 to 10%, we combined the approach with active trust management [9,13]. The intensity of the runtime enforcement by the security wrappers is adjusted according to the reputation of the observed component. To serve this purpose, a component user creates an experience report in intervals and sends it to the so-called trust information service. A positive report states that no contract model was violated by the component after sending the last report while in the case of detecting a contract violation a negative report is issued. The trust information service collects the reports from various component users and computes for each rated component a trust value (cf. [14]) stating the users' belief and disbelief in the particular component resp. their uncertainty about it. This trust value is used by the component owners to adjust the intensity of supervision by the wrappers which may reach from permanent observation via spot checks to the complete removal of a wrapper. A special trust manager component forms the link between a wrapper and the trust information service. It automates both the generation of experience reports and the control of the wrapper.

Unfortunately, the approach sketched above does not address the second security risk. On the contrary, by sending wrong negative experience reports about a component to the trust information service, a component user may easily incriminate the component and its designer. Since the trust values are not only used to control the security wrappers but also to support procurement decisions (cf. [9]), an incrimination may lead to a significant financial loss for the component designer. On the other side, a component may protect a designer of a malicious component by failing to send negative reports after detecting behavior violations.

In this paper we introduce an extension of the trust information service in order to prevent component users manipulating component trust values by issuing wrong experience reports. Now the trust information service also stores trust values of component users. The trust value of a component user is used to determine the degree, an experience report of this user is considered in computing a component's trust value. Thus, if a component user already sent false reports, a bad trust value is assigned to him and, in consequence, his experience reports are not considered for calculating the trust value of a component anymore.

In order to get decent valuations about component users, a user has to complement an experience report by a log of the events passing the interface of the evaluated component. The trust information service is supplemented by experience report checker components checking if the rating in an experience report is acknowledged by the behavior listed in the log. Moreover, by analyzing the log the experience report checker tests if the other components of the user's application fulfilled the component contract models constraining the component environment. Finally, an experience report checker tests the log for correctness. Since there are no possibilities to prevent a principal forging a log if the logged component is within the principal's control (cf. [15,16]), the experience report checker tries to reconstruct a log by running a copy of the component in a sandbox. It performs a number of runs of the component using the inputs listed in the log. If in one of the runs the outputs from the component corresponds to the log as well, the experience report checker accepts the log as correct. Otherwise, it is rejected as possibly forged. If an experience report passes all three tests the experience report checker sends a positive rating of the component user and a negative rating otherwise. The component user's trust value is calculated from these ratings.

To avoid correctness proofs of logs by reconstructing the log events, a component user may also use a so-called witness host. Here, the component in question is not executed on the system of the component user but on a remote host and incorporated to the application by means of a telecommunication service. This witness host produces an own interface log and passes it to the trust information system instead of the component user himself. Since it is trusted by the trust information service, the log is considered to be correct and experience report checker has only to perform the two other tests.

In the sequel, we give at first a short introduction into trust management and, in particular, into the computation of trust values. Thereafter, we sketch the security wrappers and their trust-based control. Afterwards, we outline the extended trust information service. Finally, we introduce the experience report checker components and the witness hosts.

2   Trust Management and Trust Value Computation

According to Khare and Rifkin [17] the World Wide Web "will soon reflect the full complexity of trust relationships among people, computers, and organizations." The goal of trust management is to include trust relations between relevant human and computer entities in the decision which security mechanisms should be used in order to protect certain principals and their assets against malicious attacks. Jøsang [14] defines two different kinds of trust relationships reflecting interactions between humans resp. between humans and computers. He calls humans *passionate entities* and computers as well as other entities without a free will (e.g., organizations) *rational entities*. One trust relationship may exist between two passionate entities A and B. Here, A trusts B if A believes that B behaves without malicious intent. The other trust relationship considers trust of a passionate entity A in a rational entity B. Since B cannot be benevolent or malicious due to the lack of a free will, this relationship states the belief of A that B will resist any malicious manipulation caused by an external passionate entity C.

Beth et al. [18] define two different types of trust. An entity A has *direct trust* in another entity B if it believes in the benevolence of B itself. In contrast, A has *recommendation trust* in B, if it believes that B gives a reliable and honest assessment of the benevolence or nastiness of a third entity C.

Some interesting approaches of trust management exist in the field of access control. Since traditional discretionary and mandatory access control models are not adequate for large distributed systems as the Internet with a large number of fluctuating participants (cf. [19]), credential-based systems like PolicyMaker [20], REFEREE [21], KeyNote [22], and the Trust Establishment Toolkit [23] gain more and more popularity. In these systems third party entities issue credentials to principals if they have direct trust in them. If a principal wants to access a resource, it passes its credentials to the resource provider. Depending on his recommendation trust in the issuers of the credentials, the resource provider decides about granting access to the owner of the credentials.

A variant of credential-based systems are label bureaus [24]. Here, web pages are labelled in order to protect children from access to objectionable Internet sites. In contrast to the previous approaches, besides of trusted authorities (third-party labels) labels may be also issued by the web site designers (first-party) or by interested web site users (second-party).

Reputation systems (cf. [25]) are another application domain for trust management. Here, an entity rates another entity according to its experience in dealing with the counterpart. A reputation system collects the ratings and publishes them either completely or encoded in a certain scheme. The ratings provide other entities with support in deciding about the trustworthiness of the rated component. A well-known example is the feedback forum of the Internet auctioneer eBay [26] where sellers and buyers can rate each other. A more recent approach is the Feedback Collection and Reputation Rating Centre (FCRRC) [27] which is used to create reputation on parties to electronic contracts. According to Dellarocas [28], reputation systems, however, are vulnerable against attacks leading to wrong reputations of principals. In particular, sellers of a good may collude with buyers in order to get unfairly high ratings themselves or to provide other sellers with unfairly low ratings. In our system, which is also a special reputation system, we rule out this vulnerability by applying the experience report checkers (cf. Sec. 5).

In order to use trust management in practice, one has to define a measure to state various degrees of trust. In [29], Jøsang introduces trust values which are triples of three probability values. Two values state the belief resp. disbelief in an entity while the third one describes uncertainty. This third value is necessary since the knowledge of an entity may be too small to give a decent assessment. A trust value can be modeled by a so-called opinion triangle (cf. Fig. 1). Here, the belief, disbelief, and uncertainty are specified by the values b, d, and u which are real numbers between 0 and 1. Since, moreover, a trust value fulfills the constraint $b + d + u = 1$, it can be denoted by a point in the triangle. A trust value stating a high degree of uncertainty is modeled by a point close to the top

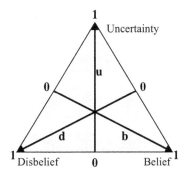

Fig. 1. Opinion Triangle (taken from [29])

of the triangle while points on the right or left bottom state great belief resp. disbelief based on large experience with the entity.

In his subjective logic [30], Jøsang extended the trust values to so-called opinions. Here, a forth probability value, the relative atomicity, was introduced. It denotes the degree of optimism or pessimism that the current uncertainty leads eventually to belief resp. disbelief. Since we do not use relative atomicity, we will apply the original trust value triples.

Trust values are used to describe both the direct trust in an entity and the trust in the recommendation of an entity about a third one. Jøsang and Knapskog introduce the following metric [31] to compute trust values from the number p of positive valuations and n of negative valuations of the entity in question:

$$b = \frac{p}{p+n+1} \qquad d = \frac{n}{p+n+1} \qquad u = \frac{1}{p+n+1}$$

The metric expresses a relatively liberal philosophy to gain trust since negative valuations can be compensated by an arbitrary number of positive assessments. Since this philosophy is probably too tolerant for some trust-management policies, we also apply the metric of Beth, Borcherding, and Klein [18]. This approach follows an unforgiving philosophy. For direct trust, the belief b is computed by the following formula v_d:

$$b = v_d(p, n) = \begin{cases} 1 - \alpha^p & : n = 0 \\ 0 & : n > 0 \end{cases}$$

Basically, v_d describes the probability that the reliability of the trust in an entity (i.e., the belief b) is larger than the value α. Thus, the larger α will be selected, the lower will be the value of b. Beth's approach does not address the distinction between the disbelief d and the uncertainty u but one can calculate d and u by means of the formulas

$$d = \begin{cases} 0 & : n = 0 \\ 1 & : n > 0 \end{cases} \qquad u = \begin{cases} \alpha^p & : n = 0 \\ 0 & : n > 0 \end{cases}$$

In this metric, a single negative experience destroys the trust in an entity forever. In contrast, like in Jøsang's approach for recommendation trust negative experience can be compensated by positive valuations which is stated as follows:

$$b = v_r(p, n) = \begin{cases} 1 - \alpha^{p-n} & : p > n \\ 0 & : else \end{cases}$$

Since, below, we do not need an explicit distinction between disbelief and uncertainty for recommendation trust, we assume that $d + u = 1 - v_r(p, n)$.

The combination of direct and recommendation trust values is addressed by Jøsang's subjective logic [30] which contains special trust combining operators. A trust value stating the direct trust in an entity x based on the recommendation of an entity r can be calculated by means of the discounting-operator $\otimes$. If the trust value $w_r = (b_r, d_r, u_r)$ describes the trust of oneself in the recommendations of r and $w_x^r = (b_x^r, d_x^r, u_x^r)$ the direct trust of r in x, the direct trust $w_{rx} = (b_{rx}, d_{rx}, u_{rx})$ of oneself in x based on the recommendation of r corresponds to the formula $w_{rx} \equiv w_r \otimes w_x^r$ where

$$w_r \otimes w_x^r \,\hat{=}\, (b_r b_x^r, b_r d_x^r, d_r + u_r + b_r u_x^r)$$

The consensus-operator $\oplus$ is used to calculate the trust value w_x stating the direct trust in an entity x from two trust values $w_{r_1 x} = (b_{r_1 x}, d_{r_1 x}, u_{r_1 x})$ and $w_{r_2 x} = (b_{r_2 x}, d_{r_2 x}, u_{r_2 x})$ which describe the trust in x based on recommendations of two different entities r_1 and r_2. The trust value w_x is computed by the formula $w_x \equiv w_{r_1 x} \oplus w_{r_2 x}$ and the operator $\oplus$ is defined by the formula

$$w_{r_1 x} \oplus w_{r_2 x} \,\hat{=}\, ((b_{r_1 x} u_{r_2 x} + b_{r_2 x} u_{r_1 x})/\kappa, (d_{r_1 x} u_{r_2 x} + d_{r_2 x} u_{r_1 x})/\kappa, (u_{r_1 x} u_{r_2 x})/\kappa)$$

where κ is equal to $u_{r_1 x} + u_{r_2 x} - u_{r_1 x} u_{r_2 x}$. Since the consensus-operator is commutative and associative, it can be used to calculate the trust of various recommendations.

By application of the metrics we can compute the trust of a particular component user in a component based on his experience reports. Thereafter, by using the discount-operator we can weight this trust value based on the recommendation trust value of the user. Finally, we can compute the trust value of the component from the recommendation trust-weighted assessments of all users by associative application of the consensus-operator.

3   Security Wrappers

In order to check that a component fulfills the security objectives specified in the models of its component contract, we put a security wrapper in between the component and its environment which checks all incoming and outgoing events for compliance with the behavior models in the contracts [10,11]. Figure 2 depicts the wrapper implementation [32] for Java Beans-based component-structured systems. An adapter bean is put in between the component to be scrutinized

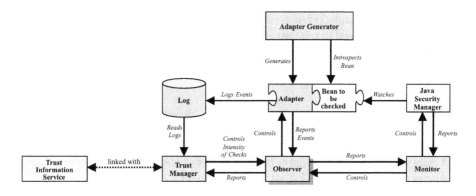

Fig. 2. Security Wrapper Architecture

and its environment. It blocks all events passing the interface temporarily and reports them to the observer beans. An observer simulates a contract model and checks if the event reported by the adapter complies with the simulated model. If the event violates the model, a report is forwarded to the monitor bean which acts as a user interface to the application administrator. Moreover, the observer notifies the adapter which seals the component until the opposite decision of the administrator. In contrast, if all observers report to the adapter that the event fulfills their models, the adapter forwards the event to its destination. Furthermore, the adapter lists all events passing the component interface in the log database in order to create a complete log of the interface behavior. The adapters are generated automatically by the adapter generator which uses the Java introspection mechanism [3] to analyze the interface of the component to be wrapped. Finally, we use also the built-in Java security manager to prevent the component using other channels than the wrapped component interface.

The intensity of the security policy enforcement is adjusted by the trust manager bean according to the current trust value of the wrapped component. The wrapped component may either be fully observed, spot checked only in times, or the supervision may be terminated[1]. As an example we introduced in [11, 13] a component-based application performing the commodity management of fast-food restaurants. In [13] we analyzed the component contracts of this application with respect to their relevance for the system security and subdivided them into three groups each containing models of a certain level of sensitivity. Afterwards, we defined for each group a wrapper management policy. According to this policy, the models of the first group describing the most sensitive security objectives have always to be fully enforced. Models of the second group may be spot checked if the belief value b of the component's trust value exceeds the value 0.999 according to the metric of Beth et al. [18] with the reliability value $\alpha = 0.99$. Moreover, if b is larger than 0.99999, the enforcement of the models

---

[1] A supervision should only be terminated if the belief in the component is very high since after the termination the wrapper cannot be reinstalled again.

may be terminated and corresponding observers may be removed. Finally, for the models of the third group we use the more tolerant metric of Jøsang and Knapskog [31] allowing spot checks for $b > 0.99$ and observation termination for $b > 0.999$. By application of these policies, the performance overhead of the wrapper for a trustworthy component could be reduced in steps from 5.4% to 3.2%.

Moreover, the trust manager forms the link between the security wrapper and the trust information service outlined below. In intervals, it reads the current trust value from the trust information service and adjusts the wrapper enforcement policy accordingly. Furthermore, on request of the trust information service it returns experience reports about the component interface behavior enclosed by the log of the behavior which is stored in the log database. If the component behavior complied with the contract models since transmitting the last report, a positive experience report is sent. If an observer detected a minor violation (e.g., in our commodity management application the violation of a contract model of the third group), a negative report is sent. In the case of a major violation (e.g., of contract models of the first or second group), the negative report is not sent after request from the trust information service but immediately. If the trust information service can verify the log or the component user is highly trusted (cf. Sec. 5), an alarm message is sent to all other users of the component in order to prevent harm on their systems. If the trust manager receives an alarm message caused by a negative experience report by another component user, it instructs the security wrapper to notify the application administrator and to seal the component.

4   Trust Information Service

Trust values of components and component users are computed by the trust information service. As delineated in Fig. 3, it is linked with component designers, with trust managers of user systems executing components, and with third-party certification authorities certifying components on behalf of component designers (cf. [33]). The trust information service consists of two parts in order to guarantee a high degree of privacy. A cipher service stores the registration data of components and component users and generates for each registered entity a unique cipher. The assessments of the entities are stored by the trust value manager which also computes and stores the trust values. Since, however, the assessments and the trust values are stored only by using the ciphers, neither the cipher service nor the trust value manager have full knowledge about the identities and trust values of the entities.

A component designer may register a component with the cipher service (cf. [9]). In order to avoid man-in-the-middle attacks, the components are sent accompanied by a digital signature to the cipher service. The cipher service creates a unique cipher of the component and forwards it to the trust value manager. Moreover, it also generates a digital signature based on a hash value of the component code and the cipher and sends it to the component designer.

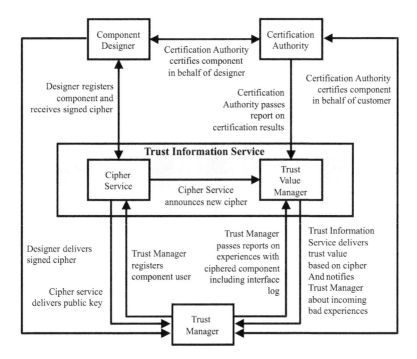

Fig. 3. Trust Information Service

Thus, neither the component designer nor anybody else may afterwards alter a component without the change being detected by the component users. The component designer may hand the signed cipher over to interested component users.

Trust managers who want to use the trust information service have to register their component users, too. Here, the cipher service also generates a unique cipher which is signed and sent to the trust manager and the trust value manager. If a trust manager is interested in a trust value of a component, it sends its cipher to the trust value manager. The trust value manager returns the two trust values calculated according the two metrics introduced in Sec. 2. Moreover, a trust manager may ask for the recommendation trust value of its own component user but — to improve privacy — not of other component users. Finally, the trust manager sends experience reports about components to the trust value manager. An experience report is accompanied by the cipher and the interface log of the evaluated component as well as the cipher of the component user.

For all registered component users $u_1, \ldots, u_n$ the trust value manager stores the number of positive and negative ratings issued by the experience report checkers which will be outlined in Sec. 5. From these ratings it computes twice the recommendation trust value ω_{u_i} of each component user u_i according to both metrics introduced in Sec. 2. Moreover, it keeps for each registered component c the experience reports of all component users. Based on this information, the

Table 1. Example for the computation of trust values

Com-ponent Users	Ratings of u_i		Rec. Trust Values ω_{u_i}	Ratings of c by u_i		Dir. Trust Values $\omega_c^{u_i}$	Trust Values $\omega_{u_i c}$	Trust Value ω_c
	pos.	neg.	Jøsang	pos.	neg.	Jøsang	Jøsang	Jøsang
u_1	12	4	(.71,.23,.06)	7	0	(.88,.00,.12)	(.62,.00,.38)	
u_2	15	0	(.94,.00,.06)	8	0	(.89,.00,.11)	(.84,.00,.16)	(.84,.04,.12)
u_3	6	9	(.37,.57,.06)	2	5	(.25,.63,.12)	(.09,.23,.68)	
	pos.	neg.	Beth	pos.	neg.	Beth	Beth	Beth
u_1	12	4	(.08,.92)	7	0	(.07,.00,.93)	(.01,.00,.99)	
u_2	15	0	(.14,.86)	8	0	(.08,.00,.92)	(.01,.00,.99)	(.02,.00,.98)
u_3	6	9	(.00,1.0)	2	5	(.00,1.0,.00)	(.00,.00,1.0)	

trust value ω_c of c can be calculated for both metrics using the discounting and consensus-operators of the subjective logic [30]. At first for each metric the value $\omega_c^{u_i}$ of the trust of u_i in c is calculated. Thereafter, the trust value manager computes the trust value $\omega_{u_i c}$ stating the trust in c based on the recommendation of u_i by application of the formula $\omega_{u_i c} = \omega_{u_i} \otimes \omega_c^{u_i}$. Finally, ω_c is computed from these trust values by means of the formula $\omega_c = \omega_{u_1 c} \oplus \omega_{u_2 c} \oplus \ldots \oplus \omega_{u_n c}$.

To clarify the approach, Tab. 1 delineates an example computation of the trust value ω_c of a component c based on the experience reports of three component users u_1, u_2, and u_3 based on both metrics. The example points out that the negative rating of the component c by user u_3 has no significant influence on the trust value of c since u_3 has a very bad recommendation trust value resulting from various questionable experience reports. Moreover, the example clarifies that the metric of Beth et al. with the selected reliability $\alpha = 0.99$ is much more conservative than the one of Jøsang and Knapskog. While the belief value of ω_c according to Jøsang's metric is already relatively close to 1 indicating great belief in c, it remains very close to 0 in Beth's metric showing nearly complete uncertainty.

Besides of trust managers, the trust value manager is also interested in experience reports from trusted third party certification authorities (cf. [33]). Therefore, component designers may send certificates of their components during registration or later. Then, the cipher service asks the certification authority to send an assessment report describing the results of the certification process to the trust value manager. Since the certification process tends to be more profound (but also more expensive) than policy enforcement by security wrappers, we weight these valuations like 50 ordinary reports from component users.

Finally, the trust value manager uses the recommendation trust values of component users to decide about forwarding alarm messages. If a component user u reports a severe security violation by a component, alarm messages to other component users are only generated immediately if the belief b of u's trust value exceeds 0.9999 according to the metric of Beth et al. [18] which is reached after 917 positive valuations. Otherwise, the log passed with u's report has to be

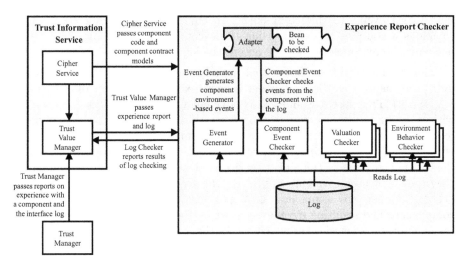

Fig. 4. Experience Report Checker

checked by an experience report checker before warning the component users. By this policy we try to make a compromise between informing component users early about security risks and preventing wrong incriminations of component designers which would be fostered by unfounded alarm messages.

5   Component User Evaluation

The recommendation trust of component users is computed based on the correctness of their experience reports which are validated by using the logs of the events passing the component interface. An experience report checker validates an experience report by carrying out three different tests. If the tests are passed, it sends a positive rating of the component user to the trust value manager and otherwise a negative rating.

The structure of the experience report checker is delineated in Fig. 4. The valuation checkers are used to perform the first test. They check if the experience report complies with the log. Similarly to the observers in the security wrapper (cf. Sec. 3), a checker simulates a model of the component contract but, in contrast to the observers, uses the log as an input. If the component user sent a positive experience report, all valuation checkers have to state that their simulated contract models were not violated by the log. If the experience report is negative, at least one valuation checker has to detect a violation of the simulated model according to the log.

In the second test the log events triggered by the component environment have to be checked for compliance with the component contract models constraining the interface behavior. This test is necessary since a component user may easily provoke wrong behavior by inducing an environment component to send wrong events to this component. An environment behavior checker also simulates a contract model by using the events listed in the log. The test is passed if all environment checkers accept the log entries.

Finally, the third test reflects that nobody can prevent a component user to forge a log as long as the component is executed under the control of this user (cf. [15,16]). Therefore it would be easy to change a log in a way that it complies with a wrong experience report. To detect this kind of fraud, the experience report checker tries to reconstruct the log by running the component in a sandbox environment. From the cipher service it loads the component code which due to the digital signature of the cipher service is identical with the code running on the component user's system (cf. Sec. 4). The event generator creates the events of the component environment according to the log entries and sends them to the component. The resulting events triggered by the component are forwarded to the component event checker which checks them for compliance with the events listed in the log. If an event does not correspond with the corresponding log entry, the run is discarded. We laid down that a test run may be repeated nine times in order to treat nondeterministic component behavior. The test is passed if at least one of these runs is consistent with the log.

The third test causes a severe problem. A component developer may build a nondeterministically behaving component in order to harm the reputation of component users since experience report checks of this component will often fail the third test and, in consequence, the recommendation trust values of the users will get worse. To prevent this problem, we introduced an alternative solution for proving the correctness of logs, too. It utilizes the possibility to execute a component-structured application on a distributed system. In particular, the component in question may be executed on a remote host. Here, on the application site a proxy is running instead of the component itself. The application site is linked via a network with the site executing the component and the proxy organizes the transmission of incoming and outgoing events through this link. In our Java-based solution we use the communication protocol RMI (Remote Method Invocation, [34]) to perform the transmission of the event objects. Furthermore, the log of the component interface behavior may be created not only on the application site but also on the remote host. Here, we use special witness hosts which are trusted by the trust information service. Since these trusted hosts send the logs to the trust value manager instead of the component users, the trust value manager can accept the correctness of the log without an experience report checker performing the third test. Thus, if a component user feels that he got an unjustified bad recommendation trust value since his experience reports often failed the third test, he can forward components to witness hosts. Thereafter, his experience reports will pass the tests and his trust value will recover.

The tests performed by the experience report checker rule out the collusion of component designers and users in order to manipulate trust values of components by sending wrong experience reports to the trust information service (cf. [28]). The manipulations will be detected and, in consequence, the experience reports will not be considered in the computation of component trust values anymore. Thus, we avoid the addressed security risk that components and their designers may be falsely incriminated.

Since the trust information system extension is not yet finished now, we cannot identify the exact performance requirements of the experience report checkers. We estimate the duration of the first and second tests as limited since the contract models can be simulated based on the log entries without the expenditure of running a real component. In contrast, the third test is considered more expensive, in particular, if the log reconstruction runs have to be repeated. This test, however, is only needed if no witness hosts are used. If not all experience reports can be checked in the time between two rounds of inquiring component user valuations, we skip the checks of the remaining reports. To guarantee that the most relevant checks are performed, we carry them out in the following order: At first, we check reports about severe security violations in order to send alarm messages as early as possible. Thereafter, we check the other negative experience reports since they are more relevant for wrong incriminations of component designers than positive reports. We give priority to reports from users with a low belief-value b in their recommendation trust values. Finally, we check positive experience reports where again users with a low value b are preferred.

6   Concluding Remarks

We proposed our approach for the fair trust-based enforcement of component-structured software. The amount of enforcement depends on the trust values which are computed based on reports stating the experience of running a component in question. Moreover, we check the validity of the experience reports and calculate recommendation trust values of component users based on these checks. By discounting experience reports of users with a bad recommendation trust value, we tackle the security objective of incriminating components and their designers wrongly by issuing false reports. Of course, our approach is still vulnerable against time bomb attacks where a principal behaves correctly for a while to get good ratings and thereafter carries out attacks (cf. [25]). Therefore, we recommend to define conservative security wrapper management policies in order to allow a reduction of the runtime enforcement only if time bomb behavior is not sensible anymore since correct behavior of a component leading to a good reputation renders a higher profit to the component designer than the gain based on a successful attack. This is reflected in our commodity management example [13], where we enforce the most crucial component contracts permanently.

References

1. Szyperski, C.: Component Software — Beyond Object Oriented Programming. Addison-Wesley Longman (1997)

2. Beugnard, A., Jézéquel, J.M., Plouzeau, N., Watkins, D.: Making Components Contract Aware. IEEE Computer **32** (1999) 38–45
3. Sun Microsystems: Java Beans Specification. Available via WWW: java.sun.com /beans/docs/spec.html (1998)
4. Lüer, C., Rosenblum, D.S.: WREN — An Environment for Component-Based Development. Technical Report #00-28, University of California, Irvine, Department of Information and Computer Science (2000)
5. Sun Microsystems: Enterprise Java Beans Technology — Server Component Model for the Java Platform (White Paper). Available via WWW: java.sun.com/products /ejb/white_paper.html (1998)
6. Microsoft: The Microsoft COM Technologies. Available via WWW: http://www. microsoft.com/com/comPapers.asp (1998)
7. Object Management Group: CORBA Component Model Request for Proposals (1997)
8. Lindqvist, U., Jonsson, E.: A Map of Security Risks Associated with Using COTS. IEEE Computer **31** (1998) 60–66
9. Herrmann, P.: Trust-Based Procurement Support for Software Components. In: Proceedings of the 4th International Conference on Electronic Commerce Research (ICECR-4), Dallas, ATSMA, IFIP (2001) 505–514
10. Herrmann, P., Krumm, H.: Trust-adapted enforcement of security policies in distributed component-structured applications. In: Proceedings of the 6th IEEE Symposium on Computers and Communications, Hammamet, IEEE Computer Society Press (2001) 2–8
11. Herrmann, P., Wiebusch, L., Krumm, H.: State-Based Security Policy Enforcement in Component-Based E-Commerce Applications. In: Proceedings of the 2nd IFIP Conference on E-Commerce, E-Business & E-Government (I3E), Lisbon, Kluwer Academic Publisher (2002) 195–209
12. Fraser, T., Badger, L., Feldman, M.: Hardening COTS Software with Generic Software Wrappers. In: Proceedings of the 1999 IEEE Symposium on Security and Privacy, IEEE Computer Society Press (1999) 2–16
13. Herrmann, P.: Trust-Based Security Policy Enforcement of Software Components. In: Proceedings of the 1st Internal iTrust Workshop On Trust Management In Dynamic Open Systems, Glasgow (2002)
14. Jøsang, A.: The right type of trust for distributed systems. In: Proceedings of the UCLA Conference on New Security Paradigms Workshops, Lake Arrowhead, ACM (1996) 119–131
15. Schneier, B., Kelsey, J.: Cryptographic Support for Secure Logs on Untrusted Machines. In: Proceedings of the 7th USENIX Security Symposium, San Antonio, USENIX Press (1998) 53–62
16. Bellare, M., Yee, B.: Forward Integrity for Secure Audit Logs. Technical report, Computer Science and Engineering Department, University of California at San Diego (1997)
17. Khare, R., Rifkin, A.: Weaving a Web of Trust. World Wide Web Journal **2** (1997) 77–112
18. Beth, T., Borcherding, M., Klein, B.: Valuation of Trust in Open Networks. In: Proceedings of the European Symposium on Research in Security (ESORICS). Lecture Notes in Computer Science 875, Brighton, Springer-Verlag (1994) 3–18
19. Blaze, M., Feigenbaum, J., Ioannidis, J., Keromytis, A.D.: The Role of Trust Management in Distributed Systems Security. In Vitek, J., Jensen, C., eds.: Internet Programming: Security Issues for Mobile and Distributed Objects. Springer-Verlag (1999) 185–210

20. Blaze, M., Feigenbaum, J., Lacy, J.: Decentralized Trust Management. In: Proceedings of the 17th Symposium on Security and Privacy, Oakland, IEEE (1996) 164–173
21. Chu, Y.H., Feigenbaum, J., LaMacchia, B., Resnick, P., Strauss, M.: REFEREE: Trust Management for Web Applications. World Wide Web Journal **2** (1997) 127–139
22. Blaze, M., Feigenbaum, J., Ioannidis, J., Keromytis, A.D.: The KeyNote Trust Management System, Version 2. Report RFC-2704, IETF (1999)
23. Herzberg, A., Mass, Y.: Relying Party Credentials Framework. Electronic Commerce Research Journal (2003) To appear.
24. Shepherd, M., Dhonde, A., Watters, C.: Building Trust for E-Commerce: Collaborating Label Bureaus. In Kou, W., Yesha, Y., Tan, C.J., eds.: Proceedings of the 2nd International Symposium on Electronic Commerce Technologies (ISEC'2001). LNCS 2040, Hong Kong, Springer-Verlag (2001) 42–56
25. Resnick, P., Zeckhauser, R., Friedman, E., Kuwabara, K.: Reputation Systems: Facilitating Trust in Internet Interactions. Communications of the ACM **43** (2000) 45–48
26. eBay Inc.: Feedback Forum. Available via WWW: pages.ebay.com/services/forum /feedback.html (2002)
27. Milosevic, Z., Jøsang, A., Dimitrakos, T., Patton, M.A.: Discretionary Enforcement of Electronic Contracts. In: Proceedings of the 6th IEEE International Enterprise Distributed Object Computing Conference (EDOC 2002), Lausanne (2002) 39–50
28. Dellarocas, C.: Immunizing Online Reputation Reporting Systems Against Unfair Ratings and Discriminatory Behavior. In: Proceedings of the 2nd ACM Conference on Electronic Commerce (EC'00), ACM Press (2000) 150–157
29. Jøsang, A.: An Algebra for Assessing Trust in Certification Chains. In Kochmar, J., ed.: Proceedings of the Network and Distributed Systems Security Symposium (NDSS'99), The Internet Society (1999)
30. Jøsang, A.: A Logic for Uncertain Probabilities. International Journal of Uncertainty, Fuzziness and Knowledge-Based Systems **9** (2001) 279–311
31. Jøsang, A., Knapskog, S.J.: A metric for trusted systems. In: Proceedings of the 21st National Security Conference, NSA (1998)
32. Mallek, A.: Sicherheit komponentenstrukturierter verteilter Systeme: Vertrauensabhängige Komponentenüberwachung. Diplomarbeit, Universität Dortmund, Informatik IV, D-44221 Dortmund (2000)
33. Voas, J.: A Recipe for Certifying High Assurance Software. In: Proceedings of the 22nd International Computer Software and Application Conference (COMPSAC'98), Vienna, IEEE Computer Society Press (1998)
34. Sun Microsystems Palo Alto: Java Remote Method Invocation — Distributed Computing for Java. Available via WWW: java.sun.com/marketing/collateral /javarmi.html (1999)

Trust Management Tools for Internet Applications

Tyrone Grandison and Morris Sloman

Department of Computing, Imperial College London,
Huxley Building, 180 Queen's Gate, London SW7 2AZ, UK
{tgrand, m.sloman}@doc.ic.ac.uk

Abstract. Trust management has received a lot of attention recently as it is an important component of decision making for electronic commerce, Internet interactions and electronic contract negotiation. However, appropriate tools are needed to effectively specify and manage trust relationships. They should facilitate the analysis of trust specification for conflicts and should enable information on risk and experience information to be used to help in decision-making. High-level trust specifications may also be refined to lower-level implementation policies about access control, authentication and encryption. In this paper, we present the SULTAN trust management toolkit for the specification, analysis and monitoring of trust specifications. This paper will present the following components of the toolkit: the Specification Editor, the Analysis Tool, the Risk Service and the Monitoring Service.

Keywords: Trust Management Tools, Trust Specification, Trust Analysis, Risk Service, Trust Monitoring Service.

1 Introduction

Trust management is becoming an important topic as indicated by the substantial number of research projects that have been initiated in the last few years and the efforts by leading software and hardware vendors to incorporate trust management into their products. The impetus behind the interest in this field is the fact that trust is crucial to Internet business transactions, but these do not permit personal, face-to-face interactions, so methods have to be devised to engender trust without these important human elements. The perception of customers that vendors' products are often insecure and not trustworthy has also fuelled research into trust management. The need for software agents to traverse smoothly through a web of interconnected networks in a trustworthy manner and the benefits from separating trust management code from application code are all factors contributing to the present popularity of trust management research.

Current trust management projects, e.g. KeyNote [1-3], REFEREE [4, 5], SD3 [6], etc., have been readily accepted by mainstream corporate entities. The vast majority of these projects are primarily concerned with public key authorization, authentication and access control but do not consider experience, risk and trust analysis. The reason for this overemphasis on a small part of the trust management problem lies in the state of affairs in the security world in the mid-90s. At the time, cryptography was used as

P. Nixon and S. Terzis (Eds.): Trust Management 2003, LNCS 2692, pp. 91–107, 2003.

a solution to the Internet's security shortcomings. However, the problem with cryptography was that it required a complex key management infrastructure. The solution to this problem was to create Public Key Infrastructures (PKIs). The trust in the certificate authority and the keys in a PKI led to another problem. This is what came to be seen as the trust management problem.

According to Blaze et. al. [7], trust management is "a unified approach to specifying and interpreting security policies, credentials, relationships which allow direct authorisation of security-critical actions". This has been the dominant view of trust management since the mid-90s. However, from the definition and subsequent implementations, we can see that the focus is on the problem of managing public key authorisation, and ignores 1) the analysis of trust relationships, 2) the use of auxiliary factors, such as risk and experience, in trust decision making, and 3) the fact that trust is a dynamic concept that evolves with time. All these solutions assume that public key infrastructures (PKIs) will be the basis of future security solution, but this may not be a prudent assumption, due to the problems of large-scale deployment of PKIs for the Internet.

In this paper, the view taken of trust management is that it is "the activity of collecting, codifying, analysing and presenting evidence relating to competence, honesty, security or dependability with the purpose of making assessments and decisions regarding trust relationships for Internet applications" [8, 9]. Evidence could include credential such as certificates for proof of identity or qualifications, risk assessments, usage experience or recommendations. Analysis includes identification of possible conflicts with other trust requirements. Thus, trust management is concerned with collecting the information required to make a trust relationship decision, evaluating the criteria related to the trust relationship as well as monitoring and re-evaluating existing trust relationships.

This paper presents a description of the architecture and basic use of the SULTAN Toolkit, which is a set of tools for specifying trust relationships, analyzing them, evaluating risk and monitoring the conditions of trust relationships. A more detailed discussion on the application of the toolkit is given in [8]. In section 2, we present the basic concepts of trust and highlight the SULTAN trust model and abstract architecture. Section 3 introduces a scenario that will be used in our discussion of the tools. Section 4 provides an overview of the SULTAN Specification Editor, while section 5 provides a discussion on the Analysis Tool. In section 6, we present a discourse on the Risk Service and highlight the Monitoring Service in section 7. Section 8 contains information on related work and we look at conclusions and future directions in section 9.

2   Overview of the SULTAN Trust Management Model

In this section, we will present the basic notions concerning trust. We will also give a brief introduction to the SULTAN Trust Management Model.

Trust is normally specified in terms of a relationship between a *trustor*, the subject that trusts a target entity, which is known as the *trustee* i.e. the entity that is trusted. Each trust relationship must be defined with respect to a particular scenario or context, can be viewed as a mathematically-defined binary relation, must have an associated trust level, can be stated as adhering to some property and has auxiliary factors that influence it (see [9] for more details). Our view of trust is that it is "the quantified belief by a trustor with respect to the competence, honesty, security and dependability of a trustee within a specified context". Quantification reflects that a trustor can have various degrees of trust (distrust), which could be expressed as a numerical range or as a simple classification such as low, medium or high. Competence implies that an entity is capable of performing the functions expected of it or the services it is meant to provide correctly and within reasonable timescales. An honest entity is truthful and does not deceive or commit fraud. Truthfulness refers to the state where one consistently utters what one believes to be true. In this context, to deceive means to mislead or to cause to err (whether accidentally or not), while fraud refers to criminal deception done with intent to gain an advantage. A secure entity ensures the confidentiality of its valuable assets and prevents unauthorised access to them. Dependability is the measure in which reliance can justifiably be placed on the service delivered by a system [10]. Thus by definition, we see that a dependable entity is also a reliable one. Timeliness is an implicit component of dependability, particularly with respect to real-time systems. Depending on a specific trust context, particular attributes of honestly, competence, security or dependability may be more important. For example, the competence of a doctor may be the most important aspect for a trust relationship. As stated in [11], it was not possible to use these attributes to classify trust relationships so there was no point in modeling them in the trust relationship. Instead they are reflected intuitively in the trust context specification.

Distrust is essential for revoking previously agreed trust for environments or when entities are trusted by default. We define distrust as "the quantified belief by a trustor that a trustee is incompetent, dishonest, not secure or not dependable within a specified context". The view of trust (and distrust) taken by some researchers has led to the terms trust, access control, authorisation and authorisation being confused and used interchangeably. The fact that Tony trusts Darren to perform network security testing does not necessarily imply that Tony will allow Darren access to the network. The principle is simple: trust does not necessarily imply access control rights and vice versa. Authorisation is the outcome of the refinement of a (more abstract) trust relationship. For example, if I develop a trust relationship with a particular student, I may authorise him to install software on my computer and hence set up the necessary access control rights to permit access. Authentication is the verification of an identity of an entity, which may be performed by means of a password, a trusted authentication service or using certificates. There is then an issue of the degree of trust in the entity, which issued the certificate. Note that authorisation may not be necessarily specified in terms of an identity. Anonymous authorisation may be implemented using capabilities or certificates. This leads us to the SULTAN Trust Management Model (Figure 1).

The SULTAN Trust Management Suite consists of four primary components: 1) The Specification Editor – which integrates an editor for trust specifications, a compiler for the SULTAN specifications, and auxiliary tools for storage, retrieval and translation of the specifications, 2) The Analysis Tool, which integrates a Query Command Builder, basic editor and front-end to Sicstus Prolog, 3) The Risk Service, which allows for the calculation of risk and the retrieval of risk information, and 4) The Monitoring Service, which updates information relating to experience or reputation of the entities involved in the trust relationships.

The Specification Editor is used by the system administrator to encode the initial set of trust requirements. He may also perform analyses on the specifications he has entered. This information is then stored in the system. Over time, applications present SULTAN with new information regarding the state of the system, experiences or even risk information. Whenever a decision is to be made, the SULTAN system may be consulted to provide information that will enable one to make a better decision. We will not be discussing SULTAN trust consultation in this paper. The architecture that supports this model is shown in Figure 2.

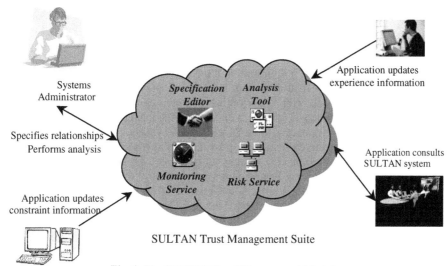

Fig. 1. The SULTAN Trust Management Model

Constraint, risk and experience information are stored in a state information server, and specifications are stored in a Specification Server.

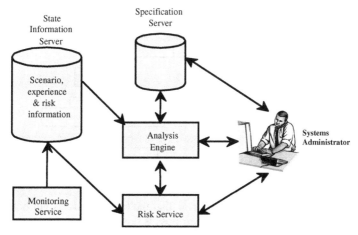

Fig. 2. Abstract Architecture for the SULTAN Trust Management System

The Analysis Tool is a front-end for the Analysis Engine, which uses the state information, specifications and risk information to determine the existence of conflicts. The Risk Service is allowed to only retrieve information from the State Information Server, and the Monitoring Service can only add or change state information. For the prototype the servers are implemented as whole structures. Fragmentation and distribution issues would serve to complicate our main goal. However, these issues will be addressed in later releases.

In the following section we use a simple scenario to elaborate on the concepts of the SULTAN system.

3   Scenario

This scenario is based on an online multimedia station. We will consider the management of the trust relationships relating to employee data access and client service provision. We will refer to our online station as JamRock. JamRock provides streaming audio and video to clients with either broadband or dialup connections. Only registered users have access to JamRock's stock of forty thousand titles.

To register, a prospective client must provide a valid name, a valid email address add credit card information. IP address information for a user's last login is automatically taken. Credit card information is taken only to ensure that minors do not have direct access to the adult content section of JamRock's library. Once the name, email and credit card information are provided, a unique, randomly-created password is sent to the client.

JamRock is a small business run by Tom Hackett. Tom employs a system administrator, Calvin, a programmer, Steve and two marketing people to help in the day-to-day running of JamRock. For legal reasons, Tom must maintain records about his employees, for tax purposes, etc. Thus, there are databases required for JamRock's employee information, its client base and its content. All three databases are considered separate entities. In Figure 3, we see the organizational structure of JamRock, which we will be referring in sections to follow.

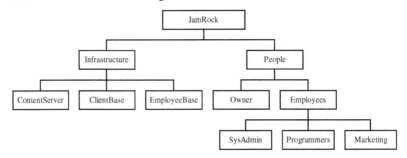

Fig. 3. Organizational Structure of JamRock

Calvin has the enviable task of ensuring that the client's trust is not betrayed, that the employees trust in the integrity of their boss is protected and that the owner's trust in his ability to ensure that only valid clients use the system is never compromised. Clients trust that their personal data will not be misused. Employees trust that the owner will use their data for legitimate purposes only. The content base should be used by legitimate clients only.

We will now discuss the SULTAN specification framework to see how Calvin can explicitly specify his trust requirements in the SULTAN specification notation.

4   Specification Editor

The Specification Editor is a composite toolkit for creating, storing, retrieving, editing and translating SULTAN Specifications. In this section, we will look at the language used by the SULTAN Editor, the compiler framework and a few other features of the Editor.

The Specification Language

In the specification language, one can specify trust, distrust, negative recommendation and positive recommendation statements. Entity names are assumed to be abstract. Thus, relationships can be defined between IP addresses, domains, public keys, software agents or even router ids. Concrete names are assigned when trust specifications are refined into a lower-level framework for purposes of security and or privacy enforcement. A trust/distrust statement has the following form:

PolicyName : **trust** (Tr, Te, As, L) ← Cs;
>   Tr trusts/distrusts Te to perform As at trust/distrust level L if constraint(s) Cs is
>   true.

PolicyName is the unique name for the assertion. Tr is the trustor, i.e. the entity that is trusting. Te is the trustee, i.e. the entity is to be trusted. As is the action set, i.e. a colon-delimited list of actions (function names) or action prohibitions. The first parameter in an action name specifies the entity the action is performed on (whether on the trustor, or the trustee, or some other entity that is a component of either). L – is the level of trust/distrust. L can be an integer or a label. Labels are converted to integers for analysis and management. For integer values of L, $-100 \leq L < 0$ represents distrust assertions and $0 < L \leq 100$ represents trust assertions. Cs is the constraint set, i.e. a set of delimited constraints that must be satisfied for the trust relationship to be established. The delimiters are the logical and (&) and logical or (|). Cs must evaluate to true or false. Examples of SULTAN trust statements are given below.

CustomerVer: trust(Supplier, Customers, view_pages(Supplier), _X)
>   ← _X > 0 & GoodCredit(Customers) &
>   *risk*(Supplier, Customers, _) <= 2;
>   *Interpretation:* Supplier trusts Customers to perform view_pages(Supplier) at trust level
>   _X if _X is greater than 0, if GoodCredit(Customers) is true and if the risk that the
>   Supplier will undertake in interacting with Customers is less than or equal to 2. Note that
>   the view_pages function is performed on Supplier by Customers.

This example shows the use of two features of the notation: variables and auxiliary functions. A variable in SULTAN is a series of characters with the underscore prefixed. In the above example, _X is a named variable that is used to refer to the trust level. The anonymous variable is represented by the underscore and it signifies a value that we have no interest in. There is an anonymous variable in the risk auxiliary function used in the constraints section

Realtor: trust (Jenny, Realtor, send_deals(Realtor, Jenny), HighTrust)
← trust (Jenny, Tom, ProvideInfo(Jenny), MediumTrust) |
    trust (Tom, Realtor, send_deals(Realtor, Tom), MediumTrust);
Interpretation: Jenny trusts Realtor to perform send_deals(Realtor, Jenny) at trust level HighTrust if Jenny trusts Tom to perform ProvideInfo(Jenny) at trust level MediumTrust or if Tom trusts Realtor to perform send_deals(Realtor, Tom) at trust level MediumTrust.

PDA: trust (Morris, Symantec, do_definition_update(Morris, Computer), HighTrust)
←DefinitionState(Symantec) = "old";
Interpretation: Morris trusts Symantec to perform do_definition_update(Morris) at trust level HighTrust if DefinitionState(Symantec) = "old".

A negative/positive recommendation statement has the following format:

PolicyName : **recommend** (Rr, Re, As, L) ← Cs;
Rr recommends/does not recommend Re at recommendation level L to perform As if constraint(s) Cs is true.

PolicyName is the unique name of the rule being defined. Rr is the recommendor, i.e. the name of the entity making the recommendation. Re is the recommendee, i.e. the name of the entity that the recommendation is about. L is the recommendation level, i.e. the level of confidence in the recommendation being issued by Rr. L can either be a label or an integer. All labels are translated to integers for analysis and management. L is $\geq$ –100 and < 0 for negative recommendations and L is > 0 and $\leq$ 100 for positive recommendations. As is the recommended action set, i.e. a colon delimited set of actions or action prohibitions that Rr recommends Re be trusted/distrusted to perform. Each action name stipulates the entity on which the action is performed. Cs is the constraint set, i.e. a delimited set of constraints that must be satisfied for the recommendation to be valid. Delimiters include the logical and (&) and logical or (|). One should be aware that: 1) The recommendation level and trust level are assumed to be independent of each other, unless otherwise specified, and 2) A recommendation may result in a trust specification (i.e. a recommendation may be the basis for one's trust specification). However, the trust level need not correspond to the recommendation level. Example recommendations include:

Credit: recommend (NatWest, Clients, GetCreditCard(NatWest), HIGH)
← Balance(Clients) > 10000;
Interpretation: NatWest recommends Clients at recommendation level HIGH to perform GetCreditCard(NatWest) if Balance(Clients) is greater than 10000.

AttPol: recommend (UCL, OpenU, do_research(OpenU), -10)
← Researchquality(OpenU) <= 3 ;
Interpretation: UCL does not recommend OpenU at recommendation level –10 to perform do_research(OpenU) if Researchquality(OpenU) is less than or equal to 3.

For details about the intricacies of the components of trust and recommend statements, please see [9].

Now that we know how to specify statements in SULTAN, let us codify Calvin's trust requirements for JamRock. We will use the abstract names from the leaves in the tree in Figure 3. His first task is to ensure that the client's trust is not betrayed. This means the client believes that the data collected by JamRock is not being used by any unauthorized individuals, for unscrupulous pursuits. It is JamRock's policy that only the owner is trusted to view their data (nothing else). Let us codify this as:

ClientPrivacy1: trust(JamRock, Owner, view_client(ClientBase, _AnyEntity) , 50);

At times, users may forget their login information or may have queries about their data. At this point Calvin may need to provide this information to them provided they have been sufficiently authenticated. One could represent this as:

ClientPrivacy2: trust(JamRock, SysAdmin, provide_info(ClientBase, _Client, _Inf), 50)
← auth_tokens_provided(_Client) & is_registered(_Client) &
   is_Information(_Client, _Inf);

Calvin's requirement concerning the employees' trust in the integrity of the boss relating to their personal records may be expressed in SULTAN as:

EmpTrust1: trust(Employees, Owner, _X, 50)
← defined_on_for(_X, EmployeeBase, _EmployeeY) &
   not_compromised(_EmployeeY);
Interpretation: Employees trust Owner to perform an action _X (at trust level 50), if this _X is an action defined on _EmployeeBase and concerns EmployeeY and _EmployeeY is not compromised by this action being performed.

Calvin's final trust requirement is to ensure that the Owners' trust in his ability to ensure that only valid clients use the system. This requirement must be stipulated in two statements. The first stating that the Owner trusts the SysAdmin and the second stating that only valid clients can access the content database. These can be specified in SULTAN as:

ClientAccess1: trust(Owner, SysAdmin, _A, 50)
← defined_on_for(_A,_ContentServer, _Y) & not_abuses(_A, JamRock);
ClientAccess2: trust(JamRock, _AnEntity, get_stream(ContentServer, _ConnType), 50)
← is_registered_client(ClientBase, _AnEntity) &
   has_Connection_Type(ClientBase, _AnEntity, _ConnType);

After typing these specifications into the editor, Calvin can then compile them, save them and translate them to Prolog to start performing analysis on them. Note that the trust levels in the examples for JamRock are arbitrarily set to 50. Let's take a quick look at the compiler.

The SULTAN Compiler Framework

Figure 4 shows the SULTAN Compiler Framework. The main modules of the compiler are based on a LALR(1) parser, which was generated by SableCC, an object-oriented Java parser generator[12]. The syntactic and semantic phases produce a intermediate representation of the code entered, which is essentially the abstract syntax tree with an added label. We have produced a translator from SULTAN to Prolog in order to analyze SULTAN specification. It is also possible to translate to other Trust or policy tools.

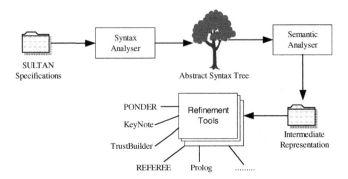

Fig. 4. SULTAN Compiler Framework

Fig. 5. Compiled version of Specifications for JamRock

Figure 5 shows the results of using the SULTAN Compiler on Calvin's specifications. Let us now look at the other features of the Editor.

Other Features

The Editor also includes an Abstract Syntax Tree Viewer (Figure 6). This is included as an aid for translator developers.

Fig. 6. Abstract Syntax Viewer for specs for JamRock

Once translators have been created then the Editor provides a facility to specify the file and its location and have it integrated as a part of the Editor. Figure 7 shows the dialog used to do this integration.

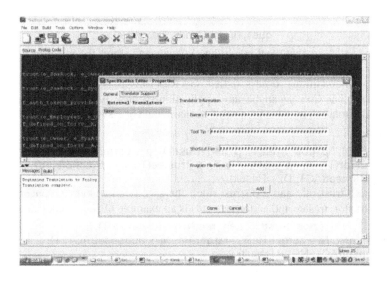

Fig. 7. How to integrate translators into the Editor

Let us turn our attention to the Analysis Tool.

5   Analysis Tool

The Analysis Tool is a front-end for both the Analysis Engine and Sicstus Prolog. The Analysis Tool encapsulates the Analysis Engine, which is the bridge between the Sicstus Prolog System, the Specification Server, the State Information Server and the Risk Service. The Analysis Tool allows the administrator to produce simulation analysis and property analysis. Simulation analysis is performed by using the Analysis Tool to directly add information to the Prolog System (with an option to store them to the State Information Server) and then using one's own knowledge of Prolog or the built-in SULTAN Analysis Model to ask questions. Property analysis involves checking whether specified properties hold on trust and recommendation rules. The properties can be with respect to the specification source, which is essentially program reasoning. Source analysis ignores the constraints, i.e. assumes they are true. The properties can also be with respect to examining trust relationships to identify scenarios of interest. Scenario analysis involves reasoning about the state of the system, and the current state of constraints. For example, in recommendation Credit, the system must have a value for Balance(Clients) in order to evaluate the constraint. The monitoring system would be responsible for updating this information.

The prototype for the analysis model is implemented in Prolog because this allows arbitrary application specific analysis to be performed to meet the requirements of a particular organization. To perform an analysis query, we use the rules in the analysis model. A query is a predicate which defines the property that the administrator is interested in, and is used to retrieve a set of results. The format of this construct is:

query(Vars, Conds, ResultSet).

This finds all Vars that meet condition(s) Conds and stores the result in ResultSet, where Vars are the variables to be collected that must be used in the Conds section; Conds are the conditions to be satisfied and ResultSet is the set of Vars that meet Conds. Note that Conds can be any application-specific predicate defined by the administrator relating to the source rules, scenario data or a system integrity check.

Examples:

query([T,D], (**p_pos_trust**(T), **p_neg_trust**(D), **p_trustor**(Tr,T),
   p_trustor(Tr, D), **p_trustee**(Te,T), **p_trustee**(Te, D), **p_actionset**(ACT, T),
   p_actionset(ACT, D)), Result).

Is there a trust rule and a distrust rule, the specification source, concerning the same trustor, trustee and actionset? This is an example of source code analysis.

query([T, NR], (**pos_trust**(T), **neg_rec**(NR), **subject**(Rr,T),
   subject(Rr, NR), **target**(Re,T), **target**(Re, NR), **actionset**(ACT, T),
   actionset(ACT, NR)), Result).

Is there a scenario in which there is a trust relationship and a recommendation that concern the same subject, target and actionset? This is an example of actual scenario analysis.

It is important to highlight that the Analysis Tool starts with the SULTAN Analysis Model, the state information, the domain's specifications and a template of common conflicts and redundancies that may be of interest loaded into its current memory.

Let's suppose that Calvin wishes to find out if there are any potential conflicts of interest in his specifications. This can be specified in the SULATAN analysis notation as:

query([X, Y], (**p_pos_trust**(X), **p_pos_trust**(Y), **p_target**(Te,X), **p_target**(Te, Y), **actionset**(A, X), **actionset**(A, Y)), Result).

The above asks if there are two policies that have the same trustee and actionset. Figure 8 shows such a query. From the Tool, one sees that the specification does contain such potential conflicts.

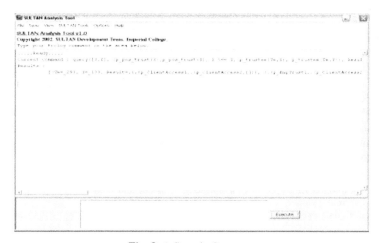

Fig. 8. A Sample Query

The results in Figure 8 show that trust policies ClientAccess1 and ClientAccess2 (amongst others) may pose a conflict of interest (this is based on analysis of the source code only). More complex queries can be built using the Query Statement Builder (shown in Figure 9).

Fig. 9. SULTAN Query Statement Builder

The value of the Analysis Tool increases over time, as it acquires new information and is able to provide the administrator with less obvious results. Note that our discussion on the Analysis Tool excluded details on cycle detection, resolution and on the use of abduction to enable queries concerning the constraints yet to be satisfied. These topics are covered in [9]. We now turn our attention to the Risk Service and its operation.

6   Risk Service

Risk is a measure of the probability of a transaction failing. In general, if there is a high risk associated with a service provider or business partner, then the lower the trust in the entity. However risk is also related to the value of a transaction. A client may trust a supplier who is considered a high risk when the services supplied only cost $10 but may not trust a medium risk supplier when purchasing goods for $10,000.

The Risk Service has two primary functions. The first is to retrieve any risk information stored in the State information Server. The second is to perform a risk calculation based on the information provided to it. When asked to retrieve risk information the Service is passed information on about the subject, target and action set in question. The following algorithm is used in this task:

Search the State Information Server for the information.
If the risk information is present for the subject, target and action(s) then simply return the information found.
If there is risk information present for the target and the actionset, then calculate the cumulative risk for the target-action pair information and provide this as a guide.
If there is no risk information present, then perform a risk calculation and return the result as a guide.

The Risk Calculation Model uses a list of common risks (e.g. receipt of malicious code, refusal to produce goods, service failure, theft of information, fraud, etc.) and their probability of occurring (likelihood), a list of action dependencies, a list of trustors and their maximum allowable losses and risk thresholds and a list of the system resources and their values to help in doing its job. Additional risks could be added as required. The model also incorporates the use of Josang's Opinion and the Asset Evaluation Model (AEM) [13, 14].

When risk is to be calculated, the service is given subject, target, action(s) and risk id. A risk value is returned after the following steps have been performed:

Use the target action information to find the Maximum Allowable Loss (MAL) and Risk Threshold (RT) for the target.

Uses the risk id to search for the probability of the risk occurring (p).

If the action(s) are dependent on others, then the risk values for all dependent subject-target-action triples are converted to Opinions and a consensus Opinion is created. The new value of p is the belief value produced is used as the new probability.The potential loss of the transaction (L) is either the cost of the transaction or (if a resource) calculated using modified AEM equation. For the prototype, it is assumed that the potential loss is always with respect to a resource. The Expected Loss (EL) is the product of L and p.

If EL < MAL, then the risk value is ((EL/MAL) * 100) else it is 100.

A design decision was made in situations where dependent actions were identified. As evident from the algorithm, in such a case, a new probability value is calculated using Opinions and not Bayes' Rules. This is done because Bayes' Rules often require information on other dependencies, which the system may be ignorant of.

The architecture of the risk service is based on client-server technology. Risk Service clients run as daemons on user machines and connect to a Risk Service Server when the Service is called upon to perform a task. Any application that can open a socket, read from it and write to it will be able to access the Service (once properly authenticated).

Ignoring the details of authentication, applications can send the following requests to the Risk Service:

✓ (**get**, subject, target, actionset) – this retrieves risk information on the specified subject, target and actionset.
✓ (**calcRV**, subject, target, actionset, riskID) – this calculates the risk value
✓ (**calcEL**, subject, target, actionset, riskID) – this calculates the expected loss

Out of curiosity, Jane, one of the marketing personnel at JamRock wants an estimation of the risk involved when the owner views her data. Her machine sends the request (**calcRV**, Jane, Owner, view_emp(ClientBase, Jane), 3). Risk id 3 represents "Theft of Information". Following the algorithm used by the Risk Service Server. The MAL and RT, which are retrieved for Jane regarding the view_emp action, are £3,000 and 0.3 respectively (These figures are gathered by the Monitoring Service and/or by the system administrator). The probability, p, of risk id 3 occurring is 0.3 (the risks and the probability of occurrence are garnered from E-Commerce studies. Though they are initially set by the system, they can be modified by the administrator). Since this action is not dependent on others, there is no need for the re-calculation of p. L, the loss, is determined by looking at the relative weighting of the associated asset, in this case information, to the other assets in JamRock. Total Assets in JamRock are worth £60,000 and information contributes 0.10 of this figure (this information is stored in the asset repository). Thus, the loss may be, at worse, £6,000. Thus the expected loss is £1,800 (6,000 * 0.3). Since the EL is lower than the MAL, the risk value would be 60. So, it is fairly risky for Jane. Let us now discuss the Monitoring Service

7   Monitoring Service

The monitoring service provides the State Information Server with up-to-date risk, experience and system state information. The architecture of the Monitoring Service is similar to that of the Risk Service. However, communication is uni-directional. No response is returned to the user application. However, upon adding state information, the Monitoring Service Server performs an analysis of the information in the State Information Server and the Specification Server, against the template of conflicts and ambiguities supplied with the SULTAN System. If a potential conflict is detected then the system sets a flag to alert the administrator the next time the Specification Editor or Analysis Tool is used by him.

The Monitoring Service client has two interfaces: A GUI-based one, which is accessible only to the system administrator, and the socket connection. Information sent to the Monitoring Service client may have the following format:

(risk, subject, target, actionset, riskvalue) – provides risk information

(experience, subject, target, actionset, expvalue) – provides experience information

(attribute, value) – provides state information

It is the monitoring service that enables the system to adapt. Suppose, Tom is a new employee at JamRock and he is skeptical about the owner. Initially, the default setting for a skeptical new employee would be not_compromised(Tom) is false. This would imply that the owner is not trusted to manipulate Tom's employee's files (however, this does not stop the owner from doing so anyway). Over time, Tom's confidence in the owner's integrity may increase and at a certain point, the not_compromised(Tom) attribute may be set to true. Note that trust and access control are not concerned with the same entities. Trust is only viewed in terms of access control when one is using trust policies for refinement to access control policies. .

8   Related Work

SULTAN trust management is a culmination of work from the fields on logic-based formalisms of trust and on trust management.

All the logic-based frameworks that have attempted to deal with the issue of trust (namely, Jøsang's subjective logic [13-16], Jones and Firozabadi's model [17], Rangan's model [18], etc) suffer from one or more of the three basic problems: 1) their underlying assumptions make them non-applicable to the distributed framework, 2) there is no associated tool support, or 3) they address a subsection of the trust management problem. The SULTAN Trust Management Framework deals with a large subset of the trust problem, makes no assumptions that may render it unusable in reality and comes with software support.

The trust management solutions developed in the last century (namely, AT&T's PolicyMaker and KeyNote, REFEREE, IBM Role-based Access Control Model [19], Poblano [20], etc.) have the following problems: 1) the responsibility of checking the conditions of the establishment of a trust relationship is entirely the application developer's concern, 2) the relationships are assumed to be monotonic 3) these solutions do not learn from the information available to them and 4) the emphasis is on access control decisions rather than general analysis of trust, whereas SULTAN (with Ponder) can cater for both.

9   Conclusions and Future Work

Trust management is the activity of collecting, codifying, analysing and presenting evidence relating to competence, honesty, security or dependability with the purpose of making assessments and decisions regarding trust relationships for Internet applications. The SULTAN Toolkit contains four tools that facilitate this, namely: the Specification Editor, the Analysis Tool, the Risk Service and the Monitoring Service. This document highlighted the basic system design and use of each of the tools and presented the two primary important concepts employed in the SULTAN system, namely: 1) the incorporation of the notions of experience and monitoring, which ensures that the SULTAN system models the dynamic nature of a trust relationship, and 2) the inclusion of risk evaluation, which facilitates the use of risk information in trust decision-making.

The future direction of the SULTAN project involves moving the system from a proof of concept to a production line system. This involves organizing the bases by namespaces to allow context-specific facts to be stored, viewed, analysed and manipulated together. The SULTAN system will also be modified to facilitate reasoning under uncertainty. A generic trust establishment framework, which not only allows SULTAN trust rules to be used for establishing relationships, but also allows the use of other trust establishment protocol systems (e.g. Trustbuilder [21]), is to be included in the toolkit. Automated refinement from SULTAN specifications to Ponder policy statements is also a future goal. This is possible solely because SULTAN operates at higher level than current security policy languages.

Acknowledgments. We acknowledge the help of our colleagues in the Policy Group at Imperial College who provided comments on this work, namely, Naranker Dulay, Emil Lupu, Alessandra Russo and Marek Sergot. We acknowledge financial support from Microsoft and BT.

References

1.   Blaze, M., J. Feigenbaum and A. D. Keromytis: KeyNote: Trust Management for Public-Key Infrastructures. Security Protocols International Workshop (1998). Cambridge, England.
      http://www.cis.upenn.edu/~angelos/Papers/keynote-position.ps.gz
2.   Blaze, M.: Using the KeyNote Trust Management System. : AT&T Research Labs (1999).
      http://www.crypto.com/trustmgt/kn.html
3.   Blaze, M., J. Feigenbaum, I. J. and K. A.: RFC2704 - The KeyNote Trust Management System (version 2). 1999. http://www.crypto.com/papers/rfc2704.txt
4.   Chu, Y.-H., J. Feigenbaum, B. LaMacchia, P. Resnick and M. Strauss: REFEREE: Trust Management for Web Applications. AT&T Research Labs (1997).
      http://www.farcaster.com/papers/www6-referee/
5.   Chu, Y.-H.: Trust Management for the World Wide Web. Massachusetts Institute of Technology. MEng Thesis (1997).
      http://www.w3.org/1997/YanghuaChu/
6.   Jim, T.: SD3: a trust management system with certified evaluation. IEEE Symposium on Security and Privacy (2001). Oakland, California, USA. IEEE Computer Society.
      http://www.research.att.com/~trevor/papers/JimOakland2001.pdf
7.   Blaze, M., J. Feigenbaum and J. Lacy: Decentralized Trust Management. IEEE Conference on Security and Privacy (1996). Oakland, California, USA.
      http://www.crypto.com/papers/policymaker.pdf
8.   Grandison, T. and M. Sloman: Specifying and Analysing Trust for Internet Applications. 2nd IFIP Conference on e-Commerce, e-Business, e-Government (2002). Lisbon, Portugal. http://www.doc.ic.ac.uk/~mss/Papers/I3e2002.pdf
9.   Grandison, T.: Trust Specification and Analysis for Internet Applications. Imperial College of Science, Technology and Medicine, London. MPhil/PhD Report (2001).
      http://www.doc.ic.ac.uk/~tgrand

10. Verissimo, P. and L. Rodrigues: Distributed Systems for System Architects: Kluwer Academic Publishers, 2001. ISBN: 0-7923-7266-2.
11. Grandison, T. and M. Sloman: A Survey of Trust in Internet Applications. IEEE Communications Surveys and Tutorials **4**(4), 2000.
    http://www.comsoc.org/pubs/surveys/
12. Gagnon, E.: SableCC: An Object-Oriented Compiler Framework. MSc. Thesis (1998). McGill University, Montreal, Canada.
13. Jøsang, A.: Artificial Reasoning with Subjective Logic. 2nd Australian Workshop on Commonsense Reasoning (1997).
    http://www.idt.ntnu.no/~ajos/papers.html
14. Jøsang, A.: Prospectives for Modelling Trust in Information Security. Australasian Conference on Information Security and Privacy (1997).
    http://www.idt.ntnu.no/~ajos/papers.html
15. Jøsang, A.: A subjective metric of authentication. 5th European Symposium on Research in Computer Security (1998). http://www.idt.ntnu.no/~ajos/papers.html
16. Jøsang, A.: The right type of trust for distributed systems. ACM New Security Paradigms Workshop (1996). http://www.idt.ntnu.no/~ajos/papers.html
17. Jones, A. J. I. and B. S. Firozabadi: On the characterisation of a Trusting agent - Aspects of a Formal Approach. Workshop on Deception, Trust and Fraud in Agent Societies (2000).
18. Rangan, P.V.: An Axiomatic Basis of Trust in Distributed Systems. Symposium on Security and Privacy (1988). Washington, DC. IEEE Computer Society Press.
19. IBM: IBM Trust Establishment Policy Language. Internet. Technical Report.
    http://www.haifa.il.ibm.com/projects/software/e-
    Business/TrustManager/PolicyLanguage.html
20. Chen, R. and W. Yeager: Poblano: A Distributed Trust Model for Peer-to-Peer Networks. Sun Microsystems Technical Report (2000).
    http://www.ovmj.org/GNUnet/papers/jxtatrust.pdf
21. Winsborough, W., K. Seamons and V. Jones: Automated Trust Negotiation: Managing Disclosure of Sensitive Credentials. Transarc White Paper (1999).

Trust-Based Filtering for Augmented Reality

David Ingram

University of Cambridge Computer Laboratory
15 JJ Thompson Avenue, Cambridge, CB3 0FD, United Kingdom
`dmi1000@cam.ac.uk`

Abstract. *This paper presents a design for an "Augmented City" tourist guide. The application is designed to be shared by large numbers of users, who may all contribute new annotations attached to physical objects. The key aspect is the need to filter content to avoid information overload in a cluttered augmented environment, without human moderators. To do this I draw on work from the SECURE project [9] which aims to model trust and risk explicitly in a global computing framework. This enables trust-based filtering with distributed recommendations to help distinguish between pseudonymous principals.*

1 Introduction

Large-scale outdoor Augmented Reality (AR) systems have been proposed as an aid for surveyors, tourists or anyone navigating city streets for some time [4,5].

These generally use a tracking technology such as differential GPS or radio triangulation as well as inertial trackers and digital compasses to establish the user's position and heading. They then present relevant navigational information and annotations, either overlaid optically on the user's view of the real world or displayed on a hand-held device such as a PDA. Of course in addition to viewing annotations in situ such a system can generally be accessed remotely without position tracking, if we wish to study an area (virtually) prior to an actual visit.

Work on the technological and user interface problems in this domain is ongoing; in this paper I shall concentrate instead on questions of information sharing and filtering. This will be illustrated by presenting a concrete design for an "Augmented City" application. The purpose is to allow users to attach virtual post-it notes to geographic locations, describing what may be found there. This has many possible uses such as restaurant recommendations, tour guide information, finding local amenities, and advertising special events.

The endpoints are networked so that all users access a combined database of notes. Anyone is allowed to create new notes, which are then readable (but not modifiable) by all. Notes consist of a physical location, their author's name, creation date, a class (to be described later) and the note's content.

2 Filtering

When there are large numbers of notes and the deliberate lack of a central moderator, the system will be prone to *clutter*, which leads to variable quality

P. Nixon and S. Terzis (Eds.): Trust Management 2003, LNCS 2692, pp. 108–122, 2003.

and information overload. Note density will increase over time, and in practice there may be hundreds placed close to the user. I found this also became a serious problem when deploying a wide-area indoor AR system [6]. We therefore need some automatic filtering mechanisms which allow the system to silently discard notes the user is unlikely to be interested in, and display the rest.

2.1   Location Filtering

At the simplest level, notes are obviously filtered based on geographic proximity to the user's point of view. The AR system may also need to know route information, such as travel times along possible routes by foot/bike/car. This will allow it to do effective *location filtering* when searching for relevant notes.

2.2   Task-Directed Filtering

It is very likely that a useful AR solution will include task relevance considerations (and detailed classification) — e.g. "show me fast food restaurants", "show me toy stores". There will be fewer things in each of these narrow categories, which greatly reduces clutter. However, there may still be components from many different principals, so clutter cannot be completely avoided this way. We therefore combine it with trust-based filtering.

2.3   Trust-Based Filtering

The SECURE framework allows us to employ trust-based filtering, so that notes can be selected based on the degree to which we trust their author to write relevant, accurate comments. We could statically configure a list of trusted authors (role-based access control), but this would prevent us seeing public notes which might be very useful. In particular if an author is currently unknown to us, but the system can determine that they have a good reputation (perhaps they are a travel journalist or a hotel inspector) we would like their notes to be displayed.

To help automate this, the system will incorporate feedback, so we can rate how useful notes were after reading them. These ratings have an effect on our trust in the author of each note, enabling the system to learn our preferences and start to filter. Furthermore this information will be forwarded by the system to others who haven't yet encountered the authors in question, in the form of **recommendations**. These can be used to determine a trust value for authors we have not encountered before.

3   Trust and Risk in the SECURE Project

The SECURE project [11,9] has been investigating ways of modelling **trust** in other principals, and how to use this information to make access control decisions.

3.1   Framework

All entities which can communicate and which it is meaningful to trust or distrust are **principals** (they may be human or otherwise). Principals are assumed to be identified, but unknown (**pseudonymous**). This means that they have been authenticated and possess an identification string which we can prove is theirs, but we may know nothing about their location or real-world identity.

Applications are broken down into sequential **actions**. These are the points at which distinct trust-based security decisions must be made by one or both parties. Actions always involve two principals, the **initiator** and **executor**, and have a set of possible **outcomes**. The executor must make a security decision at the start of the action; if they choose to go ahead the action may then take some time and the outcome will be known at the end.

Each outcome is considered to have a **likelihood** and a **cost** which quantifies the benefit or harmful consequences for the principal concerned. **Benefit** is seen as negative cost. The situation is asymmetric, so the set of outcomes as well as the associated costs will in general be different for each participant (initiator and executor) as well as for each type of action.

Often costs are not known precisely and must instead be described with a **cost-PDF**, that is, a probability density function for the cost of a particular outcome. Likelihoods are estimated using **trust** (see below).

Once the set of costs and likelihoods are known, principals make the decision to authorise an action by performing a **risk analysis**. **Risk** is defined to be the combination of cost and likelihood; the risk of an action is the sum of the risks of all the possible outcomes.

Each principal has a **security policy** which maps the risk onto an **answer set**. This says how to make the (trust-based) security decisions required by the action. The answer set is often just {permit, deny} but we allow more than two values, for cases where several possible responses are available, or to indicate low confidence in the answer ("not sure").

A key benefit of our approach is that uncertainty (in costs and probabilities) is measured explicitly and carried through to the end of the calculation.

The security policy may be based on expected cost, or include variance and maximum possible loss. This depends on the type of risk analysis which is called for by the application. For example, if one of the principals is a company there may be a maximum loss value which they cannot risk incurring at all (the value of the company). Non-linearity in mapping financial loss to perceived cost is quite possible and represents the principal's **risk sensitivity**.

3.2   Trust

The likelihood of an outcome is estimated using the **trust** held in the other participant. **Trust** is a quantified predictor of the **principal**'s future **behaviour** based on **evidence** of previous interactions.

Evidence consists of personal **observations** and **recommendations**. **Observations** and **behaviour** both relate to a **principal**'s conduct when participating in **actions**.

Each principal has a **trust policy**, which is a set of rules that state how to determine **trust values**. Some parts of this are mutable as new data is collected, others are configured based on the user's long-term policies.

Once a security decision has been made, some interaction may or may not take place and sometime later there will be feedback from that interaction in the form of an observation, which is used to update the trust values appropriately.

In some applications the action and feedback are not only separated by a time delay but may not directly correspond at all. The outcome could be unobservable, or perhaps a poor indicator of behaviour (for example, in a distributed file backup scenario it is better to test hosts' retrieval reliability methodically than to rely on the presumably rare events corresponding to actual file recovery operations).

3.3   Recommendations

Formally, a **recommendation** is information passed from principal W, the witness, to principal R, the receiver, describing their judgement of principal S, the subject.

The use of recommendations increases the amount of evidence we have regarding the subject's expected behaviour, thus reducing the chance that we will predict it incorrectly. Recommendations do introduce a new risk however, since we must decide if we can trust the advice itself.

Our **recommendation integrity** or **meta-trust** in another principal measures their truthfulness, i.e. the accuracy of their **recommendations** (whereas the ordinary trust values represent their behaviour performing **actions**).

The situation is more complex if information is received indirectly. Recommending information which was itself received as a recommendation can help scalability but must be clearly marked as such to avoid counting the same evidence twice.

There are two ways in which information can be forwarded. Where possible we prefer to *relay* information. In this case the client goes back to the original source of the recommendation for confirmation, and hence does not have to trust anyone in the relay chain.

The alternative is to form a recommendation chain, in which the information at each stage is reinterpreted ("discounted") based on the receiver's trust in the sender, and then reissued as if it were a recommendation coming from the receiver. This dilutes the information but is necessary if the client has no trust value for the original observer themselves.

It is worth noting that trust transmission via recommendations may not occur on demand, for scalability reasons in large systems. That being so our model for the trust life-cycle is based on four asynchronous parallel processes executing on each node. Depending on the implementation these may be partly synchronised or some of them may run entirely as background tasks:

1. Action processing. Incoming requests cause the trust model to be invoked, generating information on which to base risk analysis and admission control.
2. Feedback from observations.
3. Trust transmission to other nodes.

a) Behavioural recommendations
b) Truthfulness recommendations

If trust transmission does occur on demand, it may be *pulled* when a request is made for relevant recommendations, or *pushed* if a principal wishes to broadcast a misdemeanor it has observed.

Asynchronous trust transmission is performed instead with ongoing *exchanges* of information. The essential problem is that observations are indexed within the distributed system by *observer*, and need to be looked up by *subject*. If the distributed system is large we need to store partial information, for example by exchanging among a randomly selected group of peers (which can be changed periodically). Communication groups are helpful for bootstrapping newcomers to the system, since they can decide who to trust by correlating the opinions of multiple strangers; this technique works if the proportion of trustworthy principals in the population is sufficiently high.

3.4   Behaviour Models

When we try to assess the likelihood of a principal behaving in a certain way whilst performing an action, we must have a model for that principal's behaviour [8,3]. This will depend on numerous factors, some of which are not observable, such as whether they are in a good mood, in a hurry, following someone else's advice etc. For this reason although they are presumed to be rational it is justifiable to model them as behaving *randomly*, with a certain expected probability of choosing each option available to them. We seek to estimate these parameters.

A quite different model is to select between two hypotheses, as is common in statistics. This is useful in cases where we say that trust is **brittle**. This means that we expect complete reliability from principals we are prepared to collaborate with in a given action, except under extraordinary (statistically insignificant) circumstances out of their control. The hypotheses then are H_0: P is fully trusted, and H_1: P is *not fully* trusted. This is what is required for a large class of applications, such as those including electronic cash or safety critical aspects. The choice of behaviour model motivates the way we map observations onto trust values.

The usefulness of recommendations depends in part on whether behaviour is peer-specific. That is to say, whether it is a function of who the principal is dealing with, in addition to the action, environment and random element. Peer-dependent behaviour may still be consistent across a range of pseudo-anonymous strangers, so we *can* compare recommendations about a certain principal from a randomly selected cross-section of witnesses who are unlikely to collude.

3.5   Trust Value Formats

Trust values may take various forms; some of the most common are frequency counts, belief and disbelief, and probabilities.

Belief and disbelief are described in Shafer's book [10]. Dempster-Shafer theory generalises probabilities so that varying degrees of *uncertainty* can be expressed explicitly. Jøsang [7] presents mappings which can be used to translate between these representations, and Yu and Singh [12] have applied Dempster-Shafer to trust information.

Usually it is better to store the evidence itself rather than derived trust attributes, since transformations potentially lose information and the mapping can easily be performed late in a context-specific way. The trust values can be seen as bridging the gap between the evidence space and probabilities/access rights.

If the behaviour in question is not observable (or even if it is), the best predictor for it may be a function of various other observables.

4 Augmented City Terminology

Because this application is a "recommendation system" and of course involves SECURE's notion of recommendations as well, there is the potential for serious confusion between recommending principals and recommending the objects which the application is concerned with. We shall avoid this by using the words **comment** or **note** for the latter case. The principal who creates the note is called the **author**. The word **recommendation** will only be used in its technical SECURE sense (information passed from a witness to the receiver regarding their trust in the subject).

We will therefore never say "restaurant recommendation", preferring "restaurant *comment*", although we may certainly "*recommend* a restaurant comment author". Although this departs slightly from most natural English usage, experience shows that chaos ensues if we are less clear about this.

5 Object/Application Classification

A given principal may be an expert on ancient buildings but know little about pizza restaurants. This means that trust in one context cannot be applied unmodified in another, and we must regard the Augmented City application as a collection of related but different "sub-applications". Each one corresponds to a type of object that one might comment on. These "sub-applications" are referred to as **application classes**, or simply **classes**. For now we shall assume that classes are distinct, i.e. each note falls within precisely one class.

The following application classes were chosen for the Augmented City:

1. Restaurants
2. Clothes shops
3. Other shops
4. Buildings/Architecture/College courts
5. Gardens/Parks/Grounds/Countryside
6. Useful amenities (post boxes, phones, taxi ranks etc)
7. Special (swimming pools, museums, theatres, clubs etc)

There will be a **class affinity** matrix A to represent the similarity between classes. The value $A_{ijz} \in [0,1]$ signifies to what extent expertise "of type z" in C_i implies likely expertise of type z in C_j. Types of expertise are explained later when we discuss the structure of trust vectors.

6   Naming

The system doesn't constrain which objects can be commented on (since we wish the users to be able to comment on objects which the designers didn't initially include in the database). This puts the burden of object classification on the comment writer (and our trust logic must know how to deal with the possibility that an author classifies one of their notes incorrectly).

Recall that a comment consists of a (location, author, class, creation date, note content) tuple. Comments are indexed by the first four fields and there is no "physical object" field (except the description of what the comment is about in the report body, obviously); i.e. we shall not attempt to specify a naming scheme for the objects which notes might be describing.

Note bodies are in free text format, and do not assign any kind of numeric value to attractions and facilities, so the system cannot parse them itself; hence we believe little is lost by not being able to tell when two proximal notes from different authors describe the same object.

Modifying Notes

In reality, facts go out of date and/or opinions change, but we don't allow subsequent editing of notes. However authors may delete their own notes, so corrections can be made by deleting a note and creating a new one with modified content. The system does not make any kind of connection between the deleted note and the new one (other than the facts that they will have the same author and presumably be in similar locations, of course).

7   Data Structures

7.1   Trust Values

Basic **trust values** in this application will take the form (ν, n) where ν is the fraction of "successes" observed in a count of n events ($\nu \in [0, 1]$). Successes might correspond to "good" notes, for example. In general we shall use greek letters for proportions of successes and a corresponding roman letter for the event count.

If we wish to score some notes in a non-binary way, we can easily count them as partial successes, $s \in [0, 1]$. The trust value is then updated as follows: $n' = n + 1$ and $\nu' = (\nu n + s)/(n + 1)$.

7.2   Trust Vector

The three components which form a **trust vector** are all **trust values**:

- **Relevance** indicates whether notes are correctly categorised (put in the right class) and have sufficient importance (non-triviality). Denoted by (ρ, r).
- **Accuracy** is a measure of factual correctness — whether notes contain true or false information. Denoted by (α, a).

- **Opinions** measures how much you agree with the non-factual claims in notes (subjective, taste). Denoted by (σ, s).

The complete local state is then as follows. Each participant maintains a list of **principals**. For each **principal** they record a list of **trust vectors**, one for each application class, together with a single **recommendation integrity** value. There is also a **recommendation cache** to store trust vectors received from others.

8   Observations

Observations consist of scoring a note in the three categories of relevance, accuracy and opinions. Observations affect trust values directly, by adjusting the percentage and incrementing the event count. If a note isn't considered **relevant** we choose not to update **accuracy** or **opinions** at all (since it could be in the wrong class).

The user interface should aim to present the scoring widgets on the same screen as the note itself so it can be rated quickly and easily. The user may choose not to fill in all fields (for example, if a note happens to be purely factual in content, only the accuracy should be reported, since it provides no evidence for or against the opinions of the author). The scoring is obviously less important if we already have lots of information about this author. Also we might choose to input scores for only a random sample of the notes displayed, to impact less on the user's experience (after all, everyone can draw on all the other users' scores as well, via recommendations).

It is important to realise that scoring will often not be possible when a note is *read*. The **relevance** component can always be ascertained on reading, but **accuracy** and **opinions** cannot unless the user is already familiar with the object in question. Otherwise they may not be able to comment until they have had a chance to visit it for themselves. Because of this we will allow scoring to be postponed (the system may follow up some time later asking for ratings of previously viewed notes, for instance).

9   Analysis

We apply the risk analysis technique described in Section 3.1 to the application. There is only one type of action (deciding whether or not to display a note).

One unusual aspect of the Augmented City is that one of the participants in an action (the author) is unaware of the identity of their readers. This means that the author *cannot* "behave differently" (i.e. write different content) depending on the peer. Recommendations are therefore fully transferable apart from the subjective "opinions" component.

- Outcomes, costs and benefits:
  (a) Don't display the note. Cost 0
  (b) Display an irrelevant note. Cost 1

(c) Display an accurate note. Cost $-X$
(d) Display a misleading note. Cost X
The parameter X can be calibrated by the user to set the amount of clutter at an acceptable level. This is a way of finding out the perceived ratio between the cost of their time (reading notes) and the benefit of more complete information in this domain.

– Risk: $\sum_{o \in Outcomes} Probability(o) * Cost(o)$
– Policy: display the note for the user to read if the expected benefit is positive. Alternatively we could have two thresholds, and choose to display some notes together with a "low confidence" warning sign.

A helpful note may of course not contain information which is new to this particular reader; they may already be aware of it from a source outside the system, for example. However we shall perform the risk analysis on the assumption that helpful notes actually are of benefit, and misleading ones do cause mistakes. This is partly because it is difficult to describe the probability of encountering familiar information, but also because the user's mental model can easily cope with the idea that the system is trying to be helpful without knowing what they already know, and hence interpret the responses correctly.

10   Making Decisions

Assume for the moment we have plentiful direct observations of the principal in question, acting in the correct application class, stored in the trust vector. E.g. $min(r, a, s) \geq T$ for some appropriate level of evidence T.

The trust vector can then be converted into scalar probabilities for each of the outcomes, to be passed into the risk calculation, as follows:

$P(\text{irrelevant}) = 1 - \rho$, $P(\text{misleading}) = \rho(1 - \alpha)$, $P(\text{helpful}) = \rho\alpha$

Currently this analysis ignores the **opinions** component σ. There are two ways this could be used: Firstly, we could display all factually correct notes but mark those from authors with similar opinions to oneself with the addition of an icon. The reader could then separate opinions from facts and discount opinions on unmarked notes. This would require another risk analysis to determine the cost of incorrectly placed marks. Secondly, we could ask authors to label all their comments as either facts, opinions or both and decide whether to use α or σ on that basis.

11   Transferring Trust between Classes

Recommendation integrity is implemented as a shared value between all classes, so there is no need to transfer it. However, **relevance**, **accuracy** and **opinions** are all per-class, with varying degrees of "transferability" between classes (probably high, medium and low respectively).

The components of the trust vector correspond with the "types of expertise" which we mentioned earlier when defining the class affinity matrix A. If we don't know what the similarity between classes is to begin with, we can set the initial values to zero: $A_{ij\rho} = A_{ij\alpha} = A_{ij\sigma} = 0$ $\forall i \neq j$. The system can determine values for these by cross-correlating the local state (observations and recommendation cache) periodically.

It is important to keep track of information inferred from other classes separately from direct observations (which we do by simply re-evaluating the former from the related class observations every time it is required). When we have a lot of observations in the right class we can completely ignore inferred trust from other classes.

12   Recommendations

There are two levels at which trust transmission must succeed. Level 1, dissemination of information, is successful if it puts one in touch with people who claim to have relevant information about the subject principal of interest. This is a distributed systems and scalability problem. Level 2, recommendation integrity, is successful if you get high-quality information which you can rely on.

12.1   Simplifications

The problem of interpreting recommendations is simplified, because we make two restrictions to its scope:

1. All principals make recommendations based only on information *they* have directly observed (no forwarding evidence gained from other recommendations).
   For this to work the system will have to make it easy to discover the identity of lots of principals to ask for recommendations (a broad, shallow search rather than a narrow, deep one).
   Note: we *do* want the system to be implemented in such a way that it could scale to a city the size of London, say — with many inhabitants and visitors.
2. Recommendations contain the event counts, so they are backed by evidence which says *why* we have placed trust in someone, not just *how much*.

$1 \Rightarrow$ There can be no cycles and we won't accidentally count the same piece of evidence twice (except in the weaker sense that multiple recommenders and ourselves may have independently rated the same note).

$1+2 \Rightarrow$ We know exactly which principals and classes were involved in all the events that we count towards a trust assignment. We haven't summarised or lost any information except for the record of precisely which notes were involved in the events, so we effectively have all the information about events which is relevant.

Hence, the only question affecting the validity of recommendations is whether a recommender is lying (or has incorrectly configured software, leading to meaningless output), since we agree on the format of the information and what it means (there's no scope for interpretation error).

We don't need to consider if they

- are gullible or a poor judge of character (because of 1)
- have misinterpreted their data and drawn the wrong conclusions from it (because of 2)
- have bad taste (except for recommendations about **opinions**; see below)

12.2   Dissemination of Information

Scaling considerations create a trade-off between speed, local storage requirements and acting on partial information. If the system decides that recommendations are required, there are various implementation choices for getting this information. Here are some possibilities:

1. Request recommendations every time (a staggering amount of network traffic and latency, if we are panning around an area with thousands of comments and wish to broadcast for recommendations for each one from thousands of principals).
   Requests are infeasible for this application due to speed considerations.
2. Access a central "trust engine" which knows everyone's trust values.
   This doesn't scale, and can't be trusted!
3. Try to replicate trust information in a methodical way continuously by passing recommendations around in a background thread.
   This is closer to what we need. Group multicast can be used to help this scale. The problem is that to replicate a large database we can only store partial copies, and have to form trust chains to reach the data we need. Batching requests could help.
4. Store the results of requests in a local recommendation cache which is consulted first.
   I currently choose to adopt this method.

The key observation is that the Augmented City must make numerous trust decisions per principal per second, which rules out queries and recommendation relays (there's no time to verify the original sources). I have also chosen to rule out recommendation chains [1] for simplicity reasons.

Rather than attempting to prove that we can access a slice of relevant information, I decided on a random distribution method to fill a recommendation *cache* for each principal. By employing a form of Least Recently Used cache line replacement algorithm the system will aim to keep the cache full of useful information. Each cache line consists of information from a given witness, organised as a list of observations of other subjects (so the cache is two-dimensional).

If a peer-to-peer overlay network is available then deterministic methods could be applied instead, for example the *P-Grid* system [2].

12.3   Recommendation Integrity

Trust values are transferred from W to R (re: S) based on R's **recommendation integrity** value for W.

The transfer of **opinions** also depend on R's **opinions** of W (this is because W is not telling R how much they think R will approve of S's opinions, just what W thinks of them personally). Recommendations of opinions are therefore usually a weaker form of evidence than accuracy or relevance.

The recommendation integrity (rec. int.) "bit" which we store for each known principal has three possible states: True, False or Unknown. Initially these are set to Unknown. In this application recommendation integrity is considered to be a **brittle** quantity. This avoids complex weighting functions and limits which are otherwise needed to prevent one big lie from biasing a trust calculation, since the data is considered to be either fully trusted or not.

The approach we take to trusting recommendations is to believe those which correspond well with others people's recommendations. This policy works provided *most* people are honest (if they are not then a trust system isn't much use anyway). When we can't find enough relevant recommendations to form a consensus opinion we use the rec. int. bits to determine who to trust. The bit's value is changed for future reference whenever we decide to use or discard a recommendation from that principal. We don't attempt to store a history of these values. Full details are given in Figure 1.

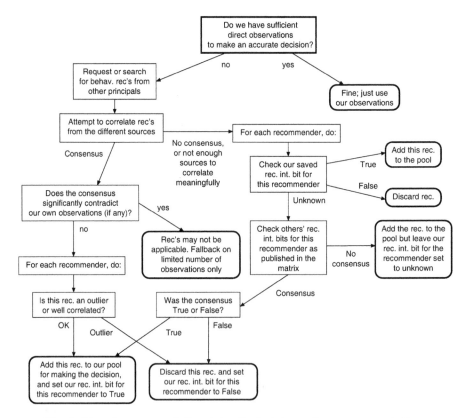

Fig. 1. Use of recommendation integrity in interpreting recommendations

13   Putting It All Together: Combining Evidence

We need to combine evidence from three sources: direct observations, observations in other classes, and via recommendations.

In *most* SECURE applications, when we have a lot of relevant direct observations, we should stop using recommendations entirely. This is a good idea because subjects may well act differently depending on who they are dealing with, so recommendations don't correspond perfectly. In this case however, authors don't know who is going to read their notes, so this consideration doesn't apply. However we shall still choose to diminish the effect of recommendations to nothing as personal observations accumulate, for efficiency reasons and to eliminate the risk of untruthful recommendations.

Notice that when we have *some* direct observations which apply to the situation at hand, we do not immediately stop using evidence from recommendations altogether. If we have a few observations and a great body of knowledge in the form of recommendations it would be foolish to assume that "we know better" straight away.

Our goal will be to accumulate evidence equivalent to T observed events, where T might be 20 or so (considerably less in a small-scale system). Beyond this point we shall not try to add any more information from further sources, to increase efficiency and reliability. The precision achieved in estimating probabilities is $1/T$. Increasing T increases *precision* but may decrease *accuracy* if less trusted sources of information must be added to the pool. Ideally this should be quantified and included in the risk analysis; for now T is a constant configured out-of-band.

The strategy will be to initially use all the direct observations we have. If there are enough of those, no other sources are added. Otherwise, we add evidence from related classes. If the combined information is still less than T event equivalents, we search the cache for recommendations. Finally, if we still need more data we also use recommendations based on related classes (the most tenuous of all).

Giving related class observations priority over recommendations is somewhat arbitrary. If the additional data results in a weight of evidence greater than T, we will scale down the last source so that it brings it exactly to T. This has the nice effect of reducing the weight of related classes and recommendations as our quantity of direct observations increases.

Calculation of Probabilities

Our input consists of direct observations, observations in related classes, and recommendations from different principals (each with an associated recommendation integrity). Related class event counts are discounted according to the class affinity matrix A. Event counts are also adjusted as described above to bring the number of observations up to the required level T.

The final expected probability is then calculated as the normalised weighted sum of all the observed "fractions of successes", with the modified event counts as weights. In the special case of no evidence at all we have no choice but to unconditionally display the note (and hope to learn from this).

14   Conclusion

Trust models are the basis for an emerging field of distributed algorithms, used to mediate interactions between unknown participants in peer to peer networks. We have shown how these ideas could be applied to a large-scale collaborative Augmented Reality system. Further work is necessary to validate the design, but the approach seems to be fruitful.

The alternatives would be to manually authorise every interaction (impractical for naïve, busy users), to trust everyone (insecure), or no-one. In the absence of a trust model, architectures must be more centralised, which places control in the hands of a few completely trusted service providers and reduces the potential functionality of the Internet in emerging peer to peer applications.

Acknowledgements. This work was funded by the European Commission Information Society Technologies SECURE project, IST-2001-32486. I would like to thank my colleagues at the University of Cambridge Computer Laboratory, at BRICS in the University of Aarhus, the Trinity College Dublin DSG, Université de Genève Object Systems Group and SmartLab at the University of Strathclyde.

References

1. A. Abdul-Rahman, S. Hailes. "Using Recommendations for Managing Trust in Distributed Systems". *Proceedings of the IEEE Intl. Conference on Communication*, Malaysia, November 1997.
2. K. Aberer, Z. Despotovic. "Managing Trust in a Peer-2-Peer Information System". *Proceedings of the 10th Intl. Conference on Information and Knowledge Management*, 2001.
3. C. Castelfranchi, F de Rosis, R. Falcone, S. Pizzutilo. "A Testbed for investigating personality-based multiagent cooperation". *Proceedings of the Symposium on Logical Approaches to Agent Modeling and Design*, August 1997.
4. K. Cheverst, N. Davies, K. Mitchell, A. Friday. "Experiences of developing and deploying a context-aware tourist guide: the GUIDE project". *Proceedings of the Sixth Annual International Conference on Mobile Computing and Networking*, August 2000.
5. S. Feiner, B. MacIntyre, T. Höllerer, T. Webster. "A touring machine: Prototyping 3D mobile augmented reality systems for exploring the urban environment". *Proceedings of the First International Symposium on Wearable Computers (ISWC)*, October 1997.
6. D. Ingram, J. Newman, A. Hopper. "Augmented Reality in a Wide Area Sentient Environment". *2nd International Symposium on Augmented Reality (ISAR)*, October 2001.
7. A. Jøsang. "A Logic for Uncertain Probabilities". *International Journal of Uncertainty, Fuzziness and Knowledge-Based Systems*, Vol 9, No. 9 June 2001.
8. F. de Rosis, R. Falcone, E. Covino, C. Castelfranchi. "Bayesian Cognitive Diagnosis in Believable Multiagent Systems". *Frontiers of Belief Revision*. Kluwer Applied Logics Series, 1999.

9. SECURE: Secure Environments for Collaboration among Ubiquitous Roaming Entities. *EU Project IST-2001-32486*, December 2002.
   `http://secure.dsg.cs.tcd.ie/`
10. G. Shafer. *A Mathematical Theory of Evidence*. Princeton Univ. Press, 1976.
11. B. Shand, N. Dimmock, J Bacon. "Trust for Transparent, Ubiquitous Collaboration". *First IEEE Annual Conference on Pervasive Computing and Communications*, 2003.
12. B. Yu, M. Singh. "An Evidential Model of Distributed Reputation Management". *Proceedings of the 1st Intl. Joint Conference on Autonomous Agents and Multiagent Systems*, Italy, July 2002.

Towards the Intimate Trust Advisor

Piotr Cofta[1] and Stephen Crane[2]

[1] E-Business & Security – Mobile Software, Nokia Group, Helsinki, Finland
Piotr.Cofta@nokia.com
[2] Trusted Systems Laboratory, Hewlett-Packard Laboratories, Bristol, UK
Stephen.Crane@hp.com

Abstract. In an increasingly automated and networked world humans are facing new problems stemming from the introduction of machine-intensive communication. The natural human ability to asses, accumulate and evaluate trust in other humans through direct interpersonal communications is significantly impaired when humans interact with systems alone. The development of applications that rely on trust, like electronic commerce, is significantly affected by this fact.

This paper outlines a joint project that Nokia and Hewlett-Packard have just begun which analyses a) the ability of technology to replace the traditional notion of human-evaluated trust with a measure of trust that can be evaluated for the human by automated systems, and b) how this measurement can be communicated to the human by a personal appliance that we call an *Intimate Trust Advisor* (ITA).

1 Introduction

As the world becomes more saturated with technology, direct face-to-face communication becomes an expensive rarity, being replaced by indirect communication means. The Internet and cryptography enable fast and secure information exchange, but reduce the natural human ability to evaluate and establish trust between communicating parties, ending the paradox: "more trust can be placed in technology than in the goodwill of the information recipient".

Trust is seen as the "lubricant of the social life" [1] and a critical factor affecting the introduction of several new technologies, e.g. mobile commerce [2]. A lack of trust caused by deficiencies in technology itself may significantly hamper its future adoption.

However, what technology breaks, technology can mend. This paper discusses the ability of technology to substitute for the naturally developed sense of trust that exists and works well in interpersonal contacts, with trust that can be evaluated by computer systems and then communicated to the human.

Special emphasis is placed on the 'lone user' case. This is the situation where the user is surrounded by technology but also alienated from it, does not understand it and is afraid of it. Users need to balance not knowing what possible risks may exist with the desire to carry out a given action. Such situations are quite common in modern

P. Nixon and S. Terzis (Eds.): Trust Management 2003, LNCS 2692, pp. 123–135, 2003.

business and personal life, and will become more so as technology dominates our environment.

The authors envisage the addition of special functionality to personal devices that will convert them into Intimate Trust Advisors (ITA). The ITA advises its owner on the level of trust that can be placed in specific technical components in the environment. Such devices will utilise vast computational resources that form the trusted (probably remote) supporting environment in order to evaluate the level of trust.

This paper presents the foundation of a joint research project being undertaken by Nokia and Hewlett-Packard. We set out by presenting our assumptions and discussing why these are fundamental to our research. A reference architecture that we have developed for the project is also explained in which we focus on the role of the ITA and the supporting environment. Use cases further clarify scenarios that are of special interest for the project.

Other planned work items within this research project that will be reported in due course, including a more detailed analysis of the issues and challenges presented, and a practical demonstration of a working implementation.

The word "trust" is a homonym; it can take on many different interpretations. It is important that in our research we recognise this fact and establish the context in which we operate. This paper defines and discusses the concept of *computational trust*, a sub-class of *relational trust* that can be evaluated with the help of computing systems.

The set of research questions that we have defined for this project concentrates on the ability of the ITA to provide reasonable pragmatic advice to the owner on the trustworthiness of their immediate technical environment.

2 Themes

The strength of this project lies in its unique approach that combines both research and practical advancements. The project builds on the rich foundations of theoretical works on trust by developing a unique methodology that focuses on issues that can be addressed with today's technology without compromising the breath that a more general approach offers.

This project demonstrates how trust can be evaluated by an autonomous co-operative (i.e. trusted) system on behalf and for the benefit of the user, and how this evaluation can be communicated to the user. It builds on five major themes, as described below.

2.1 Computability of Trust

The elusive nature of trust has led to several definitions of trust, as well as references in taxonomies (e.g. [10]). Most of the published works concentrate on generalisations that cover most (if not all) of the possible meanings of trust.

The authors believe that for a definition of trust to be of any use in a technology-rich environment it should take into account the limited computational capabilities that exists in many current devices. Therefore, the proposed definition explicitly calls for trust that can be not just evaluated but evaluated efficiently.

For this project a working definition of trust has been chosen (presented later in section 5) that, whilst derived from theoretical works, allows us to expose the unexplored areas of trust, namely its efficient and effective computability. Most existing proposals for trust computation (e.g. [6], [7]) are based on expressiveness and coverage rather than efficiency. They therefore overlook the practical limitations that the state-of-art in device development imposes. This is especially the case for hand-held devices.

2.2 Evaluation of Trust

Several existing works (e.g. [4]) attempt to determine how to increase a user's trust in the device or system (e.g. an Internet site) with which they interact, yet relatively little has been done to assist the users in determining that the device (or system) is worthy of the trust that it claims.

The idea behind the ITA is to empower users with the means to carry out their own assessment of the trustworthiness of their environment. This approach is closer to the general idea of trustworthiness (e.g. as noted in [3]) than to the idea of trust alone, since our expectation is that the Intimate Trust Advisor will be capable of evaluating the real quality of the environment.

There already exists an established body of works regarding the calculation of trust (e.g. [12]), including the algebra of trusts [7]. The definition of computational trust that is used within this paper does not provide guidelines regarding the exact function(s) that should be used to calculate trust. Further into the project the authors will propose certain subsets of functions to serve as examples of the larger possible set. The authors believe that there is a wide class of possible functions that can be implemented by each entity depending on its own preferences and capabilities.

2.3 Architecture

Existing works (e.g. [5]) concentrate on Internet-style computation where the user's (untrusted) computer has reasonably unlimited access to others' resources and communication channels.

The reference architecture (presented in section 3) is asymmetric in that it defines a portable trusted ITA that seeks co-operation with a possibly large supporting environment. This asymmetry permits separation of both the workload and trust computation functionality. The ITA is responsible for local data gathering, user communication and final assessment, while the supporting environment processes the bulk of the available data and handles remote communication.

Special consideration is given to address limitations that are inherent in current mobile communication devices, e.g. relative lower bandwidth, communication drop-outs and limited computational resources.

2.4 Context Awareness

The ITA is unlikely to have a perfect understanding of the intended action of the user. Nor will it be perfect in understanding the environment in which the action is undertaken. There are several environmental (or working) parameters that can be used as an input to calculate trust. We recognise that not all of them are easily accessible by the ITA, and that not all of them are important or always relevant.

The project recognises these limitations and addresses them by allowing for additional robustness in the trust evaluation process. Specifically, the co-operation of the local context-aware ITA with the ability of the remote environment to provide independent context analysis is explored.

2.5 User Communication

The complexity of the environment means that a user cannot make the judgement by himself on the basis of technical properties alone. In fact, the user is more likely to be confused if presented with too much information. Conversely, giving too little information leaves the user with the feeling of being controlled by the machine.

There are works (e.g. [8]) that attempt to determine the most useful way to communicate trust to the user, including cases examples of decision-making processes (e.g. [13]). There is also a reasonable body of common experience (e.g. with Web browsers) regarding how security is communicated to the user.

This project assumes that the ITA performs the role of advisor, leaving the user to make the final judgement on whether to proceed. The project examines the methods used to communicate the trustworthiness from the ITA to the user. Specifically, methods are to be explored that provide the user with meaningful information without reaching information overload .

3 Reference Architecture

If we are to work effectively with the multitude of possible interactions that may occur between a user and their technology-rich environments, then we require a simplified reference architecture. It is the intention of this project to concentrate on a reference architecture that can be applied to several interesting scenarios in the expectation that our findings can be applied to other architectures as well.

The reference architecture used throughout the project is depicted in Fig.1.

The architecture consists of two layers: the *interaction layer* and the *trust layer*. The interaction layer deals with the configuration of components and assumed interaction channels between them. The trust layer exposes necessary trust relationships, expectations and the computation of trust.

3.1 Interaction Layer

The user operates the ITA (a). The authors envisage an ITA as a personal handheld device with some communication capabilities, e.g. mobile phone or PDA.

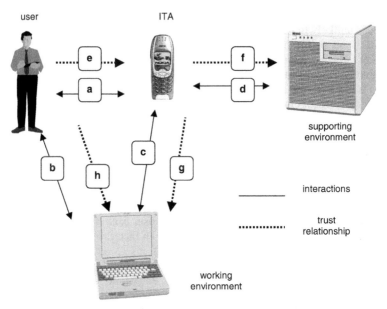

Fig. 1. Reference architecture

The working environment can be either local (e.g. the physical environment) or remote (e.g. the remote server). This environment is unknown and to a certain extent non-trusted, i.e. it can behave in a friendly way or it can be hostile. Despite this uncertainty the user is willing to (or simply must) operate through and within this environment (b).

The ITA is aware of the working environment the user deals with and the actions the user undertakes (c). It can be reasonably expected that the ITA will perform an important role in the user's activity, acting as the user's personal trusted device, intermediating the communication.

Further, the ITA has access to the supporting environment (presumably remote) that is not directly accessible to the user (d). The communication between the ITA and the supporting environment may rely on the working environment, but there are sufficient protective measures so that the ITA can entirely rely on this communication.

Within this architecture the user consults the ITA (or otherwise relies on the ITA's judgement) as to whether it is wise to proceed with a certain action within the current working environment. The ITA presents the user with its own assessment of the trustworthiness of the working environment.

3.2   Trust Layer

It is assumed that the user trusts his ITA at least when it comes to its assessment of the trustworthiness of the local environment (e). It is further assumed that the ITA trusts the supporting environment, but that the way in which the ITA accesses the supporting environment (f) also has a bearing on the level of trust.

The operation proceeds as follows: The ITA assesses the trustworthiness of the local environment (i.e. the trust it would put in the local environment) (g). The ITA presents the results to the user in order to help the user with the judgement regarding the local environment. The user preferably accepts the ITA's judgement as a part of his overall assessment of the trustworthiness of the local environment (h).

4   Use Cases

The project is looking at several use cases to understand how trust can be evaluated and communicated. Special interest is put on the set of 'lone user' cases, situations where the person is surrounded by technology but is alienated from it, does not understand it and is even afraid of it, yet still must perform certain desired actions. It is believed that such situation is quite common in modern business and personal life, and will become even more common as technology comes to dominate our environment.

The following use cases are considered within this project. Each use case is described by a configuration that matches the reference architecture and address different issues faced by the user. All the use cases are taken from the reality of the modern business life.

For each use case the following is highlighted: the ITA, the working environment, the desired action, the supporting environment, and the trust-related question. Further, an outline of the possible action undertaken by ITA to evaluate the trust is presented.

4.1   Business Trip

The user is on the business trip and decides to use his computer to communicate (action) with the home office system (supporting environment) through the Internet hook-up in his hotel room (working environment). The user has his ITA (mobile phone with local connection) that is normally used to authenticate him to the home office system through the local Bluetooth connection.

The attached instruction asks the user to install some code/settings from the accompanied CD in order to enable the use of the hotel's hook-up. The question the user faces is: is the working environment trusted enough to install the required software?

The ITA is able to directly communicate with the office system (e.g. making the wireless data connection) so that this question can be passed to the system that can respond according to the corporate policy, taking into account the reputation of the hotel, prior experience, required certificates, etc. This response is communicated to the user.

4.2   Wireless LAN

The user is equipped with the personal communication device (that acts also as an ITA) and is within reach of a wireless LAN that is free to use but unknown to her (working environment). She wants to use this opportunity to surf the Internet (action), but she is not sure whether the network can be trusted, both in terms of security and reputation. She trusts her regular wireless LAN provider (supporting environment).

The ITA can evaluate both the security features of the working environment (e.g. the level of security) and the reputation (as reported by the regular wireless LAN provider) and provide certain advice to the user. Note that the ITA relies on the working environment to access the supporting one, and that the connection between them is presumed to be secured in an end to end fashion.

4.3 Visiting the Office

The user is visiting the office of her client. While preparing for the presentation she realises that some of the files are missing. She can use the client's computer (local environment) to access her corporate network (supporting environment) but she is not certain whether such an arrangement is trusted enough as all her credentials may be recorded by the local environment and used later on to re-enter the corporate network.

She consults her wireless phone (ITA) that makes a direct call to the corporate network. The corporate network does not trust the client enough, but the ITA may be able to arrange the document to be delivered to the client's network over the unprotected channel. The ITA informs the user that the action is possible but not recommended. The user, upon consulting ITA, decides not to proceed.

4.4 Ad Hoc Network

The user plans to engage in the ad-hoc network (e.g. over Bluetooth) in the office he is visiting to (working environment) in order to print certain documents on the Bluetooth-enabled printer (action) with the intention to pick up copies and leave no trace of the text printed (which is presumably of the confidential nature). Due to the omni directional nature of the Bluetooth carrier and its relatively long range the user is uncertain whether the documents will reach only the printer or whether they can be intercepted/overheard by some other pieces of the infrastructure.

The mobile phone, incorporating ITA functionality, is used as a Bluetooth modem. It is consulted in order to see whether the action should be conducted. The ITA evaluates technical properties of the Bluetooth link (e.g. security, range) vs. other possible options understanding that the office environment can be intentionally hostile. The ITA is able to extract further information from the document itself regarding the required confidentiality level. Further, the ITA obtains information about the identity of the office (temporary, secure, competitor's, subcontractor's) and compares it remotely (e.g. though the wireless connection) with information stored in the corporate office (supporting network).

Consolidated results of the sophisticated evaluation are presented to the user who then can make the final decision whether to continue with the action.

5 Definitions

Trust is a homonym, a word that encompass more than one meaning. The literature brings a significant number of interesting definitions (e.g. [9]) as well as some overviews of those that describe a classification typology (e.g. [10]).

This project requires definitions that will cover the possibly wide area of the semantics of the word 'trust' but which at the same time fit the reference architecture and use cases. Specifically, the computational aspect of trust should be included. The phrase 'computational trust' has been developed to define an approach to trust that is important to the project.

The authors have decided to clarify and explore two definitions of trust: one that is believed to be generic enough to encompass all the relationships of trust within the reference model and another that stresses the computational aspect of it. The project will focus on exploring trust issues that arise from the second definition.

The authors have intentionally avoided definitions of trust that address one's inner emotional state (referred to as 'Dispositional' in McKnight's typology) since these are considered out of scope for this project. Some trust relationships, as explained in the architecture, provide working assumptions about user's disposition of trust. Similar approaches to the definition of trust in a global sense can be found, e.g. in [14].

The definition of computational trust, as provided below, refers to the relationship (g) in the reference architecture, i.e. the assessment by the ITA of the extent to which the user should trust the local environment. This assessment may be computed from data known by the ITA itself as well as from data gathered or calculated by the supporting environment. It is assumed that the definition of computational trust can be applied to every trust assessment or trust computation within this process.

Relationships (e) and (f) are implied by the model chosen while the relationship (h) is the propagation of the relationship (g). Relationships (e), (f) and (h) can be identified as relational trusts.

5.1 Definition 1 – Relational Trust

Relational trust is one's expectation that the outcome of the other's unobservable or incomprehensible behaviour is favourable.

This generic definition sets the scene. There is the entity A that may receive certain outcomes from another entity B. The entity A expects the outcome to be favourable to itself even though A may not comprehend its value. Further, the entity A cannot observe the behaviour of B and cannot determine in advance what the outcome might be.

The definition of relational trust encompasses categories of 'Impersonal/Structural' and 'Personal/Interpersonal' according to McKnight's typology.

5.2 Definition 2 – Computational Trust

Computational trust is one's supported expectation that can be expressed as the computationally effective function, that the outcome of others' unsupervised behaviour is favourable according to one's understanding.

This definition stresses the rational aspect of trust ('Cognitive State' aspect of trust according to McKnight's typology). The entity A expects an outcome from B, and A trusts B if A expects that the outcome from B is favourable according to its understanding. There are no restrictions on foundations of the expectations, be it reasoning, statistical model or firm belief as long as the expectation looks rationally to A.

The definition assumes that A is satisfied with an outcome that is favourable to A according to A's understanding. It assumes that A can reasonably express what is favourable and can judge whether an anticipated outcome is indeed favourable.

Note that if A can perfectly and effectively predict every action of B, then A no longer needs to trust B. In this case one can say that A possess complete knowledge of B or that trust is replaced by knowledge. Note further that if A can effectively control B at every stage of it's the activity, then A need not trust B as A can always 'steer' B towards the desired outcome . In this case the trust is replaced by control [11].

6 Technical Architecture

The technical architecture presented below is used only to illustrate one of the possible implementations of the reference architecture. The value of the proposed implementation lies in the use of common components, each directly related to a project theme, to simplify significantly the overall design.

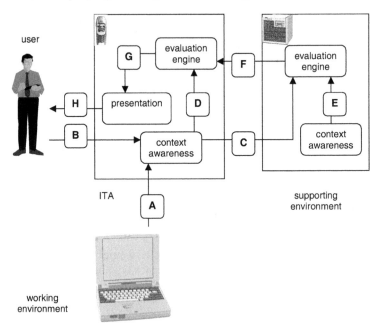

Fig. 2. Technical architecture

6.1 Components

The architecture assumes the existence of three types of components: a *context awareness* component, an *evaluation* engine and a *presentation* component. Following is a short description of these components.

It is expected that the design of the components will be portable and scaleable across all the platforms that they are supposed to work on, so that they form building blocks that can be used to populate the entire configuration. This is especially important in the case of more complex supporting environments, as discussed later in this paper.

Context Awareness. The role of the context awareness component is to collect all the relevant information about the function that is going to be performed and the current context of the device, including such items as user preferences or communication properties, if appropriate. Even though it is obvious that the context awareness component will never be able to collect all the information, the expectation is that it will be able to capture the most relevant ones.

The context awareness component is located on the ITA not only to collect information related to the function, local environment and user preferences but also to gather information about the quality of the supporting environment. The context awareness component at the supporting environment collects information about the environment itself (e.g. its preferences). It can be also used in more complex configurations to assess the quality of other environments.

Context awareness component reflects the fourth theme of the project: context awareness.

Evaluation Engine. The evaluation engine encapsulates the core of trust evaluation as it implements the selected trust evaluation function. It processes inputs from various available sources (context awareness component and other evaluation engines) and comes out with the synthetic assessment of trust, according to policies defined for the evaluation engine.

Evaluation engine is covered by the second theme of the project: evaluation of trust.

Presentation Component. The presentation component is unique to the ITA and is responsible for the presentation of the evaluation in a form that is well understood by the user. The presentation component drives the trust indicator, the element of the user interface that provides the synthetic statement of trust.

Presentation component reflects the fifth theme of the project: user communication.

6.2 Information Flow

The context awareness component of the ITA collects information about the context from the working environment (A), from the user (B) and adds information about the ITA and its supporting environment. The complete context information is sent to the supporting environment (C) and to the local evaluation engine (D).

Within the supporting environment the separate context awareness component produces information about preferences (E) which, together with contextual information from the ITA is sent to the evaluation engine that processes the consolidated trust indicator and sends it back to the ITA (E). Another evaluation engine at the ITA collects this input and combines it with its own evaluation into the consolidated trust indicator. This indicator is then sent to the presentation component (F) and eventually presented to the user (G).

6.3 Configurations

Several possible configurations can be considered, depending on the availability of the supporting environment, its robustness and configuration, and alike.

If the supporting environment is not available, the ITA is still able to process information by itself by passing information directly from its context engine to its evaluation engine. The evaluation engine takes into account that such an evaluation is local.

Alternatively, the complexity of the evaluation engine in the ITA can be greatly reduced if the ITA is designed not to support trust evaluation. In such a case it is the supporting environment that performs the majority of trust evaluation.

The supporting environment provides the essential trust processing components, but this may not be the only place where trust is processed. The structure of the supporting environment may be modular in nature, with several interlinked evaluation engines. Alternatively, the supporting environment may ask for opinions from other environments.

The technical architecture provides support for such configurations. The context awareness component in the ITA may forward its output to several evaluation engines while each evaluation engine may accept input not only from its own context awareness component but also from other evaluation engines.

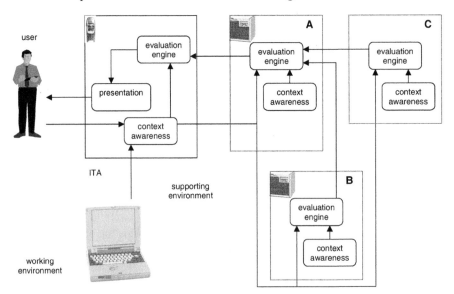

Fig. 3. Complex architecture

Fig.3. presents an example of a more complex architecture where the supporting environment consists of three evaluation engines (A, B and C), each with its own context awareness components. Information from the ITA is distributed to all three evaluation engines, while the trust indicators are consolidated by engine A before being sent to the ITA.

7 Conclusions

This joint research project between Nokia and Hewlett-Packard studies the important issue of whether a lack of inter-personal trust can be replaced with computed trust in the environment that the mobile industry workforce experiences every day.

This paper presents the initial approach that the project is taking and use cases to identify the project's scope. The project concentrates on five major themes: *definition of trust, evaluation of trust, architecture, context awareness* and *user communication*. From these themes, initial results based on our definitions and architecture are presented.

Our unique approach that combines theoretical and pragmatic approach promises very interesting results.

References

1. Fukuyama F: Trust: The Social Virtues and the Creation of Prosperity, Touchstone Books; ISBN: 0684825252; (June 1996)
2. Egger F. N.: Towards a Model of trust for E-Commerce System Design. In Proc. of the CHI2000 Workshop: Designing Interactive Systems for 1-to-1 E-commerce; also in http://www.zurich.ibm.com/~mrs/chi2000/contributions.egger.html
3. Egger F.N.: "Trust Me, I'm an Online Vendor": Towards a Model of trust for E-commerce System Design. In: Szwillus G.& Turner T. (Eds.), CHI2000 Extended Abstracts: Conference on Human Factors in Computing Systems, The Hague, April 1–6, 2000: 101–102.; also in: http://www.ecommuse.com/research/publications/ chi2000.PDF
4. McKnight D.H., Chervany N.L.: Conceptualizing Trust: A Typology and E-Commerce Customer Relationships Model. In: Proc. of the 34th Hawaii Int. Conf. on System Sciences 2001.
5. Grandison T., Sloman M.: Specifying and Analysing Trust for Internet Applications. In: Proc. of the 2nd IFIP Conference on E-Commerce, E-Business and E-Government, Oct 7–9, 2002, Lisbon, Portugal; also in http://www.doc.ic.ac.uk/~tgrand/ TrustPaper.pdf
6. Mui L., Mohtashemi M., Halberstadt A.: A Computational Model of Trust and Reputation. In Proc. of the 35th Annual Hawaii International Conference on System Sciences, 7–10 Jan. 2002, Big Island, HI, USA.
7. Grandison T., Sloman M.: SULTAN – A Language for Trust Specification and Analysis. In: Eighth Workshop of the HP OpenView University Association, June 2001, Berlin, Germany; also: http://www.hpovua.org/PUBLICATIONS/PROCEEDINGS/8_HPOVUAWS/Papers/Paper01.2-Grandison-Sultan.pdf
8. Urban G.L., Sultan F., Qualls W.: Design and Evaluation of a Trust Based Advisor on the Internet. In: http://ebusiness.mit.edu/research/papers/Urban.pdf.
9. Gerck E.: Toward Real-World Models of Trust: Reliance on Received Information. In http://www.mcg.org.br/

10. McKnight, D. H., Chervany N. L: The Meanings of Trust. In
    http://www.misrc.umn.edu/wpaper/wp96-04.htm
11. Castelfranchi C., Falcone R.: Trust and Control: A Dialectic Link. In:
    http://alfebiite.ee.ic.ac.uk/docs/papers/D3/ 4._TrustControl.pdf.
12. Marsh S. P.: Formalising Trust as a Computational Concept. Doctoral dissertation, Univ.
    of Stirling, Scotland; also in http://www.iit.nrc.ca/~steve/Publications.html
13. Muir B. M.: Trust between humans and machines, and the design of decision aids. In: Int.
    J. Man-Machine Studies (1987). Vol.27, p. 527–539.
14. Chopra K., Wallace W.A.: Trust in Electronic Environments. Submitted to: Hawaii
    International Conference on System Sciences (HICSS-36), 2003.

Trusting Collaboration in Global Computing Systems

Colin English, Waleed Wagealla, Paddy Nixon, Sotirios Terzis,
Helen Lowe, and Andrew McGettrick

Department of Computer and Information Sciences
University of Strathclyde, Glasgow, Scotland.
Colin.English@cis.strath.ac.uk

Abstract. A significant characteristic of global computing is the need for secure interactions between highly mobile entities and the services in their environment. Moreover, these decentralised systems are also characterised by partial views over the state of the global environment, implying that we cannot guarantee verification of the properties of the mobile entity entering an unfamiliar domain. Secure in this context encompasses both the need for cryptographic security and the need for trust, on the part of both parties, that the interaction will function as expected. In this paper, we explore an architecture for interaction/collaboration in global computing systems. This architecture reflects the aspects of the trust lifecycle in three stages: trust formation, trust evolution and trust exploitation, forming a basis for risk assessment and interaction decisions.

1 Introduction

The future of distributed computing is likely to bring a massively networked world supporting a diverse population of hardware and software entities [1]. In this global computing environment, many of these will be mobile entities that stand to benefit from the ability to interact and collaborate in an ad-hoc manner with other (possibly unknown) entities and services to succeed in the tasks allocated to them. In such large systems, spanning multiple administrative domains, autonomous operation is an essential characteristic of entities that cannot rely on specific security infrastructures or central control to help in security related decisions. The composition and characteristics of these systems will be both highly dynamic and unpredictable. Entities will have to deal with unforeseen circumstances ranging from unexpected interactions to disconnected operation, often with incomplete information about other principals and the environment.

Freedom for collaboration between entities is an important benefit of such a dynamic environment. Collaboration can be defined as a joint interaction between two or more principals (P), which must perform one or more specific actions (A) on one of the principals' resources.

- E.g. Simple collaboration: (A, P_1, P_2)
  $\Rightarrow P_1$ (initiator) must decide if P_2 (executor or requesting entity) is authorized to carry out A.

P. Nixon and S. Terzis (Eds.): Trust Management 2003, LNCS 2692, pp. 136–149, 2003.
© Springer-Verlag Berlin Heidelberg 2003

To allow a secure collaboration to proceed, it is necessary to predict the behaviour of other principals. The current security focus on the protection of data in transit using cryptographic measures does not address the issues of undesirable behaviour of entities at either end of the communication channel. Entities must be able to make autonomous decisions about entering into a collaboration and configure themselves dynamically according to changes in expected behaviour.

The remaining sections of the paper are arranged as follows. Section 2 provides an insight into the human phenomenon of trust as a security mechanism for the type of system considered in this paper. Section 3 describes a computational model of trust, which, in conjunction with the trust information structure outlined in section 4, forms the basis for a collaboration model architecture. The collaboration architecture discussed in section 5 incorporates a trust box, which encapsulates the trust model and implements the trust information structure, to allow a principal's trustworthiness to be established based on the available information. Section 5 also describes a risk model, which utilizes the established trust to perform risk assessment upon which to base the decision to collaborate. Sections 6 and 7 consist of ongoing work and conclusions respectively.

2 Trust

In real life, humans use the mechanism of trust to cope with the inherent risks when dealing with only partial information about people and the environment. Accepting risk via this mechanism allows humans to interact on the basis of available evidence, assigning privileges or tasks to others accordingly. Similarly, computational interactions require an adequate level of trust between the principals, which is currently pre-configured by a system administrator. We assume that the administrator will not be present and measures must be in place to allow entities to form their own opinions of the trustworthiness of others. The pre-configured, coarse and static configuration of trust in traditional systems is not consistent with human intuitions of trust as a subjective and situation specific notion [2], being an individual's opinion of another entity. Trust is also dynamic, as an individual's opinion can evolve and develop based on the evidence available for subjective evaluation. Due to the complex subjective nature of trust, people have formed many different views of what exactly trust is. While this makes it difficult to form an exact definition, we assert that a model of trust can be developed in sufficient detail for use in a security model.

Within this paper distrust is not considered, as in the type of global systems considered here, it is possible for entities to change identity when they are distrusted in order to avoid negative evidence. Distrust is therefore not represented to reduce the incentive for change of identity.

It is proposed that the development of trust-risk based security architecture for collaboration incorporating a dynamic model of trust will provide devices with the ability to operate and make security-related decisions autonomously, on the basis of changing evidence. With the use of explicit representation trust, enhanced information is available on which to base decisions. It is proposed that the collaboration architecture can be used either to augment other security mechanisms or as a basis for unencrypted interactions.

2.1 Sources of Trust

There are three main sources of trust information about another entity. Personal observations of the entity's behaviour, through recording the outcome of an interaction, are essential for the subjective evaluation of trustworthiness. Recommendations from trusted third parties provide the possibility for trust regarding unknown entities to be propagated in a similar manner to the deferment of trust as seen in current trust models (e.g. [3]). Recommendations are based purely on the recommender's personal observations and as such it is possible to associate a measure of trust in the opinion of the recommender (this is not the same as trust in the recommender for other actions). The reputation of an entity can be consulted in the absence of experience or recommendation. Reputation is anonymous in the sense that it is an aggregation of trust information from different sources (including recommendations that are passed to us via intermediate parties) and as such we cannot associate a level of trust with the opinion expressed. Trust information relevant to specific action can be of more use than trust information about general activities, thus a notion of context is necessary to incorporate the situational nature of trust. A strong basis for trust is established through an entity's subjective observations and the collection of such evidence. Recommendations may be evaluated subjectively within a similar context to the recommendation evidence source. Clearly personal experience influences trust to a greater degree than recommendation, therefore it is important to weight the evidence dependant on the source of the information. The process of recommendation becomes more important in cases where we have no personal experience with the entity in question. Requesting recommendations allows us to consider interacting with unknown entities. The paper does not currently consider reputation for simplicity although this will be examined in future work by the authors.

2.2 Dynamic Aspects of Trust

The subjective nature of trust based on evaluated evidence has been introduced. The dynamic aspects of how trust is formed, how trust evolves over time due to available information and how trust can be exploited are equally important in striving for an intuitive representation of trust. These aspects of the model are collectively referred to as the trust lifecycle [4] and will provide an entity with the ability to reason about and make security-related decisions autonomously. This dynamic view of trust will result in a more flexible model able to represent trust in a manner that captures human intuitions, such that positive outcomes of interactions will preserve or amplify trust, while trust erodes without periodic interactions or recommendations.

Evaluating the trustworthiness of a principle is referred to as trust formation. An entity's trustworthiness can be synthesized from available evidence of past interactions, to be used when allocating privileges for specific tasks. Evidence relevant to the current context will carry the most weight, in particular subjective observations made by the entity itself about previous interactions. Initially new entities have no evidence of past behaviour to establish a base for interaction. Recommendations may be used to establish collaboration between entities that have never met, but who trust a common third party.

The evolution process takes place, as additional evidence becomes available. Accumulation of evidence with experience of new interactions must modify the level of trust to be placed in an entity, incrementing the trust information to maintain accuracy. Evidence from the outcome of interactions must be evaluated against the expected behaviour of the principal.

The essential problem in exploitation is to determine behaviour on the basis of trust, by determining the risk of interacting with a particular principal for a particular action. The calculated trust values enable a full assessment of risk to be carried out to allow a decision whether or not to collaborate to be made. The decision to collaborate will be determined by the security policy or the particular entity. Through the evolution process outlined above, there is feedback from this risk assessment process, demonstrating the cyclic nature of the relationship between trust and risk.

The next section introduces the basis of trust in the collaboration model that can represent trust in this dynamic manner.

3 The Trust Model

The basis for the collaboration architecture is a formal model of trust developed by Mogens Nielsen et al in [5]. Each principal in the system has a trust box, a component that processes evidence and principals to return trust values. The trust box has a state, represented by the trust information structure detailed later. Within the trust box, the model represents trust values as elements of a domain forming a complete lattice. This allows two new structures to be constructed based on intervals for all subsets of the lattice of trust values. The actual set of trust values used may be application independent. For example, if we use the simple set of integers from 0 to 100, the interval [10, 50] means that the appropriate trust value lies somewhere in the range of from 10 to 50, but we cannot be more precise given the information we have.

The first new structure is a lattice of intervals lifted from the lattice of trust values, providing an interval ordering (trust ordering) that allows the qualitative comparison of trust intervals. The second new structure is a complete partial ordering (trust information ordering) on intervals to represent quantity of trust evidence for a principal. For example, an unknown entity has the complete lattice of trust values as an interval such that its trust value could be anything. The narrower the interval, the less possible trust values we have. This serves as the basis for least fixed-point calculations to pinpoint an entity's trust value. The local trust policy of each entity determines how it computes trust. The collection of all local policies determines a global trust function, which serves as basis for least fixed-point calculations to determine trust in others. The following section describes the structure developed to represent trust information, which in conjunction with this trust model facilitates the evaluation of dynamic trust values.

4 Trust Information Structure

The idea of a trust information structure is to provide information representing the state of the trust box in the trust based security model. The use of a layered structure (Figure 1) to store trust information provides a greater depth of information upon which to base any decision than merely storing the individual trust values relating to the entity in question. Each entity has one trust information structure, the basis of which is the store of all trust information available on every other entity with which it has been associated.

The structure has four layers: the collection of all known trust information in the first layer, the relevant separated evidence relating to personal experience and recommendations in the second layer, separate trust values (Tv_{OBS} and Tv_{REC}) derived from personal experience and recommendation in the third layer and a fourth layer containing general trust values. The goal behind these layers is to provide more fine-grained levels of trust information on entities for which we are unsure about the accuracy of the stored trust value. While the structure allows trust values to be used without further examination of available evidence in situations such as low risk assessment or high stored trust values, it may be necessary to re-evaluate trust afresh. If further information is required, the desired number of previous experiences can be examined, particularly those relevant to the currently requested action. If the final collaboration decision does not yield a positive result it is possible to seek further supportive evidence to re-evaluate a higher trust value.

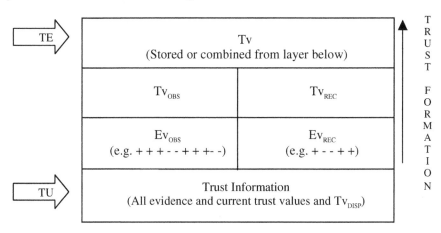

Fig. 1. The Trust Information Structure

The following points discuss these layers of trust information in more detail:

1.   The base layer contains all of the trust information available to the entity, comprising of personal experience, recommendations and stored trust values. To prevent this stored information growing to an unmanageable quantity with new evidence, the information may be temporally limited to allow out of date information to be discarded. This layer also contains information on the entity's trusting disposition (Tv_{DISP}), i.e. whether or not it is generally trusting. This information can be used to initiate interaction in the absence of evidence, by selecting a node from the whole lattice of trust values. This dispositional trust may also be of use in the evaluation of evidence offered as a recommendation. After an interaction has terminated, the evaluation process will update this layer with evidence of the outcome, to keep the store of trust information up to date.

2.   The information in the second layer is dynamically extracted from the trust information layer below upon request and contains evidence relevant to the re-

quested action. In the absence of evidence related to the specific action, general evidence for the requesting entity may be extracted to provide some basis for the trust evaluation to proceed. The approach taken is that rather than have two separate structures for experiences and recommendations, one structure is used, and the recommendations are treated in a different manner to personal observations. This is necessary to ensure that the process of recommendation does not become merely delegation of trust values from other entities, and that the information passed can be evaluated subjectively, dependant on the trustworthiness of the recommender.

3. The third layer in the structure contains trust values specific to observation/experience evidence and recommendation evidence. From evaluation of each of the two sources of relevant trust information, trust values can be established to represent personal opinion/belief and the opinion/belief from other parties, as to the trustworthiness of the entity in question. Trust values will take the form of intervals on the trust lattice and can be compared both quantitatively (quantity of information supporting the values) and qualitatively (comparison of values directly) using the two orderings described in the trust model. This allows representation of how much recommendations and experience influence the final decision individually.

4. The fourth and top layer contains the final trust value upon which to base a decision in the risk model. This layer may contain the stored trust value for the requesting entity, extracted directly from the base layer of trust information on the fly or combine the separate trust values from the layer below in a suitable manner to derive a single value for trust. A consensus operator (described in the trust formation section below) combines the two trust values, taking into account the quantity of evidence that has contributed to the evaluation of each individual trust value. In any collaboration, when the stored trust value of the requester is high we can use that trust value without re-evaluating the other two lower layers, or seeking new evidence. Evaluating the trustworthiness from base trust information upon each request requires more processing to extract the necessary information relating to a particular entity than if the trust value itself were used on the fly. This overhead is acceptable only when further evidence has become available or must be sought to enable the interaction to proceed.

There are some additional points that should be considered, which are outlined here. Each piece of trust evidence in the trust information store must be linked to the action type from which the evidence originated, whether this is a personally observed outcome, or a recommendation from a trusted third party. This is merely to provide a simple notion of context, to represent the situational nature of trust by evaluating only the pieces of evidence of relevance to the currently requested action. It should also be possible to base the trust evaluation on all the pieces of evidence relating to an entity, to provide additional support for the decision if necessary.

The representation of evidence from experience and recommendations must be carefully considered. Each piece of evidence may take the form of a tuple containing the evaluated outcome or recommendation and parameters to represent the action. The exact representation of personal observations will depend upon the function used to evaluate the outcome of an interaction, such as comparison of the expected outcome with the actual outcome of the interaction (e.g. determination of cost incurred relative to the cost-PDF predicted by the Risk Model). It may be reasonable to consider any deviation from expected outcome should be deemed unsatisfactory and reduce trust because the outcome is not what was expected, regardless of whether the outcome is positive or negative. Recommendations may take the form of personal evidence offered for evaluation or trust values offered for evaluation. The use of separate trust values based on experience and recommendation allows an entity to offer the trust value based on its own experience as a recommendation, to ensure that the value passed is based purely on the personal experience of the recommender, rather than just hearsay (e.g. a police investigator, needs to know what you saw, not what someone else told you they saw). Also, if trust values based on recommendations from other entities down a chain are passed, we run the risk of double counting trust information and distorting the final trust decision. It is likely that the transfer of trust recommendations will take place through the use of certificates, to allow verification of the source. For example, it will be possible for each entity to offer the other collaborator a certificate containing its opinion of the outcome, which could be used as a recommendation in future interactions.

Evolution of trust values and update of evidence is an important part of the dynamic nature of trust, and the trust structure must facilitate both these functions. After any interaction, the store of trust evidence should be updated (TU in Figure 1) to contain the new evidence as a result of collaboration evaluation. The evolution function (TE in Figure 1) should provide the functionality to alter the stored trust value without the excess overhead of full re-evaluation. In situations where trust must be re-evaluated afresh due to the availability of new evidence, the trust formation process can be re-invoked. The following section will detail the collaboration model architecture, which uses the trust information structure and trust model outlined above to model the lifecycle of collaboration.

5   Collaboration Architecture

The collaboration architecture outlined in Figure 2 is an expanded version of work by David Ingram et al in [6], with the addition of the notion of the trust lifecycle to provide dynamic secure collaboration support. This architecture shows how we model these dynamic aspects of trust, in terms of the available trust evidence both from personal observations and recommendations from trusted entities. The architecture outlines how trust is exploited in the process of risk assessment [6], to allow security decisions to be made on the basis of probable cost of the outcome of an action. The lifecycle of the collaboration follows a series of steps described in the following subsections. These are entity recognition, trust formation, risk assessment, collaboration monitoring and collaboration evaluation. These steps incorporate the functionality of the trust lifecycle of formation, evolution and exploitation, through the use of a trust box, which encapsulates the trust model and the trust information structure defined above.

5.1   Collaboration Request Analyser

Upon receiving a collaboration request, we must analyze the contents of the request to determine whether we have the necessary resources to allow the action to take place.

If the resources are not available, no further processing of the request is carried out, and a message is sent to notify the requesting entity. This message may also contain information recommending another entity, which can fulfill the request. Another important feature of the request analyzer is the process of entity recognition described below.

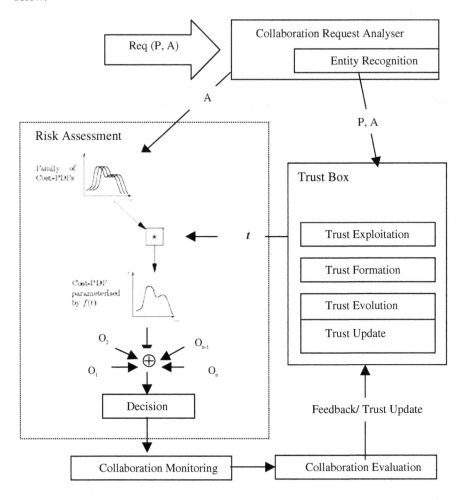

Fig. 2. The Collaboration Lifecycle (an extension of figure 1.1 in [6])

5.2 Recognition Mechanism

It may be impossible to establish the identity of unknown entities via intersecting certificate hierarchies, when entities roaming between administrative domains may be disconnected from their home network. Even when authenticated identity can be established in this manner (e.g. PKI [8]), as in most security mechanisms on the Internet, it conveys no a priori information about the likely behaviour of an entity. Work by J. M. Seigneur et al in [7] is relied upon to provide entity recognition in the collaboration architecture. It is proposed that all entities be assumed virtually anonymous, placing importance on recognition of entities rather than identity. In this way, the necessity for prior configuration of collaborative entities is removed, allowing unforeseen interactions to take place as the need arises. Recognition based on previous experiences allows the relevant evidence to be linked to the relevant entity. Auto configuration and dynamic enrolment measures must therefore be in place to remove the reliance on centralised certification authorities and allow the formation of an initial level of trust (dependant on an entity's trusting disposition) when entities meet for the first time, allowing enrolment in an initial low risk collaboration. This will provide the necessary evidence for future recognition.

A number of entity recognition mechanisms may be available, each trusted to different degree. One of these mechanisms must be selected to establish the level of trust in the recognition infrastructure. End-to-end trust in a particular collaboration then combines both trust in the underlying recognition infrastructure and trust between the principals determined by the trust model. If the final trust evaluation is trust insufficient for collaboration to take place, it is possible to look for a more trustworthy recognition mechanism to increase the end-to-end trust.

5.3   Trust Formation

From the set of all available trust evidence, we extract the set of experiences that represent personal observations and the set of experiences that represent recommendations. Upon receiving a collaboration request, we can dynamically filter the available trust evidence to retain only that relevant to the requested action. If there is no evidence for a principal regarding the specific action, it is possible use available trust evidence from other actions with the principal. This can be seen in the trust information structure section as the second layer of the diagram. Recommendation evidence is treated separately from evidence based on personal experience as the latter has a greater influence on the trust value.

If the stored trust value (Tv) is high enough an entity may decide to use that value without performing any further investigation of the evidence. An extreme case of this is that absolute trust may lead to collaboration without assessment of the risks involved, and absolute distrust might lead to automatic rejection.

If no evidence is available for an entity from experience or recommendation we must establish an initial trust value to encourage low risk collaborations. This collaboration will provide further evidence upon which to base future trust formation. There are several schemes available for determining the initial trust value. These include:

- Selecting the minimum trust value for any entity in the trust information structure, or
- Exploit the trusting disposition of the entity to select a suitable interval from the trust model.

Trust Formation Function (TFF): For evidence relating to personal observations, there exists a set of possible experience values Ex, which consists of two subsets, Ex_{NEG} and Ex_{POS} to represent negative and positive outcomes of interactions respectively.

Each element $ev \in Ev_{OBS}$ takes a value from the set Ex. To assist in the evaluation of a trust value based purely on the set of observation evidence (Ev_{OBS}) we will use the TFF.

$$TFF = (\#\{ev_i \mid ev_i \geq 0\} - \#\{ev_i \mid ev_i \leq 0\}) / i$$

The TFF gives a value to indicate the strength of positive evidence relative to negative evidence to support collaboration. This value (TFF), in conjunction with the total quantity of observation evidence ($\#Ev_{OBS}$), allows us to determine an interval on the lattice of trust value intervals ordered by the trust information ordering (Tv_{OBS}). $\#Ev_{OBS}$ determines the width of the interval, while the TFF allows the pinpointing of the exact interval on the lattice, dependant on how positive or negative it is.

Recommendation Trust Operator (RTO, $\oplus$): This operator is used to combine all of the evidence obtained via recommendation. Recommendations will only be considered based on first hand experiences from a trusted entity, to avoid the possibility of double counting trust evidence from entities further down the recommendation chain. This is referred to as recommendation independence, avoiding second hand recommendations. When we have insufficient evidence from personal observations or when the evidence we have is not relevant to the collaboration request, we may seek the relevant additional recommendations to encourage collaboration. The RTO seeks consensus between the Tv_{OBS} values from trusted entities, collected as elements of a set of recommendations Ev_{REC}. Assuming that we have two recommendations for principal $X \in P$, R_X^A and R_X^B (where $R_X^A = Tv_{OBS}$ for X, from principal $A \in P$), then the RTO reaches a consensus for Tv_{REC} as follows:

$$Tv_{REC} = R_X^A \oplus R_X^B$$

Trust Consensus Operator (TCO): The two trust values, Tv_{OBS} and Tv_{REC} are combined according to the TCO, in a manner inspired by Audun Josang's work on combining beliefs [9]. The use of Josang's consensus operator assumes the consistency of evidence underlying the opinions; therefore we make a similar assumption, that the requesting entity behaves in a uniform manner when interacting with all other principals. This consensus will strike the relevant balance between trust from experience and trust from recommendation and may also give more weight to the narrowest interval (which by definition must have been determined from more evidence). It is only necessary to use evidence in the form of recommendations if there is not enough evidence from personal observations. Thus, if Tv_{OBS} is a very wide interval, we will consider Tv_{REC} in order to narrow the interval to obtain a more accurate final Tv.

5.4   Trust Exploitation for Risk Assessment

Having established the relevant trust value for the requesting entity, this is passed to the risk model [6], in order to determine whether the risks are acceptable to enable collaboration to proceed. The evaluation of risk involves a combination of the probabilities and costs of the possible outcomes of action. An assumption is that all possible outcomes of an interaction are known and that cost or benefit associated with each can be determined. The range of possible costs for each outcome can be expressed as a cost-probability density function. For each possible outcome, the trust value is used to select one from a family of cost-pdfs, to represent possible costs or benefits, should this outcome occur. The appropriate cost-pdfs for all possible outcomes are combined and analysed according to security policy, to facilitate a decision on accepting the collaboration. The answer set can contain more than one response if necessary, or contain a moderator to express low confidence in the response.

5.5 Collaboration Monitoring

The goal of this stage is to monitor the progress of the individual actions of which the collaboration is composed. Defining policy for an interaction does not guarantee the secure execution of that interaction; therefore monitoring plays a crucial role. This is essential to ensure that the interaction is progressing towards the desired outcome rather than towards a negative outcome predicted during the risk assessment for that interaction. Moreover, we can measure the state and behaviour of principals during the interaction process, in order to terminate prematurely when a security infringe-ment or some other form of incorrect behaviour occurs, resulting in a drastic reduc-tion in trust. This protects resources immediately rather than waiting for the interac-tion to complete and then modifying trust levels. While modifying the trust level is important, it is also important to ensure that an action can be terminated without fur-ther damage being permitted. Monitoring offers further opportunity for the exploita-tion of trust values. If trust in a principal is very high, it may be your policy not to monitor the interaction to reduce processing overheads. The monitoring process is of increased importance for interactions established with unknown entities.

5.6 Collaboration Evaluation

After the interaction is finished, the outcome will be recorded and an evaluation will be carried out. The outcomes of the interaction will be evaluated with respect to the range of outcomes established during risk assessment, recording any deviation from the expected outcomes. Based on this evaluation, each action should be classified as a positive or negative experience according to the overall outcome. This information is recorded for each action, but may be grouped together in terms of the overall collabo-ration within which the action took place. This evaluation of the experience can be fed back into the trust lifecycle and used to evolve the trust value for the entity in ques-tion. Our work in this area contemplates a similar approach to the work of Catholijn Jonker and Jan Treur [10], but differs in that update affects only the trust information, not the trust value. The view of evolution here also differs from [10] concerning the narrowing and pinpointing of intervals on the trust information ordering. The evalua-tion of an interaction as a negative (Ex_{NEG}) or positive (Ex_{POS}) experience will update the stored trust evidence layer of the trust information structure for possible re-evaluation in future interactions.

Trust Update (tu). After each evaluation the outcome, in the form of experience evi-dence must be added to the store of trust information in the base layer of the trust in-formation structure. The store contains the set of all trust evidence, Ev, to which we add the latest experience, an element (ex) from the set of all possible experiences, Ex, to produce an updated set of trust evidence, Ev'. This can be represented as follows:

$$tu : Ev \times Ex \to Ev'$$
$$tu \ (Ev, ex) = Ev'$$

By updating the trust evidence in this manner, it is possible to re-evaluate trust values based on the most recent evidence, by following the procedure of trust formation again.

Trust Evolution (te). It is also important to allow the evolution of trust values over time to take place on the fly without incurring the processing overhead of trust formation. For this reason, we define the Trust Evolution function, which takes a new piece of evidence from experience (ex) and modifies the stored trust value (Tv) directly, producing a new trust value (Tv'). The function can be represented as follows:

$$te : Ex \times Tv \to Tv'$$
$$te \ (ex, Tv) = Tv'$$

To recap, this collaboration architecture will facilitate the establishment of secure interactions between autonomous entities, showing how it is possible to base the decision to collaborate with another entity on evaluation of trustworthiness. The following section will introduce some of the open issues for the model and examples of ongoing work.

6   Open Issues and Ongoing Work

The work in this paper is still in progress and as such there remains many open issues to be addressed. Examples of such issues include the examination of the notion of reputation and how to represent this. It clearly should convey less reliable information than the other two sources of trust evidence highlighted in the paper. The idea of second hand recommendations based on the Tv_{REC} of a recommender may constitute one view reputation, but the aforementioned issues of double counting of trust evidence must be addressed.

The process of monitoring requires some notion of how to model a principal's behaviour over the range of possible incorrect and correct behaviours with respect to the expected outcomes of an action.

Work is in progress to examine further the use of a set of policies, which affect the manner in which a decision is taken, dependant on existing trust values. The dynamic selection from a set of policies affords greater flexibility in decisions than hard-coded behaviours. For example, a family of evolution and update functions may exist, parameterized by policy, further increasing the flexibility of the system.

A scenario to explore an example implementation of the collaboration lifecycle is currently in development. In section 3.4 of [11], a smart space scenario is outlined, a context-aware distributed system that gathers context information about individuals. In a smart university campus or department, smart applications allow the tracking of student and staff activities through effective use of the context information. For example, staff and students can use the system via PDAs or mobile phones, to check the availability and location of colleagues for a meeting. An issue of growing concern in these systems is security and privacy. It is crucial to provide secure access to context information in order to prevent its misuse and breach of users' privacy. This challenge motivates the consideration of smart spaces as an application scenario for the application of trust-based security mechanisms. This scenario has characteristics such as different methods of information sharing and a large number of possible principals, which will be important in addressing aspects of complicated collaborations. An example interaction that may occur in this scenario, involves a student (P_1) wishing to access the supervisor's calendar (P_2) in order to book an appointment (A), which involves a variety of risks to security and privacy. More complex collaborations composed of interdependent interactions may impact upon the functions outlined in the paper, and will be the focus of future work. The scenario will also provide useful information on the practicality of such complex lifecycle processes in the context of smart environments using small devices with limited processing capability.

Also in development is a simulation framework, where entities are represented by agents, for the investigation of trust and collaboration lifecycle issues. The model will be tested using simulations rather than implementation scenarios, as this allows control over independent variables and a range of complex behaviours to be studied. We are unlikely to be able to run "real-life" experiments of more than a few cases even if these were desirable in the first instance. In real life we cannot control independent variables so failure (of our model to live up to expectations) would tell us little. Also, we could only test very benign scenarios where no one was really going to suffer as a result of their behaviour. Simulation is, therefore, an important weapon in our armoury. The simulations will test the applicability and scalability of all aspects of the model and address issues such as the use of a dropping window of evidence to limit the trust evidence considered in trust formation, the use of time limited evidence to represent out of date information and the issues involved in more complex interactions with multiple principals performing different actions, which may rely upon one another. It may be possible to examine the correctness of assumptions such as agents always behave in a rational manner and examine the effects on the system when such assumptions are removed. Work started with an implementation of two specific scenarios, an agent-based file sharing facility and trust based dynamic routing in ad-hoc networks, which we are now generalizing to produce the simulation framework. It is also hoped that privacy implications of propagating trust information will become clearer through these investigations.

7   Conclusion

The new paradigm of global computing requires a new methodology for tackling the problem of security of interaction. Conventional hard coded security mechanisms lack the flexibility required for use in such systems, where only incomplete information is available on which to base security decisions. A more flexible mechanism is the application of trust based security models to cope with the risk inherent in interactions in this environment. Current security mechanisms with pre-configured representation of trust fail to capture the notion and its relation to risk in a manner suited to systems with no form of central control. This paper proposes an architecture with the characteristics necessary to provide a basis for reasoning about trust in security related decisions for these systems. Although it is clear there are open issues, these will only be fully determined by the continuing work, which is expected to address these problems.

Acknowledgements. The work in this paper is supported by the EU FET project SECURE: Secure Environments for Collaboration among Ubiquitous Roaming Entities (IST-2001-32486) funded by the Global Computing Initiative: [http://secure.dsg.cs.tcd.ie]. The scenario ideas originated with the EU FET project GLOSS: Global Smart Spaces (IST-2000-26070).

References

1. EU Future Emerging Technologies, Global Computing Initiative.
    http://www.cordis.lu/ist/fetgc.htm
2. S. Marsh: "Formalising Trust as a Computational Concept". Ph.D. Thesis, University of Stirling, 1994.
3. A. Abdul-Rahman: "The PGP Trust Model" Department of Computer Science, University College London, 1996.
4. C. English, P. Nixon, S. Terzis, A. McGettrick and H. Lowe: "Security Models for Trusting Network Appliances". In Proceedings of the 5th IEEE International Workshop on Networked Appliances, pp 39–44 October 2002.
5. M. Carbone, O. Danvy, I. Damgaard, K. Krukow, A. Møller, J. B. Nielsen, M. Nielsen: "SECURE Deliverable 1.1: A Model For Trust", December 2002.
6. J. Bacon, N. Dimmock, D. Ingram, K. Moody, B. Shand, A. Twigg: "SECURE Deliverable 3.1: Definition of Risk Model", December 2002
7. J. M. Seigneur, S. Farrell, C. Jensen, E. Gray and C. Yong: "End-to-end trust in pervasive computing starts with recognition". To appear in the Proceedings of the First International Conference on Security in Pervasive Computing, 2003.
8. U. Maurer: "Modelling a Public-Key Infrastructure". In Proceedings of the 1996 European Symposium on Research in Computer Security, Lecture Notes in Computer Science, vol. 1146, pp. 325–350, 1996.
9. A. Jøsang: "The Consensus Operator for Combining Beliefs" Artificial Intelligence Journal, 142(1–2), p.157–170, Oct. 2002.
10. C. M. Jonker, J. Treur: "Formal Analysis of Models for the Dynamics of Trust Based on Experiences" Modelling Autonomous Agents in a Multi-Agent World 1999 European Workshop on Multi-Agent Systems. pp. 221–231, 1999.
11. C. Bryce, V. Cahill, G. Di Marzo Serugendo, C. English, S. Farrell, E. Gray, C. Jensen, P. Nixon, J-M. Seignuer, S. Terzis, W. Wagealla, C. Yong: "SECURE Deliverable 5.1: Application Scenarios", September 2002.

Trust, Reliance, Good Faith, and the Law

Daniela Memmo[1], Giovanni Sartor[2], and Gioacchino Quadri di Cardano[2]

[1] Department of Legal Sciences „A. Cicu", University of Bologna,
Via Zamboni n° 33, 40126 Bologna
dmemmo@alma.unibo.it
[2] CIRSFID, University of Bologna, Via Galliera n° 3, 40126 Bologna
{sartor, gquadri}@cirfid.unibo.it

Abstract. This paper aims to show the importance of the function assumed by trust in the present society, and to provide an overview of the main interaction patterns between trust and private law. We shall start by trying to give a definition of trust according to the socio-cognitive theory. Then we shall examine the most important private law principles involved with both trust and reliance, such as good faith, and shall particularly focus on the so-called appearance principle and its main applications by jurisprudence and doctrine[1].

1 Trust from a Legal Perspective

In this short contribution we will discuss the topic of trust from a legal perspective, focusing on Italian law. As is well known, trust has recently become the object of an increasing attention on the part of psychologists, sociologists and computer scientists. This attention is well deserved since trust is an essential component of the functioning of social institutions (both human and artificial ones). It is a basic mechanism which contributes to the development of social co-operation. Trust is good for trusters and trustees to whom it opens larger possibilities of interaction. Moreover, in a society that is based upon extensive exchanges and forms of cooperation between its members (as is required by the division of labour, and by democratic politics), trust also is a public good. If there was no trust, co-operation would end, and the whole fabric of society would collapse.

Given the social importance of trust, we should not be surprised that the law, being the most important mechanism for ensuring social co-operation, takes a special interest in trust.

However, law and trust have frequently been opposed one to the other. Some authors viewed law (formal rules) and trust as alternative, opposed mechanism for social regulation. From this perspective law is required in a society exactly because reciprocal trust is insufficient: formal rules and sanctions are a rigid and brutal mechanisms that unfortunately becomes necessary where sense of community and attachment to social norms are insufficient to restrain the opposed egoisms, to ensure mutual trust. We believe that this vision of the relationship between law and trust is basically mis

---

[1] Daniela Memmo and Giovanni Sartor are authors of paragraphs 1-7, while paragraph 8 has been written by Gioacchino Quadri di Cardano.

P. Nixon and S. Terzis (Eds.): Trust Management 2003, LNCS 2692, pp. 150–164, 2003.

taken. Rather then a conflict there is usually a cooperation between law and trust. The law does not aim at substituting trust, but rather on the one hand may provide the basis for trust to exist (even in large and anonymous societies), and on the other hand frequently recognises and supports those trust relationships which autonomously emerge or which are based upon non-legal norms. It is true that sometimes the law may disrupt trust: this happens when either the law admits behaviour which violate reciprocal trust and spontaneous cooperation (consider, for example, laws condoning fraudulent managerial practice), when it forces individuals to act against one another rather then reinforcing their spontaneous bonds (the extreme case being represented by totalitarian regimes requiring the use of informers, up to the extreme vision of Orwell's 1984), or when it only requires a formalistic application of its prescription, disregarding and conflicting with that   genuine attention for other people's interests which represents the basic ingredient of social trust (goal adoption, as Castelfranchi [8] and Falcone [9,10] call it). We believe, however, that the cases we have just considered may be viewed as a degeneration of different patterns, in which law facilitates and supports trust, as we hope to show in the following pages.

2   Trust and the Law: Main Patterns of Interaction

Relationships between trust and the law can take various shapes, so that it is difficult to classify them into a few clearcut patterns of interactions. We shall anyway make an attempt. Let us first introduce a notion of trust. We start with the well known notions provided by Castelfranchi and Falcone [8. 9]. According to these authors we can distinguish the two components in trust, core trust and reliance.
Core trust includes the following:

1. The truster has a certain goal, i.e. is interested in the production of a certain result,
2. The truster believes that the trustee is able to bring about that goal (competence belief)
3. The truster believes that the trustee is willing to bring about the goal (disposition belief)

Reliance includes the following:

4. The truster believes that it needs to rely on the trustee for the achievement of the goal (it would be impossible or inconvenient to achieve it directly) (dependence belief)
5. The truster believes that the goal will really be achieved, thanks to the action of the trustee.

3   Behaviour-Trust and Situation-Trust: Classification

The definition of trust we have considered only considers trust in the behaviour of an agent. Let us call it behaviour-trust.

Equally important for the law is reliance on the existence of preconditions for the achievement of the legal results on which the agent is interested, and the corresponding reliance on having achieved such result. Let us call it situation-trust. Situation-trust is similar in many regards to the behaviour trust. The difference is that it concerns not people's behaviour, but the fact that under certain conditions (given certain clues or certain appearances, or traces) certain legally relevant situations exist. Consider for example, the situation of a buyer who wants to enter in an Internet-contract. The buyer needs to put some trust in the behaviour of the seller (i.e. he should expect that the seller will not use improperly his credit card number or his personal data), but he also needs to trust that those preconditions exist under which the sale is fully effective (that the person who appears to be the seller really is the seller, that he really is the owner of what he is selling, etc.). And after completion of the purchase, the buyer trusts that it has been effective (that he has acquired the good).

The two aspects of trust we have just described are connected, since trust in certain clues or appearances may be related to the trust in the fact that nobody has falsified such clues or appearance, or even that nobody has allowed them to exist without the existence of the corresponding conditions. However, those two aspects of trust need to be distinguished, when looking at the phenomenon of trust from a legal perspective, since they may be protected in different ways.

When considering behaviour-trust we need to focus, first of all, on the fact that the law establishes duties upon certain persons in order to protect corresponding rights of other persons. This happens most clearly, as we shall see, in two domains.

The first concerns those legal rules which protect the integrity of the individual person and of his property. Expectation that such rules are legally binding, and are going to be enforced by public authorities, if necessary, provides a minimum of security (reliance that my fellows are not going to harm my person or my property) which is the essential precondition for avoiding an Hobbesian nightmare.

The second concerns those rules which allow the parties to enter into legally binding agreements (contracts). This allows the parties to ground their trust on the performance on the other party, also on the fact that such performance is required by the law. This also means that if the other party does not wilfully perform it may be forced to do so, or anyway, it may be forced to restore the damage that the truster has suffered. In both areas, the law increases a right-holder's reliance on the rightful behaviour the other party. Reliance is facilitated in two ways.

First of all the law increases what Castelfranchi and Falcone [8] call disposition belief. The duty-holder knows that if he defaults, he risks being punished, and this provides a powerful incentive to fulfil his duties. The public nature of the legal process (and in particular of judicial proceedings) provides a further incentive to rightful behaviour: the defaulting duty-holder is at risk of seeing his reputation so compromised that nobody is going to trust him.

Secondly, the law diminishes risk related to trust. The right holder knows that if the other parties default, he may get compensation, and therefore avoid the losses which he would otherwise suffered as a consequence of relying on the performance of the other party.

In the cases we have just considered trust is put upon the fulfilment of a legally binding rule: the law comes first, and the truster relies on the execution of a certain behaviour for the very reasons (beside possible other reasons) that it is legally mandated. We will not consider specifically this pattern of legally-based trust, since its implications seem on the one hand quite obvious and on the other hand adequately analysable in the framework provided by trust research: law only is one additional ground upon which trust-related expectation (in particular disposition-belief) can be based.

4 Behaviour-Trust Grounded upon Legal Rules

A different pattern is more interesting to us, always within the domain of what we called behaviour-trust. This concerns the case where the very fact that one party puts his trust in a certain behaviour is the reason why the law provides for its protection, by requiring that the trustee behaves in such a way that the truster is not damaged because of his trust. In such cases trust come first, and law comes after. In those conditions the truster is protected by the law against the trustee's default exactly because he has justifiedly put his reliance upon the trustee's behaviour. So reliance is the ground for legal protection (rather then the opposite). The behaviour that is required to prevent damage to the truster can usually be identified by reference to the idea that the trustee needs to behave according to the standard of good faith. As it is well known, good faith identifies the requirement of an honest and correct behaviour, a requirement which includes the need that one takes care to prevent damage to others because of their reliance on one's behaviour. Consider for example, the legal requirement that parties behave towards one another according to the principle of good faith when they are contracting (before the contact is made). This does not mean that they have any obligation to make the contract. However, they certainly have the obligation to prevent the other party suffering losses for having justifiedly relied on the conclusion of the contract. Note, however, that the law does not protect every hope or expectation concerning other people's behaviour: there must be both a sincere and reasonable trusting attitude, and the legal protection is especially intense when such reliance was caused by the trustee's behaviour.

Another general principle which supports the protection of trust (at least in legal systems which are based upon a general clause for tortious liability), as we shall see is provided by the need to restore „unjust damage" which one has caused to other (this is the expression which is used by article 2043 of the Italian civil code). The violation of the other party's reasonable trust, which is based upon the trustee's behaviour, can certainly be viewed an unjust damage.

As we said above, we will not discuss the obvious fact that the existence of legal obligations (established by law or by contract) may lead people (and especially rightholders) to trust that such obligation will be fulfilled. However we need to mention that there are some cases where the word „trust" (or „fiducia") is specifically used for referring to legal obligations. This is when one is legally bound to use his property for some specific interests (or goals) which have been set by somebody else (not that this corresponds to that element of trust which Castelfranchi and Falcone call goal-adoption).

This is the notion of „trust" as it is used in commercial and property law in common law systems, a notion which corresponds in civil law system to the Roman notion of „reliance with a friend" (fiducia cum amico). This covers what is called in Italian law „proprietà fiduciaria" (ownership with trust), and on the other hand „contratto fiduciario" (contract with trust).

1) *Proprietà fiduciaria*[2] . This concerns the case where a person (the trustee) becomes the holder of a property right which he is entitled to use not for his own interest, but for the interest of the truster (for example, the property right which is exercised by a manager of an association without legal personality, or by the owner of an inherited property subject to an obligation stated in the will, called fideicommissum, etc.).

2) *Contratto fiduciario*[3]. This is a contact, usually concerning property rights, where the parties, besides transferring such rights, establish special obligations between them which ensure that those rights are exercised for determined purposes (which are not typical for that contract). For example, in the compravendita fiduciaria (sale with trust) the buyer (trustee) of a property undertakes the obligation to transfer that property in the future to a third party or back to the seller or to use that property for a certain time according to the instructions of the seller (truster).

5   The Legal Protection of Reliance and Good Faith

Let us now move to the second pattern we have considered, i.e. to those cases where the law protects reliance of the truster upon the behaviour of the trustee. In this sense the idea of trust is related to the idea of good faith. To understand how the law protects reliance we need to examine two different uses of the notion of good faith (buona fede)[4]. In Italian law those two notions are respectively called „*buona fede in senso soggettivo*" (good faith in the subjective sense) and „buona fede in senso oggettivo" good faith in objective sense (good faith in the objective sense).

a) Good faith in the subjective sense is especially relevant in the law of property and possession, and is usually defined as   „*not knowing that one is violating other people's rights*"[5]. In fact it frequently happens that a person who violates the rights (or

---

[2]   This topic has many connection with the Anglo-Saxon institute of trust. See De Angelis [16], Lupoi [28] and Malaguti [29].

[3]   See the researches of Ferrara sr. [20], Gambini [25] and Grassetti [26], as well as Trimarchi [38]

[4]   The traditional researches of Bigliazzi Geri [5-7] have been recently continued by Nanni [30-33].

[5]   As defined by art. 1147 of the civil code. According to the jurisprudence of the Supreme Court, in order to acquire the possession it is necessary that ignorance is not due to a lack of

the legitimate interests) of other people without being aware of that, enjoys a certain degree of protection by the law. For instance, in Italian law the possessor of a thing that belongs to somebody who believes that he is the rightful owner enjoys a better position than the possessor who knows that his possession is against the law. Similarly, when one person buys a thing from somebody who is not the owner, and acquires the possession of that thing believing that the seller was entitled to sell, then that person acquires the property of that thing. On the contrary, if the buyer was not acting in good faith (he knew that the seller was not the owner) the contract would not be effective.

b) Good faith in the objective sense is usually said not to consist in a purely subjective state (a mental state) of an agent but in the fact that the agent behaves correctly.[6] Therefore it is also said that good faith is a standard of behaviour. Such standard is to be identified not only with reference to legal rules, but also with reference to social norms and to reasonableness. This is the sense in which good faith (correctness) is required in the fulfilment of an obligation, in the negotiation of a contract, in the interpretation of a contract.[7]

It is easy to see that both good faith in the subjective sense and good faith in the objective sense can be viewed as specific ways of protecting trust. More specifically, good faith in the subjective sense can be viewed as a way of protecting situation-trust: the agent who sincerely believes that he is not violating other people's rights (who trusts that there exists a legal situation which is favourable to what he is doing) enjoys a legal advantage that he would not have otherwise. In some cases that protection is so strong that this person will obtain exactly those results which he would obtain if the situation he believes to exist was really there.

On the other hand good faith in the objective sense can mainly be viewed as a way of protecting behaviour-trust. The agent may safely expect that his counterparty will behave correctly, since the law protects such expectation. Moreover, one of the most important requirements of correctness is that one does not let down those who have put their trust in oneself. Therefore, objective good faith requires, in many cases, that the trustee takes care to avoid damage to the truster, especially when the trustee's behaviour induced the truster's reliance.

It is interesting to remark a general tendency in the way in which trust is protected. While protection of behaviour-trust usually is provided by an obligation of the trustee to compensate damage suffered by the truster (because of his reliance), the protection of situation-trust is provided by allowing the truster's false belief in the existence of a certain situation (in the appropriate circumstances) to produce the same legal result (in favour of the truster) that would have been produced by that very situation.

---

that ordinary prudence and diligence that would have permitted to the purchaser to understand that he was violating somebody's right: *"non intelligere quod omnes intellegunt"* is an unforgiveble error that is not compatible with the concept of good faith itself (Cass. civ., sez. II, 7-05-1987 n. 4215, Cass. civ., sez. II, 7-05-1987 n. 4215)

[6] Bessone[3] and D'Angelo [14 - 15] are the most important authors that have written about this topic, but the studies of Del Bene [19] and Franzoni [22] are relevant too.

[7] See art. 1337 of the civil code that states that „*the parties must act according to good faith*" and art. 1366 that obliges the parties to interpret the contract according to good faith, that means that the declarations of the parties must be assigned the sense that the average man would assign them.

6 Protection of Situation-Trust and Connection with Behaviour-Trust

Finally, we need to consider what we called situation-trust. This, as we said, concerns the truster's belief that a certain situation exists, which has a positive relevance for his situation and interests. For example, a buyer is certainly interested in the fact that the seller is the owner of what he is selling to him (or was authorised to sell by the owner). If this was not the case, he would not be able to buy what he wants. However, the buyer's sincere and reasonable belief (his good-faith) in the existence of such situation is protected by the law: the person having such belief would acquire the good even if the seller did not own the goods.

We need to focus on situation-trust, since we need to consider the special form which the legal protection of the trusting party usually takes. Protection of situation-trust often justifies the following: one person's erroneous belief that a certain state of affairs exists is attributed the same legal effect which the existence of that state of affairs would have had. For example, in contract law, one party's erroneous belief that the counterparty made a certain declaration (which the counterparty did not make) or had a certain intention (which the counterparty did not have) can sometimes produce the same effect that the counterparty's making that declaration or having that intention would produce. This happens to protect the party who was justified in believing that the counterparty made that declaration or had that intention (who put its trust in this belief). However, one cannot invoke the protection of trust as the justification for allowing the effects of a certain situation (in the absence of that situation), when nobody believed in the existence of that situation, or when it was completely unreasonable to believe that it existed. Moreover, usually one party's erroneous belief that a (mental or physical) state of affairs exists can be equated to the existence of that state of affairs, only when the counterparty contributed to producing that erroneous belief (as in case of deceit and misprestentation)

The idea of situation-trust, and the form of protection which it enjoys can be seen also in contexts which lawyers do not label under the heading of good faith (in the subjective sense). In fact there are various circumstances in which a person relying in the existence of a certain situation (which may concern both external circumstances or circumstances pertaining to the counterparty) can achieve exactly the result which would have been produced by that situation, even when it does not obtain. For example, protection of reliance may prevail over the principle according to which a party may be bound only by a contract which that party wanted, and wanted on the basis of a rational volitional process which was not affected by mistake, violence or deceit. Correspondingly, a contract which is affected by the mistake of one party remains valid (has the same legal effect which the contract would have had if there was no mistake) if the contract did not and could not recognise the mistake. Similarly, the contract which was made by a person who has not the capacity of making contracts is valid if the other party relied on the validity of the contract. Consider that, on the contrary, a unilateral juristic act (such as a will) can always be voided when it damages the incapable author of that act, since in such a case there is no reliance that needs to be protected. Similarly, an only simulated contract (which should in principle be ineffective, since the parties did not agree to make it, but only to create the appearance that they made it) produces its effect in regard to the third parties who, relying on the validity of the simulated contract, acquired rights which depended on it. So, if A and B organize a fake sale of A's house to B, and subsequently B makes a contract with C, for selling A's house to C, the latter contract is valid, and C rightfully acquires the ownership of the house, since C relied on the validity on the sale contract between A and B (C would obtain, on the basis of his reliance on the fact that the contract between A and B was valid, the same effect which he had obtained if that contract was valid).

The law can not always protect the party who has relied on the existence of certain conditions by ensuring to that party the same results which would have obtained if those conditions really existed. When this is not possible, however, the law frequently establishes upon the party who failed to provide such conditions a duty to compensate damage which the truster has suffered as a consequence of his reliance. This is the case for example, when a contractor suffered damage for relying on the validity of a contract with which was invalid because of the other party's behaviour.

Obviosuly, a duty to compensate damage is the only protection which can be provided to the truster in the case of behaviour-trust. An instance of this can be seen in the case where during negotiation one party was induced to rely on the future conclusion of the contract. The party who abandoned negotiation without justification violates the standard of correctness (good faith in an objective sense) and is therefore bound to restore the damage which the other party (the truster) has suffered.

Even though the law often protects a truster, we cannot assume that the law establishes a general duty to restore any damage which a truster has suffered because of his reliance on the trustee's behaviour (or in the existence of situations which pertained to the trustee's sphere). However, we may say that in general the trustee may be bound to compensate the damage of the truster, when the trustee induces (either intentionally or negligently) the truster to rely on his behaviour.

With reference to the Italian law, we may also say that person who has put a reasonable reliance on somebody, can be considered to have a legally protected interest. The violation of such interest produces an unjust damage, for which compensation can be requested, when the damage was intentionally or negligently caused, by suing the violator for tort. In Italian law this can be done on the basis of art. 2043 of the Civil code which is viewed as establishing a general principle of tort law.

Moreover, we need to consider that in some cases the truster is protected even when his reliance in a certain appearance is not due to the fault of the other party. Under those circumstances, however a justification may be found in the fact that the law puts upon the other party the risk for the innocent reliance of the truster, where by risk one means „the negative effect on an activity which a subject undertakes in his own interest".

Finally, we need to consider that according to the law, only reasonable trust is protected. This means that the truster is only protected only when circumstances exist that justify his expectations (behaviour trust) or his beliefs (situation-trust). When situation-trust is at issue, the circumstances which create a reasonable belief in the existence of the facts on which the truster relies are said to provide the appearance (apparenza) of such facts. The problem of legally relevant appearance will be considered in the following paragraph.

7 The Limits of the Legal Protection of Trust

As we have seen above, the law does not always ensure the protection of trust. Reliance as a mental state is not always relevant to the law (besides the the cases of good faith in a subjective sense which we mentioned above). On the other hand there is not always a duty to act in such a way as to protect other people's reliance (unless this is required by the principle of correctness).

There are two limitations to be considered.

First, usually the law only protects the truster when his reliance is justified by objective circumstances. Reliance must be reasonable and legitimate. It is frequently said by jurists that the law protects reasonable people, not silly or credulous ones.

Secondly, the law needs to balance the protection of reliance with the interests of other people. For example, in deciding when and to what extent we need to protect the buyer's reliance on the validity of the contract (on the fact that the seller is entitled to sell), the law also needs to consider the interests of the real owner, by considering that the seller may be a thief.

Therefore, the protection of reliance is not an absolute exceptionless rule, but rather a principle that needs to be balanced with other values, interests and principles, it is a standard to be used (along with others), to adjudicate conflicts of competing interests. Moreover, by choosing to protect the reliance of one party, in certain specific circumstances, the law does not only aim at the generic objective of increasing social trust: it may also, and more significantly, aim at specific objectives. Protecting the reliance of one party appears to be a technique for privileging certain parties and certain interests, against other parties and other interests, i.e., for providing a legal discipline for certain conflicts of interests. For example, protection of the buyer corresponds to the idea of facilitating trust, but is more significantly a way of adjudicating the conflict between the buyer (from a false owner) and the real owner. The ways in which this conflict is solved in the Italian legal system, i.e. by protecting the reliance of the buyer in good faith, clearly correspond to the purpose of facilitating commercial transactions, eliminating the risk that the real owner may attack the buyer.

We are aware that our discussion of law and trust is inadequate and does not exhaust its subject matter. There are many other areas of the law where the idea of the protection of trust is relevant, besides the one we have just mentioned. There are also many other theories of trust in specific areas of the law with we have not examined. There are also many connections between the law and trust studies which we have failed to consider. We are aware that our work is a preliminary declaration of intent, and we shall try to address more deeply the issues pertaining to the legal protection of trust in the future. We are also aware that we have only considered Italian law, while the assessment of the legal relevance of trust needs a comparative analysis, though we tend to believe that different legal system (at least in Continental and Anglo American legal families) tend to approach the trust issue in very similar ways.

We hope, however, that our short discussion may have illustrated the need that trust studies focus their attention also on the legal domain. The law has much to learn from the current discussion on trust, since it seems to lack a clear and coherent framework for approaching this subject. However, it has also to offer an invaluable collection of cases, problems, and patchwork that which can provide a very significant input to trust studies. We strongly believe that here there is the possibility for a very fruitful interdisciplinary cross-fertilisation.

8 Appendix: The Principle of Legal Appearance in Italian Law

The topic of the juridical appearance is quite recent and was almost unknown by Roman law, that just considered the case[8] of the apparent heir who alienates an hereditary good to a third, who could be protected as a bone fide possessor.

Indeed it was only in the 19th century that French scholars[9] elaborated a wide number of theories that turn on the idea that law must protect all those who have guiltless relied on appearance. By this way the principle of juridical appearance has been used to solve different problems such as the apparent domicile, the *marriage apparent,* [10] the apparent society and so on. We must however point out that all the cases where the appearance principle is invoked must be considered as exceptions which are called to compensate the imperfections of the publicity systems that permit the application of the general rules and –by this way- to assure equity and justice.

We have a very different situation in Germany, since the BGB decrees the victory of the mechanism based upon delivery, publicity and formality over the consensual principle, and the scholars follow the declaration dogma without giving importance to the will[11]. The bona fide holder who has acquired something from who results as the heir apparent on the heredity certificates, or from who is indicated as the owner in the property register is always directly protected by law, and so the appearance principle is superfluous. However German scholars[12] elaborated the complex theory of Rechtsschein to explain the reason of this rigorous formalism that implies that „ju-

---

[8] In D. 5, 3, 25, § 17, also if this solution is not followed in public law by D. 1, 14, 3 that discusses the case of Philippus Barbarius, who was nominated praetor although being a slave. We must however point out that this concerns the efficacy of the praetorial measures adopted by the praetor (edicts) and, finally, is a problem of certainty of law.

[9] DEMOLOMBE, Cours, Paris-Bruxelles, 1847-1876, II, p. 293 e ss; AUBRY et RAU, Cours, Paris, IV, 1873, p. 439 e ss.; MERLIN, Répertoire, V, Paris, 1836, voce Héritier, III ; CREMIEU, De la validité des actes accomplis par l'héritier apparent, in Revue Trimestrielle de Droit Civil, 1910, 39 ; COLIN, CAPITANT et JULLIOT de la MORANDIERE, Traité, Paris, 1957, n. 873, p. 517 e ss.

[10] It is the simple *more uxorio* cohabitation, that has originated in our legal system the paradigms of the „unione di fatto" and of the „famiglia di fatto".

[11] The two greatest theorics of this theory were NAENDRUP, *Begriff des Rechtsscheins und Aufgabe der Rechtsscheinsforschungen,* Münster, 1910; and KRUCKMANN, *Sachbesitz, Rechtsbesitz, Rechtsschein in der Theorie des gemeinen Reghts,* in *Arch. f. d. civ. Praxis,* vol 108, 1902.

[12] See GIERKE, *Deutsches privaterecht,* I, Liepzing, 1895, pag. 187 e ss.

ridical reality always corresponds with the results of the publicity instruments preset by the legislator. In the German legal system the third parties can rely onto publicised facts because he is safeguarded also if they do not correspond to reality, and so he does not have to fear the coming up of circumstances that he previously ignored. This solutions comes from the ascertainment that the publicity results correspond almost always to the real state of things and so the sacrifice of the interested of the legitimate holder of a right can only happen in very marginal cases"[13] .

Finally under Anglo-Saxon right the liquidation of the hereditary goods is made by an administrator or an executor whose legitimisation and powers directly arise from a specific grant of probate or from specific letters of administration, which do not leave any protection to unaware third parties. While the other cases where the continental have recourse to the appearance remedies, are usually solved with some equity rules and some applications of the estoppels.

In Italy ever since in the codification of 1865[14] the *„rights acquired by bone fide third parties in force of onerous conventions stipulated with the apparent heir"* are declared save, while article 1242 assigns a redeeming effect to the bone fide payment made to the possessor of credit. Nevertheless the inspiring model of the reform of private law is still the French one, firmly bond to the dogma of the will, with regard to which the two above mentioned cases must be considered two exceptions that reveal that the protection of collective interests to private one's detriment is not considered as meritorious of protection yet.

Scholars were strongly divided between those[15] who affirmed that *„appearance has the same charm as the things we do not know very well, and we should refuse to assent to such a bizarre theory"* and who was persuaded that *„the interest of third parties becomes an element so strong that forces the creation of opposite canons where the necessities of the crowds are more relevant of individual ones"*.

It was the jurisprudence that created the appearance principle into our legal system, especially after Sen. Mariano d'Amelio [20-22], the First President of the Cassation Court, authoritatively took sides for the French theory of appearance in 1934 and this principle was subsequently acknowledged by the Supreme Court and by the Italian magistracy. D'Amelio's theory does not lies in simple *„analogical interpretation of article 933 of the civil code, but it is rather the recognition of a principle that was affirmed to resolve a specific relation and that becomes a part of the general system and can be consequently be invoked to regulate other juridical situations. Between the two principle, the first affirming that nobody can transfer to others more rights that he actually got, and the other one proclaiming the protection of the bone fide third party in the contractual domain, it is not exact to say that they are each one's exception; we'd rather say that, according to the case, they replace each other and that they both work jointly in their respective fields of application"*.

So under this point of view, which was widely followed by the Italian courts, the problem that arises for the jurist is to determinate in every single case whether the

---

[13] This topic has been recently studied by Rajneri [54]

[14] Art. 933 of the Civil Code, in the sense that what distinguishes the apparent heir is *„the external appearance towards third parties, the opinion that the others or the public have"* apart from his good faith, as affirmed by Bonfante [10].

[15] Among the others we remember Stolfi [60]

principle of the certitude of law must prevail of if, instead, the good faith must be predominantly protected.

In the case law of the last decade, the theme of appearance prevalently concerns the topic of representation and the problems produced by the behaviours of the falsus procurator. According to a constant opinion[16] , indeed, *„the application of this principle to the contractual representation requires that appearance is based onto objective elements that are suitable to justify the erroneous conviction of who invokes the principle that the apparent situation reflects the juridical reality; that this conviction is reasonable and arises from an excusable error and not from fault; and that the appearance is produced by a guilty behaviour of the apparent represented. So the apparent representation can be a case of appearance of law only if we can prove not only the existence of the apparent power of a subject to represent an other one and the lack of fault of the third party to whom this situation appears, but also the existence of a guilty behaviour of the appearing represented that determines the arising of this appearance".*

Similarly the jurisprudence generally affirms that *„both the common fund of the association and the members of an unrecognised association that have acted in the name and interest of the association are responsible for the obligations contracted with others by the members of the association, according to article 38 of the civil code. In fact since our legal system does not make provision for publicising the power of representation, those third parties for whom it is objectively impossible to verify the representative capacity of the counterpart can only be protected by the application of the appearance principle according to which the persuasion, that is not generated by a faulty mistake, to be in front of somebody legitimised to represent the association is a sufficient condition to make valid the stipulation of the contract and the creation of the consequent obligations both for the third party and for the unrecognised association. Obviously that does not imply that the above mentioned lack of representative power can not produce the legal liability of the member towards the other members and towards the association".* [17]

While who wants to have recognised a right against the joint-ownership must call in action who was invested of the representative power by the assembly of the joint-owners, and cannot consider what results from documents other than the official minutes. [18] In fact the principle of appearance can not be invoked in those situations where the law prescribes particular forms of publicity by which it is possible to check, using normal diligence, the real extent of somebody's representative power, because this principle stems from the legitimate entrustment of third parties onto a reasonably reliable situation (although not corresponding to reality) which can not be controlled if not by its exterior manifestations. [19]

---

[16] Cass. civ., sez. III, 22.04.1999, n. 3988; Cass. civ., sez. I, 29.04.1999, n. 4299 and Cass. civ., sez. II, 21.03.2000, n. 3301.

[17] Cass. civ., sez. lav., 16 maggio 2000, n. 6350. Cfr. anche Cass. civ., sez. III, 18 maggio 2000, n. 6461.

[18] Cass. Civ. sez. III, 4.01.2002, n. 65

[19] Cass. civ., sez. I, 7.03.1997, n. 2093; Cass. civ., sez. II, 3.04.1999, n. 3287; Cass. civ., sez. lav., 24.02.2000, n. 2127.

Two classic examples are art. 1189 c.c. that redeems the bone fide debtor that has paid to the apparent creditor, as well as art. 1415 and 1416 that concern the effect of the simulation of the contract.

The protection of appearance can also be found in our family law, especially in the complicated domain of the validation in Italy of the judicial decisions on marital topics that are given by canonical courts.

Indeed the homologation of the canonical decision that declares the inexistence of the canon marriage due to the exclusion by only one of the spouses of one of the bona matrimonii (in the specific case, the exclusion of the duty of fidelity) can find and obstacle in the Italian law and order whenever this exclusion remained unexpressed in the psychic domain of its author without never being externated (or without being otherwise recognised or recognisable) by the other spouse, according to the binding principle of the protection of good faith and unconscious reliance.

The Supreme Court[20] however specified that „*this principle, although always binding, is connected to an individual value that belongs to the availability of the subject and is consequently invoked to protect this value against unfair external attacks, and not against the will of its titular, to whom we must recognise the right to chose whether to conserve or not a relationship which is defected by an act of the other part, what means that this obstacle does not exist when the spouse (that ignored or could not be know the will flaw of the other) requires the exequatur of the ecclesiastic decision by the Court of Appeal, or does not make opposition against this declaratory*".

An other interesting case that was discussed by the Court of Cassation is that of the appearing society, whose existence is configured every time two or more persons externally act in such a way that bona fide third parties are inducted to believe the existence of a social relationship that does not exist really.

We must however warn that „*the topic of the apparent social relationship must not be confused with that of the hidden one nor with the different situation of the de facto society: we call apparent society that one that appears as existing to third parties although there is not a real social contract, while the de facto society is that one where the social contract does not result from a deed or from an other kind of written act, but results as such by facta concludentia*". So in the case of the apparent society, in force of the principle of the juridical appearance whose reason of being can be found in the necessity to protect third parties' reliance, to make possible the legal extension of the liability for the social obligations to the subject who acts as a partner, it is just required that the externalisation of the social bond happens in such a way to reasonably persuade third parties of the real existence of the social bond.[21]

It now must be clear that the protection of the reliance aroused by appearance is the ratio of numerous legal rules, and there are many other ones that share the same goal. The reliance onto the simulated contract is protected by art. 1415, comma I and 1416, comma 1 of the civil code; the one who purchases in bona fide from the possessor – which is definitively who externally appears as the owner of the good- is strongly pro-

[20] Cass. Civ. sez. I, 28.03.2001, n. 4457; Cass. Civ. sez. I, 8.01.2001, n. 198; Cass. Civ. sez. I, 16 maggio 2000, n. 6308.
[21] Cass. civ., sez. I, 9.08.1996, n. 8168; cfr. anche Cass. civ., sez. I, 26.07.1996, n. 6770 e Cass. civ., sez. I, 12.09.1997, n. 9030.

tected, as well who –without fault- has entrusted on somebody's will declaration that was affected by an obstative error.

However, according to Prof. Francesco Galagano (*Diritto Civile e Commerciale*, vol. II t.1, Padova, 1999, p. 393) this cannot and must not be considered enough to affirm the existence of a general *„principle of appearance"*, which should enable appearances always to prevail over legal reality, in every situation.

Indeed there are many rules that defend the entrustment onto reality rather than onto appearance, as art. 1416 c. II by which, in case of conflict between the creditor of the simulated purchaser and that of the simulated seller, the latter is preferred if his credit is antecedent.

In fact, as Galgano observes, the Supreme Court[22] has made clear that *„the appearance, outside of the specific cases of protection of the reliance it can generate that are contemplated by law, does not integrates a general institute, with firm and clear characteristics, but only operates in those specific juridical relationships, according with the different tolerance decree that they accord to the prevalence of appearance over reality"*.

In fact almost all the cases of apparent procurator or of apparent society where third parties are protected by the law are cases of tacit simulated proxy or of simulation of the social contract, where one may also appeal to the principle of the protection of good faith.

References

1   AA.VV., Casi scelti in tema di buona fede nei contratti speciali, a cura di ALPA e PUTTI, Cedam, Padova, 1996.
2   ALPA, BESSONE, FUSARO, Poteri dei privati e statuto della proprietà, Roma, 2002.
3   BESSONE e D'ANGELO, Buona fede, in Enciclopedia Giuridica, Treccani, Roma, 1988.
4   BIANCA, La nozione di buona fede quale regola di comportamento contrattuale, in Rivista di Diritto Civile, 1983.
5   BIGLIAZZI GERI, Buona fede nel diritto civile, in Digesto Civile, II, Torino, 1988.
6   BIGLIAZZI GERI, L'interpretazione del contratto, in Il codice civile – Commentario, Milano, 1991.
7   BIGLIAZZI GERI, Note in tema di interpretazione secondo buona fede, Pisa, 1970.
8   CASTELFRANCHI e FALCONE, Socio-Cognitive Theory of Trust, Roma, 2001.
9   CASTELFRANCHI e FALCONE, Towards a Theory of Delegation for Agent-based Systems, Robotics and Autonomous Systems, Roma, 1998.
10   CASTELFRANCHI, The social nature of information and the role of Trust, Roma, 2002.
11   D'AMELIO, L'apparenza del diritto nella giurisprudenza francese, in Monitore dei Tribunali., 1934.
12   D'AMELIO, Sull'apparenza del diritto, in Monitore dei Tribunali, 1934.
13   D'AMELIO, Voce «Apparenza del Diritto», in Nuovo Digesto Italiano, Torino, 1937 e Novissimo Digesto Italiano, Torino, 1957.
14   D'ANGELO, La clausola generale di buona fede, in Contratto e Impresa, 1990.
15   D'ANGELO, La tipizzazione giurisprudenziale della buona fede contrattuale, in Contratto e impresa, 1990.

---

[22] Cass. civ. 17.03.1975, n. 1020; Cass. civ. 4 .12.1971, n. 3510.

16 DE ANGELIS, Trust e fiducia nell'ordinamento italiano, in Rivista di diritto civile, 1999.
17 DE LUCA, Poteri del mandatario in situazioni eccezionali, cooperazione del mandante e giudizio di buona fede come tecnica di analisi dei rischi contrattuali, in Rivista di Diritto Commerciale, 1998.
18 DE MAURO e FORTINGUERRA, La responsabilità precontrattuale, Padova, CEDAM, 2002.
19 DEL BENE, Notazioni critiche sull'effettività del canone ermeneutico ex fide bona tra tutela dell'affidamento e presupposizione, in Giustizia Civile, 1997.
20 FERRARA sr., I negozi fiduciari, in Studi in onore di Scialoia, Milano, 1905.
21 FORCHINO, «Pactum fiduciae» e mandato senza rappresentanza: due figure giuridiche a confronto, in Giurisprudenza italiana, 2000.
22 FRANZONI, Buona fede ed equità tra le fonti di integrazione del contratto, in Contratto e impresa, 1999, 83
23 GALGANO, Atlante di diritto privato comparato, XIII, Milano, 1992.
24 GALINDO, Derecho, confianza e Internet, Saragozza, 2001.
25 GAMBINI, Il negozio fiduciario negli orientamenti della giurisprudenza, in Rassegna di diritto civile, 1998.
26 GRASSETTI, Del negozio fiduciario e della sua ammissibilità nel nostro ordinamento giuridico, in Rivista di Diritto Commerciale, 1936.
27 LUHMANN, La fiducia, Bologna, Il mulino, 2002.
28 LUPOI, Il trust nell'ordinamento giuridico italiano dopo la Convenzione dell'Aja del 1° luglio 1985, in Vita notarile, 1992.
29 MALAGUTI, Il Trust, in Atlante di diritto privato comparato, XIII, Milano, 1992.
30 NANNI, La buona fede contrattuale nella giurisprudenza, in Contratto e impresa, 1986.
31 NANNI, La buona fede contrattuale, Cedam, Padova, 1988.
32 NANNI, La buona fede contrattuale, in I grandi orientamenti della giurisprudenza civile e commerciale, Cedam, Padova, 1989.
33 NANNI, Scelte discrezionali dei contraenti e dovere di buona fede, in Contratto e impresa, 1994.
34 OPPO, Profili dell'interpretazione oggettiva del negozio giuridico, Bologna, 1943.
35 RAJNERI, Il principio dell'apparenza giuridica, in Rassegna di Diritto Civile, 1997.
36 STELLA RICHTER, La responsabilità precontrattuale, Torino, UTET, 1996.
37 STOLFI, L'apparenza del diritto, Modena, 1934.
38 TRIMARCHI, Il negozio fiduciario, in Enciclopedia del diritto, vol. XXI, Milano, 1994.
39 VALENTE, Nuovi profili della simulazione e della fiducia. Contributo ad un superamento della crisi della simulazione, Milano, 1961.

Social Capital, Community Trust, and *E*-government Services

Michael Grimsley[1], Anthony Meehan[2], Geoff Green[1], and Bernard Stafford[3]

[1] Centre for Regional, Economic and Social Research, Sheffield Hallam University,
Pond Street, Sheffield, UK, S1 1WB
{m.f.grimsley, g.green}@shu.ac.uk
[2] Security and Requirements Group, Computing Department, The Open University,
Walton Hall, Milton Keynes, UK, MK7 6AA
a.s.meehan@open.ac.uk
[3] Department of Economics and Related Studies, University of York,
York, UK, YO10 5DD
b.stafford@york.ac.uk

Abstract. This paper analyses data from two large-scale community surveys to explore the relationship between community trust relations, as an expression of social capital, and perceptions of the quality of locally available government services. The analysis leads to a model of trust propagation within communities. The factors which connect different forms of trust suggest information and communication technologies for the public sector have an important role to play in mediating trust relations in the community. We indicate some implications for designers, managers and developers of these technologies.

1   Introduction

Our interest in trust arises from a desire to make explicit the connection between trust relations and social capital and thus the link between trust and community wellbeing and sustainability. We explore this link through analyses of two large-scale surveys conducted in the South Yorkshire region of the UK.

Social capital is one of four forms of capital in a community [1]. *Fixed capital* represents the buildings, plant and machinery used in the production of goods *and* services. *Environmental capital* includes natural resources, greenspace, bluespace, and may be broadened to include housing, estate design, and community amenities (especially social amenities). *Human capital* is the sum of the skills and knowledge in a community. This is a narrow definition which constrains human capital to 'fitness for work' in terms of (educational) qualificatios and training. A broader definition includes health and all forms of skill and knowledge that contribute to community wellbeing, including community governance. *Social capital* may be considered as the productive investments in social relations [2] and has been described as the 'glue' holding all other forms of capital together [1]. Adequate levels of all four forms are essential for sustainable community development [1].

Coleman recognises that social capital makes possible the achievement of community ends that would not be attainable in its absence [3]. We observe that trust facilitates the same ends. Warren suggests that social capital provides four antecedents of social cooperation; information, influence, certification of trustworthiness and reinforcements for commitments [2]. All of these can be related to trust factors and mechanisms. 'Information' can be connected to notions of reputation; 'influence' to notions of dependability and enforcement; 'certification' to reliability (of information) and reputation; 'reinforcement' to a community's institutional frameworks for applying rewards and penalties in relation to trust-based obligations, either met or not met.

Trust enables both a division of labour (people may trust each other to perform specialised roles in a community) and sharing of labour roles (people distribute responsibilities in time, e.g., sharing child supervision). Community-based trust relations are an expression (possibly the principle expression) of a community's capacity to cooperate to achieve a better quality of life than would otherwise be available if its members acted merely individuals. This 'trust capacity' can be valorised, hence it is a form of capital.

The remaining sections of this paper are organised as follows. In section 2, we identify three research questions to be addressed in analysing the survey data. In section 3, the survey methodology and the results of the analyses are described. Section 4 contains a discussion of the results. Section 5 identifies some of the implied challenges for the design of information and communication systems related to public interaction with community services, including the problem of secure access.

2   Research Objectives

Braithwaite and Levi, amongst others, suggest that it is possible to differentiate between vertical and horizontal community trust relations [4]. *Vertical trust* reflects the quality of relations between citizens and the institutions of community governance and their associated services (e.g., elected councils, housing, police and justice, health, education, transport). *Horizontal trust* reflects social cohesion between members of a community (e.g. between friends, family, neighbours, work colleagues). The first objective of this research is to look for evidence of this distinction. (If such a distinction is established, the focus of this paper will fall upon vertical trust as this is the principle trust relation between the community, the policy makers, and the providers of electronically mediated e-government services.)

Rothstein conjectures that there is a further distinction to be made between vertical trust as it relates to representative fora which develop policy and determine service provision ("input" vertical trust) and vertical trust in relation to agencies providing government services ("output" vertical trust) [5]. The second objective of the research is to seek evidence for this distinction.

Finally, we seek to relate social capital and trust by seeking evidence of a connection between selected antecedents of cooperative activity and community trust levels. We take two of Warren's antecedents, [amount and quality of] information and [sense of] influence, and add a third antecedent, a 'sense of control/autonomy', that we conjecture is significant in facilitating community action. Autonomy is defined 'a person's sense of their ability to control their own life in the community'.

3   Survey Methodology and Analysis

In this section we first describe the surveys that provided the data and then present the results of these analyses.

3.1   Community Surveys

The data used in this analysis was captured as part of two sample surveys of economically deprived communities in the UK's South Yorkshire coalfields. The South Yorkshire Social Capital Survey was commissioned primarily to evaluate UK government's South Yorkshire Health Action Zone and European Union Single Regeneration Budget 5 strategies. It was designed and supervised by a local consortium of agencies and interviews were undertaken by 50 trained members of the local communities surveyed. It elicited responses from 4220 individuals in homes within nine distinct communities with one adult selected per randomly sampled household [6].

The Housing and Regeneration in Coalfield Communities (HARCC) Survey was commissioned by the Housing Corporation and the South Yorkshire Coalfields Health Action Zone. This was a postal survey which covered eight similar, but not the same, communities. The main research thrusts of this investigation were the links between the nature of housing, particularly social housing, health and sustainable community regeneration. More than one person per household was sampled and social housing households were over represented by design. Responses were obtained from 1341 individuals [7].

Non–weighted analysis would emphasise single person household responses over households with two or more persons. Accordingly, the main results from the Social Capital survey are based on data weighted by number of adults per household. The weighted maximum number of returns were thus 7727[1]. Confirmatory analyses of HARCC survey data were not weighted.

In both surveys, respondent's levels of trust were expressed on five-point ordinal, or Likert, scales.

---

[1] Unweighted results do not appear significantly different from weighted findings.

3.2   Data Analysis

In each survey, the analysis of the data was structured as follows. First, a measure of trust among community members was derived and the issue of whether there was evidence to support a distinction between horizontal trust and vertical trust was explored. Second, the relation between satisfaction with community services and the level of community trust was explored. Third, the relationship between each of the three antecedents of cooperative action identified above (information, autonomy/control, influence) and levels of trust was explored. We present the results of the analyses in parallel, addressing each of the steps in this analysis in turn.

3.2.1 Forms of Community Trust

Six measures of trust featured in each survey. In the Social Capital survey, the measures related to trust in local government politicians, local council administration, employers, family, friends and neighbours. In the HARCC survey the measures related to trust in national politicians, local politicians, the local council administration, family, friends and neighbours. The method of oblique principal component factor analysis was used to identify the underlying dimensions of the trust measures used. This analysis suggests two underlying dimensions to the level of trust expressed. The first two components (Tables 1a and 1b) accounted for 56.5% and 68.3% of total variance respectively.

Table 1a. Social Capital survey: dimensions of community trust

Trusted Party	Component (Dimension)	
	1	2
Local Politicians	0.887	-0.059
Local Council	0.888	-0.078
Employers	0.511	0.116
Neighbours	0.133	.625
Friends	-0.016	.803
Family	-0.090	.700

Table 1b. HARCC survey: dimensions of community trust

Trusted Party	Component (Dimension)	
	1	2
National Politicians	0.867	0.002
Local Politicians	0.936	-0.015
Local Council	0.869	0.015
Neighbours	0.129	.670
Friends	-0.045	.841
Family	-0.061	.733

In both tables the squared values of the coefficients (in columns) indicate the unique contribution of each of the six measures to each of the two components or dimensions. Thus, in each survey, component 1 relates to institutions of community government and is interpreted as vertical trust; factor 2 relates to peers in the community (friends, family and neighbours) and is interpreted as horizontal trust.

Oblique rotation facilitates non-orthogonal factors and thus may express a correlative relation between factors. On this occasion the method gives the factor correlations of 0.183 and 0.215 for the Social Capital and HARCC surveys, respectively, which are both significant at the 0.01 level (2-tailed).

Having thus established sound evidence of two distinct, but correlated, dimensions of community trust (vertical and horizontal) the analyses that now ensue examine these dimensions independently, focussing on the vertical trust relation in relation to each question (as indicated in Section 2, above).

3.2.2 Community Services and Trust

Both surveys examined respondents' satisfaction with community services. A number of services were considered. The Social Capital survey elicited responses for health services, police and transport services. The HARCC survey examined health facilities, transport and schools. In each case, satisfaction was expressed on a five-point ordinal scale. In presenting the results for each service in turn we will concentrate on the relation between perceptions of the service and the level vertical trust.

Health services and facilities. The relation between satisfaction with health-related service levels and vertical trust is illustrated in Figs. 1a and 1b. In both surveys there is a strong, positive, relationship between satisfaction with health service/facility levels and vertical trust. The relation to horizontal trust was weaker, but both relationships are statistically significant.

Transport. The relation between satisfaction with public transport services and vertical trust is illustrated in Fig. 2(a-b). In both surveys there is a strong, positive, relationship between satisfaction with transport service levels and vertical trust. A relation to horizontal trust was not evident.

Police. The strong positive relation between satisfaction with the police service and vertical trust is illustrated in Fig. 3. The relation to horizontal trust is weaker, but still significant.

Schools. The relation between satisfaction with local schools and vertical trust is illustrated in Fig. 4. There is a strong, positive, relationship between satisfaction with the schools and vertical trust. The relation to horizontal trust is weaker, but still significant.

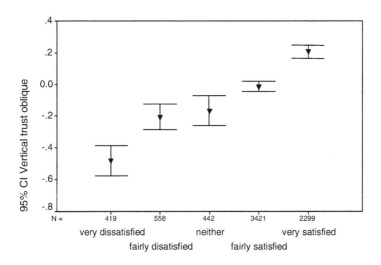

(a)

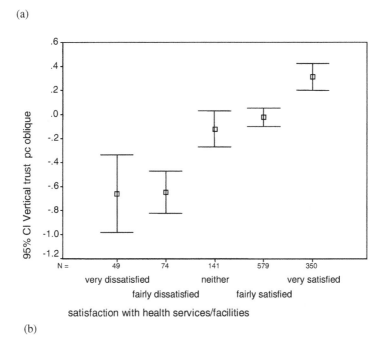

(b)

Fig. 1. Relation between satisfaction with health-related services/facilities and vertical trust. (a) Social Capital survey; (b) HARCC survey

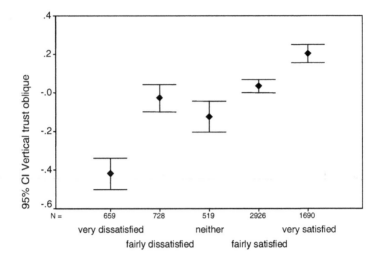

(a)

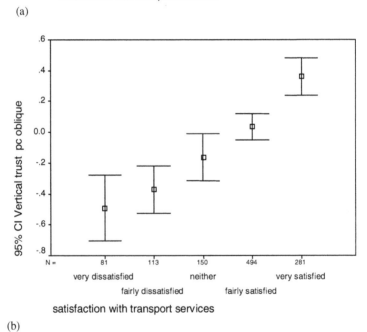

(b)

Fig. 2. Relation between satisfaction with transport services and vertical trust. (a) Social Capital survey; (b) HARCC survey

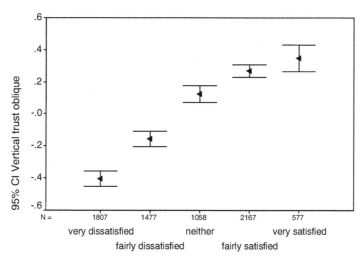

Fig. 3. Relation between satisfaction with police service and vertical trust (Social Capital survey only)

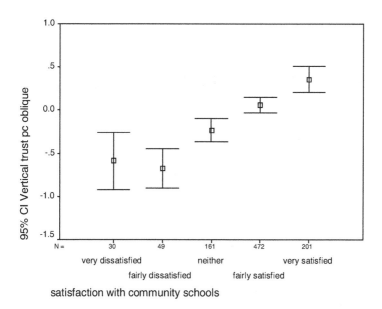

Fig. 4. Relation between satisfaction with local school services and vertical trust (HARCC survey only)

3.2.3 'Antecedent' Factors Determining Community Trust Levels

The Social Capital survey allows an analysis of three factors that may influence levels of community trust: *information* (the extent to which individuals had suffient and reliable information about the local community), *control* (the extent to which individuals felt they enjoyed personal autonomy or control in the conduct of their community life) and *influence* (the extent to which individuals felt they were able to influence or shape community life). The results for each are presented in turn.

Information. Fig. 5 illustrates that the relationship between perceptions about the quantity and quality of information about community life and vertical trust levels. There is a strong, positive, relationship between how well informed individuals are and the levels of both vertical and horizontal trust.

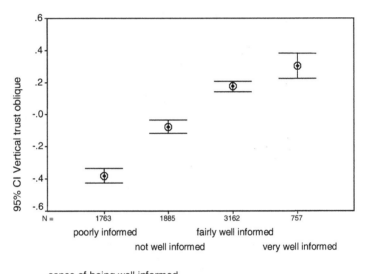

Fig. 5. Relation between how well informed individuals are and vertical trust

Control. Fig. 6 illustrates the relation between perceptions of personal control and vertical trust levels. There is a strong, positive, relationship between perceptions of personal control and the level of vertical trust. The relation to horizontal trust is weaker.

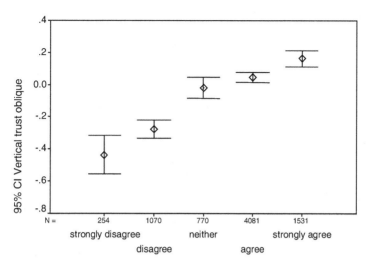

Fig. 6. Relation between perceptions of personal control and both vertical and horizontal trust. The positive relation is statistically significant in both cases

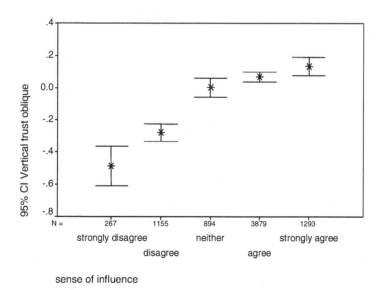

Fig. 7. Relation between perceptions of personal influence and both vertical trust. The positive relation is statistically significant for both vertical and horizontal trust

Influence. Fig. 7 illustrates the relation between perceptions of personal influence and levels of vertical trust. There is a strong, positive, relationship between perceptions of personal control and the level of vertical trust. The relation to horizontal trust is weaker.

4   A Trust Propagation Cycle

The results above provide answers to the questions we had posed in relation to community trust, the possibility of there being distinct forms of such trust, and factors that might influence the levels of trust in a community.

There seems to be clear evidence from both surveys that the distinction between vertical and horizontal trust is well founded and that these are correlated (Tables 1(a) and (b), above). Further, the legitimacy of distinguishing between vertical trust in representative institutions (*input* vertical trust) and trust arising from experience of the services provided (directly or indirectly) by such institutions (*output* vertical trust), as conjectured by Rothstein, is also supported. Whilst it might have been anticipated that satisfaction with community services promoted vertical trust, it is of some interest that, in nearly all cases, this was also translated into horizontal trust.

The association between the three antecedents of cooperation conjectured and vertical trust is also supported. Here, the strength of the relationship between the antecedent factor, *information*, and *both* vertical and horizontal trust is, perhaps, striking. The relationship of the other antecedent variates, *control* (autonomy) and *influence*, to trust levels is also significant for both forms of trust but particularly for vertical trust.

These results suggest a *trust cycle* that propagates trust within a community (Fig. 8). Levels of 'input' vertical trust are promoted by a sense of influence over the policies determined (and managed) by representative institutions. In the UK, the policies are determined by a number of fora. Examples of these, at a local level, are directly accountable (elected) City and Borough Councils, indirectly accountable agencies such as the not-for-profit hospital and health-care trusts and school governors.

Satisfactory experience of the resulting community services and amenities reinforces 'output' vertical trust. Here, two experiential factors are at work, the quality and quantity of information about the services available and the extent to which the services facilitate personal control or autonomy over one's life in the community. As we have noted, satisfaction with some community services and amenities also promotes horizontal trust.

It is tempting to suggest a causal connection between the three factors, *influence*, *information*, *control/autonomy* and the respective forms of vertical trust and this is reflected in the figure presented (Fig. 8). A mechanism that underpins the weak but statistically significant positive correlation between vertical and horizontal trust remains to be elucidated.

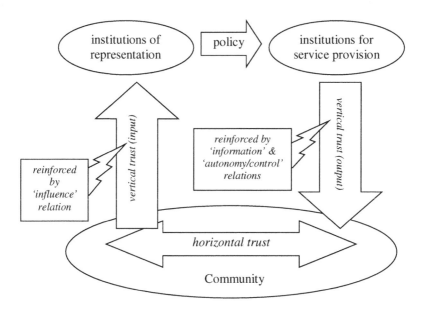

Fig. 8. Proposed *Trust Cycle* for community government and service-related trust propogation. The reinforcment relations are only suggested but seem natural at this stage

5   Some Implications for *E*-government Information Systems

We have seen that, from the point of view of community members, trust relations, and especially two forms of vertical trust, are partially determined (in a statistical sense) by three variates:

i.   *information*: the quantity and quality of information about community government, its agencies and services;

ii. *control/autonomy*: the extent to which individuals feel these services give people a feeling of control over their lives;

iii. *influence*: the extent to which people feel able to influence the institutions, agencies and services provided within the community.

The identification of these variates, and their role in promoting trust-based expressions of social capital, suggests that they should each be explicitly addressed in the planning, management and delivery of government services. If designers and managers of public sector information systems are to turn these factors into levers which can enhance community trust and social capital, then an information and communication model that translates human experience of levels of information, control and influence into dimensions of human experience of information and communication systems which mediate access to community services is needed.

5.1 Levels of Interactivity

The model we propose achieves this through a mapping from information, control and influence to *levels of interactivity* (Table 2).

Table 2. Mapping trust factors to levels of interactivity with electronically mediated access to community services

Trust Factor	Level of Interactivity	Expression (and examples)
Information: Quality and quantity of information circulating within a community.	*Low*: (Zero interactivity) individuals get access to personal information; restricted *intranet* access rights	Government agencies and services provide information which can be accessed but not directly altered by members of the community, e.g., parental monitoring of a child's progress at school, patient's monitoring of their progress in a queue for hospital admission.
Control/Autonomy: The extent to which individuals feel able to control their own lives in the community.	*Medium*: (Constrained) additionally, restricted ability to *modify* (personal) data and contract to use resources	Services provide information which can be accessed and directly altered but in a predetermined form, e.g., booking an appointment with doctor, submitting a domestic dwelling planning application, reporting vandalism, posting community notices
Influence: The degree to which individuals can influence the government (and its agencies) in their community.	*High*: (Unconstrained) additionally, ability to access and analyse 'raw' data; e-government moves towards teledemocracy	Government and services provide electronic fora for contributing to policy formation, e.g., parental input to school governance, determination of health or crime prevention priorities, patterns of public transport provision. This form of interaction may extend to determination of policy by electronic referenda/voting.

Facilitating these levels of interactivity for different individuals and community organisations poses significant problems of security as progressively 'deeper' access and greater interactivity is granted on a selective basis. Security issues relate chiefly to maintaining confidentiality and integrity of information and ensuring that individuals have the necessary authority/entitlement to access services at a given level of interactivity.

Trust metrics provide a means to determine (dynamically) levels of authority/entitlement of access for individuals and groups in the community. For example, entitlement to make online appointments might depend upon responsible use of such facilities: failure to keep appointments, and perhaps the making of unnecessary appointments, is untrustworthy behaviour and should, perhaps, result in diminution of entitlement. Government and service agencies may wish to distinguish between different recipients of information, perhaps reflecting levels of sensitivity/confidentiality of the material and/or the 'representative' status of community organisations (e.g., school governors/boards, residents' associations). Individual or collective breaches of confidentially are also breaches of trust.

6   Conclusion

On the basis of two large-scale surveys of local communities we have presented evidence to support a distinction between different forms of trust within a community. Horizontal trust is expressed between family friends and neighbours. Vertical trust exists between members of a community and its institutions providing governance and services. Vertical trust is seen to be related both to satisfaction with services but also to the extent to which members of the community feel they have sufficient reliable information about community services and function, the extent to which their experience of services engenders a sense of control over their own lives and the extent to which they feel able to influence governance and the provision of services to the community.

On the basis of this evidence, we have advanced a cycle of community trust propagation that attempts to relate the different forms of trust and the factors which may influence them.

Given the significance of the role of community related information in fostering both vertical and horizontal trust, we have attempted to explore how community members' relation to information-based services might be structures in order to promote levels of two other variates promoting trust levels, a sense of autonomy or control, and a sense of influence.

The communities studied are distinctive, both geographically, economically and culturally. This should be kept in mind when considering these results. However, we are confident that there are many similar communities in the UK, Europe, the United States and possibly elsewhere.

References

1. Grootaert, G.: Social Capital: The Missing Link. World Bank. SCI Working Paper No.2, April 1998
2. Warren, M.E.: Social Capital and Corruption. In: Dario Castiglione: Social Capital: Interdisciplinary Perspectives. EURESCO conference on Social Capital, Exeter, UK, 15–20 September 2001, http://www.ex.ac.uk/shipss/politics/research/socialcapital/
3. Coleman, J.: Foundations of Social Theory. Harvard University Press, Cambridge, MA. 1990.
4. Braithwaite, V., Levi, M. (eds): Trust and Governance. New York: Russell Sage Foundation, 1998
5. Rothstein, B.: Dept. of Political Science, Goteborg University, Sweden. (personal communication).
6. Green. G., Grimsley, M., Suokas A., et al: Social Capital, Health and Economy in South Yorkshire Coalfield Communities. CRESR, Sheffield Hallam University, Oct 2000, ISBN 0 86339 918 5
7. Green, G., Grimsley, M., Stafford, B.: Capital Accounting for Neighbourhood Sustainability,CRESR, Sheffield Hallam University 2001, ISBN 0 863 399 568

Simulating the Effect of Reputation Systems on E-markets

Audun Jøsang, Shane Hird, and Eric Faccer

Distributed Systems Technology Centre*
Queensland University of Technology, GPO Box 2434, Brisbane Qld 4001, Australia
{ajosang, shird, efaccer}@dstc.edu.au

Abstract. Studies show that reputation systems have the potential to improve market quality. In this paper we report the results of simulating a market of trading agents that uses the beta reputation system for collecting feedback and computing agents' reputations. The simulation confirms the hypothesis that the presence of the reputation system improves the quality of the market. Among other things it also shows that a market with limited duration rather than infinite longevity of transaction feedback provides the best conditions under which agents can adapt to each others change in behaviour.

1 Introduction

Individuals and organisations take risks by participating in e-commerce. Transactions are often conducted with people or organisations who are strangers to each other and who often have an unknown record of past behaviour. This situation provides plenty of opportunities for irresponsible and fraudulent players to provide low quality or deceitful services resulting in a large number of complaints about e-commerce players being reported [5]. A study by Consumers International [3] involved researchers from 11 countries placing 151 orders at sites in 17 countries. They found that 9% of goods ordered never arrived. In 20% of cases the amount actually charged was higher than expected, and there were problems obtaining a refund in 21% of purchases, despite the fact that the sites in question advertised that refunds were available. When little or no information about potential transaction partners can be obtained honest players are left in the dark when making decisions about e-business transactions. Hence, there is a need to design and introduce systems for recording the behaviour of e-market participants and make it available to potential transaction partners for decision making purposes. This is in essence the role of reputation systems.

A reputation system gathers and aggregates feedback about participants behaviour in order to derive measures of reputation. In the centralised approach which we will use in our market simulation study, feedback is received and stored by a feedback collection centre. Fig.1 below shows a typical reputation framework where X and Y denote transaction partners.

---

* The work reported in this paper has been funded in part by the Co-operative Research Centre for Enterprise Distributed Systems Technology (DSTC) through the Australian Federal Government's CRC Programme (Department of Industry, Science & Resources).

P. Nixon and S. Terzis (Eds.): Trust Management 2003, LNCS 2692, pp. 179–194, 2003.

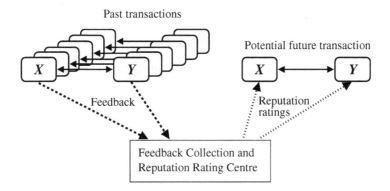

Fig. 1. General framework for a centralise reputation system

After a transaction is completed, the agents provide feedback about each other's performance during the transaction. The reputation centre collects feedback from all the agents and continuously updates each agent's reputation rating as a function of the received feedback. Updated reputation ratings are provided online for all the agents to see, and can be used by the agents to decide whether or not to transact with a particular agent. The two fundamental aspects of reputation systems are:

1. *Propagation mechanism* that allow participants to provide feedback about transaction partners, as well as to obtain reputation measures of potential transaction partners.
2. *Reputation engine* that derive measures of reputation for each participant based on transaction feedback and other information.

Studies show that reputation systems can improve the quality of e-markets, and that the reputation of a particular agent can have positive effects on the agent's gain as a result of participating in the marketplace. The quality of the market can for example be defined in terms of efficiency and honesty as described by Bolton *et al.* (2002) [1].

The quality of the market and the gain of individual participants as described above represent very specific and easily measurable properties. Reputation systems thus address both the overall welfare of communities and the prosperity of individual participants. To stimulate environments where reputation can develop thus seems to be a promising way of creating healthy markets. The purpose of this study is to analyse the effect of using a reputation system in a simulated e-market.

2   The Reputation System

This simulation study was done using the Beta Reputation System [4] which provides a flexible framework for integrating reputation services into e-commerce applications. The reputation rating described in Section 2.2 is based on the beta probability distribution function which will be briefly described next.

2.1   The Beta Distribution

The beta distribution function can be used to derive probability distributions based on observations of past events. The mathematical analysis leading to this result can be found in many text books on probability theory, e.g. Casella & Berger 1990[2] p.298, and we will only present the results here.

The beta-family of distributions is a continuous family of distribution functions indexed by the two parameters α and β. The beta distribution $f(p \mid \alpha, \beta)$ can be expressed using the gamma function Γ as:

$$f(p \mid \alpha, \beta) = \frac{\Gamma(\alpha + \beta)}{\Gamma(\alpha)\Gamma(\beta)} p^{\alpha-1}(1-p)^{\beta-1} , \quad \text{where } 0 \leq p \leq 1, \ \alpha > 0, \ \beta > 0, \quad (1)$$

with the restriction that the probability variable $p \neq 0$ if $\alpha < 1$, and $p \neq 1$ if $\beta < 1$. The probability expectation value of the beta distribution is given by:

$$E(p) = \alpha/(\alpha + \beta). \tag{2}$$

Let us consider a process with two possible outcomes $\{x, \overline{x}\}$, and let r be the observed number of outcome x and let s be the observed number of outcome $\overline{x}$. Then the probability distribution of observing outcome x in the future can be expressed as a function of past observations by setting:

$$\alpha = r + 1 \quad \text{and} \quad \beta = s + 1, \quad \text{where} \quad r, s \geq 0. \tag{3}$$

As an example, a process with two possible outcomes $\{x, \overline{x}\}$ that has produced $7 \times x$ and $1 \times \overline{x}$ will have a beta distribution expressed as $f(p \mid 8, 2)$ which is plotted in Fig.2.

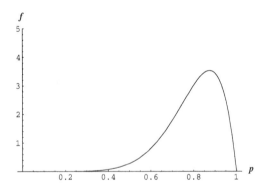

Fig. 2. Beta function of event x after 7 observations of x and 1 observation of $\overline{x}$.

This curve expresses the uncertain probability that the process will produce outcome x during future observations. The probability expectation value according to Eq.(2) is $E(p) = 0.8$. This can be interpreted as saying that the relative frequency of outcome x in the future is somewhat uncertain, and that the most likely value is 0.8.

The variable p is a probability variable, so that for a given p the probability density $f(p \mid \alpha, \beta)$ represents second order probability. The first-order variable p represents the probability of an event, whereas the density $f(p \mid \alpha, \beta)$ represents the probability that the first-order variable has a specific value. Since the first-order variable p is continuous, the second-order probability $f(p \mid \alpha, \beta)$ for any given value of $p \in [0, 1]$ is vanishingly small and therefore meaningless as such. It is only meaningful to compute $\int_{p_1}^{p_2} f(p \mid \alpha, \beta)$ for a given interval $[p_1, p_2]$, or simply to compute the expectation value of p. Below we will define a reputation rating that is based on the expectation value. This provides a sound mathematical basis for combining feedback and for expressing reputation ratings.

2.2   The Reputation Rating

The concept of probability distribution is ideal for mathematical manipulation, but less so for communicating a reputation rating to human users. A more simple representation than the probability distribution is therefore needed. Most people are familiar with the notion of a probability value, and the probability expectation value $E(p)$ from Eq.(2) therefore seems very suitable. This would give a reputation rating in the range $[0, 1]$ and this will be used in the simulations. It should be noted however that the reputation rating can be scaled to any range as mentioned in [4].

The reputation rating will depend on the feedback as well as a base rate that will be equal for all participants in a market. This will be implemented using base rate parameters denoted by $(r_{\text{base}}, s_{\text{base}})$. This will replace the fundamental base rate of $1/2$ of the beta probability distribution. The base rate and the feedback parameters will together determine the reputation rating according to the expression below.

Definition 1 (Reputation Rating). *Let $(r(Z), s(Z))$ represent target Z's reputation parameters, and $(r_{\text{base}}, s_{\text{base}})$ represent the base rate parameters. Then the function* $\text{Rep}(Z)$ *defined by:*

$$\text{Rep}(Z) = \frac{r(Z) + r_{\text{base}}}{r(Z) + s(Z) + r_{\text{base}} + s_{\text{base}}} . \qquad (4)$$

is called Z's reputation rating.

The reputation rating can be interpreted as a measure of reputation, that may be used as an indication of how a particular agent is expected to behave in future transactions. The parameter $r(Z)$ represents the amount of positive feedback about Z, and the parameters $s(Z)$ represents the amount of negative feedback about Z.

2.3   Combining Feedback

Reputation systems must be able to combine feedback from multiple sources. In the beta reputation system this can be done by simply accumulating all the received r and s parameters from the feedback providers. Assume two agents X and Y giving feedback about the same target Z. Target Z's reputation parameters by X and by Y can then be expressed as $(r^X(Z), s^X(Z))$ and $(r^Y(Z), s^Y(Z))$ respectively. By simply adding the reputation parameters for Z the combined reputation parameters emerge.

Definition 2 (Combining Feedback).
Let $(r^X(Z), s^X(Z))$ and $(r^Y(Z), s^Y(Z))$ be two different sets of reputation parameters on Z resulting from X and Y's feedback respectively. The reputation parameters $(r^{X,Y}(Z), s^{X,Y}(Z))$ defined by:

$$
\begin{aligned}
&1. \quad r^{X,Y}(Z) = r^X(Z) + r^Y(Z) \\
&2. \quad s^{X,Y}(Z) = s^X(Z) + s^Y(Z)
\end{aligned}
\tag{5}
$$

is then called Z's combined reputation parameters by X and Y.

2.4 Providing and Collecting Feedback

After each transaction, a single agent can provide both positive and negative feedback simultaneously, in the form of the parameters $r \geq 0$ and $s \geq 0$ respectively. The purpose of providing feedback as a pair (r, s) is to reflect the idea that an agent's performance in a transaction can, for example, be partly satisfactory. This could be expressed through a feedback with $r, s = 0.5$ which carries the weight of 1, whereas a feedback with $r, s = 0$ is weight-less, and would be as if no feedback was provided at all. In general the sum $r + s$ can be interpreted as the weight of the feedback.

In our simulation the buyers will provide the feedback $(r, s) = (1, 0)$ in case the item is shipped, and the feedback $(r, s) = (0, 1)$ in case the item is not shipped, so that the weight will always be 1.

2.5 Feedback Longevity

Old feedback may not always be relevant for the actual reputation rating, because the agent may change its behaviour over time. What is needed is a model in which old feedback is gradually forgotten or diminished. This can be achieved by introducing a feedback longevity factor $\lambda \in [0, 1]$ which can be adjusted in order to determine how fast feedback will diminish. The feedback longevity principle is very similar to the feedback forgetting principle described in [4]. The idea is that neither a feedback longevity $\lambda = 0$ (where all feedback is immediately forgotten) nor a feedback longevity $\lambda = 1$ (where all feedback is remembered forever) will result in a healthy market. Rather, the longevity factor must have a value which allows market players to, for example, repair a damaged reputation by improving their behaviour.

Let Z's reputation parameters resulting from feedback received after i transactions be denoted by $(r_i(Z), s_i(Z))$. The feedback longevity factor $\lambda \in [0, 1]$ can be introduced so that when adding feedback from transaction $(i + 1)$ denoted by $(r(Z), s(Z))$ the new updated reputation parameters can be computed as:

$$
\begin{cases}
1. \quad r_{i+1}(Z) = (r_i(Z) + r(Z)) \cdot \lambda \\
2. \quad s_{i+1}(Z) = (s_i(Z) + s(Z)) \cdot \lambda
\end{cases}
\quad \text{where } 0 \leq \lambda \leq 1.
\tag{6}
$$

This is a recursive algorithm which makes it possible to keep the reputation parameters of all agents without having to store every single feedback.

3   Description of the Market Simulation

3.1   Computing Transaction Gains

The market consists of 3 sellers and 10 buyers who trade the same commodity item. The market activity is structured into sessions of 10 rounds each. In each round every buyer will attempt to buy exactly one item. A transaction only happens when a buyer finds a seller satisfying his buying criteria. A buyer who receives the item provides a positive feedback $(r(S), s(S)) = (1, 0)$, and a buyer who does not receive it provides negative feedback $(r(S), s(S)) = (0, 1)$. The seller's reputation is then updated using Eq.(6), and the change becomes visible to the market at the beginning of the next round.

At the start of each session each seller S defines the selling price $\mathrm{Prc}(S)$ and honesty level $\mathrm{Hst}(S)$. Every seller S will also have a reputation rating $\mathrm{Rep}(S)$. Items are shipped with probability $\mathrm{Hst}(S)$, and not shipped with probability $(1 - \mathrm{Hst}(S))$.

The production cost per item is $\mathrm{Cst}_{\mathrm{prod}} = \$80$. In case the item is shipped the actual transaction gain of seller S can be computed as:

$$g^{\mathrm{T}}(S) = \mathrm{Prc}(S) - \mathrm{Cst}_{\mathrm{prod}} . \qquad (7)$$

The seller will thus make a positive gain $g^{\mathrm{T}}(S)$ from a transaction as long as $\mathrm{Prc}(S) > \mathrm{Cst}_{\mathrm{prod}}$. By defining a selling price the seller is in fact defining the gain per transaction because the production cost is fixed. In case the seller does not ship the item, the actual transaction gain is simply the selling price according to:

$$g^{\mathrm{T}}(S) = \mathrm{Prc}(S) . \qquad (8)$$

The intrinsic value of the item to every buyer is denoted by $\mathrm{Val} = \$260$. The buyers are faced with the risk that the seller does not ship, and the buyer's expected transaction gain when dealing with a specific seller S is denoted by $g^{\mathrm{T}}_{\mathrm{Exp}}(S)$ which can be computed as:

$$
\begin{aligned}
g^{\mathrm{T}}_{\mathrm{Exp}}(S) &= (\mathrm{Val} - \mathrm{Prc}(S)) \cdot \mathrm{Rep}(S) - \mathrm{Prc}(S) \cdot (1 - \mathrm{Rep}(S)) \\
&= \mathrm{Val} \cdot \mathrm{Rep}(S) - \mathrm{Prc}(S) .
\end{aligned}
\qquad (9)
$$

At the start if each session all the buyers will define the *risk aversion* denoted by $\mathrm{Avs}(B) \in [0, 1]$ where $\mathrm{Avs}(B) = 0$ means that the buyer is happy to take any risk, and $\mathrm{Avs}(B) = 1$ means that the buyer does not want to take any risk at all. By setting a risk aversion the buyer B requires that the seller S has a reputation rating satisfying:

$$\mathrm{Rep}(S) \geq \mathrm{Avs}(B) . \qquad (10)$$

A buyer will thus choose the seller who yields the highest expected gain according to Eq.(9) and for whom also Eq.(10) is satisfied.

In case the seller ships the item the buyer's actual transaction gain is given by: $g^{\mathrm{T}}(B) = \mathrm{Val} - \mathrm{Prc}(S)$. In case the seller does not ship the item the buyer's loss is given by: $g^{\mathrm{T}}(B) = -\mathrm{Prc}(S)$. In case no deal satisfies Eq.(10) the buyer will not transact in that particular round and the gain is zero.

After every session the sellers and buyers will compute the profit made as a result of trading during that session.

3.2   Market Strategies

Each seller S is initialised with selling price $\text{Prc}(S) = 100$, honesty $\text{Hst}(S) = 0.9$, and base rate reputation parameters $(r_{\text{base}}, s_{\text{base}}) = (9, 1)$. Each buyer B is initialised with risk aversion $\text{Avs}(B) = 0.9$. These parameter values (except the base rate reputation) are subject to change which represents the agents' strategies for optimising their profit.

Seller Mutation. For each seller the session gain $g_k^S(S)$ will be compared with the previous session's gain $g_{k-1}^S(S)$. The seller parameter values that generated the highest gain are used as basis for defining new and possibly better parameters which will be used in the subsequent session $k + 1$. The new parameters are defined as follows:

The price $\text{Prc}(S)$ is increased by Δ_{Prc} with probability $\text{Prob}_{\text{Prc}}^+$, decreased by Δ_{Prc} with probability $\text{Prob}_{\text{Prc}}^-$, and remains unchanged with probability $\text{Prob}_{\text{Prc}}^=$, where:

$$\text{Prob}_{\text{Prc}}^+ = 0.33, \quad \text{Prob}_{\text{Prc}}^- = 0.33, \quad \text{Prob}_{\text{Prc}}^= = 0.34 \quad \text{and} \quad \Delta_{\text{Prc}} = \$1 . \quad (11)$$

The honesty $\text{Hst}(S)$ goes up by Δ_{Hst} with probability $\text{Prob}_{\text{Hst}}^+$, goes down by Δ_{Hst} with probability $\text{Prob}_{\text{Hst}}^-$, and remains unchanged with probability $\text{Prob}_{\text{Hst}}^=$, where:

$$\text{Prob}_{\text{Hst}}^+ = 0.33, \quad \text{Prob}_{\text{Hst}}^- = 0.33, \quad \text{Prob}_{\text{Hst}}^= = 0.34 \quad \text{and} \quad \Delta_{\text{Hst}} = 0.02 . \quad (12)$$

Seller Intelligence. Under certain conditions the seller mutation is overruled by a set of simple rules.

1. If a seller has not conducted any transactions during the last session, the selling price $\text{Prc}(S)$ is decreased by Δ_{Prc}, and the honesty $\text{Hst}(S)$ is increased by Δ_{Hst}.
2. The minimum selling price is zero, thus allowing sellers to transact with loss in order to regain reputation and get back into the market.
3. The maximum and minimum honesty is 1 and 0 respectively.

Buyer Mutation. For each buyer the session gain $g_k^S(B)$ is compared with the previous session's gain $g_{k-1}^S(B)$. The buyer risk aversion that generated the highest gain are used as basis for defining a new and possibly better risk aversion which will be used in the subsequent session $k + 1$. The new risk aversion is defined as follows:

The risk aversion $\text{Avs}(B)$ is increased by Δ_{Avs} with probability $\text{Prob}_{\text{Avs}}^+$, is decreased by Δ_{Avs} with probability $\text{Prob}_{\text{Avs}}^-$, and remains unchanged with probability $\text{Prob}_{\text{Avs}}^=$, where:

$$\text{Prob}_{\text{Avs}}^+ = 0.33, \quad \text{Prob}_{\text{Avs}}^- = 0.33, \quad \text{Prob}_{\text{Avs}}^= = 0.34 \quad \text{and} \quad \Delta_{\text{Avs}} = 0.01 . \quad (13)$$

Buyer Intelligence. Under certain conditions, the buyer mutation is overruled by a set of very simple rules.

1. If the buyer has not conducted any transactions during the last session, then the risk aversion $\text{Avs}(B)$ is decreased by Δ_{Avs}.
2. If the buyer has made a loss in the previous session, then the risk aversion $\text{Avs}(B)$ is increased by $\Delta_{\text{Avs}} \times$ *the number of times the item was not received*.
3. The maximum and minimum risk aversion is 1 and 0 respectively.

4 Simulation Results

We ran 3 different simulations in order to compare the performance of market with and without the beta reputation system.

We simulated a market without a reputation system by defining a feedback longevity value $\lambda = 0.0$ which means that all feedback is immediately forgotten before it contributes to the reputation rating. We simulated a market with a reputation system by setting $\lambda = 0.99$ which causes feedback to be slowly forgotten. With this longevity value, the maximum reputation rating is also 0.99. We also simulated a market with $\lambda = 1.0$ in order to study the effect on the market when feedback is never forgotten. All 3 simulations ran for 1000 sessions and the graphical illustrations presented below are based on data obtained from those 3 simulation runs.

4.1 Honesty and Reputation

In this section we look at how well the reputation rating follows the honesty of an individual seller. The honesty represents the sellers personal and private state of mind whereas his public reputation rating can be interpreted as an estimate of his honesty. Idealistically the reputation rating should be equal to the honesty, but that can never be achieved. The reliability of the reputation system can be measured by how well the reputation rating follows the real honesty.

Fig.3 illustrates honesty and reputation rating for Seller 1 in a market without feedback.

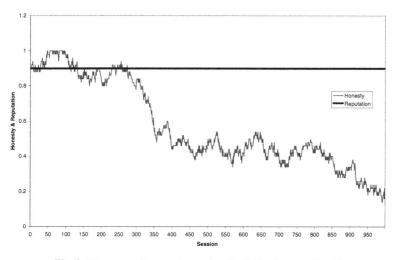

Fig. 3. Honesty and reputation rating for Seller 1 where $\lambda = 0$

Because all feedback is immediately forgotten the reputation rating remains constant at the base rate 0.9. This allows the sellers to reduce their honesty, thus to be more fraudulent, without suffering a loss of reputation. This causes the market to deteriorate.

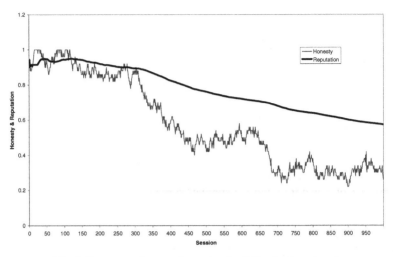

Fig. 4. Honesty and reputation rating for Seller 1 where $\lambda = 1$

Fig.4 below illustrates a market where $\lambda = 1$, and where the rating suffers.

In Fig.4 it can be seen that the reputation rating follows the honesty fairly well in the beginning of the trace, but that it deviates more and more further out in the trace. When feedback is never forgotten, the reputation rating becomes less sensitive to new feedback. In the end it becomes possible to reduce honesty without suffering a loss in reputation in the short term. The simulation shows that the seller exploits this effect to reduce honesty and become fraudulent, thus causing the market to deteriorate.

Fig.5 illustrates the evolution of the honesty and reputation rating for seller 1 in a market with diminishing feedback, i.e. with feedback longevity factor $\lambda = 0.99$.

It can be seen that the reputation rating tracks the honesty fairly well. As a result, when honesty for example is reduced it will have an effect on sales in two ways: 1) it will lead to short term increased profit for the seller because some items are not shipped, and 2) it will lead to long term reduced sales because the reputation rating will suffer relatively quickly. The balance between these two effects keeps the honesty within a range of 0.75 - 1.0 during the simulation. This reflects a much more healthy market than when all feedback is either immediatly forgotten ($\lambda = 0$) or never forgotten ($\lambda = 1$).

Fig.6 illustrates the evolution of the honesty and reputation rating for one seller with diminishing feedback during the sessions 50-150.

The figure which represents a close zoom-in on Fig.5 is included to show in detail how the reputation rating follows the honesty when the longevity factor $\lambda = 0.99$. It can be seen that during sessions 65-70 when the honesty is 1.0 the reputation approaches its maximum before dropping again.

The fact that the reputation rating follows the honesty in a rather erratic way is of course due to the fact that the reputation rating is a result of feedback which is a result of a probabilistic decision to ship or not to ship in individual transactions. It is thus

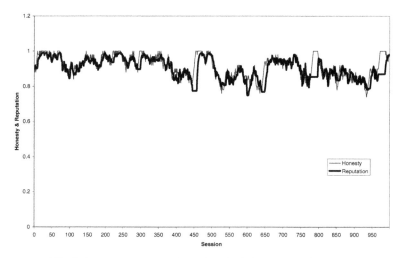

Fig. 5. Honesty and reputation rating for Seller 1 where $\lambda = 0.99$

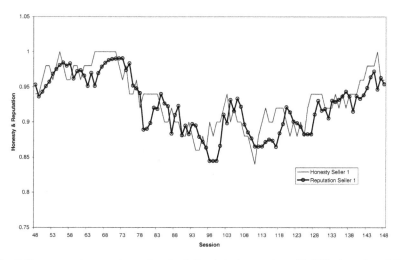

Fig. 6. Honesty and reputation rating for Seller 1 during sessions 50-150 where $\lambda = 0.99$

possible that even though the honesty is 0.90 the seller might for example ship only 5 out 10 items in any given session.

4.2   Snapshot of Seller Strategy, Rating, and Transactions

The seller strategy is defined by the honesty and the selling price. The tracing of these two parameters together on the same plane can be called a "genetic walk" if we consider the parameters as the "genes" that define the nature of the seller. In Fig.7 below we have traced the genetic walk for all three sellers during the sessions 600-620.

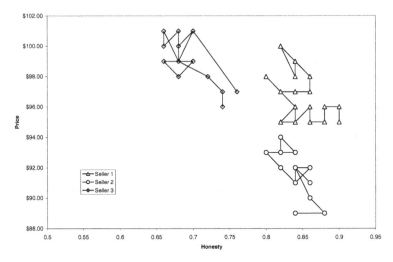

Fig. 7. Seller strategy evolution during sessions 600-620 where $\lambda = 0.99$

It can be observed that in this period seller 1 and 2 are competing with comparable honesty levels whereas seller 3 operates with a lower honesty level. The resulting reputation rating for the 3 sellers in the same period can be seen in Fig.8 below.

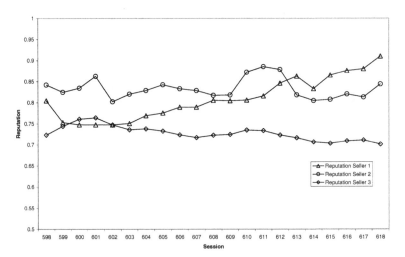

Fig. 8. Seller reputation rating during sessions 600-620 where $\lambda = 0.99$

It can be observed that seller 3 has the lowest reputation rating overall, and that the reputation ratings of sellers 1 and 2 in fact are crossing each other at session 613. The combination of selling price and reputation rating determines the number of transactions that each seller will get during a session. Fig.9 shows the number of transactions of each seller in the same period.

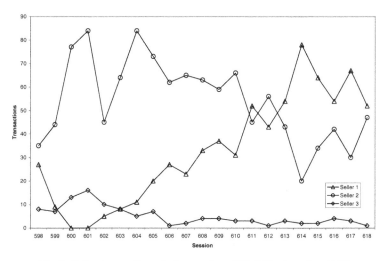

Fig. 9. Seller transactions during sessions 600-620 where $\lambda = 0.99$

As expected it can be seen that seller 3 has the lowest number of transactions due to his relatively low reputation rating and high selling price.

4.3   Market Honesty

Market Honesty measures the number of shipped transactions divided by the number of total number of transactions. We will measure the market honesty for each session and trace the honesty as a function of session number.

In Fig.10 which illustrates the market honesty when feedback is ignored, it can be seen that the sellers notice that their base rate reputation rating of 0.9 is not influenced by cheating, so that they in fact can improve their profit by reducing the honesty level. The increase in market honesty (around session 550) can be explained by the buyers getting more risk averse and thus buying less, resulting in reduced business for all the sellers. By increasing the honesty the sellers will get more business and increase profit, and the seller mutation process is somehow able to implement this strategy. Even though the general market honesty increases in the period after session 550, it can be seen that there are brief periods of very poor market honesty, which never occurred in the period before session 550. The market around session 800 thus seems to be in a worse state than around session 200, even though the general market honesty level is equal at both instants.

In Fig.11 which illustrates the market honesty when feedback is permanent, i.e. $\lambda = 1$, it can be seen that the honesty steadily deteriorates. The difference between this and the previous graph (where feedback was immediately forgotten) can be explained

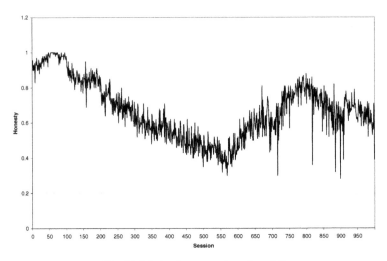

Fig. 10. Market honesty where $\lambda = 0.0$

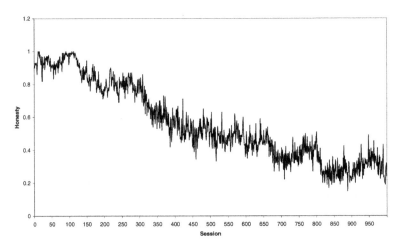

Fig. 11. Market honesty where $\lambda = 1.0$

by the fact that the sellers are unable to improve business by increasing honesty because of the stiffness of their reputation ratings. Due to their myopic view of the world (only the two last transactions matter) the sellers are unable to keep increasing their honesty long enough to notice that it influences their reputation in a positive way.

Fig.12 above illustrates the market honesty with feedback longevity $\lambda = 0.99$. It can be seen that when the feedback is slowly forgotten the market honesty remains significantly higher than is the case when feedback longevity $\lambda = 0$ or $\lambda = 1$.

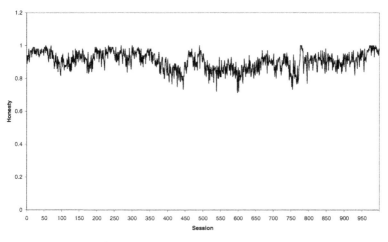

Fig. 12. Market honesty where $\lambda = 0.99$

4.4 Profit

Fig.13 illustrated the average profit of sellers and buyers for each session in a market where the feedback longevity $\lambda = 0.99$.

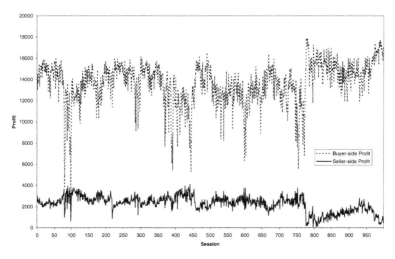

Fig. 13. Profit of sellers and buyers in the market where $\lambda = 0.99$

Two effects can be observed:

– In general the curves are mirrors of each other, meaning that when sellers make more profit over a period, then the buyers make less profit, and vice versa. The periods of high seller profit can be described as seller's market, and the periods of high buyer profit as buyer's market. One explanation of why the simulation has periods of seller's market and buyer's market is there is an unstable balance between the sellers' and buyers' opposing strategies for maximising profit.

– There are brief periods when there is a sharp profit drop on both seller and buyer side. This is obviously caused by a sharp drop in the number of transactions caused by the sellers' reputation rating dropping below the buyers' risk aversion so that the buyers decide not to transact. These periods are brief because the sellers are programmed to reduce price and increase honesty and the buyers are programmed to reduce risk aversion when no transactions occur, so that the market quickly picks up again. These sharp drops in profit often initiate a period of buyer's market.

5   Discussion and Conclusion

In our study we simulated a market of selling and buying agents where the buyers provide feedback about the sellers after each transaction. We were able to demonstrate some fundamental properties of markets of selling and buying agents:

1. A market without reputation system where strangers transact with each other without knowing each others past behaviour record will be unhealthy.
2. A market with a reputation system in place has the potential to become healthy.
3. A market with a reputation system can only become healthy when the record of past behaviour is slowly forgotten.

Conclusion (3) above intuitively makes sense because most people would judge it unreasonable to put equal weight on behaviour observed in a distant past as on behaviour observed yesterday. It is interesting to notice that the Feedback Forum used on eBay[1] uses a mixture of permanent and forgetting indicators. The overall number of positive minus the overall number of negative feedback is presented together with the number of positive, negative and neutral feedback from the past 6 months, from the past month and from the past 7 days. The reputation rating derived by the beta reputation system represents similar information in a much more condensed form which can be used directly for decision making.

The buying agents in our simulation have a strong ability to forgive sellers' sins of the past, even too strong one might say. For example when a buyer has been cheated, he provides a negative feedback, increases the risk aversion by $Avs(B)$ and a part from that could perfectly well trade with the same dishonest seller in the next transaction as long as the buying criteria are satisfied.

Typical sayings are that it takes many good impressions to cancel out one bad impression, that you never get a second chance to make a first impression, and that once your reputation is lost it is almost impossible to regain. Our trading agents certainly have a significantly more positive view of the world than these proverbs suggest. It thus indicates that the sellers are able to maintain a lower honesty and still survive in the market than would have been possible in the real world.

---

[1] eBay is the most successful electronic market that uses a reputation system. (http://ebay.com)

The buyer side in our simulation consists of only 10 buyers, and even when they have been ripped off by dishonest sellers and their risk aversion stops them from transacting for a few sessions they quickly return to the market as the eternal optimists they are. In the real world, buyers who have been seriously ripped off might leave the market and never return. In the real world there is also a steady stream of newcomers to the market whereas our simulation used a fixed set of players. We deliberately gave the buying agents a positive world view in order to have a functioning market that can produce transaction data. We also thought this was a simple way to implement the combination of pessimistic players who leave and new players who arrive. It would be interesting so observe how the market would be influenced by giving the buyers a more human pessimistic attitude, as well as have a flux of leaving and arriving players.

The simulation results presented here are the first obtained with our market implementation, and we plan to continue our study by changing the market parameters and by analysing other aspects of the market in order to learn more about the ability of reputation systems to influence markets.

The real benefit of reputation systems will emerge as software agents evolve into intelligent entities that are able to automatically make decisions and perform transactions on behalf of their human masters. We believe that software agents will have characteristics of social entities which are able to follow strategies for interactions with other agents for mutual benefit while resisting exploitation by malicious agents. Reputation systems can thus be seen as "navigation instruments" for software agents to find optimal transaction partners and to avoid dangerous encounters. In a nutshell, the goal of reputation systems can be defined as that of optimising the quality of the market and the gain of individuals.

References

1. Gary Bolton, Elena Katok, and Axel Ockenfels. How Effective are Online Reputation Mechanisms? Discussion Papers on Strategic Interaction 25-2002, Max-Plank-Institut, 2002.
2. George Casella and Roger L. Berger. *Statistical Inference*. Duxbury Press, 1990.
3. Consumers International. *Consumers@shopping: An international comparative study of electronic commerce*. Consumers International's Programme for Developed Economies and Economies in Transition, http://www.consumersinternational.org/campaigns/electronic/e-comm.html, September 1999.
4. A. Jøsang and R. Ismail. The Beta Reputation System. In *Proceedings of the 15th Bled Electronic Commerce Conference*, Bled, Slovenia, June 2002.
5. US FTC. Boom in E-Commerce Has Created Fertile Ground for Fraud. US Federal Trade Commission, http://www.ftc.gov/opa/2001/05/iftestimony.htm, May 2001.

Integrating Trustfulness and Decision Using Fuzzy Cognitive Maps

Cristiano Castelfranchi, Rino Falcone, and Giovanni Pezzulo

Institute of Cognitive Sciences and Technomogies - CNR
viale Marx, 15 - Roma
{castel, falcone, pezzulo}@ip.rm.cnr.it

Abstract. The aim of this paper is to show how relevant is a trust model based on beliefs and their credibility. We will also show how the Fuzzy Cognitive Maps are convenient and practicable for implementing and integrating trustfulness and delegation.

1   Introduction

In this paper we will show a possible implementation and advance of the socio-cognitive model of trust developed in [1, 2]. This implementation uses a fuzzy approach (in particular, it uses the so-called Fuzzy Cognitive Maps - FCM [3]).

One of the aims of this paper is to show how relevant is a trust model based on beliefs and their credibility. In addition, given that the credibility of a belief directly depends from the credibility of its sources, we also analyse the different nature of the belief sources and their trustworthiness.

The richness of the referred model (trust is based on many different beliefs) allows to distinguish between internal and external attributions (to the trustee) and for each of these two attributions it allows to distinguish among several other sub-components such as: competence, disposition, unharmfulness and so on.

Another important aim of this paper is to show how the FCMs are really convenient and practicable for implementing and integrating the two mechanisms of the evaluation of trust (trustfulness) and of the decision to delegate.

1.1   Why the Fuzzy Approach

We have chosen an approach based on the Fuzzy Logic for several reasons. First, we want to model some graded phenomenon like trust that is difficult to estimate experimentally. The qualitative approach of the Fuzzy Logic is very useful because it is intuitive to start the analysis with natural language labels (this doctor is *very skilled*) that represent intervals rather than exact values. More, the behavior of these systems (e.g. their combinatorial properties) seems to be good in modelling several cognitive dynamics [3], even if to find "the real function" for a mental operation and to estimate the contribution of convergent and divergent belief sources remain open problems.

P. Nixon and S. Terzis (Eds.): Trust Management 2003, LNCS 2692, pp. 195–210, 2003.

We have used an implementation based on a special kind of fuzzy system called Fuzzy Cognitive Maps (FCM); they allow to compute the value of the trustfulness starting from belief sources that refer to trust features. The values of those features are also computed, allowing us to perform some cognitive operations that lead to the effective decision to trust or not to trust (e.g. impose an additional threshold on a factor, for example risks). Using this approach we describe beliefs and trust features as approximate (mental) objects with a strength and a causal power one over another.

2   Scenarios

In order to exemplify our approach and system we will apply it to an interesting scenario, that is one of the application scenarios identified within the Alfebiite Project [4]. The scenario we are going to study is medical house assistance in two particular instances: a) a doctor (a human operator) visiting a patient at home and b) a medical automatic system for supporting the patient (without direct human intervention).

The case studies under analysis are:

- an **emergency situation**, in which there is the necessity of identifying an occurring danger (for example, a hearth attack) as soon as possible to cope with it; we consider in this case the fact that the (first) therapy to be applied is quite simple (suppose just a injection);

- a **routine situation**, in which there is a systematic and specialist therapy to apply (with quite a complex procedure) but in which there is no immediate danger to cope with.

We will show how the factors that produce the final trust for each possible trustee are dependent on:

- the initial strength of the different beliefs (on which trust is based) but also

- how much a specific belief impacts on the final trust (the causality power of a belief).

It is through this second kind of factors that we have the possibility also of characterizing some personality traits of the agents [5, 6, 7].

3   Belief Sources

In our model trust is an "*evaluation*" and an "*expectation*" (i.e. in our theory special kinds of beliefs) and also an (affective) attitude and disposition. They are based upon more specific beliefs which are both *basis* of trust and its *sub-components* or *parts*: which/how is our trust in (evaluation of) the trustee as for his/her/its competence and ability? Which/how is our trust in (evaluation of) the trustee as for his/her/its intention and reliability? Which/how is our trust in (evaluation of) the trustee as for his/her/its goodwill and honesty? And so on.

Those beliefs are the analytical account and the components of trust, and we derive *the degree of trust* directly from the *strength* of its componential and supporting beliefs. More precisely in our model [2] we claim that *the degree of trust is a function of the subjective certainty of the pertinent beliefs*. We used the degree of trust to formalize a rational basis for the decision of relying and betting on the trustee. Also in this case we claimed that the "quantitative" aspect of another basic ingredient is relevant: *the value or importance or utility of the goal g*, will obviously enter the evaluation of the risk, and will also modify the required threshold for trusting. In sum, *the quantitative dimensions of trust are based on the quantitative dimensions of its cognitive constituents.*

When we have a belief we have to evaluate:

- the value of the content of that belief;

- who/what the source is (another agent, my own inference process, a perceptive sense of mine, etc.);

- how this source evaluates the belief (the subjective certainty of the source itself);

- how the trustier evaluates this source (with respect to this belief).

Those beliefs are not all at the same layer. Clearly some of them are meta-beliefs, and some of them tune, modulate the value and the impact of the lower beliefs. The general schema could be described as a cascade having two levels (see Figure1); at the bottom level there is the single belief (in particular, the value of the content of that specific belief; this value should be used (have a part) in the trustier's evaluation of some trustee's feature); at the top level there is the composition of the previous value with the epistemic evaluations of the trustier. At this level all the contributions of various sources of the same type are integrated.

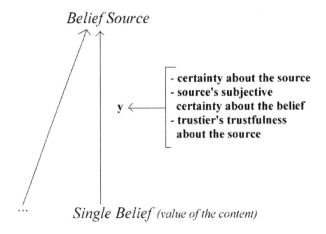

Fig. 1. From single beliefs to the belief source

4   Modelling Beliefs and Sources

Following a belief-based model of trust [1] we can distinguish between trust in the trustee (be it either someone –e.g. the doctor- or something –e.g. the medical automatic system-) that has to act and produce a given performance thanks to its internal characteristics, and the (positive and/or negative) environmental conditions (like opportunities and interferences) affecting the trustee's performance, that we call "external factors".

In this paper we take into account:

- Three main beliefs regarding the trustee: an ability/competence belief; a disposition/availability belief, and an unharmfulness belief.

- Two main beliefs regarding the contextual factors: opportunity beliefs and danger beliefs.

4.1   Beliefs and Sources Overview

Which are the meanings of our basic beliefs in the case of the doctor and in the case of the medical automatic system?

For the *medical automatic system* the internal and external factors that we consider are:

- *Internal factors – ability/competence beliefs*: these beliefs concern the efficacy and efficiency of the machine; its capability to successfully apply the right procedure in the case of correct/proper use of it. Possibly, also its ability to recover from an inappropriate use.

- *Internal factors – disposition/availability beliefs*: these beliefs are linked to the reliability of the machine, its regular functioning, its easiness of use; possibly, its adaptability to new and unpredictable uses.

- *Internal factors – unharmfulness beliefs*: these beliefs concern the absence (lack) of the internal/ intrinsic risks of the machine: the dangers implied in the use of that machine (for example side effects for the trustier's health), the possibility of breaking and so on.

- *External factors – opportunity beliefs*: concerning the opportunity of using the machine, independent of the machine itself, from the basic condition to have the room for allocating the machine to the possibility of optimal external conditions in using it (regularity of electric power, availability of an expert person in the house that might support in its use, and so on).

- *External factors – danger beliefs*: these beliefs are connected with the absence (lack) of the systemic risks and dangers external to the machine that could harm the user: consider for example the risk for the trustier's privacy: in fact we are supposing that the machine is networked in an information net and the data are also available to other people in the medical structure.

For the *doctor* the internal and external factors that we consider are:

- *Internal factors – ability/competence beliefs*: these beliefs concern the (physical and mental) skills of the doctor; his/her ability to make a diagnosis and to solve problems.

- *Internal factors – disposition/availability beliefs*: these beliefs concern both the willingness of the doctor to commit to that specific task (subjective of the specific person or objective of the category), and also his/her availability (in the sense of the possibility to be reached/informed about his/her intervention).

- *Internal factors – unharmfulness beliefs*: these beliefs concern the absence (lack) of the risks of being treated by a doctor; namely the dangers of a wrong diagnosis or intervention (for example, for the health of the trustier).

- *External factors – opportunity beliefs*: concerning the opportunities not depending on the doctor but on conditions external to his/her intervention. Consider for example the case in which the trustier is very close to a hospital in which there is an efficient service of fast intervention; or again, even if the trustier is not very close to a hospital he/she knows about new health policies for increasing the number of doctors for quick intervention; and so on. Conversely, imagine a health service not efficient, unable to provide a doctor in a short time; or, again, a particularly chaotic town (for the car traffic, for the frequent strikes in it) that could hamper the mobility of the doctors and of their immediate transfer in the site where the patient is.

- *External factors – danger beliefs*: these beliefs concern with the absence (lack) of the risks and dangers which do not depend directly on the doctor but on the conditions for his/her intervention: for instance, supposing that the trustier's house is poor and not too clean, the trustier could see the visit of a person (the doctor in this case) as a risk for his/her reputation.

Each of the above mentioned beliefs may be generated by different sources; such as: direct experience, categorization, reasoning, and reputation. So, for example, ability/competence beliefs about the doctor, may be generated by the direct knowledge of a specific doctor, and/or by the generalized knowledge about the class of doctors and so on.

5   Overview of the Implementation

We describe an implementation that uses Fuzzy Cognitive Maps (FCM) [3]. In order to design the FCM and to assign a value to its nodes we need to answer four questions: which value do I assign to this concept? How sure am I of my assignment? Which are the reasons of my assignment? How much does this concept impacts on an other linked concept?

We address the first and the second question above assigning numeric values to the nodes representing the belief sources. The nodes are causal concepts; their value varies from -1 (true negative) to $+1$ (true positive). This number represents the value/degree of each single trust feature (say ability) by combining together both the credibility value of a belief (degree of credibility) and the estimated level of that feature. Initial values are set using adjectives from natural language; for example, "I believe that the ability of this doctor is *quite good* (in his work)" can be represented using a node labeled "ability" with a little positive value (e.g. $+0.4$). For example, the value $+0.4$ of ability either means that the trustier is *pretty sure* that the trustee is *rather good*, or that he/she is *rather sure* that the trustee is *really excellent*, etc.

We address the third question above designing the graph. Some nodes receive input values from other nodes; these links represent the reasons on which their values are grounded. Direct edges stand for fuzzy rules or the partial causal flow between the concepts. The sign (+ or -) of an edge stands for causal increase or decrease. For example, the Ability value of a doctor influences positively (e.g. with weight $+0.6$) his Trustfulness: if ability has a positive value, Trustfulness increases; otherwise it decreases.

We address the fourth question above assigning values to the edges: they represent the impact that a concept has over another concept. The various features of the trustee, the various components of trust evolution do not have the same impact, and importance. Perhaps, for a specific trustee in a specific context, ability is more important than disposition. We represent the different quantitative contributions to the global value of trust through these weights on the edges. The possibility of introducing different impacts for different beliefs surely represents an improvement with respect to the trust basic model. FCMs allow to quantify causal inference in a simple way; they model both the strength of the concepts and their relevance for the overall analysis. For example, the statement: "Doctors are *not very accessible* and this is an *important factor* (for determining their trustfulness) in an emergency situation" is easily modelled as a (strong) positive causal inference between the two concepts of Accessibility and Trustfulness. FCMs also allow to sum up the influence of different causal relations. For example, adding another statement: "Doctors are *very good* as for their ability, but this is a *minor factor* in an emergency situation" means adding a new input about the Ability, with a (weak) positive causal influence over Trustfulness. Both Accessibility and Ability, each with its strength and its causal power, contribute to establish the value of Trustfulness.

6   Description of the Model

Even if FCMs are graphs, ours can be seen as having four layers. As we have previously seen, the first layer models the influence of the "beliefs sources": Direct Experience (e.g. "In my experience…"), Categorization (e.g. "Usually doctors…"), Reasoning (e.g. "I can infer that…"), Reputation (e.g. "A friend says that…"). Their value is meant to be stable (i.e. it does not change during computation), because these nodes could be assumed being the result of an "inner FCM" where each single belief is represented (e.g. Direct Experience about Ability results from many nodes like: "I was visited *many times* by this doctor and he was *really good* at his work", "*Once* he made a *wrong* diagnosis", …). So their value not only represents the strength of the feature expressed in the related beliefs, but also their number and their perceived importance, because belief sources represent the synthesis of many beliefs. The second layer shows the five relevant basic beliefs: Ability, Accessibility, Harmfulness, Opportunities and Danger. These basic beliefs are distinguished in the third layer into Internal Factors and External Factors. Ability, Accessibility and Harmfulness are classified as Internal Factors; Opportunities and Danger are classified as External Factors. Internal and External factors both influence Trustfulness, which is the only node in the fourth layer. For the sake of simplicity no crossing-layer edges are used, but this could be easily done since FCM can compute cycles and feedback.

6.1   Running the Model

Once the initial values for the first layer (i.e. belief sources) are set, the FCM starts running[1]. The state of a node N at each step s is computed taking the sum of all the inputs, i.e., the current values at step s-1 of nodes with edges coming into N multiplied by the corresponding edge weights. The value is then squashed (into the –

---

[1] We have used a slightly modified implementation of the Fuzzy Cognitive Map Modeler described in [12].

1,1 interval) using a threshold function. The FCM run ends when an equilibrium is reached, i.e., when the state of all nodes at step s is the same as that at step s-1. At this point we have a resulting value for Trustfulness, that is the main goal of the computational model. However, the resulting values of the other nodes are also shown: they are useful for further analysis, where thresholds for each feature could be considered.

6.2   Experimental Setting

Our experiment shows the choice between a doctor and a medical apparatus in the medical field. We assume that the choice is mainly driven by trustfulness. We have considered two situations: a "Routine Visit" and an "Emergency Visit". We have built four FCMs representing trustfulness for doctors and machines in those two situations. Even if the structure of the nets is always the same, the values of the nodes and the weights of the edges change in order to reflect the different situations. For example, in the "Routine Visit" scenario, Ability has a great causal power, while in the "Emergency Visit" one the most important factor is Accessibility. It is also possible to alter some values in order to reflect the impact of different trustier personalities in the choice. For example, somebody who is very concerned with Danger can set its causal power to *very high* even in the "Routine Visit" scenario, where its importance is generally low. In the present work we do not consider those additional factors; however, they can be easily added without modifying the computational framework.

6.2.1   Routine Visit Scenario
The first scenario represents many possible routine visits; there is the choice between a doctor and a medical apparatus. In this scenario we have set the initial values (i.e. the beliefs sources) for the Doctor hypothesizing some direct experience and common sense beliefs about doctors and the environment.

    Most values are set to zero; the others are:
- Ability – Direct Experience: quite (+0.3);

- Ability – Categorization: very (+0.7);

- Accessibility – categorization: quite negative (-0.3);

- Unharmfulness – categorization: some negative (-0.2);

- Opportunity – Reasoning: some (+ 0.2);

- Danger – Reasoning: some negative (-0.2).

    For the machine we have hypothesized no direct experience. These are the values:
- Efficacy – Categorization: good (+0.6);

- Accessibility – Categorization: good (+0.6);

- Unharmfulness – Categorization: quite negative (- 0.3);

- Opportunity – Reasoning: some (+0.2);

- Danger – Categorization: quite negative (- 0.3);

- Danger – Reasoning: quite negative (-0.3).

We have also considered the causal power of each feature. These values are the same both for the Doctor and the Machine. Most values are set to mildly relevant (+0.5); the others are:

- Ability: total causation (+1);

- Accessibility: only little causation (+0.1);

- Unharmfulness: middle negative causation (-0.4);

- Opportunity: only little causation (+0.1);

- Danger: little negative causation (-0.2).

The results of this FCM are shown in Figure 4: Trustfulness for the Doctor results good (+0.57) while trustfulness for the machine results only almost good (+0.22).

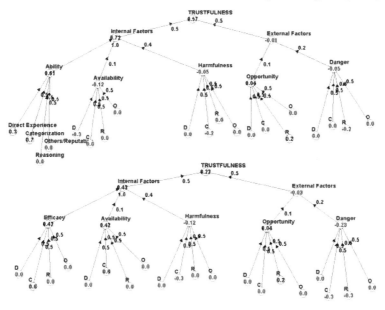

Fig. 2. Routine Visit FCMs for the Doctor (top) and the Machine (bottom)

The FCMs are quite stable with respect to minor value changes; setting Machine's Accessibility – Direct Experience to good (+0.6), Accessibility – Categorization to really good (+0.8) and Danger – Categorization to little danger (-0.5) results in a non dramatic change in the final value, that changes from *almost good (+0.23)* to *quite good (+0.47)* but does not overcome the Doctor's Trustfulness. This is mainly due to the high causal power of Ability with respect to the other features. We can also see the influence of different personalities. For example, if we assume that Doctors are supposed to involve high external risks (Danger – Reputation: +1), with the usual values, the trustier's Trustfulness does not change very much (*good (+0.47)*). But if the patient is somebody who gives high importance to Danger (danger: *total causality (-1)*), the Doctor's Trustfulness decreases to *negative (-0.42)*.

6.2.2 Emergency Visit Scenario

We have hypothesized an emergency situation where somebody needs a quick visit for an easy task (e.g. a injection). In this scenario the values for the nodes are the same as before, but some edges drastically change: Reliability becomes very important and Ability much less. The values for the edges are:

- Ability: little causation (+0.2);

- Willingness: very strong causation (+1);

- Unharmfulness: strong negative causation (-0.8);

- Opportunity: middle causation (+0.5);

- Danger: quite strong causation (+0.6).

The results also change drastically: Trustfulness for the Doctor is *only slightly positive (+0.02)* and for the Machine it is *quite good (+0.29)*. The FCMs are very stable; altering some settings for the Doctor (Ability – Direct Experience: *very good* and Danger – Categorization: *only little danger*) results in a change in the Trustfulness value that become *almost good* but does not overcome the Machine's one. We obtain the same results if we suppose that Doctor's Ability - Direct Experience: *perfect* and Ability's Causal Power: *very strong*. On the contrary, if we introduce a big danger (+1) either internal (*harmfulness*) or external (*danger*) in each FCM the trustfulness values fall to *negative* in both cases (respectively -0.59 and -0.74 for the doctor; and -0.52 and -0.67 for the machine).

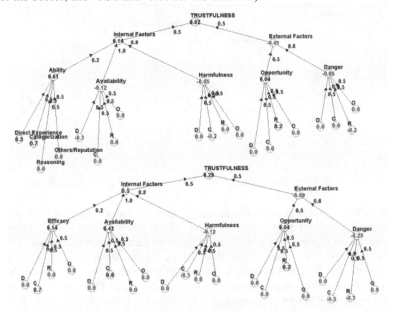

Fig. 3. Emergency Visit FCMs for the Doctor (top) and the Machine (bottom)

7   Trustfulness and Decision

At the end of its run phase, an FCM shows a value for Trustfulness and a value for each one of the relevant factors: Ability, Availability, Unharmfulness, Opportunity and Danger. All these factors are relevant in order to make the final choice (e.g. between a doctor and a machine in our scenarios) and to decide about delegation. Many choices are possible: to delegate the doctor, to delegate the machine, or not to delegate at all. For this decision, we have to take into account mainly the Trustfulness value, even if the final decision is affected by a set of other relevant factors and by their reciprocal relationships.

More precisely, the trustier is endowed with at least a goal (in our case, to maintain his/her health), and can evaluate the utility of each possible result of the selected action.

So we should consider the following abstract scenario (Fig. 4) where we call:

$U(X)$, the trustier's utility function, and specifically:

$U(X)_d{}^+$, the utility of the doctor's success performance (the utility due to the success of the delegated action to the doctor);

$U(X)_d{}^-$, the utility of the doctor's failure performance (the damage due to the failure of the delegated action to the doctor);

$U(X)_m{}^+$ the utility of the machine's success performance (the utility due to the success of the delegated action to the machine);

$U(X)_m{}^-$ the utility of the machine's failure performance (the damage due to the failure of the delegated action to the machine);

$U(X)_0$ the utility of to do nothing.

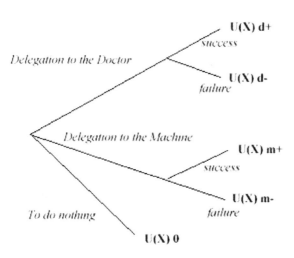

Fig. 4. Evaluation of the utilities.

More precisely, we have:

- $U(X)_d^+$ = Value(g) + Cost [Delegation(trustier, doctor, time)],

- $U(X)_d^-$ = Cost [Delegation(trustier, doctor, time)] + Additional Damage for failure

- $U(X)_m^+$ = Value(g) + Cost [Delegation(trustier, machine, time)],

- $U(X)_m^-$ = Cost [Delegation(trustier, machine, time)]+ Additional Damage for failure

where is supposed that we attribute a quantitative value (importance) to the goals and where the costs of the actions (delegation) are supposed to be negative.

For each comparison between two branches of the above scenario we have introduced in a previous work [2] the formula:

$T_{XY\tau} * U(X)_{d1}^+ + (1 - T_{XY\tau}) U(X)_{d1}^- > T_{XZ\tau} * U(X)_{d2}^+ + (1 - T_{XZ\tau}) U(X)_{d2}^-$

Where $T_{XY\tau}$ (with $0 \leq T \leq 1$) is the trustfulness of the trustier X on the trustee Y about the task τ. Y•Z. Y and Z could be the doctor, the machine, or nobody.

The above formula follows the classical Decision Theory useful for calculating in the actual scenario the best action to perform on the basis of all the parameters involved in the calculus (the trustfulness values of the different trustees, the value of the goal to achieve, the different costs of action results, and so on).

In any case this procedure only considers the best global hypothesis; it does not permits to take in consideration the possibility of saturation effects such as too high costs. In other words, it is very important to consider the values of some parameters independently from the values of the others. This fact suggests to introduce some saturation-based mechanism to influence the decision, some threshold.

For example, cost value can represent a problem for the decision: even if the costs-benefits relationship is maximal, sometimes we cannot delegate to the trustee (in our case, doctor or machine) because the cost is too high. In some sense is how if we are introducing a sort of threshold on a specific parameter.

Many other factors can have a role as thresholds in the decision process: in fact, each evaluation on the trustee's features could have a maximum or minimum value: ability, reliance, danger, etc. We can fix a threshold for one or more features and inhibit a choice even if trustfulness is acceptable. In other words, given the same trustfulness value, many different compositions of the internal ingredients are possible for that final value of trustfulness. Not all these possibilities are cognitively acceptable because some of them could be cut from saturation mechanisms that we will implement by thresholds. For example, someone very concerned with dangers can decide not to delegate, even if the trustfulness value is good, because there are too many risks in that specific case.

It is important to distinguish between the trust evaluation (trustfulness) and the final decision; we can make our evaluation even if there are some factors that constrain the decision; for example we can evaluate the quality-price ratio of something even if we know we have not enough money to buy it. An FCM alone cannot take into account all the *necessary conditions* for a decision: this result can be reached only adding additional thresholds. This seems to us a good cognitive feature: even if there is an evidently unsatisfied *necessary condition*, humans could compute a trust value; may be this calculation waste time and resources but in some situation it is necessary for collecting elements and founding better the final decision. For example, even if I know I do not have enough money to pay a specific doctor, it would be possible (and sometimes useful) to evaluate his competence. In the decision process, this attitude can lead to counterfactuals (e.g.: *I Trust him, and I would have asked him to cure me if I have had enough money*).

A (positive) trust judgment do not force the decision, even if costs conditions are satisfied: we can judge something trustable but decide not to trust it. This depends from the thresholds that I can assign to other factors. For example, in the game of poker, we can judge that a bet is a good action, and even do it if not so much money is involved; but we can decide not to do it if too much money is involved (the risk of loosing the money is too high for us). In this case we do not think that it is not a good action; we judge the bet a good action to do, but we simply could not take the risk.

In order to distinguish between different thresholds, consider these two different situations, where I consider a bid a good action but I do not bid:

- I do not have enough money to bid (if I had enough money, I would have bid);
- I have enough money but the risk is too high (if the bet was not so high, I would have bid).

In the two cases, two different thresholds values are considered: the first one is a cost threshold; the second one is a danger/opportunity threshold.

7.1   Decide Not to Delegate

Not all decisions are between two choices (as between a doctor and a machine in our scenario); in some cases, if neither of the two choices is satisfying, I can decide to not to delegate at all. This can be due to some unsatisfied threshold or to the fact that "doing it by myself" has a cost-benefit value greater than any other choice.

The solution of "do not decide" is another applicable rule: in this case "doing nothing" has a cost-benefit value greater than any other choice. Sometimes I am just waiting for some constraints being satisfied: for example, I can revise my opinion and decide in presence of new information.

There is another, interesting reason for deciding not to delegate: feeling that we need more information. This is an ambiguous aspect, because sometimes it is easy to decide how much information we have with respect to the total information available; but sometimes this is not true. More, sometimes the problem is not how much information I have, but how it is relevant or how it is reliable: an information from a very trusted source, even if there can be more information available, is sufficient. So, this ignorance measure depends both from quantitative (how much information I have) and qualitative (sources trustfulness and information relevance) factors.

In our FCM models evaluation and epistemic issues are mixed up (from a certain layer up); so a low trustfulness value, as well as low features values, can derive both from quantitative and qualitative reasons; sometimes poor information means poor trust, but only because we feel that we need more information. We use the same parameter (trustfulness value) as a first threshold for deciding to delegate, so deciding not to delegate can derive both from an explicit negative evaluation or from an estimation about ignorance[2].

---

[2] However, if we need do know why the final value is poor we can trace back the calculation in order to split evaluation, epistemic and quantity factors and decide which factor was more or less important.

8   Trustfulness, Decision, and Personality Factors

Some personality factors are involved both in the trustfulness value computation and in the following decision process.

In the Trustfulness value computation (trough an FCM), some personality factors are important in order to assign the values for some links in the FCMs at different layers.

At the first layer level the links represent the "causal power" of the beliefs sources over the features. Some personality factors are involved: for example, somebody who is self-confident could assign a strong importance to direct evidence and underestimate reputation (others' opinions).

At the second layer, personality factors can be involved in assigning the causal power of each single features over trustfulness; for example, somebody who particularly cares about his safety can overestimate the impact of danger and harmfulness.

There is not a fixed (rational) rule for assigning link values, but many contingent factors can have a "causal power" over them. In the FCM computations we assume link values as (already) fixed; but how are they obtained? As we have shown in Fig.1, in the case of beliefs sources building, even link values are computed by another (inner) FCM, whose nodes represent rational motivations as well as personality factors. In the case of building belief sources from single opinions, each opinion is "weighted" by certainty and trustfulness of the single font. So, personality factors can have important consequences into the values of the edges, i.e. impact factors.

Maybe it can be surprising that personality factors can assume in our analysis the same role of "more motivated" beliefs, as those concerning the current situation: but in a cognitive perspective, all the factors that contribute to building a meta-belief like trust (or to fix its fuzzy value) are equally important; they all have a "causal power". No special claim is done about the type of factors that are relevant to a given computation, only their strength and their impact are considered[3].

8.1   Personality Factors in the Decision

Some personality factors have a role even in the decision process, because they can contribute to fix the threshold for each factor. The costs-benefits ratio is not necessary a linear relationship (in other words, not always is true that if the risk increases as much as the benefit the relationship does not change). In the real situations, saturation mechanisms are introduced such as in the case of a not acceptable risk (independently by the goal) or in the case of a not sacrificable goal (independently by the risk). The personality factors can play a role for defining these thresholds. Obviously we have to consider that there is a difference between the objective risk and the perceived risk (such as between the perceived benefit and objective benefit). So we can also consider different kinds of personalities on the basis of the perception ability.

---

[3] Choosing the heuristics for summing up the different kinds of relevant factors (especially diverging opinions) is an open problem: it involves complex cognitive strategies (e.g.: choosing only the most trustworthy font, choosing only the most competent font, ...) and meta-rules derived from reasoning, past experience and personality factors. In the present work we simply sum up all the factors; but it is not a cognitive claim, it is only a temporary (and mathematically simple) solution.

8.2   Some Personalities

At the end of the analysis, we can say that personality factors have a strong "tuning" role in the FCM computation and even for the final decision; each personality factor can lead to different trust values and different decisions even with the same set of initial values for the beliefs sources.

At this point, we can try to show some simple examples of Personalities involved in our scenario. Many of them are possible, each with its consequences for the FCM; for example: *Prudent*: high impact for danger and unharmfulness; *Too Prudent*: high impact for danger and unharmfulness, additional threshold on danger and unharmfulness for decision; *Focused on Reputation*: high reputation impact, low impact for the other beliefs sources; *Auto*: high direct experience and categorization impact, low impact for the other beliefs sources.

There is another interesting point about personalities: normally we humans do a sort of reverse-engineering from others' decisions in order to guess their personality. For example, assuming that we all take into account the same factors in a decision process, if we observe that somebody has overestimated (in our terms) danger, we assign him the label "prudent" (and we can also use this sort of judgements in order to "tune" his opinions)[4].

8.3   Emotional Factors

Personality factors are strongly related to emotional components, too. They can lead to important modifications of the dynamics of the FCM, for example modifying the choice of the heuristic for combining homogenous and heterogeneous fonts or systematically underestimate or overestimate some factors. "Hot" computation, especially when oneself is involved, can lead to surprising results that are not directly due to misinformation but to some changes in the dynamics of the computation itself.
An example: a pessimistic mood can constraint the system behaviour in a very low level way, for example leading to a systematic overestimation of negative evidence in a decision process.

The emotional component adds another level to our analysis: sometimes the emotional impact itself can be seen as a motivation or it is an obstacle. For example, the decision to jump with a base-jump rope can involve many factors: normally, I trust the rope and the whole apparatus (I could even bit that the next man who jumps will have no injury); I can decide not to jump because the risk is too high compared to the benefit, or because even if I do not have injuries the situation is emotionally too strong for me.

8.4   Some Experiments with Personalities

In order to show some effects of personalities introduction in the FCM computation, we present here some examples; these experiments do not contain empirical data but

---

[4] This cue can be used in order to define user models in MAS systems

their main goal is to evaluate how much our methods are able to take into account cognitive phenomena.

Consider for example the FCM for the Emergency Visit Scenario; it is a risky situation and Danger and Harmfulness values are high. But perhaps a *Prudent* can overestimate them, fixing them at the maximum values (1). This has very little consequences (the trustfulness value of the Machine changes from 0.29 to 0.28), because the impact values have a little change and the node values are low. Probably this change has no consequences even for the Decision phase. But a Very Prudent may decide to fix a threshold on Danger and Harmfulness. If this threshold is fixed at -0.5 (little danger), the Danger value of the Machine exceeds it (it is -0.23); as a consequence of this threshold, in the Decision process the choice to delegate the Machine is inhibited.

In the same Emergency Visit Scenario, if we consider the *Auto* personality, that accords a high value to his own knowledge (represented both by the Personal Experience and Categorization Belief Sources) the final trustfulness values change drastically: the trustfulness value of the Doctor becomes 0.07 and the trustfulness value of the Machine becomes 0.75.

Since we have set all the Belief Sources about Reputation to zero, experiments with a personality like *Focused on Reputation* (that assigns high impact to reputation and low to all other sources) lead to very low final values for trustfulness, probably the final values are not enough for the decision to delegate in both senses, so the best choice can be not to delegate. This can represent the fact that somebody having such a personality feels that he needs more information in order to decide; even if the decision is absolutely necessary (as in the case of emergency), the feeling of "risky decision without enough knowledge" remains (and maybe this can lead to anxious states that feedbacks on the process).

9 Conclusions

In this paper we have described an approach to trust based on beliefs and their credibility. Trustfulness value derives from the value of the beliefs about its main features as well as their impact depending on the scenario; evaluation and epistemic factors, belief fonts and impacts are described in the paper. However, obtaining a trustfulness value is only the first step; a decision about to delegate or not to delegate is the successive phase, based on motivational factors that rely outside the knowledge level. This second step is described together with its main components, costs and utilities. Some considerations about personality and emotive factors, as well as many heuristics (that drive, among the others, the processes of summing up convergent and divergent belief fonts), are considered. In general, they show that a simple one-dimensional analysis (as a simple mathematical formula is) is not sufficient for a complex phenomenon like trust.

It has to be taken into account that considering the knowledge level alone leads to a poor analysis of the trust phenomenon; we distinguish the trustfulness computation phase (using FCMs) and a successive decision phase, driven by the motivational apparatus. So, what we need is not only a flat mathematical formula but a cognitive architecture that takes into account even motivations (and emotions). More, many heuristics (driven by the motivational apparatus, too) intervene at different levels:

combining converging and diverging fonts; setting relevance and impact factors and in general tuning the system; deciding thresholds; and so on. All these heuristics are fundamental in order to obtain a cognitively plausible behavior; simply embodying them into the system (as in many approaches) leads to a one-dimensional analysis.

References

1. Castelfranchi, C; Falcone, R., Principles of trust for MAS: Cognitive anatomy, social importance, and quantification. In Proceedings of the Third International Conference on Multi-Agent Systems, pages 72–79, Paris France, 1998.
2. Falcone R., Castelfranchi C., (2001). Social Trust: A Cognitive Approach, in *Trust and Deception in Virtual Societies* by Castelfranchi C. and Yao-Hua Tan (eds), Kluwer Academic Publishers, pp. 55–90.
3. Kosko, B. Fuzzy Cognitive Maps. International Journal Man-Machine Studies, vol. 24, pp.65–75, 1986.
4. http://www.iis.ee.ic.ac.uk/~alfebiite/ab-home.htm
5. J Carbonell: Towards a process model of human personality traits. *Artificial Intelligence, 15,1980.*
6. Castelfranchi C., de Rosis F., Falcone R., Pizzutilo S., (1998) Personality traits and social attitudes in Multi-Agent Cooperation, *Applied Artificial Intelligence Journal.*, special issue on "Socially Intelligent Agents", n. 7/8, vol.12, pp. 649–676.
7. C Elliott: Research problems in the use of a shallow Artificial Intelligence model of personality and emotions. *Proceedings of the 12th AAAI*, 1994.
8. C. Jonker and J. Treur (1999), Formal Analysis of Models for the Dynamics of Trust based on Experiences, Autonomous Agents '99 Workshop on "Deception, Fraud and Trust in Agent Societies", Seattle, USA, May 1, pp.81–94.
9. M. Schillo, P. Funk, and M. Rovatsos (1999), Who can you trust: Dealing with deception, Autonomous Agents '99 Workshop on "Deception, Fraud and Trust in Agent Societies", Seattle, USA, May 1.
10. Dragoni,A. F., 1992. A Model for Belief Revision in a Multi-Agent Environment. In *Decentralized AI - 3,* Y. Demazeau, E. Werner (eds), 215–31. Amsterdam: Elsevier.
11. Castelfranchi, C. 1996. Reasons: Belief Support and Goal Dynamics. *Mathware & Soft Computing, 3.* 1996, pp. 233–47.
12. http://www.users.voicenet.com/~smohr/FCMApplication.htm

Methodology to Bridge Different Domains of Trust in Mobile Communications

Zheng Yan[1] and Piotr Cofta[2]

[1] Nokia Research Center, Nokia Group, Helsinki, Finland
[2] E-Business – Security – Mobile Software, Nokia Group, Finland
{zheng.z.yan, piotr.cofta}@nokia.com

Abstract. Trust is playing an important role in communications and transactions. Based on different reasons of trust, different trusted domains, possibly disjoint, are formed in mobile communications, preventing complete systems from working properly. What is lacked therein is a bridge that can link domains, across trust gaps to establish a complete trusted mobile communication system. In this paper, the authors propose a generic method to analyze and model a mobile communication system into a number of trusted domains. In order to overcome the trust gaps among the originally disjoint domains, the authors further propose three approaches to bridge different domains and demonstrate the use of mobile Personal Trusted Devices, such as mobile handsets to act as the said bridge.

1 Introduction

Trust is an important aspect in the design and analysis of secure distributed systems [1]. Recently, trust modeling is paid more and more attention in mobile communications.

Actually, trust is such a subjective and dynamic concept that different entities can hold different opinions on it even while facing the same situation [2]. Based on different trust perception, different trusted domains can be formed also in the area of mobile communications. For example, a trusted domain that contains a security element (such as a smart card) and its issuer is formed if the issuer trusts the security element due to its tamper resistance. A trusted domain containing a personal mobile device (e.g. a mobile phone) and its holder can be constructed if the device holder trusts the device because its brand has a good reputation. An operator trusts its SIM (Subscriber Identity Module) card due to the embedded cryptography inside. A SIM card trusts the phone it is inserted into because otherwise it has no chances to operate.

In today's mobile communications, we can find many cases in which a system is actually formed by a number of the trusted domains and the communications and transactions are actually conducted among and across those domains. Significant problem may arise from the fact that different domains must cooperate in order to provide a complete service even though they may not share the same concept of trust. Specifically, security problems may be caused by the deficiency of trust among domains. This deficiency is likely one of the major barriers that prevents the proliferation of the mobile communications and transactions. The deficiency of trust is visible as gaps between the trusted domains established by different entities. For

P. Nixon and S. Terzis (Eds.): Trust Management 2003, LNCS 2692, pp. 211–224, 2003.

example, the proper arrangement for secure interaction between a smart card that belongs to a trusted domain of the card issuer and a terminal based application that belongs to a trusted domain of an application developer has been causing a lot of problems for a very long time. As another example, identification of autonomous and potentially malicious nodes in an ad-hoc network is both a security and a trust challenges that have raised many arguments.

There are several methods to bridge the trust gap, e.g. legal, contractual, and risk management based solutions. The authors believe that technology is one of the most important methods. In this paper, a technical method to bridge the trust gap is provided. The authors propose a methodology to analyze and bridge the trust domains and then study the use of mobile Personal Trusted Device to work as a trusted bridge for certain use cases derived from the mobile communications and transactions area.

The rest of the paper is organized as follows. Section two provides an overview of related trust schemes in literature. Section three introduces necessary definitions while the next section proposes the method to bridge the trusted domains in the mobile communications. In section five, the applicability of the proposed method is illustrated by applying it to some realistic examples. Finally, conclusions are provided in the last section.

2 Related Work

Current academic work related to the trust covers wide area of interest ranging from such aspects as perception of trust [4, 5], problem analysis of current secure systems [11, 12], trust modeling [7, 8, 9, 10], to trust quantification and specification in digital systems [3, 6].

The concept of trust is defined in various ways in the literature [2, 4, 5, 11, 14, 16]. It is widely understood that the trust itself is a comprehensive concept, which is hard to narrow down. The trust is subjective because the level of trust considered sufficient is different for each entity. The trust is also partly objective as it is affected by those factors that we cannot monitor.

Several papers discuss the role and models of trust applied to electronic communication. For example, a trust model for a secure multi-agent marketplace in [13] is based on a concentric sphere structure. The core of this model is the physical security. A security infrastructure is located in middle sphere: an internal and an external security infrastructure. In outer sphere, this model uses complex aspects of the trust such as fairness, reliability, reputation and loyalty to provide a complete model of basic trust for marketplaces. Unfortunately, this work did not illustrate how to apply the model into real systems.

Another interesting work in [8] provides a generic model of transaction trust for electronic commerce. This model is based on separating the mostly subjective party trust and mostly objective control trust. In the authors' opinion, party trust + control trust = transaction trust. If the level of the transaction trust is not sufficient for the transaction then the party trust should be possibly complemented by the control trust in order to reach the required level. This work focuses on the Internet based transactions. It did not consider the scenarios of the mobile communications.

Further, work in [14] gears towards trust management and describes an authentication trust model, as well as a schema for managing access control in a multi-agent system. The trust model and trust management framework proposed can take advantages of a number of trust management schemas, such as SPKI (Simple Public Key Infrastructure), RBAC (Role Based Access Control) and Kerberos, for delegation of authorizations. Similarly, in [10], a model for trust is proposed based on distributed recommendation. These work do not examine their applicability for the mobile communications. In addition, they cannot solve the trust gap problem.

As it can be seen from the short discussion above, none of the existing work tried to address trust in the mobile communications that have its own salient characteristics, and where mobile devices play a very important role by supporting communication mobility and flexibility. Further, no work considered or dealt with the trust gap problem that can be found. A new methodology to bridge different domains of trust is therefore needed to overcome these issues.

3 Definitions

Due to multiplicity of meanings associated with the word 'trust' and its derivatives, it is essential to establish certain set of definitions that can be used throughout the paper.

The working definition of trust used in this paper bases on [16] where the trust is defined as the confidence of an entity on another entity based on the expectation that the other entity will perform a particular action important to the trustor, irrespective of the ability to monitor or control that other entity. Note that the methodology presented in this paper is not sensitive to the exact definition of trust.

3.1 Trusted Domain

The trusted domains are not the entirely new concept in the literature, but so far, the authors have not found a concrete definition in available references. Herein, the following definition of the trusted domain is used throughout the paper.

Definition 1. Trusted Domain

> A trusted domain is a set of domain entities (e.g. service providers), defining statements and domain components (e.g. devices) such that all domain entities share certain defining statements regarding their trust definition for specified purpose, and all domain components adhere to such trust definition and implement the statements. The defining statement identifies requirements of the domain entities that must be fulfilled by the domain components to be trusted.

In Fig.1, an example of three trusted domains is presented. Domain $D1$ consists of an entity A and two statements $s1$ and $s2$. The statement $s1$ does not define any existing component (i.e. there are no components that fulfill the statement) while the statement $s2$ defines two components a and b. Domain $D2$ contains entity B and two statements. The statement $s1$ (identical with one of the statements from the domain $D1$) defines component c while statement $s3$ defines component d. Finally domain $D3$ has two entities: C and D with two statements. Statement $s4$ defines two components d and e, in which the former is shared with the domain $D2$. Statement $s5$ defines two components *e* and *f*, in which the former is also defined by the statement *s4*. Note that the component *d* fulfills both the statement *s3* and *s4*, so that the *D2* and *D3* are naturally bridged by the component *d*.

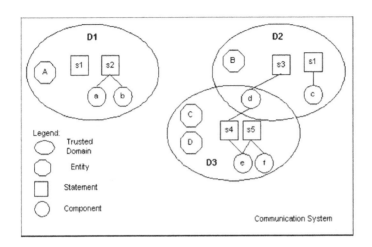

Fig. 1. An example of three trusted domains in a communication system

In other words, a trusted domain is established whenever some entity or entities (such as a user, an operator or a service provider) trusts some components for the specific purpose, regardless of the reasons for the trust that can be both subjective and objective, either rational or irrational. In this paper, special interest is placed in the domains where their components are hardware or software components in a digital system.

For example, the mobile operator creates its own domain of trust that includes, among others, SIM cards. The operator may trust the SIM cards that are fitted in mobile phones for the purpose of user authentication. The reason the operator trusts its SIM cards is likely to be rational and may come from the understanding of physical and cryptographic properties of the card as well as the quality of personalization process. The user defines his/her own domain of trust. The user may also trust the SIM card for the purpose of billing relationship due to effective user authentication. However, this trust may be less rational but rather driven by the popularity of technology or the visibility of the operator's brand. In this example the operator forms its own domain that is built on its understanding of trust while the user forms another domain on the basis of the user's defining statement. The SIM cards exist in both domains, thus enabling the mobile communication.

In another example, the user attempts to roam in another country where no roaming agreement exists between the user's home operator and current operator. Even though the configuration is technically identical, the current operator does not trust the user's SIM. Effectively, the user's SIM is out of the operator's trust domain and the user cannot use the mobile network.

3.2 Trusted Bridge

Based on the above definition and examples of the trusted domain, we can see that the full trust is retained inside the trusted domain while the trust may be missing among the domains. This may cause the trust gap in places where the trusted domains do not overlap.

For the success of the mobile communication systems, all the trusted domains that are essential for the complete system must intersect, i.e. there must be at least one component (or a chain of them) that is trusted by the entities communicating with each other. If it is not the case, a bridging solution should be identified and on that basis the bridging component must be created. Such trusted bridge can be as simple as the component that is trusted by both domains, or complex, with its own respective entities, statements and components that can bridge the disjoint trusted domains.

Definition 2. Trusted Bridge

A trusted bridge is a component or a set of components that is/are trusted by more than one domain. Therefore such component(s) can work as a bridge to establish the trust among those domains. Note that if any of the bridged domains contain more than one statement, it is sufficient for the trusted bridge to implement one of those statements for each of the domains it is bridging.

In Fig.1, the domains *D1* and *D2* are disjoint and no trust can be readily established by any technical means, while the domains *D2* and *D3* intersect so that the component *d* can be used to establish the trust between them.

As illustrated by the previous example, the SIM card operating in the home network acts as a bridge between the operator's domain and the user's domain. If, for example, the operator extends its domain to cover some digital content merchants, they can immediately benefit from the existing trusted bridge.

3.3 Personal Trusted Device

Most of use cases in the section five explore the applicability of a Personal Trusted Device (PTD) to bridge the trust gap. Certain references to the concept of PTD can be found in [16]. Due to the fact that there is no formal definition of the PTD, the working definition is provided below.

Definition 3. Personal Trusted Device (PTD)

PTD is a platform device that accepts multiple technologies with special focus on mobile communications and is personal to its user.

Further it will be demonstrated that by exploring the above properties the PTD can become a trusted bridge for the multiplicity of services thus acquiring desired trust property that has been intentionally removed from the original definition of the PTD.

The mobile phone acting as the PTD plays an important role in the mobile communications. It has hardware support for the trust, such as a slot for the smart card. Tamper-resistant device like the smart cart inside the mobile phone offers high level of trust through security. Most of the mobile phones have a SIM (Subscriber

Identity Module) card, trusted by the mobile network operator who can audit the phone's network activities. In addition, the mobile phone can hold a WIM (WAP Identity Module) card (either as a separate card or as an application located at the SIM card) for generating digital signatures that can realize non-repudiation. With its inherent characteristics of mobility, portability and security, the mobile phone is very flexible in approaching any other devices to realize communications regardless of time and location. The PTD implemented by the mobile phone is therefore potentially the best device that can link the user, the operator and the service providers, acting as a bridge for several mobile services.

4 Methodology

In this section, the authors introduce a new methodology into the area of mobile communications. This methodology helps to analyze the trust inside any mobile communication system by modeling the system into a number of trusted domains formed by different entities. In order to solve the issue of trust gaps, the authors further propose three approaches to bridge the disjoint domains.

In any mobile communication and transaction system, we can always specify the system as a number of trusted domains. The communications and transactions are actually conducted among those domains. Inside each trusted domain, the domain entities trust the domain components according to their defining statements, for whatever reasons they find appropriate. Among the trusted domains, it is expected that the trust must be usually created and constructed logically and rationally. The authors propose the methodology to analyze the trust domains and to create the trusted bridge, effectively enabling the domains to form a complete solution. The proposed methodology is summarized as follows.

1. Model the mobile communication system by separating it into a number of trusted domains formed by different entities.
2. Analyze each domain in order to extract the defining statements and list existing domain components. The resulting graph may resemble Fig.1.
3. For each pair of disjoint domains that must trust each other for the purpose of a given service, seek bridging solution that can satisfy both domains (see the discussion below).
4. Form the trusted bridge by finding or creating the suitable component (or components), or by establishing bridging domains, depending on needs (see the discussion below).

There are several approaches to identify the bridging solution and to introduce the trusted bridge, depending on the defining statements within the trusted domains as well as on non-technical limitations. Following is a short list of those. Throughout the discussion, the domains $D1$ and $D2$ from the definition of the trusted bridge (as shown in Fig. 1) will be used to illustrate concepts.

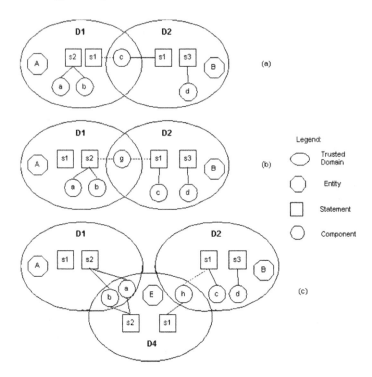

Fig. 2. Methods of bridging trusted domains

a. Use existing component (Fig.2.a.)

The analysis itself may lead to the discovery that there is already an existing component that may be trusted by more than one domain. Even though such solution may seem trivial, it is the trust-based analysis itself that is frequently needed. For example (Fig.2.a), as the domains *D1* and *D2* share the same defining statement *s1*, it is sufficient to verify that the component *c* (currently within the domain *D2*) that fulfills the statement *s1* is accepted also by *D1*.

b. Create new component (Fig.2.b.)

If the bridging component does not exist it is possible to create it. Some components may conform to only one statement so that they require the identical statement in both domains. Some components may conform to more than one statement so that they can be used to bridge the domains with different statements. Note that the meaning of the identity of defining statements requires further discussion that goes beyond the scope of this paper.

The use of multi-statement component has been already demonstrated at the intersection of the domains *D2* and *D3*. Such solution is also viable for the domains *D1* and *D2*, e.g. in a form of a component *g* that conforms to both the statements *s2* and *s1*, as shown in Fig.2.b.

c. Create separate domain (Fig.2.c.)

If there is no potential component that may satisfy the domains (e.g. the statements are significantly different), the solution may be to create a separate domain such that its domain components fulfill statements from both disjoint domains. Such domain may share existing or new components with all the domains it is bridging. The authors call the created domain as bridging domain.

For example, domain *D4* can be introduced to bridge disjoint domains *D1* and *D2*. Domain *D4* consists of the entity *E* and three components: the existing components *a* and *b* that conform to the statement *s2* and is trusted also by the *D1* and a new component *h* that conforms to the statement *s1* and is trusted also by the *D2*.

If necessary, the creation of the new domain can be repeated to form the chain of domains until the bridging is complete, i.e. until there is at least one chain of domains that links all the domains that were originally disjoint. Obviously, it is possible to get multiple solutions to bridge trusted domains. It depends on further analysis and concrete systems requirements to decide which one is the best.

The authors further propose the PTD that could be implemented by a mobile phone to work as the trusted bridge for the purpose of the mobile communications. It is obvious that the PTD which is the platform that is possibly trusted by both the user and the operator can be deployed as a component that satisfies almost all domain entities in the mobile communication systems.

It is significant that this methodology can also be applied into any system analysis and design. It provides a special approach on security analysis from the trust point of view. Based on the analysis, it is clear to know what is lacked and therefore needed in the system. It will be also potentially easier to find the proper component with appropriate technologies to bridge the trust gap that otherwise may cause the security problems. Therefore, this methodology helps us to set up a secure and trusted system and aids us to seek new business opportunities, e.g. via seeking the proper trusted bridges to find new products or novel functions.

5 Applicability

In this section, the authors will illustrate how to apply the proposed methodology into different scenarios and expound how the PTD can work as the trusted bridge to overlay the trust gaps among the trusted domains in the mobile communications.

Note that this chapter does not aim at providing complete solutions but merely to illustrate the methodology. The outcome, even though it actually conforms to historical information, should not be considered the only or the perfect solution for analyzed cases.

5.1 Mobile Trust Interaction (inside Mobile Terminal)

This case demonstrates the use of approach (a) - discovery of the existing component that can be used to bridge the domains.

Looking inside today's mobile terminals, we are facing the trust gap problem. The issue of interaction between a security element (SE) (such as a smart card, e.g. SIM) and terminal based applications has been discussed for a very long time. The lack of general solution has been slowing the development of possible exciting applications, especially in mobile commerce. The problem lies in the trust deficiency between the SE and the terminal-executed applications, such as Java MIDlets, Symbian applications and web pages.

The recent development of signed applications (e.g. Symbian application, OMA (Open Mobile Alliance) signed content and MIDP (Mobile Information Device Profile) 2.0 environment) has brought new interesting aspect into such scenario.

The common perception across the industry is as follows. The terminal application and the SE come from different trusted domains established by different entities. The signed application (e.g. a MIDlet) is trusted by its developer, which is expressed by the fact that the developer signs the application. The smart card, a SE, is trusted by the card developer. Finally, the user of mobile device basically trusts what he/she sees at the device.

All the three trusted domains enter the terminal and meet there when the application attempts to access the SE, which is usually combined with certain user interaction. Those trust domains should overlap somewhere, where the interaction between the application, the SE and the user are in place. However, one problem is that they do not overlap because there is no method to introduce the sufficient trust among those domains of those entities.

Implementing the proposed methodology, the following observations can be made, leading to the complete picture as shown in Fig.3.

1. The application developer trusts his application (*s1*) as it is him who developed it. Further, the application developer trusts (*s2*) the signing process usually derived from the PKI (Public Key Infrastructure) technology and the implementation of delivery and verification mechanisms for installing and running the application on the mobile terminal.
2. The card developer trusts the card due to its tamper-resistance (*s3*) while he/she does not necessarily trust any particular cryptographic system. The card developer trusts also the same terminal (*s4*) regarding its ability to convey correctly messages between the application and the card as well as regarding the correct handling of the user interaction.
3. The user trusts in what he/she sees on the terminal (*s5*). This trust is not based on any particular technology, but on the combination of several psychological factors.

Note that the methodology has immediately discovered three hidden statements, all applying to the terminal. Even though the three trusted domains are driven by different statements, all of them share the same component: the terminal that can be the mobile PTD. Therefore the PTD can potentially serve as the bridge to overlay the trust gap, e.g. by defining the access control mechanisms so that only certified applications can access designated objects on the card via the interaction with the user.

5.2 Mobile Services

The case of mobile services is used here to demonstrate the approach (b) - identifying the new common component.

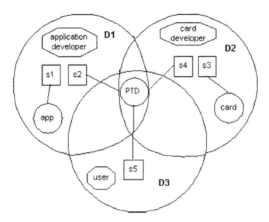

Fig. 3. Mobile trust interaction inside mobile terminal

The term 'mobile services' can be vaguely defined as services that are provided to mobile users via the mobile terminals, e.g. messaging, browsing, and shopping. Specifically, the mobile terminals such as the mobile phones and mobile PDAs (Personal Digital Assistants) are considered to be the key element of mobile services. The key problem of mobile services seems to be the identification of the user for the purpose of service delivery and billing.

As the mobile phone has already had the trust relationship ($s1$) with its operator through the existence of SIM and relevant authentication methods, the analysis leads to the outcome depicted in Fig.4 (solid lines and plain text only). Naturally the users trust their terminals ($s2$) mostly due to the good reputation of terminal manufacturers. The service provider stays out of the usual trust relationship due to the fact that no component in possession of the user falls into its domain D2.

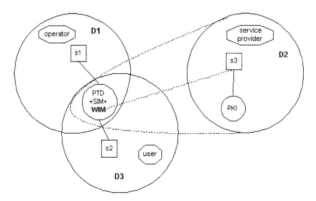

Fig. 4. Trust interaction in mobile services

The service providers have been creative to overcome the trust gap, e.g. by going with the operators and re-using the existing authentication and billing infrastructure. By doing this, the service providers effectively moved themselves into the operator's domain. Alternatively they established the independent component with the users through the sign-in process (e.g. a password), even though it has led to several inconveniences for the user.

An analysis revealed that the service provides who are not willing to move into the operator's domain are expressing significant trust in PKI technologies (*s3*). However, the use of such technologies requires an independent identification element in the terminal. Such element can be established in a form of a second card, WIM, sharing the same terminal with the SIM, as depicted on Fig.4 (dotted lines and bold text). The re-designed mobile terminal, essentially realized by the PTD, can therefore bridge the trust gap.

This scenario also demonstrates that not all solutions that are technologically sound may easily enter market. Despite of the existence of dual chip phones they are not the most popular solution for the mobile services. Alternative solutions like SWIM (Subscriber and WAP Identity Module) where SIM and WIM reside in the same card or 'white WIM' where the blank smart card owned by the user is issued to the phone are also not popular. The complete analysis of such solutions from the trust perspective that may deliver interesting observations is unfortunately beyond the scope of this paper.

5.3 Mobile Ad Hoc Networks (MANET)

This use case demonstrates the method (c) - introduction of new domains to bridge the disjoint domains.

Ad hoc networks are a new paradigm of networks offering unrestricted mobility without any underlying infrastructure. The mobile ad hoc network (MANET) is a collection of autonomous nodes or terminals that communicate with each other over relatively bandwidth-constrained wireless links. Since the nodes are mobile, the network topology may change rapidly and unpredictably over time. The network is decentralized. Thus all network activities including discovery of the topology and delivery of messages must be executed by the nodes themselves, i.e., routing functionality will be incorporated into the mobile nodes. The MANETs are generally more prone to physical security threats. The possibility of eavesdropping, spoofing, denial-of-service, and impersonation attacks increases. Significant applications of the MANETs include establishing survivable, efficient, dynamic communications for emergency/rescue operations, disaster relief efforts, and military networks that cannot rely on centralized and organized connectivity.

The problem studied here is the identification of the nodes constructed by ad hoc terminals. It is one of the most important problems of the ad hoc network, which effectively prevents such networks from wide deployment.

Applying the proposed methodology one can produce the graph as depicted in Fig.5 (solid lines and plain text only). Each node is effectively an island for itself, driven by its own statement. For example, if the node is in the possession of the user (user 1 in domain *D1*), statement (*s1*) may base on the trust on reputable brand or shared password. The nodes that reside in a corporate building attached to certain devices (domain *D2*), may be trusted by corporation (user 2) because of its semi-permanent supervised location (*s2*).

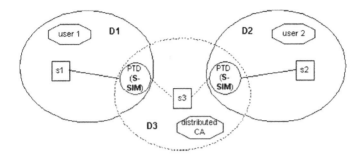

Fig. 5. Trust interaction of identification in ad hoc networks

As the nodes cannot trust each other regarding their identities, they cannot establish any meaningful service. Further, the methodology demonstrates that in the general case there is nothing in common between two nodes except for their communication capabilities. In such case the introduction of additional domain seems to solve the problem.

The authors propose to introduce the bridging domain created by a distributed CA introduced in [17] that trusts its authentication system (*s3*). The CA converts nodes into multi-statement-supported devices by adding an authentication component that can be a SIM signed by the distributed CA (called here S-SIM), as illustrated in Fig.5 (dotted lines and bold text). A centralized CA (e.g. the operator) can also work for the initialization of the ad hoc network via issuing the authentication component (e.g. S-SIM) and distributing partial secrets to the nodes. The signature signed by over a threshold number of nodes can be treated as valid. Those nodes may cooperate to behave as a distributed CA in the future, because the centralized CA most possibly may lose contact with the nodes after the network starts running. In that case, the distributed CA acted by the nodes themselves will start to play the role of CA as an essential backup.

Another challenge in the ad hoc network is that every node has to depend on other nodes to delivery data package, including routing information. At the same time every node must not readily trust any other nodes because they are more easily to be captured, compromised and hijacked. Further, attacks raised from malicious nodes inside the network are much harder to detect as they hold the correct identities.

As stated above, this use case is the illustration of the methodology, not the solution of the security problem in the ad hoc networks. Other solutions that can be derived from the same methodology can be considered as well. Specifically, trust evaluation may be of some interest, as shortly described below.

Instead of aiming at perfect identity and full trust, the node may live with partial trust because the identity can be spoofed. Based on the work in [1, 4], the trust can be evaluated and processed digitally by quantifying its variables such as transaction cost, transaction history, recommendations and reputation data. The authors hold opinion that the above trust evaluation should be conducted digitally ahead of any communication and the evaluation result should be considered for better security decision. This mechanism should be embedded into every ad hoc terminal.

Note that the node terminal fitted with the identification mechanism (such as the S-SIM) and the trust evaluation mechanism can be realized by the PTD that behaves as the trusted bridge in the ad hoc networks.

6   Conclusions

In this paper, the authors introduced a methodology to bridge the domains of trust in mobile communications. It has been proposed that any system analysis and design could include modeling the system as composed of different trusted domains that may reflect various reasons for the trust. Inside the domain, the trust relationship has been established, while among domains the trust is deficient. Thus in this way, it is easier to identify the trust and security problems hidden inside the system. In order to bridge the trust gaps, the authors further proposed three approaches and illustrate their applicability through the real industry cases.

Based on this study, it has been found that the PTD, such as the mobile phone, plays an important role in the mobile communications and transactions. It is in a unique position contributing to the system trust and security by overlaying the trust gaps among various the trusted domains with corresponding functionalities. The special role of the PTD to establish the trust claims that it fully deserves its name as the Personal Trusted Device. The applicability study further proves that the methodology is generic and helpful in the analysis and design of various mobile systems. The authors believe that it can also be applied into other areas to solve similar issues.

References

1. Diamadi, Z. Fischer, M.J.: A simple game for the study of trust in distributed systems. International Software Engineering Symposium 2001 (ISES'01), Wuhan University Journal of Natural Sciences Conference (March 2001).
2. Diego Gambetta.: Can We Trust Trust?. In, Trust: Making and breaking Cooperative Relations, Gambetta, D (ed.) Basil Blackwell. Oxford, (1990).
3. Daniel W. Manchala: Xerox Research and Technology. E-Commerce Trust Metrics and Models. IEEE Internet Computing, vol.4, no.2 p.36–44 (2000).
4. McKnight, D. Harrison, Chervany Norman L.: The meanings of Trust. In <http://www.misrc.umn.edu/wpaper/wp96-04.htm>
5. McKnight, D. Harrison, Chervany Norman L.: What is Trust? A Conceptual Analysis and An Interdisciplinary Model. In Proceedings of the 2000 Americas Conference on Information Systems (AMCI2000). AIS, Long Beach, CA (August 2000).
6. Mui Lik, Mohtashemi Mojdeh, Halberstadt Ari: A Computational Model of Trust and Reputation. In Proc. Of the 35th Annual Hawaii International Conference on System sciences, 7–10 (Jan. 2002), Big Island, HI, USA
7. Warne, D., Holland, C.P.: Exploring trust in flexible working using a new model. BT Technology Journal, vol.17, no.1, p.111–119. (Jan 1999).

8. Yao-Hua Tan. Thoen, W.: Toward a generic model of trust for electronic commerce. International Journal of Electronic Commerce vol.5, no.2, p.61–74.
9. Egger Florian N.: Towards a Model of Trust for E-Commerce System Design. In Proc. Of the CHI2000 Workshop: Designing Interactive Systems for 1-to-1 E-commerce.
10. Abdul-Rahman Alfarez, Halles Stephen: A Distributed Trust Model. In Proc. Of New Security Paradigms Workshop, ACM, New York, NY, USA (1998).
11. Gerck Ed. Overview of Certification System: X.509, PKIX, CA, PGP & SKIP. In <http://www.thebell.net/papers/certover.pdf>
12. Perlman, R.: An overview of PKI trust models. IEEE Network, vol.13, no.6 p.38–43.
13. Robles, S., Borrell, J., Bigham, J., Tokarchuk, L., Cuthbert, L.: Design of a trust model for a secure multi-agent marketplace, Fifth International Conference on Autonomous Agents, Montreal, Canada (05.2001).
14. Wu Wen, Mizoguchi, F.: An authorization-based trust model for multiagent systems, Applied Artificial Intelligence vol.14, no.9 p.909–25.
15. Mayer, R.C., Davis, J.H., Schoorman, F.D.: An Integrative Model of Organizational Trust, Academy of Management Review, Vol. 20, No 3, pp. 709–734 (1995).
16. MeT Personal Trusted Device Definition (2001) <http://www.mobiletransaction.org/pdf/R11/MeT-PTD-Def-R11.pdf>
17. L. Zhou, Z. J. Haas: Securing Ad Hoc Networks. IEEE Network, 13(6): 24–30 (Nov/Dec 1999).

A Subjective Approach to Routing in P2P and Ad Hoc Networks

Andrew Twigg

Computer Laboratory, Cambridge University, UK
andrew.twigg@cl.cam.ac.uk

Abstract. This paper presents a subjective approach to routing in peer-to-peer and ad hoc networks. The main difference between our approach and traditional routing models is the use of a trust model to mediate the risk inherent in routing decisions. Rather than blindly exchanging routing table entries, nodes 'discount' recommendations from other nodes using a distributed trust computation which allows them to avoid malicious, faulty and unreliable nodes and links in routing decisions. Adding the risk model allows energy-efficient routing decisions to be made in a wireless network, and we show how our model can be optimized for different network behaviours, including wireless networks. The model is described in the context of the DSR [1] routing algorithm, although it is equally-applicable to others, including peer-to-peer routing substrates.

1 Introduction

The game of chinese whispers is often played by a group of children (the *nodes*) sitting in a circle (the *route*). One such node (the *source*) whispers something (the *packet*) to the next node on the route, which is supposed to forward it to the next node. This continues until the packet reaches the node at the end of the route (the *destination*). At school, the source and destination are often the same, heightening the dramatic effect when the packet has been corrupted[1].

An ad hoc network has no fixed infrastructure, and the lack of implicitly trusted routers means that each node becomes part of the routing fabric. Hence the network is collaborative, since successful operation relies on nodes correctly forwarding packets which may have no direct benefit for themselves. Routing in such a network is similar to a game of chinese whispers where an entity (mobile node) must rely on other intermediate nodes to correctly forward the packet to the destination, yet in general, the intermediate nodes may have no prior contact with the sender.

In this paper, we describe how a source node can choose routes to minimize the disruption to the packets it wishes to send, by *avoiding* certain nodes. The approach is rather different to traditional routing methods. We develop a trust model that can be used to reason explicitly about routing choices and the nodes

---

[1] ScoutBase UK [www.scoutbase.org.uk/activity/games/pages/whispers.htm] report that 'once we started with "we have a new car" and ended with "someone ate a brand new car".'

P. Nixon and S. Terzis (Eds.): Trust Management 2003, LNCS 2692, pp. 225–238, 2003.

and links which constitute them. Rather than reasoning objectively, we operate in the domain of subjective logic [2] which permits uncertainty in probabilities, so nodes form *opinions* rather than storing observations. Our main contribution is that, rather than blindly exchanging routing table entries, nodes can 'discount' these recommendations from other nodes using a distributed trust computation that takes into account others' opinions about the recommender, hence avoiding both malicious and unreliable nodes and links.

The second contribution of this work is in using the trust model to mediate the risks associated with routing decisions. In a wireless ad hoc network, this allows nodes to make informed routing decisions by trading energy requirements against the reliability of a route. The work is based on a trust-based extension to the dynamic source routing algorithm presented in [3], and the work on establishing trust in peer-to-peer systems in [4,5]. Secure routing protocols for similar problems are presented in [6,7,8], though we want to consider the less 'traditional' secure notion of trust, as in [9].

The remainder of this paper is organised as follows. Section 2 briefly describes our network model, Section 3 develops the trust model and Section 4 outlines how it can be integrated with a risk model. A major part of the paper (Section 3.3) develops an inference procedure, which attempts to identify the unreliable nodes and links, given that we can only observe aggregate properties of routes.

2   Network Model

We model a *network* $\mathcal{N}$ as a set of *nodes* and a set of *links* between pairs of nodes, where packets can be sent bidirectionally across links. We model network behaviour by initially assuming that packets can be dropped at nodes only (irrespective of their source or destination). However, we show in Section 3.5 how to adapt our model to apply under the assumption that packets are instead dropped at links, which may be more useful when operating in a wireless network.

In this paper we only consider source routing, such as the dynamic source routing algorithm (DSR) [1] which is designed for mobile ad-hoc networks and forms the basis for the trust work in [3]. To send a packet from r_1 to r_n requires that the source r_1 compute the entire route $r = \langle r_1, r_2, \ldots, r_n \rangle$ and embed it into the packet. In DSR [1], each node maintains a route cache of recently used[2] routes, indexed by destination. The cache is maintained in response to changing topologies by sending 'route request' packets or 'snooping' on others' route request packets. Other types of protocol include 'hop-by-hop' (where the route is not established at source), which we hope to consider later. A good survey of peer-to-peer and ad hoc routing techniques is presented in [10].

In DSR, a 'route error' packet is sent to the source (or a timeout occurs) when the packet could not be delivered, due to an intermediate or destination node being unreachable, or as the result of an intermediate node dropping the packet (or even faking the route error packet). Such packets form the basis of the observations upon which our trust model is built.

---

[2] The cache replacement algorithm is not fixed, although LRU is often used.

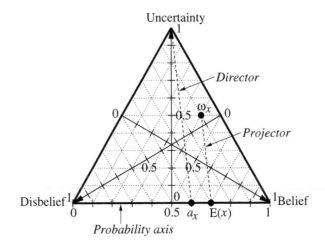

Fig. 1. The opinion space Ω showing the opinion $\omega_x = (0.4, 0.1, 0.5)$ as an example. The 'weight' of the opinion is $a_x = 0.6$, which is used to determine the expectated value $E(x)$ since the *projector* lies parallel to the *director*

3   Trust Model

"Trust is a precious commodity; easily damaged but difficult to mend."

3.1   Trust Values

Before developing the trust model, we present a few brief definitions. *Trust values* are elements of a complete lattice $(T, \leq)$, P is the set of *principals* and the *trust space* T is a partial function $\mathcal{T} : (P \rightharpoonup T)$. Initially, let P be the set of nodes in the network, hence $\mathcal{T}(u) \in T$ is our trust in node u. In Section 3.5 we show a use for other definitions of P.

How does one assign meaning to T? A starting point is to follow [3] and take trust values to be arbitrary scalars $\in [0, 1]$ where $0, 1$ represent complete distrust and trust, respectively. Using arbitrary values (in the sense that they do not represent any measurable quantity) presents problems in both understanding and analysis. Asking 'what does it mean for a node to have trustworthiness 0.5?' become subjects of philosophical debate, and asking 'how should I update the trustworthiness of a node given it performed action a in context Γ with outcome o' are open to subjective interpretation.

Subjective Logic. We take elements of T to be *opinions* in subjective logic [2]. An *opinion* $\omega = (b, d, u)$ is an element in the Barycentric *opinion space* Ω shown in Figure 1, where $b, d, u \in [0, 1]$ represent belief, disbelief and uncertainty, respectively, and $b + d + u = 1$. The horizontal line representing $u = 0$ is the *probability axis* and represents situations without uncertainty (*dogmatic* opinions), equivalent to a traditional probability model. Uncertainty is caused by lack of evidence to support either belief or disbelief, and so the opinion space provides a way of continuously distinguishing between notions of 'unknown', $(0, 0, 1)$ and 'least trust', $(0, 1, 0)$. Observations are made in the *evidence space* Φ and are transformed into the opinion space using a simple bijection, derived in [2]. Let $\varphi_r^v = (x, y)$ be an *observation* by principal v about route r where x, y are the numbers of successful and unsuccessful packet transmissions, respectively. Let the opinion corresponding to φ be $\omega(\varphi) = (b, d, u)$ where

$$b = x/(x + y + r) \tag{1}$$
$$d = y/(x + y + r) \tag{2}$$
$$u = r/(x + y + r) \tag{3}$$

where $r \geq 1$ is a parameter controlling the rate of loss of uncertainty, which can be used to tune the use of uncertainty in the model for the requirements of different scenarios (we often take $r = 1$).

Given the above and the trust space, we say that $\mathcal{T}(v)$ is our *opinion* about the proposition 'principal v forwards packets successfully', based on observations on routes containing v. We make use of three operators on opinions, the definitions of which are reproduced in Appendix A.

Unknown principals. The opinion space helps overcome the problem of unknown principals being associated with 'least trust', by assigning them the opinion $\omega = (0, 0, 1)$. As a metric to order opinions, Jøsang [2] suggests computing the expected probability value by projecting the opinion onto the probability axis, parallel to the director (see Figure 1). If the director cuts the axis at ρ ($\rho = 0.6$ in the Figure), then $E(\{b, d, u\}) = (b + u)/(b + d + u/\rho)$.

The meaning of this is to assign a 'newcomer' principal with $\mathcal{T}(v) = (0, 0, 1)$ the expectation ρ, whilst maintaining independence between the notions of 'unknown' and 'untrusted'. One could also take ρ as the expectation of some distribution representing all the current principals' expectations.

3.2   Building the Trust Model

To make a good estimate of the trust space $\mathcal{T}$, one needs a good inference procedure and a good set of observations (and, implicitly, a good way of gathering them).

The Need for Inference. In our model, observations can be made only on routes. Rather than take P to be the set of routes, we make use of an inference procedure whose job is to make estimations about *principals* given observations on *routes*. By using knowledge about principals on other routes, opinions about new unused routes can be formed.

An *inference procedure* Θ maps observations on routes to opinions about principals, i.e. $\Theta : \Phi \to (P \to \Omega)$ where Φ is the evidence space and Ω is the opinion space. Separating the inference procedure from the trust computation allows each node to have its own procedure, for example some nodes could become authorities on recommendations because they have the power to perform stronger inference, whereas nodes with less power can perform weaker inference. An inference procedure based on a least mean-squares error approach is developed in Section 3.3.

Gathering observations. A useful strategy is to supplement a node's direct observations with observations from other nodes, known as *recommendations*. Recommendations are made by piggypacking some observations onto the routing table entries (RTEs) returned in response to a route request packet. A typical set of routing table entries returned from a node v would be as in Figure 2.

$$\left\{ \left(\text{route A}, \varphi^v_{\text{route A}}\right), \left(\text{route B}, \varphi^v_{\text{route B}}\right), \left(\text{route C}, \varphi^v_{\text{route C}}\right) \right\}$$

Fig. 2. Making recommendations: route observations are piggybacked onto the routing table entries (RTEs) returned from a node v, in response to a route request packet

The advantage of using recommendations is that it removes the need to store and explore many routes, and reduces the chance that little can be inferred about a route's trustworthiness. However, we must deal with the fact that principals may lie (making bad inferences is not a problem since only direct observations are communicated).

The gathering of recommendations via the route request mechanism can be used in conjunction with a strategy for separately gathering recommendations by sending dummy packets (though one needs to consider the extra network traffic incurred). Some strategies will provide a higher amount of information than others, but this is difficult to quantify as it depends on the inference procedure too. One approach might be to gather recommendations along routes which currently have a high uncertainty, or when a node moves into a new region of space. A promising approach is to make *direct observations* of increasing length along a route (e.g. r_1 then r_1, r_2 then r_1, r_2, r_3 etc.) by sending out dummy packets.

Malicious and Colluding Principals. There are two types of threat from malicious and colluding principals. Malicious principals can collude to attempt to make each other look more trustworthy. Alternatively, principals can try to make other principals appear malicious by spreading bad recommendations. In the trust computation, we assume that principals are rational in the game-theoretic sense, i.e. that a principal makes true recommendations if they forward packets (and are trustworthy), and attempts to hide their misbehaviour by making false recommendations if they do not forward packets (and are untrustworthy). Hence $\mathcal{T}(v)$ is an appropriate discounting for the credibility of v's alleged observations.

The trust computation ensures that recommendations from colluding nodes are heavily discounted (effectively ignored) unless one of the following holds:

1. Principals we trust make good recommendations on a colluding principal;
2. We make good direct observations on a colluding principal.

Under the game-theoretic assumption, these both fail unless we also collude. In practice, a principal in a clique of colluding principals can build up one's trust by forwarding packets correctly, then use this to falsely make good observations about the others in the clique (and violating our assumption). Whether or not the assumption will be valid in reality remains a point of discussion, particularly with regard to faulty (misconfigured) principals.

One can avoid making the assumption by using separate trust spaces for 'participation' (forwarding packets) and 'recommendation' (the ability to make accurate recommendations) as in [?]. Taking this approach complicates the trust computation, but can easily be integrated into the model presented here.

Trust computation. Here we describe the local trust computation carried out at each node. Let Θ be the inference procedure used. The trust space $\mathcal{T}$ is described by an iterative fixpoint computation over the set of observations $\{\varphi^w\}$ (both our direct observations and recommendations from other nodes), as below:

$$\mathcal{T}(v) = \bigoplus_{\varphi^w} \{\mathcal{T}(w) \otimes \Theta\left(\varphi^w\right)(v)\} \tag{4}$$

where $\oplus$ is the *Bayesian consensus* operator (to combine opinions), and $\otimes$ is the *discounting* operator, defined in Appendix A.

A more descriptive view of Equation (4) is that we are trying to determine the trust value (our opinion) of principal v. Given the set of direct observations and recommendations, we apply our inference procedure to obtain opinions on principals. To account for false recommendations, these opinions are discounted by our opinion of their observer (under the assumption made earlier), and the resulting opinions combined using the consensus operator. But v's trust value affects the weighting of v's observations, and so on. The solution is analogous to eigen problems in sparse graphs (such as the WWW), so techniques similar to PageRank [11] can be employed to solve it. A similar computation and its approximate solution is described in [4]. Note that node v's direct observations are discounted by v's opinion of itself.

A consequence of having to *infer* trust values from observations, in a distributed context, is that each node may estimate the trust values in a different way, based on the same observations. It would be interesting to see if this leads to greater subjective variation of trust throughout the system (as in real life).

3.3   Inference: Spreading the Blame

The goal of this section is to develop an inference procedure to estimate principals' *prior* behaviours from *a priori* observations on routes. Assume one makes the observation $\varphi_r = (x, y)$. What can be concluded? Given no prior information about principals, the fairest is to assume each principal behaved equally badly. Perhaps an obvious solution would be to distribute the observation by uniformly shifting the uncertainty component in the opinion of each principal on the route. But the number of observations on a principal that a route observation provides decreases exponentially from the source, since each principal drops some *proportion* of its packets along the way and so fewer packets reach nodes further along the route. This section presents a theory for spreading the 'blame' or 'praise' among nodes, and uses a least-mean squares error approach.

Our inference consists of two parts. We first estimate the most likely *packet-level* behaviour of principals then use these to form new opinions on principals. An opinion about a route r can then be formed as the conjunction of the opinions of nodes in r. Consider the observation $\varphi_r = (x, y)$ along the route $r = \langle r_0, r_1, \ldots, r_n, r_{n+1} \rangle$ (where r_0 is the source and r_{n+1} the destination). Let the total number of observations, $T = x + y$. We 'explain' the observation by assuming each principal r_i successfully transmitted a *proportion* α_i of its packets, for the duration of the observation.

First, consider the behaviour of node r_1. Since T packets enter r_1 and α_1 are dropped, the estimated observation is $\varphi_{r_1} = (\alpha_1 T, (1 - \alpha_1)T)$. For principal r_2 the situation is similar, since $(\alpha_1 T)$ packets are expected to leave r_1 and r_2 is expected to successfully forward a proportion α_2 of them. Hence we have the expected observations for each principal

$$\varphi_{r_1} = (\alpha_1 T, (1 - \alpha_1)T)$$
$$\varphi_{r_2} = (\alpha_1 \alpha_2 T, (1 - \alpha_2)\alpha_1 T)$$
$$\vdots$$
$$\varphi_{r_i} = \left(\prod_{j=1}^{i} \alpha_j T, (1 - \alpha_i) \prod_{j=1}^{i-1} \alpha_j T \right)$$

One can check that this does in fact explain the observation, since $(\prod_{j=1}^{n} \alpha_j T) = x$ packets leave r_n, as observed. Transforming these from the evidence space to the opinion space gives the opinions

$$\omega(\varphi_{r_1}) = \left(\frac{\alpha_1 T}{T + 1}, \frac{(1 - \alpha_1)T}{T + 1}, \frac{1}{T + 1} \right)$$
$$\omega(\varphi_{r_2}) = \left(\frac{\alpha_1 \alpha_2 T}{\alpha_1 T + 1}, \frac{(1 - \alpha_2)\alpha_1 T}{\alpha_1 T + 1}, \frac{1}{\alpha_1 T + 1} \right)$$
$$\vdots$$
$$\omega(\varphi_{r_i}) = \left(\frac{\prod_{j=1}^{i} \alpha_j T}{\prod_{j=1}^{i-1} \alpha_j T + 1}, \frac{(1 - \alpha_i) \prod_{j=1}^{i-1} \alpha_j T}{\prod_{j=1}^{i-1} \alpha_j T + 1}, \frac{1}{\prod_{j=1}^{i-1} \alpha_j T + 1} \right)$$

This procedure can be seen as shifting the unknown component of the opinions, but relative to the expected number of observations made on a node. An interesting result is that one has to make around $(1/\prod_{j=1}^{n} \alpha_j)$ times as many observations to achieve an equal reduction in the unknown of the nth node, compared to the unknown in the 1st node. This implies that the learning rate increases with the α's, i.e. our opinions will be less uncertain when observing well-behaved routes. A similar argument can be made for shorter routes, since an observation is spread less thinly over the nodes on the route. Together, these suggest a strategy that a node should use to gather observations in order to maximise its 'information gain'.

Estimating the behaviours: picking the α_i's. So far we have not discussed how the α_i's are chosen. To *correctly* explain the observation, we must satisfy the constraint $\prod_{i=1}^{n} \alpha_i = (x/T)$. A good start would be to assume no prior knowledge of the current principals' behaviours and hence that all principals behaved equally, that is $\alpha_1 = \alpha_2 = \cdots = (x/T)^{1/n}$.

Let us now take into account the current opinions about principals. For example, if we currently have high belief in r_1 and high disbelief in r_2 and make (or receive) an observation with high disbelief, the 'best' explanation is that which most closely resembles our current opinions: that r_1 behaved well and r_2 behaved badly, rather than penalising them both equally. We now try to make this approach more formal.

Let $\beta_i \in [0,1]$ be the expected value of the current opinion of principal r_i. We want to approximate (in the least squares error sense) the β_i's with a set of α_i's (whilst obeying the constraint). Our approach is to renormalize the opinions such that they satisfy the constraint, which effectively performs a *ratio scaling* on the β's. We conjecture that by minimizing the total square change in our current opinions (β's), the least mean square error is also minimized.

The argument is as follows. Our current β's don't satisfy the constraint (if they do, then $\alpha_i = \beta_i$). Hence we can write

$$\prod_{i=1}^{n} \beta_i \neq (x/T) \tag{5}$$

Taking logs gives

$$\log \prod_{i=1}^{n} \beta_i \neq \log(x/T) \tag{6}$$

Now consider the actual value of the LHS of Equation 6; some unique $d \neq \log(x/T)$. Therefore

$$\log \prod_{i=1}^{n} \beta_i = d \neq \log(x/T) \tag{7}$$

Let $\kappa = \log(x/T)/\log \prod_{i=1}^{n} \beta_i$. Multiplying Equation (7) by κ, simplifying then removing the logs gives

$$\kappa \log \prod_{i=1}^{n} \beta_i = \log(x/T) \tag{8}$$

$$\prod_{i=1}^{n} \beta_i^{\kappa} = (x/T) \tag{9}$$

and hence $\alpha_i = \beta_i^{\kappa}$ where $\kappa = \log(x/T)/\log \prod_{i=1}^{n} \beta_i$.

One can easily check this is a generalisation of the special case described earlier. In fact, the case appears whenever our prior opinions of each principal are equal, not just when there is no knowledge. Setting $\beta_1 = \beta_2 = \cdots = \beta$:

$$\alpha_i = \beta^{\log(x/T)/\log \beta^n} \tag{10}$$

$$= \beta^{\frac{1}{n}\log_\beta(x/T)} \tag{11}$$

$$= \left(\beta^{\log_\beta(x/T)}\right)^{1/n} \tag{12}$$

$$= (x/T)^{1/n} \tag{13}$$

Finally, our inference procedure is as follows. Given an observation φ_r, it computes opinions for each principal (node) on the route r (except the source and destination). All other principals are assigned the 'unknown' opinion $\omega = (0, 0, 1)$.

Related approaches. Using arbitrary trust values naturally leads to arbitrary inference procedures. Consider the approach taken in [3]; if the packet was lost, the source node has no way of determining which node in r caused the fault, hence the best it can do is to decrease the trust value of each node on the route. Even ignoring this uniform distribution of blame and the fact that more observations are made on nodes closer to the source, no 'correct' update procedure is obvious. In practice, the values are updated 'exponentially', i.e. for a successful transmission $t = t + (1 - t)/20$ and for an unsuccessful transmission $t = t - t/20$ for each node on the route. It is difficult to make anything other than an empirical case for this procedure, and it stems from using arbitrary trust values.

3.4   Selecting Routes

Recall $\mathcal{T}(v)$ is our opinion about the proposition 'principal v forwards packets successfully'. We can form an opinion about a route $r = \langle r_0, r_1, r_2, \ldots, r_n, r_{n+1}\rangle$ by combining opinions about principals using the *conjunction* operator, $\wedge$ [2]:

$$\omega_r = \mathcal{T}(r_1) \wedge \mathcal{T}(r_2) \wedge \cdots \wedge \mathcal{T}(r_n) \tag{14}$$

The remaining problem is ordering opinions, to choose a route from those in the route cache. This is done by ordering routes according to their expected probability value $\mathrm{E}(\omega_r)$, as described in Section 3.1. To avoid overloading nodes with slightly higher trust values, the routes should be chosen with probability proportional to their relative trust expected probability values. This provides a form of trust-based load balancing, and gives previously untrusted nodes a chance to redeem themselves.

3.5   A Better Model for Wireless Networks

So far the set of principals has been the set of nodes (the *network principal space*), and we have assumed the *weak network model* where packets are dropped

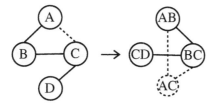

Principal=Node   Principal=Undirected link

Fig. 3. Optimising the model for wireless networks: to model the behaviour where packets are dropped on links rather than at nodes, the principal space is transformed. In the network on the left, principals represent nodes. The network on the right is equivalent in that principals are now the links from the original network. Applying the trust model to the new 'network' allows it to reason about link, rather than node, behaviours. The dashed edges show the effect of adding the physical link $A \to C$

only at nodes. Yet often it is the links rather than nodes which are the cause of network disruption, and this is particularly true for wireless networks - contrast this with the Internet, where the large distances between hops and a reliable medium mean that malicious or faulty nodes are the major concern.

We now show how the same routing model can be used in the *undirected-link network model*, where packets can be dropped at individual links rather than nodes (this corresponds to a stronger 'adversary'). This assumption can be modelled by taking P to be the set of links as in Figure 3. The source routing algorithm can be extended to include this transformation as follows. The request 'route from A to C' provides choices $\langle A, B, C \rangle$ and $\langle A, C \rangle$ from the route cache, as before. These are transformed into routes $\langle AB, BC \rangle$ and $\langle AC \rangle$ respectively in the model principal space (where a principal is an undirected link), about which opinions can now be formed as before. Observations are gathered in a similar way; an observation on a route $\langle B, C, D \rangle$ transforms to $\langle BC, CD \rangle$ in the model principal space and is handled as before.

We may consider an even stronger adversary which can block packets at links based on their direction (the *directed-link network model*), hence the model principal space induces a directed graph. More devious adversaries can block packets on links, based on the route taken *so far* of the packet. Such a network model can be simulated in the [un]directed-link network model where the model principal space is the set of possible routes to a node in the network, from all sources.

4   Risk

"There is no need to trust anyone unless there is risk involved."

Routing decisions based on trust need to be mediated by the risk of doing so. For example, less trust is needed to send a packet of low importance than to send a message whose safe arrival is critical. Previous works such as [3,4,?] consider

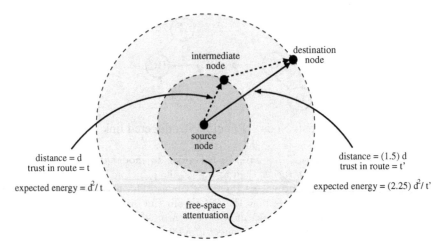

Fig. 4. Using trust to mediate the energy risks in wireless routing. Assuming Friss free-space attentuation, the energy needed for wireless transmission over distance d is proportional to d^2. The source node has two possible routes - the dashed route involving the intermediate node and the direct route. The dashed route requires less energy for the first hop, yet the direct route may have a higher probability of succeeding. Given the trust values t and t' of the routes and that the direct route is 50% further, which route should the source pick to minimize the expected energy required? Equating the two energy equations, we find the direct route is most energy-efficient if $t' \geq 2.25 \cdot t$, *i.e.* over twice as trustworthy

trust in complete isolation, and in this section we show how trust can mediate the risk-inherent action of sending packets.

Nodes in a wireless network often have limited battery power, so energy conservation is an important topic when considering routing decisions. In a sense, the *risk* to a node of sending a packet along a particular route is proportional to the energy needed to make the first hop, and the probability of that energy being 'wasted' (if the packet is not successfully sent). Since our trust values represent a meaningful quantity, *i.e.* the probability of a successful transmission, then the inverse represents the expected number of retransmissions, assuming retries are to the same node (although more complex schemes can be handled). We say that trust *mediates* the energy risks in wireless routing, as described in Figure 4.

We can also consider aggregate properties, including retransmissions and so on. Assuming that packets will be delivered after an infinite number of re-transmissions, consider the action 'send p to v within time t'. Our outcomes are likely to be {p delivered late, p delivered successfully} (the outcome 'p is not delivered' is not possible because of the retransmission assumption). Our policy will be to carry out the sub-action 'send p to node v' until we observe the outcome 'p successfully sent'. Assuming a geometric distribution, i.e. independent retransmissions[3], the expected time before we observe this is 'latency'$/(1 - \Pr($'p delivered successfully'$))$. This can be used to parameterise a distribution over the time, and calculate $\Pr($time $< t)$ from which the expected cost of the original action can be found, for a given route. This kind of reasoning permits one to justify *why* a particular route should be chosen.

5   Conclusion

This paper has presented a subjective approach to routing in peer-to-peer and ad hoc networks. The main difference between our approach and traditional routing models is the ability to reason subjectively about trust in the network through the use of opinions. Rather than blindly exchanging routing table entries, nodes can 'discount' these recommendations from other nodes using a distributed trust computation that takes into account others' opinions about the recommender. Hence malicious and faulty participants can be avoided. Finally, we showed how the model can be optimised for various uses, including wireless networks.

Source-routing algorithms such as DSR can easily be augmented with the model, and we hope to apply similar ideas to hop-by-hop algorithms such as Pastry [12].

Acknowledgements. The author wishes to thank Dave Gamble, David Ingram, Brian Shand and members of the Cambridge Computer Laboratory for interesting discussions and insightful comments. This work has been inspired by the EU-funded SECURE project (IST-2001-32486), part of the EU Global Computing initiative. As a result, the author thanks BRICS at Århus, Denmark for their initial work in developing a formal trust model [13]. The author is supported by BTexact Technologies and EPSRC.

References

1. Johnson, D., Maltz, D., Broch, J.: DSR: A dynamic source routing protocol for multihop wireless ad hoc networks. In: David B. Johnson, David A. Maltz, and Josh Broch. DSR The Dynamic Source Routing Protocol for Multihop Wireless Ad Hoc Networks. In Ad Hoc Networking, edited by Charles E. Perkins, chapter 5, pages 139–172. Addison-Wesley, 2001. (2001)
2. Jøsang, A.: A logic for uncertain probabilities. Available at citeseer.nj.nec.com/392196.html (2001)
3. Keane, J.: Trust based dynamic source routing in mobile ad hoc networks. msc. thesis, trinity college dublin. (2002)
4. Xiong, L., Liu, L.: Building trust in decentralized peer-to-peer electronic communities. In: Fifth International Conference on Electronic Commerce Research (ICECR-5), Canada. (2002)
5. Aberer, K., Despotovic, Z.: Managing trust in a peer-2-peer information system. In: CIKM. (2001) 310–317

---

[3] This is not quite true; the route may be switched if the trust values change enough during transmissions.

6. Awerbuch, B., Holmer, D., Nita-Rotaru, C., Rubens, H.: An on-demand secure routing protocol resilient to byzantine failures (2002)
7. Hu, Y., Perrig, A., Johnson, D.: Ariadne: A secure on-demand routing protocol for ad hoc networks (2002)
8. Hu, Y.C., Johnson, D.B., Perrig, A.: SEAD: Secure efficient distance vector routing in mobile wireless ad hoc networks. In: Fourth IEEE Workshop on Mobile Computing Systems and Applications (WMCSA '02). (2002) 3–13
9. Jøsang, A.: The right type of trust for distributed systems. In: C. Meadows, editor, Proc. of the 1996 New Security Paradigms Workshop. ACM, 1996. (1996)
10. Schollmeier, R., Gruber, I., Finkenzeller, M.: Routing in mobile ad hoc and peer-to-peer networks. a comparison (2002)
11. Page, L., Brin, S., Motwani, R., Winograd, T.: The pagerank citation ranking: Bringing order to the web. available as tech. Rep., computer science department, stanford university (1998)
12. Rowstron, A., Druschel, P.: Pastry: Scalable, distributed object location and routing for large-scale peer-to-peer systems. In: IFIP/ACM International Conference on Distributed Systems Platforms (Middleware). (2001) 329–350
13. Carbone, M., Danvy, O., Damgaard, I., Krukow, K., Møller, A., Nielsen, J.B., Nielsen, M.: A model for trust (2002) EU Project SECURE IST-2001-32486, Deliverable 1.1.

A   Subjective Logic Operator Definitions

Definition 1 (Bayesian Consensus). *Let* $\omega^A = (b^A, d^A, u^A)$ *and* $\omega^B = (b^B, d^B, u^B)$ *be opinions respectively held by prinicpals A and B about the same proposition. Let* $\omega^{A,B} = (b^{A,B}, d^{A,B}, u^{A,B})$ *be the opinion such that*

$$b^{A,B} = (b^A u^B + b^B u^A)/\kappa$$
$$d^{A,B} = (d^A u^B + d^B u^A)/\kappa$$
$$u^{A,B} = (u^A u^B)/\kappa$$

where $\kappa = 1 - (1 - u^A)(1 - u^B) = u^A + u^B - u^A u^B$ *such that* $\kappa \neq 0$ *(i.e.* u^A *and* u^B *cannot both be 0, otherwise one is trying to combine dogmatic opinions which leave no room for uncertainty). Then* $\omega^{A,B} = \omega^A \oplus \omega^B$ *is called the Bayesian consensus between* ω^A *and* ω^B. *Furthermore,* $\oplus$ *is commutative and associative.*

Definition 2 (Discounting). *Let* $\omega_B^A = (b_B^A, d_B^A, u_B^A)$ *be principal A's opinion about principal B, and let* $\omega_p^B = (b_p^B, d_p^B, u_p^B)$ *be B's opinion about some proposition p. Let* $\omega_p^{A:B} = (b_p^{A:B}, d_p^{A:B}, u_p^{A:B})$ *be the opinion such that*

$$b_p^{A:B} = b_B^A b_p^B$$
$$d_p^{A:B} = b_B^A d_p^B$$
$$u_p^{A:B} = d_B^A + u_B^A + b_B^A u_p^B$$

Then $\omega_p^{A:B} = \omega^A \otimes \omega^B$ *is called the discounting of* ω_p^B *by* ω_B^A. *Furthermore,* $\otimes$ *is associative but non-commutative.*

Definition 3 (Conjunction). *Let* $\omega_p = (b_p, d_p, u_p)$ *and* $\omega_q = (b_q, d_q, u_q)$ *be a principal's opinions about two distinct propositions* p, q. *Let* $\omega_{p \wedge q} = (b_{p \wedge q}, d_{p \wedge q}, u_{p \wedge q})$ *be the opinion such that*

$$b_{p \wedge q} = b_p b_q$$
$$d_{p \wedge q} = d_p + d_q - d_p d_q$$
$$u_{p \wedge q} = b_p u_q + u_q b_q + u_p u_q$$

Then $\omega_{p \wedge q} = \omega_p \wedge \omega_q$ *is called the conjunction of* ω_p *and* ω_q. *As expected,* $\wedge$ *commutes and associates.*

Trust Propagation in Small Worlds

Elizabeth Gray[1], Jean-Marc Seigneur[1], Yong Chen[1], and Christian Jensen[2]

[1] Distributed Systems Group, Department of Computer Science
Trinity College, Dublin 2, Ireland
{grayl, seigneuj, cheny}@tcd.ie
[2] Informatics and Mathematical Modelling, Technical University of Denmark
Richard Petersens Plads, Building 322, DK-2800 Kgs. Lyngby, Denmark
cdj@imm.dtu.dk

Abstract. The possibility of a massive, networked infrastructure of diverse entities partaking in collaborative applications with each other increases more and more with the proliferation of mobile devices and the development of ad hoc networking technologies. In this context, traditional security measures do not scale well. We aim to develop trust-based security mechanisms using small world concepts to optimise formation and propagation of trust amongst entities in these vast networks. In this regard, we surmise that in a very large mobile ad hoc network, trust, risk, and recommendations can be propagated through relatively short paths connecting entities. Our work describes the design of trust-formation and risk-assessment systems, as well as that of an entity recognition scheme, within the context of the small world network topology.

1   Introduction

The proliferation of mobile devices and development of vast ad hoc networks introduces the possibility of an environment where multitudes of diverse entities will partake in collaborative applications with each other. A mobile ad hoc network is an autonomous system of mobile entities connected by wireless links. All entities are free to move randomly, and the network is self-organising, which makes it highly dynamic and subject to rapid and unpredictable changes. As in traditional networks, access to collaborative resources in mobile ad hoc networks requires varying levels of control. Also, some way of authenticating an entity is needed, as well as a way of determining what access that entity may have to shared resources. Traditional authentication and access control methods fail when applied in a decentralised collaborative ad hoc environment. For example, in traditional groupware applications, access to a group is controlled by an administrator with a predefined list of names and access permissions of group members. The administrator grants access rights based on whether the requesting entity is authenticated and identified as meeting the appropriate criteria. However, in a network that is constantly changing both size and topology, this approach does not scale.

This is best illustrated by the following example. Suppose that while on the 8am commuter train every weekday, Alice joins an ad hoc wireless network to see

P. Nixon and S. Terzis (Eds.): Trust Management 2003, LNCS 2692, pp. 239–254, 2003.
© Springer-Verlag Berlin Heidelberg 2003

what collaborative gaming applications are available. One morning, she discovers a blackjack game in which Bob is the dealer, and she requests admission to the game. To Bob, Alice is an unknown entity, who may or may not be trusted to behave correctly, e.g. pay her gaming debts, if given access to his game. In the traditional model, Bob would be able to contact a centralised administrator to determine if Alice is Alice, and if she should have access rights to participate in the blackjack game. This example shows that traditional authentication methods do not scale to the large mobile ad hoc networks envisioned.

We propose a solution for this scenario based on the human notions of trust, risk, and recognition in human ad hoc collaborative networks. Every day, humans determine how to interact with known, partially-known, and unknown people. Much of the time, we do this with no assistance from a trusted, centralised third party and without the availability of complete information. Humans use the concepts of trust, risk, and recognition to help decide the extent to which they cooperate with others. In this way, mechanisms are provided for lowering access barriers and enabling complex transactions between groups.

Difficulties lie in trying to map the human concepts, which themselves are defined differently across the various fields of research, to a computational model. A first important step in this domain is given by Marsh [1], who demonstrates that the concept of human trust can be formalised as a computational model. Another critical step comes from McKnight and Chervany [2], who describe a framework for regulating trust formation, so that unambiguous conversation between computational entities can occur. We implemented McKnight and Chervany's trust framework [3], whereby a trust-based admission control system allows entities in open, diverse systems a way of directly establishing trust in one another. Within this system, as trust formation occurs, trust is measured and used to make dynamic admission control decisions. A problem arises the first time two previously-unknown entities interact, because Alice has to decide her initial trust in Bob.

Further comparisons with human networking concepts give us a possible solution to this problem, based on recommendations from mutual acquaintances. Sociologists estimate that each human has roughly 300 acquaintances with whom he is on a first-name basis. This means that there are 300 people one step away from any given person, 90,000 people two steps away, 27 million people three steps away, etc. This sociological concept is the basis for small world research [4], which describes the tendency for each entity in a large system to be separated from any other entity in the system by only a few steps. Small world research formalises human networking concepts, and gives us standard formulae with which to analyse seemingly random digital networks. We aim to describe how trust-based security measures can be furthered by developing a design against the backdrop of small world theories.

In this paper, we describe how, within the context of the small world network topology, the human concepts of trust, risk, and recognition can be applied to secure collaborative applications in mobile ad hoc networks. The structure of the paper is as follows. Section 2 is an examination of the small world theory.

Section 3 specifies the design of our trust-based security architecture within the context of small worlds. Finally, Section 4 presents conclusions and ideas for future work.

2   Small Worlds

The small world concept suggests that any pair of entities in a seemingly vast, random network can actually connect in a predictable way through relatively short paths of mutual acquaintances. The work on small world theory is of significant interest to our research on the formation and propagation of a computational notion of trust within collaborative networks that appear to be made up of completely random and dynamic connections.

In this section, we review the major research into small world theory, including Stanley Milgram's seminal work in the field as well as more recent developments from the areas of sociology, psychology, and computer science.

2.1   Small World Beginnings

In the 1960's, Stanley Milgram [5], a social psychologist at Harvard, researched the hypothesis that members of any large social network are connected to each other through short chains of intermediate acquaintances, as described in the handshaking scenario above. Milgram and Travers [6] brought small world theory to the attention of the academic community in 1969, having performed the following experiment to prove the hypothesis. They sent information packets to a few hundred randomly selected people in Nebraska and Kansas. Within each information packet was the name of one of two target persons in Boston. Each Nebraskan/Kansan was to forward the information packet onto some acquaintance known on a first-name basis, until the packet reached the target person in Boston. The famous result is one of 'six degrees of separation,' which states that any two people in the U.S. population at the time are connected by no more than six steps.[1]

This result is startling because a person's average number of acquaintances is significantly less than the size of the entire population. Milgram's results are even more surprising when we consider that a person's acquaintances are not generally spread evenly throughout the population. Instead, acquaintanceship tends to be based on common location, background, interests, etc. Therefore, most of a person's acquaintances would be in a tight network, or clique, around him. Within each clique is a high level of redundancy, i.e. within Alice's circle of friends, most of them are also friends with each other. In theory, if all human networks are based upon tight, closed, cliques, it would take far more than a few steps to link two strangers in populations of millions.

---

[1] The Department of Sociology at Columbia University is currently carrying out the first large-scale global verification of Milgram's small world hypothesis, using email rather than the postal service.

Watts and Strogatz [7] furthered Milgram's ideas by modelling small world networks as distinguished from ordered networks and random networks, as shown in Figure 1. Assuming that any network can be represented by connections existing between its members, broad classes of networks can be defined with a range between highly ordered and highly random. In the fully ordered case, the network is completely regular and cliquish. One node knows only the nodes immediately adjacent. In this type of network, many steps are required to connect non-adjacent nodes. The second case is a totally random network, wherein no cliquish behaviour is exhibited. In this type of network, a node is just as likely to be linked to an adjacent node as to a non-adjacent node. The intermediate case that Watts and Strogatz were able to model is the small world network. Randomness is introduced into a fully ordered network by randomly adding 'shortcuts', which are links from one point to another point in the network that would usually take several steps to access. In a small world, any given node has an immediate clique of adjacent connections and may or may not also be connected via a shortcut to a node in any other part of the network. In fact, just a very small number of random links is enough to 'short circuit' an otherwise huge, ordered network. For example, if only one node in 100 has a random link to any other node in the network, the average number of steps linking network node pairs decreases tenfold. Therefore, a small world network has the characteristics of a fully ordered network, but as randomness increases, the number of steps needed to link nodes decreases.

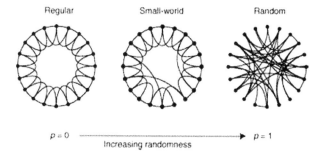

Fig. 1. Increasing Network Randomness [7]

To give a better understanding of the small world network model, Watts [8] identifies three characterising properties. The first is characteristic path length, which is the shortest path required to connect one node to another. This is averaged over all node pairs to give the characteristic path length of the whole network. The second parameter is the clustering coefficient, which measures the probability that two nodes that are connected via a mutual acquaintance will also be directly connected to one another, i.e. the cliquishness of the network. Watts shows that, according to these two parameters, highly ordered networks have long characteristic path lengths and large clustering coefficients, while random networks have short characteristic path lengths and very little clustering. A small world network exhibits characteristic path lengths approximately as short as those of random networks, but with much greater clustering. The third property is logarithmic length scaling such that for all graph sizes, as the network graph grows significantly larger, the average characteristic path length remains relatively small.

Watts and Strogatz assess three real-world networks: social, power, and neural. Each of these three networks exhibits small world topologies. For example, the connections exhibited by the social network [9] are delineated by short paths between a given actor (most notably, actor Kevin Bacon in the 'Kevin Bacon Game' developed at the University of Virginia [10]) and any other actor in the population of actors. The Kevin Bacon Game small world network exhibits significant clustering and a small characteristic path length that remains relatively small, no matter how large the database of actors grows.

Adamic [11] extends Watts' research to prove that another real-world network, the World Wide Web, is also small world. Based on a sample of .edu sites, at the site level the Web exhibits an average characteristic path length of four and a clustering coefficient significantly higher than in a random network of similar size.

2.2   Identity and Search in Small Worlds

While models such as that of Watts and Strogatz present excellent analysis of Milgram's conclusions regarding the pervasiveness of short chains in a range of real-world networks, Kleinberg [12] finds these models insufficient to explain a second component of Milgram's findings: 'that individuals using local information are collectively very effective at actually constructing short paths between two points in a social network.' Kleinberg extends Milgram's original research to illustrate that not only is it possible for networks to have short characteristic path length and local clustering, but also that it is possible for an entity to use local information to find short paths without requiring a map of the entire network.

Kleinberg defines an infinite family of random network models that generalizes the Watts-Strogatz model. For one of these models, then, he shows that there is a decentralized algorithm capable of finding short paths with high probability. Finally, he proves that there is a unique model within that family for which decentralized algorithms are effective for navigation.

Kleinberg specifically focuses on decentralised algorithms, i.e. those by which is passed sequentially from an entity to one of its local or long-range connections using only local information. It is stressed that constraining the algorithm to use only local information is crucial to this research because if an entity had knowledge of all other entities in the network, it could simply perform a breadth-first search to locate the shortest path.

Watts et al [13] incorporate similar ideas into their research of social networks. They define the concept of 'searchability,' the property of being able to find a target quickly in a networks. The model gives an explanation of social networks in terms of searchability based on recognizable personal identities, where identity is considered to be a set of characteristics measured along social dimensions. A class of searchable networks is defined, as is a method for searching which, similar to that of Kleinberg, is a decentralised algorithm based on Milgram's work whereby each entity forwards a message to its neighbour who is closer to the target entity in terms of social distance. This research suggests that searchability is a generic property of real-world social networks, and that an effective decentralised search can be conducted provided that two pieces of information are known: the characteristics of the target entity, and the current entity's immediate neighbours.

In the case of the search algorithms presented by Kleinberg and Watts, there is still the underlying assumption that each entity in a network has a findable, unchanging location. This assumption does not hold in mobile ad hoc networks, which do not rely on any fixed infrastructure. In this type of network, all networking functions must be performed by entities themselves in self-organising manner. In this regard, Hubaux et al [14] present their Shortcut Hunter algorithm, which shows that certificate chains result with high probability between two previously unknown entities using only their merged local certificate repositories. Capkun et al [15] build on Hubaux's work and propose a new approach to securing mobile ad hoc networks. The work is PGP-based, as PGP's functionality relies solely on user acquaintances, and shows that the small world phenomenon naturally emerges in the PGP system as a consequence of the self-organisation of the users. Moreover, Capkun et al argue that self-organised security systems in which entities issue certificates based on acquaintanceship will exhibit small world properties as a result of the formation of mutual trust relationships.

2.3 Summary

In this review, we find that self-organising networks, such as particular types of mobile ad hoc networks, exhibit small world tendencies. This means that we may use existing distributed algorithms, developed in small world research, to establish shortcuts between cliques in mobile ad hoc networks. Based on this premise, we see that small world characteristics become increasingly relevant to the design of a security system that incorporates the elements of trust, risk, and entity recognition. In the following section, we present our design concepts for such a system.

3   Trust-Based Security Mechanisms in Small Worlds

In this section, we present a trust-based security architecture, including the design of four components that may be used to provide security in mobile ad hoc networks: entity recognition, trust-based admission control, risk assessment, and trust management. Each component's design is heavily influenced by the concepts illustrated in small world research.

3.1 Trust-Based Security Architecture

An overview of our trust-based security framework is shown in Figure 2.

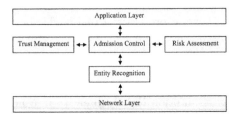

Fig. 2. Trust-Based Security Architecture

The framework consists of four main components. *Entity Recognition* observes encountered entities and decides whether they have been encountered before. *Trust-Based Admission Control (TBAC)* examines the recognised entity and decides whether sufficient trust exists to offset the risk involved with collaboration with this entity. *Risk Assessment* examines the recognised entity and calculates the risk involved with collaboration with this entity. *Trust Management* manages the recorded experiences from interactions with encountered entities.

We return to the collaborative gaming example from Section 1 in order to illustrate how these components are used. Alice wishes to join a blackjack game in which Bob is the dealer. She sends a message to Bob requesting to join the game. The entity recognition component on Bob's device determines whether Bob knows Alice from previous interactions, i.e., Bob tries to *recognize* Alice. The result from the recognition process (either "Alice" or "unknown") is passed on to the TBAC component which decides whether Alice is allowed to join or not. In order to perform its task, the trust-based security framework passes the result from the recognition process to the risk assessment component in order to determine the risk involved with interacting with Alice. Once the risk has been established, the TBAC component queries the trust management component in order to determine the level of trust that has been established from previous interactions with Alice. If the level of trust is sufficient to offset the risk, Alice is allowed to join the game. Bob's TBAC component may also consult the current players, but this protocol is beyond the scope of this paper. The four components are discussed in greater detail in the following sections.

3.2 Entity Recognition

Recognition is a notion humans use when interacting with one another. A person recognises, partially recognises, or does not recognise another person, and this helps him determine the level of trust in the other person and to assess the risk of a particular interaction.

A similar concept arises in mobile ad hoc networks, where diverse entities must interact in a highly dynamic and unpredictable environments. Traditionally, authentication is the first block to ensure secure computing [16], because, without being certain with whom an entity interacts, three fundamental properties - confidentiality, integrity and availability - can be trivially violated through interaction. Authentication, however, does not scale to the world of ubiquitous computing. We believe that, in this context, it is more beneficial to take an approach based on entity recognition [17,18], rather than solely on traditional authentication schemes such as PKI [19] or Kerberos [20].

Authentication Process (AP)	Entity Recognition (ER)
A.1. **Enrolment**: generally involves an administrator	
A.2. **Triggering**: e.g., someone clicks on a Web link to a resource that requires authentication to be downloaded	E.1. **Triggering** (passive and active sense): mainly triggering (as in A.2), with the idea that the recognizing entity can trigger itself
A.3. **Detective work**: verification of the principal's claimed identity	E.2. **Detective work**: to recognize the entity using the negotiated and available recognition scheme(s)
	E.3. **Retention** (optional): whereby there is preservation of after-effects of experience and learning to make recognition possible
A.4. **Action**: the identification is subsequently used in some way. The claim of the identity may be done in steps 2 or 3 depending on the authentication solution. (Loop to A.2.)	E.4. **Action** (optional): the outcome of the recognition is subsequently used in some way (Loop to E.1.)

Fig. 3. Comparison of Authentication and Entity Recognition[18]

In general, authentication schemes start with enrolment of entities. This is a static process, which allows a central administrator to assign permissions to a user. To allow for the dynamic enrolment of strangers and unknown entities, we propose an entity recognition process, which is compared to traditional authentication in Figure 3. Once an entity has been recognised, i.e. has been through one cycle of the entire recognition process, trust-based security mechanisms can start up. In other words, the trust-based admission control and risk assessment components described below can operate on an entity once it has been identified through the entity recognition scheme, paralleling the way in which humans assess trust and risk once human recognition has taken place.

Recognition is therefore a necessary and sufficient requirement in the formation of trust and assessment of risk. Entity recognition is based on records about previous interactions. The more relevant the information recorded about these interactions, the more accurate the trust formation and risk assessment performed upon interactions can be.

3.3   Trust-Based Admission Control

As mentioned above, humans use the notion of trust to determine how to interact using incomplete information with known, partially-known, and unknown people. In Gray et al [3], we implemented McKnight and Chervany's trust framework and showed that a computational trust framework could be implemented such that entities might simulate human trust-based interactions by forming trust measurements and using these measurements for secure admission control. In this work, trust formation is based on the results of previous interactions with other entities. The entity can then use high level policies to specify the permitted level of admission to resources based on trust values. The results of these trials show that the trust-based admission control system reacts correctly to changes in an entity's context-specific behaviour, i.e. adjusts trust value and implements admission policies in a given context correctly according to the framework, which parallels the human trust framework.

Within this framework, when a pair of entities, p_0 and p_m, interacts for the first time, trust values have not yet been formed. To allow interaction to occur, p_0 assigns very low-risk trust-based admission rights to p_m, and from this point trust can evolve based on interactions. We foresee that a recommendation component would make this process better informed and more efficient, whereby mutual acquaintances can make recommendations to assist p_0 form an initial trust value for p_m.

Based on small world research, we surmise that in a very large mobile ad hoc network, trust can be formed and propagated between a pair of unknown entities in a predictable way through relatively short paths of mutual acquaintances. In Equation 1, we present a small world trust formula to illustrate that p_0 can indeed determine how much to trust p_m upon their first meeting. This formula forms the basis for the design of a small worlds-based recommendation component, whereby trust value certificates (TVCs) can be passed along multiple connections between entities such that initial trust values may be calculated. Because in a given context, each entity calculates trust based on the same situation-specific criteria, the trust value certificates passed between entities will be meaningful and usable.

$$Tp_0(p_m) = \frac{\sum_{k=1}^{m} w_k(Tp_{k-1}(p_k))}{m} \qquad (1)$$

Where $Tp_0(p_m)$ = trust value p_0 forms for any p_m
p_0 = principal making admission control decision
p_m = principal m steps away from p_0 and requesting admission
$1 \leq 0 \leq m$ is a set of steps between connected principals
m = total number of steps connecting p_0 and p_n
k = current step
w_k = discounting factor (as k increases, w_k decreases)

To apply the formula above to, for instance, a database of film actors [21], we show the trust value one actor, Kevin Bacon, could form a trust value for another actor, Charlie Chaplin, with whom he has never interacted. (In this context, interaction means acting in the same film together.) However, small world theory shows that these two actors can be linked through mutually shared connections to other actors. Along these connections, TVCs can be passed, as follows:

1. Charlie Chaplin was in Brother Can You Spare a Dime (1975) with Orson Welles. Therefore Orson Welles can form a trust value for Charlie Chaplin and pass it as a TVC to Colleen Camp, in step 2.
2. Orson Welles was in Hearts of Darkness: A Filmmaker's Apocalypse (1991) with Colleen Camp, so Ms. Camp can form a trust value for Orson Welles and add it to the TVC Mr. Welles passed to her.
3. Colleen Camp was in Trapped (2002) with Kevin Bacon, so Mr. Bacon has a trust value for Ms. Camp based on his own interactions with her.

Kevin Bacon can then evaluate the TVC for each step separating himself from Charlie Chaplin. Three connections occur here, and according to our formula, p_0 (Kevin Bacon) would form an initial trust value for p_3 (Charlie Chaplin) by taking the average of the sum of partial trust values based on the interactions between each pair of entities in the chain of connections between p_0 and p_3, as illustrated in Equation 2.

$$Tp_0(p_3) = \frac{(Tp_0(p_1))w_1 + (Tp_1(p_2))w_2 + (Tp_2(p_3))w_3}{3} \qquad (2)$$

Each partial trust value in the sum is discounted according to how many steps it is away from p_0. This is expressed in the form of the discounting factor, w_k, which decreases as the number of steps separating entities increases.

Once $Tp_0(p_m)$ is calculated, p_0 can determine whether or not the value meets his criteria for admission. Should p_0 allow p_m admission, he may proceed with trust formation based on his own interactions with p_m.

This design addresses the difficulty in trust formation upon initial meeting between entities who are unknown to one another. At the same time, it also raises a further issue, concerning conflicting references should there be more than one trusted path connecting entities across the network. In this case, we foresee p_0 taking the most trusted of the available paths, so as to arrive at the most legitimate trust value for p_m. However, $Tp_0(p_m)$ does not distinguish interaction-based trust values from trust in an entity as a referee or recommender. Therefore, it may be necessary in future work to define a reliability factor whereby trust in correctness of recommendations is separate from other interaction-based trust calculations. The reliability factor could then be included in the TVC.

3.4 Risk Assessment

Risk is unavoidable and present in virtually every human interaction where there is uncertainty of outcomes. In many scenarios, risk can be mitigated through the use of records of every possible pattern or outcome. In this way, risk assessment can be as precise as necessary because the maximum amount of information is available for assessing new situations based on previous patterns.

In a mobile ad hoc network, an entity regularly comes into contact with other entities with which it has never interacted. In this scenario, an entity, p_0, has no firsthand information with which to assess the risk of interacting with unknown entity, p_m.

However, as in the design of the trust-based admission control component presented in Section 3.3, we are able to design a risk assessment component based on small world theory. Assuming that risk assessment information can be passed across ad hoc networks via short paths of mutual acquaintances, p_0 may be able to assess the risk, where risk is defined as the probability of an unwanted outcome from interacting with p_m, based on recommended risk information.

Calculating the risk value for p_0's initial interaction with p_m is similar to calculating initial trust values in Section 3.3. The risk of the known parts can be accessed through the chain of connections and then used to formulate an overall small world risk assessment, as described in Equation 3.

$$Rp_0(p_m) = 1 - ((1 - Rp_0(p_1))(1 - Rp_1(p_2))(1 - Rp_2(p_3)) \ldots (1 - Rp_n(p_m)) \quad (3)$$

Where $Rp_0(p_m)$ = risk assessment p_0 forms for interaction with any p_m
p_0 = principal making risk assessment
p_m = principal m steps away from p_0 and requesting interaction
$1 \leq 0 \leq m$ is a set of steps between connected principals
m = total number of steps connecting p_0 and p_n

We can apply the risk formula to the same chain of film actors in the example in Section 3.3, such that a risk value can be generated by Kevin Bacon to assess the risk of interacting with Charlie Chaplin. Along the connections between the actors, partial risk values can be assessed. Kevin Bacon can then evaluate the overall risk with interaction-based risk values for each step separating himself from Charlie Chaplin. Three connections occur here, and according to the risk formula, p_0 (Kevin Bacon) would form an initial risk assessment for p_3 (Charlie Chaplin) as follows:

1. Take the product of the complements of each of the partial risk assessments, which are based on the interactions between each pair of entities in the chain of connections between p_0 and p_3.
2. Take the complement of the resulting product to provide the final overall assessment of the risk of p_0's interaction with p_3.

According to our risk assessment design, as m increases, the level of risk also increases. Similarly, as m decreases, the lower the risk p_0 forms regarding interaction with p_m.

This design addresses the difficulty in risk assessment upon an initial meeting between entities who are unknown to one another. Upon initial interaction, p_0 can use partial risk assessments passed through a chain of mutual acquaintances between p_0 and p_m, such that initial assessment of risk of interaction may developed with more complete information than if the partial risk assessments were not available. Similar to the trust-based admission control concern above, though, an issue arises when there is more than one path connecting two entities. In this case, we foresee p_0 taking the path with the lowest overall risk value, so as to be as cautious as possible in his decision-making. There may be scenarios, however, in which this level of caution is not desirable, e.g. where higher risk is offset by higher benefits. Therefore, in future work, we envisage the risk assessment component interfacing closely with the trust-based admission control component, whereby p_0 is permitted to make context-based choices in this regard. Moreover, linking the risk assessment and trust-based admission control components would enable the ability to assess the trust in the correctness of recommendations of risk assessment.

3.5   Trust Management

The vast number of entities with potentially different distinguishing characteristics expected to be interacting in mobile ad hoc networks and the high connectivity of entities in a small world network lead to the question of scalability of the entity recognition scheme discussed above. Large amounts of data may have to be stored, such as recognition information, information associated with trust, recommendations, observations, etc, on what may be resource-constrained devices with limited available memory. Consequently, the size of the cache, the place where recognition and trust information is stored, may be bound. For example, access to online file servers may not be provided in mobile ad hoc networks, which means that each entity has to carry any information that might be needed for secure decision-making.

To cope with scalability, we propose to 'forget' about some entities (that have been previously recognised) according to an algorithm, such that only the least critical entities are 'forgotten.' Because mobile ad hoc networks exhibit small world tendencies, we are able to design the algorithm based on small world characteristics, i.e. shortcuts and clusters. The Small-wOrld-based Forgetting Algorithm (SOFA) we propose in this regard can be helpful in the maintenance of trust-based information, depending on which source of trust is considered to be most important in the given scenario, such as recommendations and observations.

Where *recommendation data* is more important than other sources of trust, it is essential that SOFA is designed to remember entities that are 'pivots,' [22] i.e. those that have significant long-range shortcuts which span communities. In this way, the stored data will be that which is most valuable, i.e. trust information about many entities throughout the network. An algorithm such as the Shortcut Hunter mentioned above can then be used to retrieve certificate chains via these entities.

Where *observation data* is more important than other sources of trust, it is important that the algorithm is designed to remember entities with whom collaboration may occur based on the next contextual cluster. Two points are key in this regard. First, as shown in Section 3.3, it is important to be able to retrieve trust-based information based on previous observations of an entity's behaviour. Second, in a small world, clusters of entities form according to different criteria, e.g. geographical location. For example, assuming that an entity, p_0, is roaming to another environment and knows specific information about this environment. p_0 will most likely wish to have available trust-based information about any p_m most likely to be present in the destination environment. Matsuo shows [23] that 'a cluster often shows the particular context,' and describes a Small-World Clustering algorithm to identify a cluster's context. Therefore, knowing in advance in which context p_0 is likely to be, p_0's cache should contain information relevant to p_m in the particular contextual cluster. The cluster may also be used to establish the probability of likely future collaborations [24], based on the cliquishness, or number of mutual acquaintances, within that cluster. Care should be taken regarding pivot entities, as they may not necessarily be directly related to the cluster to which they have shortcut connections.

It is important to note, that this algorithm should interface with the trust-based admission control and risk assessment components. Even if an entity has many shortcuts, it may not be trustworthy or worth the risk of interaction, and in these cases, the entity should be forgotten. Moreover, it may be useful to remember and avoid 'bad' entities, i.e. those which behave incorrectly. This raises an interesting paradox, however, in that if p_0 remembers a bad p_m, p_m may simply establish a new identity and his old identity could be forgotten, but if p_0 completely forgets about a bad p_m, p_m may retain his identity and it would have been worth remembering him. We have a possible solution to this paradox, but it is outside the scope of this paper.

3.6   Summary

In this section we described our trust-based security architecture and its associated components. We showed how existing small world principles, such as shortcuts, clustering, and distributed search algorithms, apply to the domain of ad hoc computing, specifically within our trust-based security framework. First, it allows quick trust formation and risk assessment through short chains of mutually-known entities. Second, it directs retention of information about entities in the cache, through the SOFA algorithm, thereby reducing the overall size of the cache.

4   Conclusions and Future Work

Because traditional security measures do not scale well in the envisaged massive, networked infrastructure of diverse entities partaking in collaborative applications with each other, we proposed the provision of trust-based security measures that make use of small world concepts. In this regard, we provided an overview of small world research, in which we highlighted areas that are relevant to the design of a trust-based security system. We found that self-organising networks, such as certain types of mobile ad hoc networks, exhibit small world tendencies.

Based on this premise, we are able to incorporate small world characteristics in the design of three security components for self-organising networks, based on trust, risk, and entity recognition. We then presented the design of these three components.

Our component designs are based on the concepts of recognition, trust, and risk, and each component parallels recognition, trust, and risk in human ad hoc collaborative environments. The component designs address the difficulty in entity recognition, admission control, risk assessment, and trust management upon initial meeting between entities who are unknown to one another in large, self-organising networks.

Applying existing ideas from small world research to a trust-based security architecture gives us the following results. First, it indicates that previously-unknown entities should be able to quickly establish initial trust in one another, based on short chains of recommendations via mutually-known entities. Second, it directs trust management, particularly by assisting an entity in determining which information is important to retain and which entities can be "forgotten," as demonstrated by SOFA. Next, with regard to small world influence in trust formation and risk assessment, we found that a given entity may be potentially provided with more complete information, via mutually-trusted entities, to be assessed than would be available in completely random networks (where decisions have to be made based on either direct observation or prohibitively-large recommendation chains). Having more complete information at its disposal, then, enables an entity to make more informed and predictable decisions regarding interaction with unknown entities. Increasing the informedness and predictability of decision-making enables the entire system to be more secure.

We identified future work in four key areas. First, an issue arises when there are more than one equally-short paths connecting two entities. In this scenario, we must refine the design of the trust and risk components such that an entity can evaluate equally-short paths and choose which path is most suitable. Here, we foresee the integration of criteria assessment for determining context-sensitive path suitability. Second, we determined that there is a need to distinguish interaction-based trust values from trust in an entity as a referee or recommender. Therefore, in future work, we foresee the definition of a reliability factor whereby trust in correctness of recommendations is separate from other interaction-based trust calculations. Third, we identified the need for all three designs to interface with each other, enabling them to work together in providing entity recognition, risk assessment, and trust-based admission control. In this way, relevant interaction-based and recommended information can be shared amongst each of the three components. Finally, we wish to explore possible solutions to the paradox regarding the retaining of information about 'bad' entities.

Acknowledgements. The authors would like to thank Raymond Cunningham for his valued input. This work is funded by the SECURE project (IST-2001-32486), a part of the EU FET Global Computing initiative.

References

1. Marsh, S.: Formalising Trust as a Computational Concept. PhD thesis, University of Stirling, Department of Computer Science and Mathematics (1994)
2. McKnight, D., Chervany, N.: The Meanings of Trust. MISRC 96-04, University of Minnesota, Management Informations Systems Research Center, University of Minnesota (1996)
3. Gray, E., O'Connell, P., Jensen, C., Weber, S., Seigneur, J.M., Yong, C.: Towards a Framework for Assessing Trust-Based Admission Control in Collaborative Ad Hoc Applications. Technical Report 66, Department of Computer Science, Trinity College Dublin (2002)
4. Matthews, R.: Six Degrees of Separation. World Link (2000)
5. Milgram, S.: The Small World Problem. Psychology Today **61** (1967)
6. Travers, J., Milgram, S.: An Experimental Study of the Small World Problem. Sociometry **32** (1969) 425–443
7. Watts, D., Strogatz, S.: Collective Dynamics of 'Small-World' Networks. Nature **393** (1998) 440–442
8. Watts, D.: Small Worlds, The Dynamics of Networks Between Order and Randomness. Princeton University Press (1999)
9. Watts, D., Strogatz, S.: Kevin Bacon, the Small-World, and Why It All Matters. http://www.santafe.edu/sfi/publications/Bulletins/bulletinFall99/ workInProgress/smallWorld.html (1999)
10. Reynolds, P.: Oracle of Bacon. (http://www.cs.virginia.edu/oracle/)
11. Adamic, L.: The Small World Web. In Abiteboul, S., Vercoustre, A.M., eds.: Proc. 3rd European Conf. Research and Advanced Technology for Digital Libraries, ECDL. Number 1696, Springer-Verlag (1999) 443–452
12. Kleinberg, J.: The Small-World Phenomenon: An Algorithmic Perspective. In: Proc. of the 32nd ACM Symposium on Theory of Computing. (2000)
13. Watts, D., Dodds, P., Newman, M.: Identity and Search in Social Networks. Science **296** (2002) 1302–1305
14. Hubaux, J.P., Buttyan, L., Capkun, S.: The Quest for Security in Mobile Ad Hoc Networks. In: Proc. of the ACM Symposium on Mobile Ad Hoc Networking and Computing (MobiHOC). (2001)
15. Capkun, S., Buttyan, L., Hubaux, J.P.: Small Worlds in Security Systems: an Analysis of the PGP Certificate Graph. In: New Security Paradigms Workshop, Norfolk, VA (2002)
16. Stajano, F.: Security for Ubiquitous Computing. Wiley (2002)
17. Seigneur, J.M., Farrell, S., Jensen, C.D.: Secure Ubiquitous Computing Based on Entity Recognition. In: Ubicomp'02 Security Workshop, Gothenburg (2002)
18. Seigneur, J.M., Farrell, S., Jensen, C.D., Gray, E., Yong, C.: End-to-end trust in pervasive computing starts with recognition. In: Proceedings of the First International Conference on Security in Pervasive Computing, Boppard, Germany (2003 [to appear])
19. ITU: Information Technology - Opens Systems Interconnection - The Directory: Authentication Framework. Number X.509 in ITU–T Recomandation. International Telecomunication Union (1993)
20. Kohl, J., Neuman, B.: The Kerberos Network Authentication Service (Version 5). RFC 1510, IETF (1993)
21. IMDB: Internet Movie Database. (http://www.imdb.com)

254 E. Gray et al.

22. Venkatraman, M., Yu, B., Singh, M.: Trust and Reputation Management in a Small-World Network. Technical report (2002)
23. Matsuo, Y.: Clustering Using Small World Structure. In: Knowledge-Based Intelligent Information and Engineering Systems, Crema, Italy (2002)
24. Newman, M.: Clustering and Preferential Attachment in Growing Networks. Phys. Rev. E **64** (2001)

Enforcing Collaboration in Peer-to-Peer Routing Services

Tim Moreton and Andrew Twigg

Computer Laboratory, Cambridge University, UK
{Tim.Moreton,Andrew.Twigg}@cl.cam.ac.uk

Abstract. Many peer-to-peer services rely on a cooperative model of interaction among nodes, yet actually provide little incentive for nodes to collaborate. In this paper, we develop a trust and security architecture for a routing and node location service based on Kademlia [1], a distributed hash table. Crucially, rather than 'routing round' defective or malicious nodes, we discourage free-riding by requiring a node to contribute honestly in order to obtain routing service in return. We claim that our trust protocol enforces collaboration and show how our modified version of Kademlia resists a wide variety of attacks.

1   Introduction

Peer-to-peer systems are global-scale distributed applications that consist of nodes or peers typically run by individuals and organisations without an out-of-band trust relationship. Despite this, most existing such systems rely on a cooperative model of node interaction. Participants join the network and use the service: other peers route their queries, serve their requests or store their data. In return, they are expected to contribute their own resources to provide the same functionality to other peers, although doing so yields no direct benefit to them.

Game-theoretic and empirical analysis of such applications [2,3] has shown that users will often defect from providing resources if it is in their personal interest to do so, while still using the service, regardless of the degradation that results. Some adversaries may even actively consume resources in an attempt to deny service to legitimate users.

The decentralized nature of a peer-to-peer system means that it is impossible to account for the validity of peer software implementing the system's protocol: a user may develop or download an alternative to any 'bona fide' implementation. In such an environment, we must assume that each peer acts as a rational, self-interested agent.

Routing substrates such as Pastry [4], Tapestry [5] and Kademlia [1] are an important class of middleware for peer-to-peer applications, and are the focus of much recent research. Being services in the same way as higher-level peer-to-peer applications, each node contributes by maintaining routing table information and carrying out either message-passing or responding to routing table requests.

P. Nixon and S. Terzis (Eds.): Trust Management 2003, LNCS 2692, pp. 255–270, 2003.

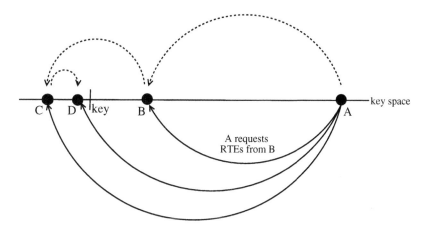

Fig. 1. Locating a node in Kademlia is reminiscent of a source-routing protocol. Node *A* wishes to route to the closest node to a key (which happens to be *D*), by learning of and querying successively closer nodes, represented by the solid lines. The dashed lines represent the conceptual routing that takes place

There is no reason to believe that peers will behave any differently in a routing service; as yet though there are no real-world deployments from which to gather evidence.

This work focuses on developing a new model for participation in routing services that are based on distributed hash tables (DHTs), and in particular Kademlia. We describe a trust protocol which forms the basis for enforcing collaboration by providing incentives for nodes to participate both in the routing service and in the trust framework.

The remainder of this paper is organised as follows. Section 2 outlines Kademlia, the routing service to which we apply our model. Section 3 describes the trust model, how to extend Kademlia to support it, and discusses attacks. Finally, we compare our approach with related work in Section 4.

2 Background

2.1 Kademlia

Kademlia [1] is a distributed hash table in which peers are assigned a unique identifier that determines the position they take in a global key space. Each node maintains a set of *routing table entries* (RTEs) organised by the distance between itself and each remote node. Kademlia offers the property common to DHTs that a node's knowledge of the key space is greater for values closer to their own identifier.

Observations made of node uptime data in traces of Gnutella networks [3] show that nodes are more likely to stay connected, the longer that they have remained connected already. Kademlia applies a least-recently-seen eviction policy to nodes in its tables, and never removes entries for nodes that respond to PING messages. This means that long-term pairwise relationships build up between peers close to each other in the key space. In our framework these relationships allow nodes to determine accurate trust information about likely first and second hops.

Unlike other distributed hash tables, Kademlia does not perform message-passing in a hop-by-hop fashion, where each node on the route forwards the request towards its destination key.

Instead, at each step, the source node picks a node B and requests B's k closest nodes' RTEs[1] . Each successive step uses routing information obtained in the previous step, until the source node can determine the identity of the destination peer; at this point they may communicate directly. Figure 1 demonstrates this process.

2.2 Service and Participation in Routing Substrates

In considering Kademlia's routing service, we distinguish three categories of participation: honest participation, and two categories of active, dishonest behaviour: free-riding and deliberate subversion:

- *Free-riders* wish to use the global service, but aim to minimise their participation costs by not contributing some or all of the resources expected of them. By threatening to exclude them from the service, we make it in free-riders' interests to participate honestly.
- *Deliberately subversive* nodes, on the other hand, actively choose to expend their own resources to deny service to other users. In this case, external motivations determine a node's self-interest. Peers acting in this way have no desire to utilise the global service except to gain a position whereby they might deny service.

Our trust model allows nodes to 'route around' both categories of dishonest peers. However, using trust to avoid poorly-contributing nodes is not sufficient. In a routing context, free-riding nodes are less likely to return responses, so fewer nodes will pass requests for routing information to them; the amount of resources they need to consume to contribute is reduced. It is then in the interest of all nodes to defect and free-ride; a global equilibrium may emerge in which no node replies to queries and the service collapses. To avoid this, we need additionally to align the incentives of free-riding nodes with participation in the routing service.

So, we aim to enforce two properties in a collaborative service:

1. Dishonest nodes do not *provide* the routing service for other valid participants (the *avoidance* property).
2. Dishonest nodes may not *use* the routing service (the *exclusion* property).

---

[1] In practice, at each step the node makes requests for RTEs from α different nodes, to mitigate the effect on the latency of the lookup from nodes that do not respond.

3   Enforcing Collaboration

3.1   Securing Messages and Routing Tables

As it stands, the Kademlia protocol is susceptible to nodes returning false information in replying to requests. Here we present techniques that restrict the class of attacks that a trust model must consider.

Pairwise authentication. Each node has an associated asymmetric keypair, which can be used to sign and verify requests and replies between nodes. As nodes in each other's routing tables tend to interact over an extended period, we are investigating a lower-overhead means of authenticating messages by hashing chains of codewords.

Secure RTEs and identifier assignment. Recall that node identifiers are assigned pseudo-randomly. It is not sufficient to allow each node to determine its own identifier, since this may allow an adversary to install a higher fraction of subversive nodes in one region of the keyspace where it wants to censor a node or a data item.

Rather, we calculate it as the hash of the concatenation of the node's public key and IP address, included to prevent identifiers being swapped between real nodes. A trusted third party Certification Agency (CA) or a similar distributed scheme signs these two unhashed values, so that it is difficult for adversaries to obtain many virtual identities. The operation of the CA and the requirements it makes on nodes (financial, proof of identity, etc.) are beyond the scope of this paper.

Testing for malicious tampering of replies. The above techniques ensure that a set of k RTEs can contain no non-existent nodes. A malicious adversary may, however, return nodes which are not among the k closest to the lookup key, by excluding legitimate entries. A *density test* proposed by Castro et al. [6] may be used to compare the spacing of identifiers in the local routing tables with the spacing of the returned entries. Given the distance between the remote node and the destination key, we can estimate the average expected spacing and range of nodes in the appropriate level of the remote routing table, and compare it to observations.

3.2   The Structure of Trust Values

Before developing the trust model, we present a few brief definitions. *Trust values* are elements of a complete lattice $(T, \leq)$, P is the set of *principals* and the *trust space* t is a partial function $t : P \rightharpoonup (P \rightharpoonup T)$. Initially, let P be the set of nodes in the network, hence we write t_B^A to denote A's trust in node B.

We separate the notions of trust into two categories: trust as a participator in the service and trust as a recommender of other principals. This avoids

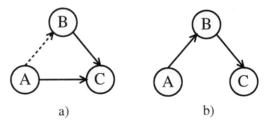

Fig. 2. How separate trust spaces permit selective transitivity in trust relationships. Principal A only trusts C as a participant if A trusts B as a recommender and B trusts C as a participant. Interestingly, A need not trust B as a participant for it to have the transitive relationship

the inherent difficulty associated with having to make an assumption about a principal's ability to *recommend*, based on their ability to *participate*. Without this independence, s service is open to the *colluding nodes* attack. Essentially a node builds up the trust of another node A (by participating), then makes false recommendations to 'transfer' A's trust into a set of malicious nodes, which A now trusts transitively via B. By separating trust in participation and recommendation, we avoid this attack, as described in Section 3.7. We now define more precisely these two notions of trust.

Let $t_{P,B}^A$ be principal A's trust in principal B as a participant of the service, *i.e.* returning valid RTEs. This is computed based on principals' (including A's) interactions with B. Let $t_{R,B}^A$ be principal A's trust in principal B as a recommender. More accurately, it is the trust A has in the proposition 'B returns accurate recommendations about other principals'.

Transitivity. Trust is not, in general, transitive [7] yet it should be transitive for small groups of principals who trust each other *in a certain way*. By separating trust in participation and recommendation, we show how trust can be transferred *selectively transitively*.

Consider the arrangement of nodes in Figure 2. If B trusts C to participate ($t_{P,C}^B$ is high) then should A trust C to participate, i.e. should the trust be transitively transferred? The answer depends on A's trust in B as a recommender (*i.e.* $t_{R,B}^A$), though *not* in A's trust in B as a participator. If $t_{R,B}^A = \top \in T$ then the trust is completely transitive, and if it equals $\bot \in T$ then A completely discounts B's recommendation and no trust in C as a participator is inferred. A value in-between describes a partial transitivity and furthermore, each trust relationship has its own degree of transitivity based on these two trust relationships.

3.3   Making Recommendations

Recommendations are made by a principal B by augmenting the RTEs returned
with B's trust in those principals. A typical set of routing table entries returned
from B would be as in Figure 3.

$$\left\{\left\langle \mathcal{C}, t_{P,C}^{B}\right\rangle, \left\langle \mathcal{D}, t_{P,D}^{B}\right\rangle, \left\langle \mathcal{E}, t_{P,E}^{B}\right\rangle\right\}$$

Fig. 3. A typical set of RTEs from a principal B. $\mathcal{C}$ represents all the lower-level data
about node C, returned by B as per the standard Kademlia protocol

3.4   Observations and Interactions

Let $\varphi_{B}^{A} = (x,y)$ represent the direct observations principal A has made on principal B where x, y are the numbers of successful and unsuccessful interactions,
respectively. 'Success' is defined to exclude as many attacks as possible on the
routing service. We consider a *successful* interaction to be one where B, when
passed a valid request for a given key, returns k *valid* RTEs, where a valid RTE
is one which:

- **refers to a node that exists:** the identifier associated with the node is
  valid; it may be signed by an out-of-band Certification Authority [1];
- **is plausibly in the set of the k-closest nodes to the key that B
  knows about:** to prevent B inserting valid but colluding nodes into the k
  entries that it returns; i.e. that it passes the *density test* [6].

No response after a certain timeout, whether because B dropped the request,
or because it was never delivered, is an unsuccessful interaction. Note that our
definition of a routing service specifies only an ability to find the node whose
identifier is closest to a given key, not an ability to interact with it.

  The exact nature of φ depends on the trust space used – it could be the
proportion of successful interactions (and hence in $[0, 1]$) as in [8,9,10] or taken
to be *opinions* in subjective logic [11], as in [12]. The advantage of a subjective
logic is that it permits a notion of uncertainty in probabilities, allowing nodes to
reason subjectively about the trust in the network and the decisions they make.
The trust model we develop in this paper makes no assumptions about the trust
values used, only that they form a complete lattice $(T, \leq)$ and that a number
of operators which obey certain properties, are well-defined (and closed) over T.
These are:

- *discounting* $\otimes$: This reduces the contribution of a node's opinion B by our
  trust in B as a recommender, and is written $t^{A:B} = t^A \otimes t^B$. We require
  that $\otimes$ be associative but not necessarily commutative. An example $\otimes$ over
  opinions in subjective logic is given in [11].

- *consensus* ⊕ : This takes two trust values and combines them, as if two agents held opinions on different events, and is written $t^{A,B} = t^A \oplus t^B$. We require that ⊕ be associative and commutative. As an example, if trust values are pairs of (successful, unsuccessful) interactions then $(a, b) \oplus (c, d) = (a + c, b + d)$.
- *agreement* ⊖ : This returns a measure of the agreement in opinions expressed in two trust values, and is written $t^{A-B} = t^A \ominus t^B$. We require that ⊖ both associates and commutes. Trust values that are very similar will have high agreement, and those which differ wildly will have low agreement.

3.5   Trust Protocol

How nodes interact. When A attempts to interact with B (i.e. by requesting RTEs), the protocol is that B satisfies the request (i.e. responds) in proportion to some combination of its trust in A as a participant *and* a recommender. Considering both trust values satisfies the *exclusion* property of the service. An initial thought is to consider just A's trust as a participant (i.e. to reciprocate A's behaviour in replying), but this fails to uphold the exclusion property since lazy nodes (see the *laziness attack*) are not penalised. Hence our protocol is for B to reply to A with probability proportional to $t^B_{P,A} \sqcap t^B_{R,A}$, i.e. the greatest lower bound of the two values.

The bandwidth cost associated with a poorly-trusted node retrying failed requests may not be sufficient on its own to cause the node to improve its participation. As such, we may also employ a *proof-of-work* scheme where a token that requires a certain amount of computation to generate, but is trivial to verify, is associated with each request; this will serve to limit the rate at which A can make requests, and so increase the relative cost of each failed one.

How nodes route. In Kademlia, A picks α nodes at random from its k closest nodes to perform the next 'hop' on the route. Our trust protocol extends this by choosing α nodes which A trusts to return accurate and valid entries. The expected proportion of accurate and valid RTEs returned from B in response to a request from A is given by:

$$t^A_{P,B} \otimes t^A_{R,B} \tag{1}$$

since $t^A_{P,B}$ is A's trust in B to reply with *valid* entries and $t^A_{R,B}$ is A's trust that the valid entries B returns are accurate.

Hence A chooses α nodes from the k about which it knows that are closest to the desired key, with probabilities proportional to their expected values as in Equation (1). This provides a form of load balancing, and offers nodes with low trust values an opportunity to increase them through successful interactions while adhering overall to the desired avoidance property.

3.6   Trust Computation

In this section, we describe how a node's trust values are computed for both participants and recommenders, and discuss their derivations and solutions.

Computing the trust in participators. We now look at how A computes its trust in B as a participant. Without the use of recommendations, the trust computation for $t_{P,B}^A$ (A's trust in B as a participant) is given by:

$$t_{P,B}^A = t_{R,A}^A \otimes \varphi_B^A \qquad (2)$$

where $t_{R,A}^A$ is A's trust in itself as a recommender (which may be $\top$). Including this may seem surprising, but it is not uncommon to not have full trust in one's observations in reality.

Now we consider how to incorporate recommendations from other principals. Let $C : B$ represent a recommendation from principal C about principal B, obtained from an RTE returned by C. Using the *discounting* operator $\otimes$, the recommendation $C : B$ with trust value $t_{P,B}^C$ (C's trust in B as a participant) is discounted (its contribution reduced) by A's trust in C as a *recommender* ($t_{R,C}^A$). This is done for each recommendation *about* B, and the discounted values are combined using the *consensus* operator $\otimes$.

This leads to an iterative fixpoint computation whose solution is the fixpoint assignment of all participating trust values. The final step is to introduce the direct observations. For $t_{P,B}^A$ all the recommendations are combined with A's direct observations on B, φ_B^A. The final trust computation for participation is given below:

$$t_{P,B}^A = \bigoplus_{\forall C \text{ s.t. } C:B} \{t_{R,C}^A \otimes t_{P,B}^C\} \oplus (t_{R,A}^A \otimes \varphi_B^A) \qquad (3)$$

Computing the trust in recommenders. Now we consider how A computes its trust in B as a recommender. Essentially what we want to do is *compare* the recommendations it makes with our view of the same, using the *agreement operator* $\ominus$ which represents the agreement between two trust values. Hence $(t_C \ominus t_B)$ is a high trust value iff t_C and t_B concur.

We can combine the results of all these 'comparisons' by using the consensus operator $\oplus$, over all the recommendations made *by* (as opposed to *about* as in Equation (3)) B, about some principal C. The computation is as below:

$$t_{R,B}^A = \bigoplus_{\forall C \text{ s.t. } B:C} \{t_{P,C}^B \ominus t_{P,C}^A\} \qquad (4)$$

It may be that $\oplus$ is not the best way to combine the comparisons in all applications. Essentially, $\oplus$ performs an 'averaging' over all the comparisons, which allows incorrect recommendations to become 'diluted' or lost if a principal makes enough good ones. The computation could be made 'more strict' by taking the

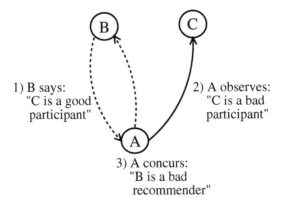

Fig. 4. Updating A's opinion about B as a recommender. In addition to A's direct observations on C, it can use other recommendations from principals it already trusts as recommenders (of course, they can be wrong but the process converges to the correct situation rapidly)

worst comparison, i.e. replacing $\oplus$ with the greatest lower bound of the observations, $\sqcap$ (which exists since our trust values form a complete lattice). It should now be clear that $\oplus$ and $\sqcap$ are just two operators in a partial order which describes how 'strict' A is about computing its trust in B as a recommender. The order includes other operators and a subset of it is given below:

$$\bot \sqsubseteq \sqcap \sqsubseteq \oplus \sqsubseteq \sqcup \sqsubseteq \top \tag{5}$$

where $\bot$ means 'ignore B's recommendations and assign it lowest trust anyway' (and the opposite for $\top$), and $\sqcup$ takes the least upper bound of the comparisons.

This is interesting since it allows each principal control over how it rates other principals, as well as how it computes the trust values. As a node, we do not care about *how* A computes its trust values, only how they compare to our and others' findings. Thus, it is in a principal's interest to accurately compute the values (to avoid being marked as lazy) whilst doing the minimum amount of computation it can 'get away with'.

Meta-recommendations. Consider the situation where A has requested RTEs from B and chooses C as the next step on the route. C returns k valid RTEs as per the protocol (and hence *participates*), but since A has no evidence of C as a recommender, it cannot discount C's recommendations. This situation will not be uncommon in large principal spaces where nodes will have only interacted and received recommendations for, a very small proportion of the principals in the space.

In the same way that principals can recommend principals' abilities to participate, we can increase the propagation of trust by considering the ability to recommend other principals' abilities to recommend. Recall that $t_{R,B}^A$ is A's

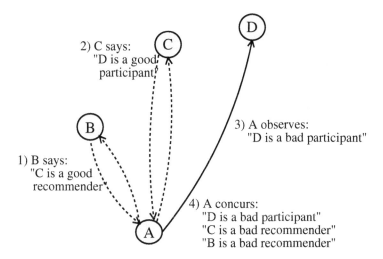

Fig. 5. How meta-recommendations are updated and propagated. A's trust in B's ability as a recommender decreases due to one of two things: C turns out to be a bad recommender, or (not shown) C could be a bad participant. Hence meta-recommendations consider the ability to *recommend in general*

recommendation about B's ability to return correct observations about other principals. A *meta-recommendation* is a recommendation about a principal's ability to recommend principals who make accurate recommendations about other principals. We make the assumption that a principal makes accurate meta-recommendations (i.e. about principals' abilities to recommend) if they make accurate recommendations, since it is the ability to *recommend* in general, not their ability to recommend about participation, that we are interested in modelling.

To handle meta-recommendations, a node returns in its RTEs its trust values of other nodes as recommenders, in addition to their trust values as participants, as shown in Figure 6.

$$\left\{ \left\langle \mathcal{C}, t^B_{P,C}, t^B_{R,C} \right\rangle, \left\langle \mathcal{D}, t^B_{P,D}, t^B_{R,D} \right\rangle, \left\langle \mathcal{E}, t^B_{P,E}, t^B_{R,E} \right\rangle \right\}$$

Fig. 6. A typical set of RTEs from a principal B with meta-recommendations. $\mathcal{C}$ represents all the lower-level data about node C, returned by B as per the standard Kademlia protocol

Fixed-point solutions to trust equations. Equations (3) and (4) are mutually-recursive - A's trust in B as a participant affects A's (and others') trust in B as a recommender, which in turn affects the weightings of B's rec-

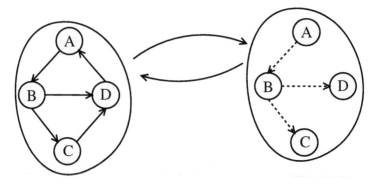

participation trust space   recommendation trust space

Fig. 7. How the trust spaces affect each other by means of the trust Equations (3) and (4). The fixed-point solution to both sets of trust values represents the 'equilibrium position' between the spaces, i.e. when the values in one do not change the values in the other

ommendations, and so on. The solution is analogous to eigen problems in sparse graphs (such as the WWW), so techniques similar to PageRank [13] can be employed to solve it. A similar computation and its approximate solution is described in [12,9].

Conceptually, the two trust spaces can be thought of as products in a two-way reaction, as in Figure 7. Essentially, the fixed-point solution to the trust equations is the equilibrium position between these spaces.

3.7   Attacks

This subsection outlines a series of possible attacks on the service, and informally describes how they are resisted.

Recall that we so far only model the aggregate property of B as a recommender of principals' participation in the service. One may consider stronger adversarial network models where nodes make false recommendations depending on the subject of the recommendation, and this behaviour can be modelled by transforming the principal space as in [12]. This type of adversarial model is particularly appropriate when one considers the colluding nodes attack.

Attack 1 (Colluding Nodes) *A node B participates in the service and makes true recommendations, except for other nodes in its collusion set, about which it falsely reports excellent observations, as shown in Figure 8.*

By treating principals as pairs of nodes, trust values resemble $t^A_{R,B:C}$ meaning A's trust in B as a recommender of C's participation. Then, even if B participates and makes good recommendations on other nodes outside its set, B cannot 'transfer' A's trust in it into the set via C, since B's correctness in

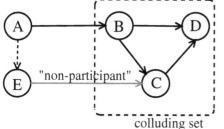

A can never build trust in C,D
as participants unless they are
observed (not necessarily by A)

Fig. 8. The colluding nodes attack. Nodes B, C, D form a set where B participates and aims to use this to transfer A's trust in it into the set, where C, D are free-riding. A has high trust in E as a recommender, who has observed C to be a free-rider. Separating trust in participation and recommendation prevents C, D from free-riding at the expense of A

recommending other nodes has no influence on A's trust in it recommending C. Only by observing (or gaining recommendations from other nodes whom A trusts to recommend C) C's participation (and therefore validating or refuting B's recommendation) can A transfer trust into the set. But if C is malicious and does not participate, B's claim is impossible to validate.

Resisting the next attack essentially relies on the system to uphold both the avoidance and exclusion properties of the service, to both avoid and exclude 'free-riders'.

Attack 2 (Free-riding) *A free-riding node B avoids participation in the service by not returning RTEs when requested, or returning invalid RTEs.*

Nodes that request RTEs from B will rapidly concur that $t_{P,B}$ is low, both by their direct observations and from recommendations of principals they trust. The avoidance *property of the service is not compromised since nodes will route around B by avoiding requesting RTEs from it, and the* exclusion *property is upheld since nodes will rapidly deny B their RTEs, ending its reign as a free-rider.*

A variation on free-riding is laziness. Although this may not be an attack in the malicious sense, we still consider it a threat to the service.

Attack 3 (Laziness) *A lazy node B participates in the service by returning valid RTEs but with random trust values since it does not wish to (or cannot) expend the resources involved in computing trust values. This is distinct from badmouthing, in that expected correlation between B's trust values and the actual values is zero, yet the values are all strongly-negative under bad-mouthing.*

On average the t_P^B values in RTEs returned by B are significantly different from those computed by non-lazy nodes (not just other honest nodes). By Equation (3), the trust values $t_{R,B}$ will be low. Hence B can be identified as a lazy node quite easily and hence avoided. The exclusion property of our service is also upheld, since other nodes will not return RTEs for B very often.

However, we certainly consider the next attack to be of malicious intent since it involves nodes spreading malicious recommendations. Unfortunately, it may be quite difficult to distinguish between bad-mouthing and lazy nodes in reality unless the attack is sufficiently long-lived.

Attack 4 (Bad-mouthing) *A node B attempts to* bad-mouth *other nodes by returning valid RTEs but with malicious trust values, often* $\perp$.

This attack is similar to the laziness attack except that B may do one of two things:

1. *Return malicious (i.e. low) trust values for all nodes;*
2. *Return lazy (i.e. random) trust values for nodes it does not bad-mouth;*
3. *Return correct trust values for nodes it does not bad-mouth.*

The first mode of attack can be detected (and treated) in the same way as for laziness. The final two modes require a transformation of the principal space so that principals represent pairs of nodes, as per Attack 1.

A possible motivation for this attack is an attempt to justify later free-riding, by claiming that nodes B bad-mouthed were poor participators, and hence B is justified in reciprocating their behaviour towards them, as if it were following the protocol honestly.

The phrase 'screw-each-server-once' has been used as an attack against systems which do not consider recommendations (where the trust is built 'locally') and therefore is fairly weak in the current context.

Attack 5 (Screw-each-server-once) *A malicious node B which does not participate nor make accurate recommendations (due to laziness or bad-mouthing) attempts to gain maximum use of the service by interacting with as many principals as possible in the hope that it stays 'ahead of its reputation'.*

The use of almost any recommendation and reputation system will counteract this attack eventually. However, the attacker may use knowledge about how the recommendations are distributed in order to maximize its benefit from the attack. Since nodes in Kademlia are distributed randomly over the key space, the graph which describes how recommendations are distributed (by other nodes performing routing) is essentially a random graph. Assuming routing requests are randomly distributed and each route discovers reputations about $O(k \log n)$ other nodes, we conjecture that a node can expect to 'screw' $O((1/k) \log n)$ servers before its reputation catches up with it.

The final attack we consider relies on subverting a particular property of Kademlia's routing protocol. That is, a node returns k valid RTEs but they do not represent the k closest nodes in the key space.

Attack 6 (Not returning the actual k closest nodes) *This can be detected using the* density test *described in Section 3.1, and the node's trust value as a participant will be reduced, excluding it from the service.*

4   Related Work

4.1   Economic and Game-Theoretic Approaches

Work on using economic models to realign nodes' incentives to participate have presented schemes that assume variable demand for services. Geels and Kubiatowicz argue in [14] that replica management in global-scale storage systems should be conducted as an economy. Nodes trade off the cost of storing data blocks with the value they are able to charge for access to them – in this context, a variable demand for blocks is essential.

However, variable demand properties may hold for human-valued commodities, such as the information stored or shared in a peer-to-peer system, but not for routing table entries. Since DHTs typically determine the allocation of items to nodes pseudo-randomly, requests for keys will also be distributed evenly, so no particular value can be conferred on any particular destination.

Currently, the lack of a scalable, low-overhead digital cash system that may be fully decentralized hampers uptake of economic models. Mojo Nation [15], a distributed file storage and trading system, used a currency 'mojo' to discourage free-riding and to obtain load balancing at servers by congestion charging, but relied on a centralized trusted third party to prevent double-spending.

Acqusti et al. [16] develop an incentive model for a distributed application that offers anonymity to its participants. They take a game-theoretic approach to analysing node behaviour and attacks in various system models. Trust is only considered as a means to ameliorate pseudo-spoofing [17] attacks, rather than as a means to provide incentives to peers.

4.2   Trust and Reputation Frameworks

Aberer et al. [10] present a system for 'managing trust' in a peer-to-peer system using a complaint-based metric. However, recommendations from other nodes are not discounted and they present a threshold technique for checking whether a node is 'untrustworthy', based on the difference between its recommendations and the 'average view'. This presents a brittle view of trust which is likely to be difficult to use to effectively reason about decisions on whether to interact.

The NICE system [18] aims to identify rather than enforce the existence of cooperative peers. It claims to "efficiently locate the generous minority [of cooperating users], and form a clique of users all of whom offer local services to the community." We take the view that such systems should work to exclude dishonest users rather than avoid them.

4.3   Levien's Stamp Trading Network

Levien proposes a stamp-trading network [19] applied to Kademlia that offers incentives to enforce end-to-end service, and is underpinned by a trust model based on constrained flow in networks. A node's owner explicitly selects other nodes whom they trust, so a trusted set of live nodes must be obtained or known before each join. *Stamps* are continually created and circulated to these nodes, which may them trade them with other nodes, and which can later be redeemed at the issuing node for service.

Trading is directed by Kademlia's key location service, but the mechanism suffers from practical difficulties. Currently, at each step in the key lookup, a node obtains a stamp to facilitate its next hop. However, stamp *exchange rates*, set to reflect the value of the service offered by nodes, require advertising before an exchange can be made. The interaction is further complicated by the Kademlia protocol usually returning k RTEs at once to reduce latency.

The system obtains feedback when a destination node 'refuses' to redeem a stamp that it issued. An audit trail is maintained in the stamp to detect double-spending; each node trading the stamp appends a signed statement to the trail. Unfortunately, this scheme suffers high overhead given the number of trades required for a stamp, and no scheme is proposed to exclude double-spending nodes.

5   Conclusion

We have presented a trust model which aims to enforce collaboration in a peer-to-peer routing service, based on Kademlia, a distributed hash table with symmetric routing properties. Our work is related to the research goals of the SECURE project [20], which aims to develop a formal foundation for trust and risk in global computing systems. We have presented an *existential* view of trust which separates how trust values are computed from what the computation represents. This methodology allows each node to compute trust approximations of differing quality, yet still be able to exchange recommendations – particularly important in mobile and pervasive computing applications.

Acknowledgements. The authors wish to thank members of the Cambridge Computer Laboratory for reading draft versions of this paper, often at short notice. Thanks also go to the reviewers for helpful comments about the general ideas within the paper. The authors are supported by EPSRC and Andrew Twigg is additionally supported by BTexact technologies.

References

1. Maymounkov, P., Mazieres, D.: Kademlia: A peer-to-peer information system based on the xor metric. In: Proceedings of IPTPS02, Cambridge, MA. (2002)
2. Adar, E., Huberman, B.: Free riding on Gnutella. In: Technical report, Xerox PARC, 10 Aug. 2000. (2000)
3. Saroiu, S., Gummadi, P.K., Gribble, S.D.: A measurement study of peer-to-peer file sharing systems. In: Proceedings of Multimedia Computing and Networking 2002 (MMCN '02), San Jose, CA, USA (2002)
4. Rowstron, A., Druschel, P.: Pastry: Scalable, distributed object location and routing for large-scale peer-to-peer systems. In: IFIP/ACM International Conference on Distributed Systems Platforms (Middleware). (2001) 329–350

5. Zhao, B.Y., Kubiatowicz, J.D., Joseph, A.D.: Tapestry: An infrastructure for fault-tolerant wide-area location and routing. Technical Report UCB/CSD-01-1141, UC Berkeley (2001)

6. Castro, M., Druschel, P., Ganesh, A., Rowstron, A., Wallach, D.: Security for structured peer-to-peer overlay networks. In: 5th Symposium on Operating Systems Design and Implementaion (OSDI'02). (2002)

7. Christianson, B., Harbison, W.: Why isn't trust transitive? In: Security Protocols Workshop, 1996, pp. 171–176. (1996)

8. Keane, J.: Trust based dynamic source routing in mobile ad hoc networks. MSc. Thesis, Trinity College Dublin) (2002)

9. Xiong, L., Liu, L.: Building trust in decentralized peer-to-peer electronic communities. In: Fifth International Conference on Electronic Commerce Research (ICECR-5), Canada. (2002)

10. Aberer, K., Despotovic, Z.: Managing trust in a peer-2-peer information system. In: CIKM. (2001) 310–317

11. Jøsang, A.: A logic for uncertain probabilities. Available at citeseer.nj.nec.com/392196.html (2001)

12. Twigg, A.: A subjective approach to routing in P2P and ad hoc networks. In: 1st International Conference on Trust Management, Crete. (2003)

13. Page, L., Brin, S., Motwani, R., Winograd, T.: The pagerank citation ranking: Bringing order to the web. available as tech. Rep., computer science department, stanford university (1998)

14. Geels, D., Kubiatowicz, J.: Replica management should be a game. In: Proceedings of the SIGOPS European Workshop. (2002)

15. Wilcox-O'Hearn, B.: Experiences Deploying a Large-Scale Emergent Network. In: 1st International Peer To Peer Systems Workshop. (2002)

16. Acquisti, A., Dingledine, R., Syverson, P.: On the economics of anonymity. Available at www.freehaven.net/doc/fc03/econmics.pdf (2003)

17. Douceur, J.: The Sybil Attack. In: 1st International Peer To Peer Systems Workshop. (2002)

18. Lee, S., Sherwood, R., Bhattacharjee, B.: Cooperative Peer Groups in NICE. In: IEEE Infocom. (2003)

19. Levien, R.: Stamp trading networks. Available at www.levien.com/thesis (2001)

20. SECURE: Secure: Secure environments for collaboration among ubiquitous roaming entities. EU IST-2001-32486 (2001)

Statistical Trustability (Conceptual Work)

Robert Kalcklösch and Klaus Herrmann

Intelligent Networks and Management of Distributed Systems
Faculty for Electrical Engineering and Computer Science
Berlin University of Technology, D-10587 Berlin
{rkalckloesch,kh}@ivs.tu-berlin.de

1 Introduction

Trust management and trust-aware applications have gained importance in recent years (e.g., [1,2]). Conventional security mechanisms are unable to cover all application domains. For example, in ad hoc networks, the frequent lack of an online connection to the Internet makes routine tasks very difficult. Trust seems to be a good way to overcome such shortcomings because it does not necessarily rely on fixed centralized infrastructures [5].

We investigate the concept of trust-based interaction in the domain of mobile ad hoc networks (MANETs) [3]. A MANET consists of mobile devices that are equipped with a short range radio interface. Two devices can only connect to each other if they are within each other's transmission range (usually between 10 and 100 meters). Since these devices are carried by mobile users, the communication network among them is highly dynamic. Connections are setup and torn down frequently. There is no preexisting infrastructure through which one device may connect to some other device reliably.

One major problem in this scenario is the disability to authenticate a communication partner properly, especially since you can not prove any certificate against a trusted third party as you may have no connection to them. Therefore, a different mechanism is needed to gauge someone's trustworthiness in a MANET.

Trust is a relation between entities that ties them together to form a complex network. As this network grows enormously with an increasing amount of entities, and since it is decentralized by its very nature, it is not possible for every individual to have an exact view on the trust network.

In the following, we develop a concept which should allow each user to maintain his own local, statistical view of the whole trust network. While he meets other users, the software on his device collects trust information about them and the people they met. This trust information is then compiled into a concise view of the user's environment. Based on this view, he is able to gauge the trustability of his communication partners in the MANET, even if he has not met them before.

We identify and analyze what is necessary to achieve this *trust network*. We uncover related problems and characterize further research topics that need to be addressed. We will describe the trust model we are intending to use and explain

P. Nixon and S. Terzis (Eds.): Trust Management 2003, LNCS 2692, pp. 271–274, 2003.

a mechanism for the exchange of trust values. Also we introduce a concept for automatic adjustment of trust values, based on exchanged information. Finally, an application scenario is presented that can benefit greatly from the proposed concepts. We conclude the paper with a short outlook to the open problems that have to be solved to implement our concept in a prototype.

2   The Underlying Trust Model

Trust is not a binary decision. There can be many shades between trust and distrust in a person. Therefore, trust has to be defined as a continuous attribute. In our model, trust values lie in the interval [-1, +1] where -1 is interpreted as maximum distrust, +1 signifies absolute trust, and a trust value of 0 is interpreted as *neutral*.

We adopt a definition of trust that incorporates three aspects which all have to be taken into account to compute a specific trust value [6]. The first aspect deals with the willingness of a user to generally trust in others. According to Marsh [6] this is called *basic trust*. The second aspect is the general trust in the actual communication partner. This is called the person's *trustability*. The third aspect is called *contextual trust* and deals with a certain context in which trust is granted. This could be a specific situation or action (e.g., a person wants to use a specific service residing on my computer or two people would like to exchanging mp3-files). For example, if two people want to exchange information on a specific topic, the contextual trust would be based on the competence of the sender with regard to the topic.

The general trust-willingness of a user is a personal attribute that he uses in any interaction that is subject to trust assessment. The other two aspects are aggregated in a two-dimensional trust value that describes trust in a specific user with respect to a specific context. Usually, in a specific interaction, a high contextual trust reveals additional information about the general trustworthiness of the communication partner, but not vice versa. If the trustability is negative, the person is said to be *hostile*.

3   Trust Storage and Exchange

As we want to exchange trust information, we first have to organize it in a certain way so that we are able to easily cope with the exchanged information. As we have explained, trust is not only related to a specific person, but also to a certain context. Thus we have to store the person and the context together with the specific trust value. Each person stores the trust information on their environment. That is, trust values for all other entities it has dealt with so far for every context it has been in. All this information also has to be exchanged in order for the entities to be able to build their local view on the trust network.

A simple approach would be to store this data in a table. As one could easily see, the scalability of this approach is very low. Assuming that the available bandwidth and storage capacity of mobile devices will increase in the future it might become less of challenge to deal with that much information, but even then it is necessary to come up with an intelligent strategy to reduce the communication overhead and waste of storage. The memory complexity of the table-driven approach is $O(\#users * \#contexts)$. The goal is clearly to reduce that. Starting from our first table-driven solution we are investigating to what extend the topology of the underlying trust network will help us to reduce the amount of storage capacity needed.

4   Adjusting Trust

To adjust the trust value in a specific context one has to consider three cases:

The first case is a communication of user A with a partner B where A has no information about B. There should be an initial trust value based on the A's basic trust.

The second case deals with trust in a new context. Here, A already has some information about B, but the context is still new. In that case A could try to adopt a trust value for a similar context and use that as a starting point to create a trust value for this specific context. Therefore, it is necessary to recognize that two context are similar.

In the third case A already has a trust value with respect to B and the current context. When A meets C who also has trust information on the same user B with respect to the same context, A and C need to exchange their trust values and adjust their own values to incorporate each others knowledge on B. The new trust value of A is a function of its old trust value, the trustability of C and B's trust value received from C. The development of this *trust function* is at the core of achieving statistical trustability.

Assuming the existence of this function the adjustment can be easily automated. As the number of interactions with other users increases, information from more and more entities is taken into account. Finally, this will lead to a statistical trustworthiness where each entity has reliable trust information about all participating entities. The trust exchange will lead to a propagation throughout the network. As a consequence a person is able to assess the trustworthiness of people whom he never met before.

In addition to the above each user has the ability to adjust all trust values manually (e.g., if he gets information from outside the system).

5   Application Scenario

In [7] we present a system for trust-based knowledge management in mobile communities, where the concepts provided here are taken into account.

We enhance an existing knowledge management system for ad hoc networks [8] by employing mobile agents [4]. In this system, mobile agents (so-called Delegents) enable users to be virtual present at numerous places at the same time. Delegents exchange knowledge without the intervention of the user. Therefore, we need a mechanism to assess this information. This is done by assigning competence values for specific topics to the users. In this scenario the topics represent contexts, and competence is a contextual trust value. Statistical trustworthiness replaces the manual assessment of incoming knowledge by the human user and allows Delegents to act autonomously on behalf of their user. Delegents are able to filter, accept and reject knowledge based on trust.

6   Conclusion and Outlook

Our approach to maintain and exchange trust information should lead to a statistical view of the over-all complex trust network that inherently connects users. It should give each individual the opportunity to make a trust-based decision on an entity he has never met before just on local information and the exchange of that information. Still, a lot of open issues have to be resolved to reach this goal. The major challenge is the adjustment of trust information. Also, the representation of context information and a similarity measure for contexts is a major issue and will be subject of our future research. Furthermore, a strategy for scalably storing trust information has to be developed to reduce resource requirements.

References

1. Karl Aberer and Zoran Despotovic. Managing trust in a peer-2-peer information system. In *CIKM*, pages 310–317, 2001.
2. T. Beth, M. Borcherding, and B. Klein. Valuation of trust in open networks. In *Proc. 3rd European Symposium on Research in Computer Security – ESORICS '94*, pages 3–18, 1994.
3. S. Giordano. *Mobile ad hoc networks. In Handbook of Wireless Networks and Mobile Computing.* John Wiley & Sons, 2002.
4. Klaus Herrmann. MESHMdl – A Middleware for Self-Organization in Ad hoc Networks. In *Proceedings of the 1st International Workshop on Mobile Distributed Computing (MDC'03)*, May 19 2003.
5. Pradip Lamsal. Understanding trust and security. http://www.cs.helsinki.fi/u/lamsal/asgn/trust/UnderstandingTrustAndSecurity.pdf, 2001.
6. S. Marsh. *Formalising Trust as a Computational Concept.* PhD thesis, Department of Mathematics and Computer Science, University of Stirling, 1994.
7. S. Schulz, K. Herrmann, R. Kalcklösch, T. Schwotzer. Towards trust-based knowledge management in mobile communities. In *AAAI Spring Symposium on Agent-Mediated Knowledge Management; Stanford University/USA*, March 2003.
8. T. Schwotzer and K. Geihs. Shark - a system for management, synchronization and exchange of knowledge in mobile user groups. In *Proceedings of the 2nd International Conference on Knowledge Management (I-KNOW '02), Graz, Austria*, pages 149–156, 2002.

An Introduction to Trust Negotiation

Marianne Winslett

Department of Computer Science, University of Illinois, Urbana IL 61801, USA,
winslett@uiuc.edu,
http://dais.cs.uiuc.edu/Winslett.html

Abstract. The last decade of improvement in service offerings over the Internet offers the hope that many kinds of sensitive interactions between strangers can be carried out electronically, without requiring physical transmission of paper credentials to establish trust. In this short paper, we describe one way of converting the current paper-based approach to establishing trust into an electronic approach that minimizes human intervention. We also describe the theoretical and systems issues that are raised by this approach.

1 Target Interactions

Last year I bought twelve shirts for my husband at a going-out-of-business sale. The lady behind the counter took my credit card, looked at the hologram on the front of the card, ran the card through her scanner, and waited while the computer behind the scanner checked to see that the card had not been revoked and that sufficient credit was available for me to buy all those shirts. Then the cash register printed out a receipt, which I signed. The lady behind the counter compared my signature to the signature on the back of the credit card. After a long pause, she said dubiously, "I *guess* they're the same."

In this manner, we two strangers carried out a face-to-face business transaction. The system we used is far from perfect, as it is vulnerable to attack at several points along the line. For example, credit cards can be forged (hence the hologram), stolen (hence the automatic phone call to a remote center to check for revocation, the example signature on the back, and the signature comparison), or expired (hence the automatic check for expiration). My privacy is not well served by the system, since the credit card company knows about all my purchases and likes to sell that information to third parties. Still, with all its weaknesses, the system seems to work fairly well.

I would like to see the same ease of interaction between strangers on line, when they come together to carry out a transaction. In this case, the interaction could be between an individual and (a representative of) an organization, as in my previous example; or it could be between two individuals, or two organizations. The scenario could involve an ordinary purchase, as in the example above; participation in an on-line auction; a request to access medical records, military data pertinent to a joint exercise, or any other kinds of sensitive documents; registration for school, for a voters' card, library card, marriage license, visa,

P. Nixon and S. Terzis (Eds.): Trust Management 2003, LNCS 2692, pp. 275–283, 2003.

passport, etc.; proof that all requirements for an adoption, change of citizenship, work permit, etc., have been met; or any other scenario where two strangers today must disclose paper credentials to carry out an interaction with some degree of sensitivity.

2   Digitization

Perhaps the most obvious starting point for this quest is to attempt to digitize our current system, while perhaps plugging a few of its most blatant vulnerabilities at the same time. For example, what are the requirements for a digital version of the shirt-purchase transaction?

1. I will need a digital version of my credit card, and some way to prove that it is *my* credit card. The digital version of my credit card should be verifiable and unforgeable.
2. The store needs to be able to recognize my credit card: it must be able to tell that the credit card was issued by someone it trusts, such as VISA, and correctly read and interpret the fields of the card. It must also know how to verify that I own the card.
3. The store needs a policy for credit card acceptance. This policy will need to specify the acceptable credit card issuers, require that ownership of the card be demonstrated, check that the card has not expired, and require that the card issuer be contacted to check that the card is not revoked and that the new charges do not exceed the available credit for the card.
4. If my credit card is to be shown automatically when needed, I will require a policy that specifies the conditions under which I am willing to show my card. For example, I might require the merchant to belong to the Better Business Bureau of the Internet, or I might want to check certain aspects of the merchant's privacy policy. To prevent my kindergartner from using my credit card on-line to buy toys, I might want my computer to check the identity of the person at the console, either through checking the login or using another authentication procedure.
5. The merchant and I need a protocol that will allow us the opportunity to show each other the credentials that are relevant for the purchase, and perhaps also to find out which credentials are relevant for the purchase.

Clearly there are ways to satisfy most of these requirements.

1. X.509 certificates could be used for digital credentials, or we could move to a more modern credential format that offers improved guarantees for privacy, non-forgeability, single- versus multiple-use, and so on (e.g., [2,4, 12]). We might choose to use one or more standard languages for expressing credential contents, such as XML [3].
2. Public Key Infrastructures (PKI) can be used to establish domains of trust. For example, VISA International could be the root authority for a PKI hierarchy devoted to VISA cards. The Better Business Bureau could be the

root authority for a PKI hierarchy that includes all the chapters of the Better Business Bureau. My employer can create its own hierarchy, used for employee ID cards and other purposes.

3. Access control policies for *every* credential and *every* service (such as my VISA card and the shirt purchase) can be codified so that they can be checked and enforced automatically whenever possible, to minimize manual intervention by the user. My access control policies describe exactly who I trust, and for what purposes. If a need arises while trust is being established, I should also be able to export my access control policies in a format that can be understood by strangers trying to gain access to my local resources, so that strangers understand what the requirements are for gaining access to the resources of interest to them. For example, I may need to know which credit cards are accepted by this merchant, and the merchant may need to find out about the access control policy that he will have to satisfy before I will disclose my VISA card to him.

4. Each party can decide which PKI authorities it trusts (VISA and the Better Business Bureau, in the shirt purchase transaction), and write its access control policies accordingly. Parties can cache credentials of interest to them personally (e.g., their employee ID, library card, credit card, certification that their employer is a state agency, and so on), so that they will be available to show to strangers as needed. Similarly, for the parts of an access control policy that require the policy's owner to actively seek out credentials (e.g., the merchant's check that my credit card is not revoked, and my check that my child is not trying to use my credit card), the party can contact the appropriate authority on line in real time.

3   Example

To make these ideas more concrete, let's look at a simple example of how things might work. The example involves a request to view Susan Jones's medical record at Busey Hospital. Busey Hospital's access control policy for that record says that the requester must be a physician at Busey Hospital, or else be the patient. The hospital also has an institutional ID that it is willing to show to anyone.

The requester, Susan Jones, has two credentials of interest. She is a patient at Busey Hospital, and she also works there as a staff physician. She will show her employee ID only to Busey Hospital. Her access control policy for her patient ID says that it can only be shown to people who work at Busey Hospital, Blue Cross Blue Shield of Illinois, or to Busey Hospital itself. For the sake of concreteness, the exact policies are given below, although the reader may prefer to skip over their contents because there are no formal definitions of the access control policy language or credential representations in this paper.

The example in Figure 1 uses descriptive names for credentials, to help the reader. In the real world, credential and access control policy names must not reveal useful information, else the disclosure of an access control policy can reveal sensitive information about the credential it protects. Also for realism,

Server (Busey Hospital) resources and their access control policies:
institutionID:
  true
medicalRecord:
  (x.type = "patient ID" $\land$ x.issuerPublicKey = publicKey("Busey Hospital")
  $\land$ x.patientNumber = "12345" $\land$ requesterAuthenticatesTo(x.ownerPublicKey))
  $\lor$
  (y.type = "employee ID"
  $\land$ y.issuerPublicKey = publicKey("Busey Hospital")
  $\land$ y.jobtitle = "Staff Physician" $\land$ requesterAuthenticatesTo(y.ownerPublicKey))

Client (patient Susan Jones and employee Dr. Sue Jones) resources and their access control policies:
employeeID:
  x.type = "institutional ID"
  $\land$ x.issuerPublicKey = publicKey("Busey Hospital")
  $\land$ x.ownerPublicKey = publicKey("Busey Hospital")
  $\land$ requesterAuthenticatesTo(publicKey("Busey Hospital"))
patientID:
  (x.type = "employee ID"
  $\land$ x.issuerPublicKey = publicKey("Busey Hospital")
  $\land$ requesterAuthenticatesTo(x.ownerPublicKey))
  $\lor$
  (y.type = "employee ID"
  $\land$ y.issuerPublicKey = publicKey("Blue Cross Blue Shield
  of Illinois") $\land$ requesterAuthenticatesTo(y.ownerPublicKey))
  $\lor$
  (z.type = "institutional ID"
  $\land$ z.issuerPublicKey = publicKey ("Busey Hospital")
  $\land$ requesterAuthenticatesTo(publicKey("Busey Hospital")))

Fig. 1. Example policies associated with patient records.

the example uses a *RequesterAuthenticatesTo* predicate, whose truth or falsity is determined at run time by whether or not the requester can demonstrate knowledge of the private key associated with the public key specified in the credential (or by another suitable authentication approach). Finally, the example uses a function *publicKey*, whose interpretation is, in practice, supplied by a call to a certification authority that publishes public keys.

We now show how Susan Jones and Busey Hospital can establish trust. The actual negotiation is conducted between Susan's and the hospital's security agents, without intervention from Susan or the hospital; for simplicity, we describe the negotiation as though Susan and the hospital were negotiating directly with one another.

1. The negotiation is triggered when Susan Jones requests to read her *medicalRecord* over the web. After she requests to read the record, Busey Hospital

sends Susan the access control policy for the hospital's *medicalRecord* resource.

2. Susan determines that her employee ID satisfies the access control policy for *medicalRecord*, and discloses her access control policy for *employeeID* to the hospital.

3. Busey Hospital determines that its institutional ID satisfies Susan's access control policy for *employeeID*, and discloses *institutionID*.

4. Susan determines that *institutionID* satisfies the access control policy for *employeeID*, and discloses her employee ID.

5. At this point, Busey Hospital receives Susan Jones's *employeeID*, which satisfies the access control policy for *medicalRecord*. Thus Busey Hospital grants access to *medicalRecord*.

The negotiation could have followed a different path, if Susan or the hospital had used different strategies. For example, Susan might have preferred to satisfy the hospital's policy by disclosing her patient ID, rather than her employee ID. If she is very eager to establish trust, she might prefer to disclose both of them.

Suppose that Susan is accessing her medical record in order to check her home address, to see if it is correct. After examining the address, she may see that it does not reflect her recent move, and ask to update the record. The access control policy for updating the address information in *medicalRecord* may state that only the patient is allowed to update the patient's address. In this case, Susan will have to learn about this new access control policy and reestablish trust, based on her patient ID rather than on her employee ID: the two IDs refer to different identities, and the hospital does not know that Susan possesses both identities.

4   Issues

A number of interesting theoretical and practical questions arise if we adopt this approach to establishing trust between strangers, revolving around such issues as autonomy, scalability, and vulnerability to attack. For example:

1. **Policy and credential capture and interpretation.** The central role of access control policies in this approach raises many software engineering and knowledge representation issues. We need good languages for expressing access control policies, as well as tools to help people write and update them. We need standard schemas for popular types of credentials, such as employee IDs and passports, so that strangers will be able to interpret their contents correctly. We also need tools to help users analyze the properties of their policies (e.g., what actions could a particular user perform?), modify them, and test the modifications.

2. **Architectures.** Can we use a trusted third party to establish trust between strangers, in a manner that does not leave the third party vulnerable to attack? Can we use a zero-knowledge approach, if there is no trusted third party?

3. **Strategies for establishing trust.** To establish trust without a trusted third party or a zero-knowledge approach, strangers will have to disclose some of their credentials, and possibly some of their access control policies as well. However, there will be many decision points while trust is being established: out of all the credentials and access control policies that I *could* disclose next (i.e., their own access control policies are satisfied), which should I actually disclose? For example, I am theoretically willing to show almost all of the credentials in my purse to a stranger (i.e., their access control policies are satisfied). However, unless the stranger demonstrates a *need to know*, I will not disclose them. For example, I did not show my driver's license or my daughter's baby pictures to the store clerk when I bought the shirts. Thus there is a strategic decision in choosing which credentials to disclose at each step of trust establishment. What is the possible range of strategic choices? Further, to support autonomy, we should not require all participants to make the same strategic choices. How can we ensure that two strangers will be able to establish trust, while still giving them autonomy in their strategic choices?

4. **Obtaining and storing credentials.** How can I obtain the credentials I need? How should I store them to keep them safe from prying eyes? If I need to find credentials that are not cached locally, how can I do so in real time while trust is being negotiated?

5. **Scalability.** How can trust establishment be automated in a highly scalable manner? Can it be made ubiquitous? How can we incorporate trust negotiation into today's popular communication substrates, such as IPSec, HTTP, TLS/SSL [5], and SOAP?

6. **Attacks.** What kinds of attacks is trust negotiation vulnerable to, and to what degree can they be mitigated? What kinds of information leaks can occur during a trust negotiation, and how can they be mitigated? What parts of trust negotiation software must be trusted, and to what degree? What kind of privacy should digital credentials provide [4]?

7. **Authentication of multiple identities.** Under this approach to automated trust establishment, each party can have many identities, each corresponding to the identity that a particular credential issuer uses to designate that individual. For example, the identities in my purse today include my patient number, my driver's license number, my employee ID number, my credit card number, my library card number, and so on. I may be asked to prove that I possess several of these identities during trust establishment. How can I do so, in a manner that prevents or penalizes collusion? How can I make the actions I take under different identities unlinkable?

5   Conclusions

For several years, a small set of researchers has been exploring the issues listed in the previous section. We have made progress on many fronts, both theoretical and practical, though many issues have not yet been addressed. Further, a new result often suggests several additional intriguing issues to investigate. Of the theoretical and practical issues listed above, we have made the most progress in the following areas:

1. Understanding the set of features needed in a policy language for trust negotiation [13,16], incorporating those features into proposed languages [9,14, 15,11], and developing policy evaluation algorithms that support distributed collection of the credentials needed to satisfy a policy [10]. The needed language features include a well-defined semantics, so two parties can agree on what a policy means and whether a given set of credentials will satisfy it; monotonicity; protection for sensitive information that can appear in policies; and support for policies that require submission of combinations of credentials, constraints that relate multiple credentials to each other, chains of credentials where the subject of one credential is the issuer of the next, transitive closure, constraints on the values of fields of credentials, external functions (e.g., time of day), local variables (i.e., references to my own environment), explicit specification of authentication requirements, and delegation.
2. Understanding the range of possible strategies for establishing trust and addressing issues related to autonomy in the choice of a trust negotiation strategy and correct interoperation of the strategies chosen by two strangers [17].
3. Investigation of basic architectural issues [1,2], and testbed implementations of trust negotiation in a variety of communication protocols and scenarios ([6,7,8]).

The interested reader is invited to look at the publications cited above and in the bibliography (or, more likely, their follow-on work) to see the directions pursued and the results that have been obtained. I do not summarize the results here, because they quickly become extremely technical.

Acknowledgements. Other people have been instrumental in exploring issues related to automated trust establishment. During the past several years, I have participated in a joint project with Kent E. Seamons of Brigham Young University. Kent and his students have been building trust negotiation prototypes and exploring systems issues that arise in implementing trust negotiation in a scalable manner. Closer to home, most of the theoretical results for which I have been a coauthor over the past few years have been proved by Ting Yu. We have also benefitted from the closely related work done by Will Winsborough of NAI Labs and Ninghui Li and John Mitchell at Stanford University.

Our portion of this work has been supported by DARPA through AFRL contract number F33615-01-C-0336 and through Space and Naval Warfare Systems Center San Diego grant number N66001-01-18908.

An earlier version of this paper appeared as "An Introduction to Automated Trust Establishment", which appeared in the Workshop on Credential-Based

Access Control, Dortmund, Germany, October 2002. A second early version appeared as "An Introduction to Trust Negotiation", which appeared in the International Conference on Multimedia and Its Applications, Agra, India, January 2003. Permission to reuse material from those papers is gratefully acknowledged.

References

1. J. Biskup, U. Flegel, and Y. Karabulut. Secure Mediation: Requirements, Design, and Architecture. *Journal of Computer Security*, 2002.
2. J. Biskup and Y. Karabulut. A Hybrid PKI Model with an Application for Secure Mediation. *Submitted for publication*, 2002.
3. P. Bonatti and P. Samarati. Regulating Service Access and Information Release on the Web. In *ACM Conference on Computer and Communications Security*, Athens, November 2000.
4. S. Brands. *Rethinking Public Key Infrastructures and Digital Certificates*. MIT Press, 2000.
5. T. Dierks and C. Allen. The TLS Protocol Version 1.0. In *http://www.ietf.org/rfc/rfc2246.txt*, January 1999.
6. A. Herzberg, J. Mihaeli, Y. Mass, D. Naor, and Y. Ravid. Access Control Meets Public Key Infrastructure, Or: Assigning Roles to Strangers. In *IEEE Symposium on Security and Privacy*, Oakland, CA, May 2000.
7. A. Hess, J. Jacobson, H. Mills, R. Wamsley, K. Seamons, and B. Smith. Advanced Client/Server Authentication in TLS. In *Network and Distributed System Security Symposium*, San Diego, CA, February 2002.
8. A. Hess and K. E. Seamons. An Access Control Model for Dynamic Client Content. In *8th ACM Symposium on Access Control Models and Technologies*, Como, Italy, June 2003.
9. N. Li, J. C. Mitchell, and W. H. Winsborough. Design of a Role-based Trust-management Framework. In *IEEE Symposium on Security and Privacy*, Oakland, May 2002.
10. N. Li, W. Winsborough, and J. C. Mitchell. Distributed Credential Chain Discovery in Trust Management. *Journal of Computer Security*, 11, February 2003.
11. N. Li, W. H. Winsborough, and J. C. Mitchell. Beyond Proof-of-compliance: Safety and Availability Analysis in Trust Management. In *IEEE Symposium on Security and Privacy*, Berkeley, California, May 2003.
12. P. Persiano and I. Visconti. User Privacy Issues Regarding Certificates and the TLS Protocol. In *ACM Conference on Computer and Communications Security*, Athens, Greece, 2000.
13. K. Seamons, M. Winslett, T. Yu, B. Smith, E. Child, J. Jacobson, H. Mills, and L. Yu. Requirements for Policy Languages for Trust Negotiation. In *IEEE 3rd International Workshop on Policies for Distributed Systems and Networks*, June 2002.
14. W. Winsborough and N. Li. Towards Practical Trust Negotiation. In *IEEE 3rd International Workshop on Policies for Distributed Systems and Networks*, June 2002.
15. W. H. Winsborough and N. Li. Protecting Sensitive Attributes in Automated Trust Negotiation. In *Workshop on Privacy in the Electronic Society*, Washington, DC, November 2003.

16. T. Yu and M. Winslett. A Unified Scheme for Resource Protection. In *IEEE Symposium on Security and Privacy*, Berkeley, California, May 2003.
17. T. Yu, M. Winslett, and K. E. Seamons. Supporting Structured Credentials and Sensitive Policies through Interoperable Strategies for Automated Trust Negotiation. *ACM Transactions on Information and System Security*, 6, February 2003.

Experience with the KeyNote Trust Management System: Applications and Future Directions⋆

Matt Blaze[1], John Ioannidis[2], and Angelos D. Keromytis[3]

[1] AT&T Labs – Research, `mab@research.att.com`
[2] AT&T Labs – Research, `ji@research.att.com`
[3] CS Department, Columbia University, `angelos@cs.columbia.edu`

Abstract. Access control in distributed systems has been an area of intense research in recent years. One promising approach has been that of *trust management,* whereby authentication and authorization decisions are combined in a unified framework for evaluating security policies and credentials. In this paper, we report on our experience of the past seven years using the PolicyMaker and the KeyNote trust management systems in a variety of projects. We start with a brief overview of trust management in general, and KeyNote in particular; we describe several applications of trust management; we then discuss various features we found missing from our initial version of KeyNote, which would have been useful in the various applications it was used. We conclude the paper with our plans for future research.

1 Introduction

The problem of controlling access to protected data or services has been a central issue in computer and network security since the early days of the computing. At a high level of abstraction, access control systems mediate access to a protected resource by only allowing authorized users to perform an operation on said resource. A traditional "system-security approach" to the processing of a request for action treats the task as a combination of *authentication* and *authorization*. The receiving system first determines *who* the requester is, typically by using an authentication protocol through which the requester digitally "signs" the request, and then queries an internal database to decide *whether* the signer should be granted access to the resources needed to perform the requested action. It has been argued that this is the wrong approach for today's ever-changing networked world [1,2]. In a large, heterogeneous, distributed system, there is a huge set of people (and other entities) who may make requests, as well as a huge set of requests that may be made. These sets change often and cannot be known in advance. Even if the question "who signed this request?" could be answered reliably, it would not help in deciding whether or not to take the requested action if the requester is someone or something from whom the recipient is hearing for the first time.

The right question in a far-flung, rapidly changing network becomes "is the cryptographic key that signed this request *authorized* to take this action?" Traditional name-key

---

⋆ This work was partly supported by DARPA and the NSF under contracts F39502-99-1-0512-MOD P0001 and CCR-TC-0208972 respectively.

P. Nixon and S. Terzis (Eds.): Trust Management 2003, LNCS 2692, pp. 284–300, 2003.

mappings and pre-computed access-control matrices are inadequate. The former because they do not convey any access control information, and the latter because of the amount of state required: given N users, M objects to which access needs to be restricted, and K variables which need to be considered when making an access control decision, we would need access control lists of minimum size $N \times K$ associated with each object, for a total of $N \times M$ policy rules of total size $N \times M \times K$. As the conditions under which access is allowed or denied become more refined (and thus larger), these products increase. In typical systems, the number of users and objects (services) is large, whereas the number of variables is small; however, the combinations of variables in expressing access control policy can be arbitrarily large. Furthermore, these rules have to be maintained, securely distributed, and stored across the entire network, with the concomitant security risks. Thus, one needs a more flexible, more distributed approach to authorization.

We give an overview of the trust management approach to authorization and access control (Section 2). We describe the KeyNote [3] trust-management system (Section 3), which has been used in a number of different projects, and give a brief description of these in Section 4. Section 5 discusses future improvements to KeyNote, as are a result of our experiences in building and using a trust management system for several years.

2   A Trust-Management Approach to Access Control

The *trust-management approach*, first introduced in [1], frames the question as follows: "Does the set C of *credentials* prove that the *request r complies* with the local security *policy P?*" The difference with access control using traditional public-key certificates is shown graphically in Figure 1.

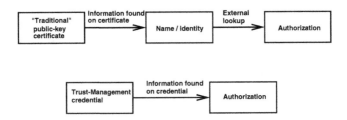

Fig. 1. The difference between access control using traditional public-key certificates and trust management.

Each entity that receives requests must have a policy that serves as the ultimate source of authority in the local environment. The entity's policy may directly authorize certain keys to take certain actions, but more typically it will *delegate* this responsibility to credential issuers that it trusts to have the required domain expertise as well as relationships with potential requesters. The *trust-management engine* is a separate system component that takes (r, C, P) as input, decides whether compliance with the policy has

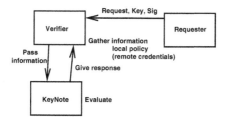

Fig. 2. Interaction between an application and a trust-management system.

been proven, and may also output some additional information about how to proceed if the required proof has not been achieved. Figure 2 shows an example of the interactions between an application and a trust-management system.

An essential part of the trust-management approach is the use of a *general-purpose, application independent* algorithm for checking proofs of compliance. Why is this a good idea? The traditional approach that products or services have taken when they require some form of proof that requested transactions comply with policies, is to use a special-purpose algorithm or language implemented from scratch. Such algorithms/languages could be made more expressive and tuned to the particular intricacies of the application. Compared to this, the trust-management approach offers two main advantages. The first is simply one of engineering: it is preferable (in terms of simplicity and code reuse) to have a standard library or module, and a consistent API, which can be used in a variety of different applications. The second, and perhaps most important gain is in soundness and reliability of both the definition and the implementation of *proof of compliance.* Developers who set out to implement a hopefully simple, special-purpose compliance checker (in order to avoid what they think are the overly complicated syntax and semantics of a universal meta-policy) discover that they have underestimated their application's need for proof and expressiveness. As they discover the full extent of their requirements, they may ultimately wind up implementing a system that is as general and expressive as the complicated one they set out to avoid. A general-purpose compliance checker can be explained, formalized, proven correct, and implemented in a standard package, and applications that use it can be assured that the answer returned for any given input (r, C, P) depends only on the input and *not* on any implicit policy decisions (or bugs) in the design or implementation of the compliance checker.

At a high level of abstraction, trust-management systems have five components:

- A language for describing *actions*, which are operations with security consequences that are to be controlled by the system.
- A mechanism for identifying *principals*, which are entities that can be authorized to perform actions.
- A language for specifying application *policies*, which govern the actions that principals are authorized to perform.
- A language for specifying *credentials*, which allow principals to delegate authorization to other principals.

- A *compliance checker*, which provides a service to applications for determining how an action requested by principals should be handled, given a policy and a set of credentials.

By design, trust management unifies the notions of security policy, credentials, access control, and authorization. An application that uses a trust-management system can simply ask the compliance checker whether a requested action should be allowed. Furthermore, policies and credentials are written in standard languages that are shared by all trust-managed applications; the security configuration mechanism for one application carries exactly the same syntactic and semantic structure as that of another, even when the semantics of the applications themselves are quite different.

2.1 PolicyMaker

PolicyMaker was the first example of a *trust-management engine*. That is, it was the first tool for processing signed requests that embodied the *trust-management* principles articulated in Section 2. It addressed the authorization problem directly, rather than handling the problem indirectly via authentication and access control, and it provided an application-independent definition of *proof of compliance* for matching requests, credentials, and policies. PolicyMaker was introduced in the original trust-management paper by Blaze *et al.* [1], and its compliance-checking algorithm was later fleshed out in [4]. A full description of the system can be found in [1,4], and experience using it in several applications is reported in [5,6,7].

PolicyMaker credentials and policies (collectively referred to as *assertions*) are fully programmable: they are represented as pairs (f, s), where s is the *source* of authority, and f is a program describing the nature of the authority being granted as well as the party or parties to whom it is being granted. In a policy assertion, the source is always the keyword **POLICY**. For the PolicyMaker engine to be able to make a decision about a requested action, the input supplied to it by the calling application must contain one or more policy assertions; these form the *trust root,* which is the ultimate source of authority for the decision about this request, as shown in Figure 3. In a credential assertion, the source of authority is the public key of the issuing entity. Credentials must be signed by their issuers, and the signatures must be verified before the credentials can be used. PolicyMaker assertions can be written in any programming language that can be "safely" interpreted by a local environment that has to import credentials from diverse (and possibly untrusted) issuing authorities. A version of AWK without file I/O operations and with program execution time limits (to avoid denial of service attacks on the policy system) was developed for early experimental work on PolicyMaker, because AWK's pattern-matching constructs are a convenient way to express authorizations. For a credential assertion issued by a particular authority to be useful in a proof that a request complies with a policy, the recipient of the request must have an interpreter for the language in which the assertion is written (so that the program contained in the assertion can be executed). Thus, it would be desirable for assertion writers ultimately to converge on a small number of assertion languages so that receiving systems have to support only a small number of interpreters and so that carefully crafted credentials can be widely used.

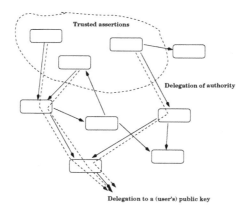

Fig. 3. Delegation in PolicyMaker, starting from a set of trusted assertions. The dotted lines indicate a delegation path from a trusted assertion (public key) to the user making a request. If all the assertions along that path authorize the request, it will be granted.

However, the question of which languages these would be was left open by the Policy-Maker project. A positive aspect of PolicyMaker's not insisting on a particular assertion language was that all the work that went into designing, analyzing, and implementing the PolicyMaker compliance-checking algorithm would not have to be redone every time the assertion language was changed or a new language was introduced. The *proof of compliance* and *assertion-language design* problems are orthogonal in PolicyMaker and can be worked on independently.

The main technical contribution of the PolicyMaker project was fully specifying and analyzing the notion of *proof of compliance*. We give an overview of PolicyMaker's approach to compliance checking here; a complete treatment of the compliance checker can be found in [4]. The PolicyMaker runtime system provides an environment in which the policy and credential assertions fed to it by the calling application can cooperate to try to produce a proof that the request complies with policy. Among the requirements for this cooperation are a method of inter-assertion communication and a method for determining that assertions have collectively succeeded or failed to produce a proof.

Inter-assertion communication in PolicyMaker is done via a simple, append-only data structure on which all participating assertions record intermediate results. Specifically, PolicyMaker initializes the proof process by creating a "blackboard" containing only the request string r and the fact that no assertions have thus far approved the request or anything else. Then PolicyMaker runs the various assertions, possibly multiple times each. When assertion (f_i, s_i) is run, it reads the contents of the blackboard and then adds to the blackboard one or more *acceptance records* (i, s_i, R_{ij}). R_{ij} is an application-specific action that source s_i approves, based on the partial proof that has been constructed thus far. R_{ij} may be the input request r, or it may be some related action that this application uses for inter-assertion communication. Note that the meanings of the action strings R_{ij} are understood by the application-specific assertion programs f_i, but they are not understood by PolicyMaker. All PolicyMaker does is run the assertions and maintain the global blackboard, making sure that the assertions do not erase acceptance records previously written by other assertions, fill up the entire blackboard so that no other assertions can write, or exhibit any other non-cooperative behavior. PolicyMaker never tries to interpret the action strings R_{ij}.

A proof of compliance is achieved if, after PolicyMaker has finished running assertions, the blackboard contains an acceptance record indicating that a policy assertion approves the request r. Some of the nontrivial decisions PolicyMaker must make include the order in which assertions should be run, the number of times each assertion should be run, and when to discard a non-cooperative assertion.

Although the most general version of the compliance-checking problem allows assertions to be arbitrary functions, the computationally tractable version that is analyzed in [4] and implemented in PolicyMaker is guaranteed to be correct only when all assertions are monotonic. (Basically, if a monotonic assertion approves action a when given evidence set E, then it will also approve action a when given an evidence set that contains E; see [4] for a formal definition. By evidence set we mean all the information an assertion uses to reach a decision; this information is typically related to the request r, but may contain additional information about the system's status *etc.*) In particular, correctness is guaranteed only for monotonic *policy* assertions, and this excludes certain types of policies that could used in practice, most notably those that make explicit use of "negative credentials" such as revocation lists. Although it is a limitation, the monotonicity requirement has certain advantages. One of them is that, although the compliance checker may not handle all potentially desirable policies, it is at least analyzable and provably correct on a well-defined class of policies. Furthermore, the requirements of many non-monotonic policies can often be achieved by monotonic policies. For example, the effect of requiring that an entity *not* occur on a revocation list can also be achieved by requiring that it present a "certificate of non-revocation"; the choice between these two approaches involves trade-offs among the (system-wide) costs of the two kinds of credentials and the benefits of a standard compliance checker with provable properties. Finally, restriction to monotonic assertions encourages a conservative, prudent approach to security: in order to perform an action, a user must present an adequate set of affirmative credentials; no potentially dangerous action is allowed by default simply because of the absence of negative credentials.

3   The KeyNote Trust-Management System

The design of KeyNote [3] followed the same principles as PolicyMaker, using credentials that directly authorize actions instead of dividing the authorization task into authentication and access control. Two additional design goals for KeyNote were standardization and ease of integration into applications. KeyNote also requires that credentials and policies be written in a specific assertion language, designed to work smoothly with KeyNote's compliance checker. By using a specific assertion language that is flexible enough to handle the security policy needs of different applications, KeyNote goes further than PolicyMaker toward facilitating efficiency, interoperability, and widespread use of carefully written credentials and policies, at the cost of reduced expressibility and interaction between different policies, compared to PolicyMaker. A sample assertion is shown in Figure 4, with keys and signatures artificially shortened for readability.

In KeyNote, the authority to perform trusted actions is associated with one or more *principals*. A principal may be a physical entity, a process in an operating system, a public key, or any other convenient abstraction. KeyNote principals are identified by a string called a *Principal Identifier*. In some cases, a Principal Identifier will contain a cryptographic key interpreted by the KeyNote system (*e.g.,* for credential signature verification). In that case, the principal can digitally sign assertions and distribute them over untrusted networks for use by other KeyNote compliance checkers. These signed assertions are also called *credentials,* and serve a role similar to that of traditional public key certificates. Policies and credentials share the same syntax and are evaluated according to the same semantics. A principal can therefore convert its policy assertions into credentials simply by digitally signing them. In other cases, Principal Identifiers may have a structure that is opaque to KeyNote. Principals perform two functions of concern to KeyNote: they request *actions* and they issue *assertions*. Actions are any trusted operations that an application places under KeyNote control. Assertions delegate the authorization to perform actions to other principals.

A calling application passes to a KeyNote evaluator a list of credentials, policies, requester principals, and an *Action Attribute Set*. This last element consists of a list of attribute/value pairs, similar in some ways to the Unix shell environment. The action attribute set is constructed by the calling application and contains all information deemed relevant to the request and necessary for the trust decision. The action-environment attributes and the assignment of their values must reflect the security requirements of the application accurately. The semantics of the names and values are not interpreted by KeyNote itself; they vary from application to application and must be agreed upon by the writers of applications and the writers of the policies and credentials that will be used by them. Identifying the attributes to be included in the action attribute set is perhaps the most important task in integrating KeyNote into new applications. The result of the evaluation is an application-defined string that is passed back to the application. This policy compliance value returned from a KeyNote query advises the application how to process the requested action. In the simplest case, the compliance value is boolean (*e.g.,* "reject" or "approve"). Assertions can also be written to select from a range of possible compliance values, when appropriate for the application (*e.g.,* "no access", "restricted access", "full access"). Applications can configure the relative ordering (from weakest to strongest) of compliance values at query time.

As in PolicyMaker, policies and credentials (collectively called assertions) have the same format. The only difference between policies and credentials is that a policy (that is, an assertion with the keyword **POLICY** in the *Authorizer* field) is locally trusted by the compliance-checker, and thus need not be signed. Assertions are structured so that the *Licensees* field specifies explicitly the principal or principals to which authority is delegated. Syntactically, the Licensees field is a formula in which the arguments are public keys and the operations are conjunction, disjunction, and threshold.

The "programs" in KeyNote are encoded in the *Conditions* field and are essentially tests on action attributes. These tests are string comparisons, numerical operations and comparisons, and pattern-matching operations. We chose a simple language for KeyNote

```
KeyNote-Version: 2
Authorizer: "rsa-hex:1023abcd"
Licensees: "dsa-hex:986512a1" || "rsa-hex:19abcd02"
Comment: Authorizer delegates read access to
         either of the Licensees
Conditions: (file == "/etc/passwd" &&
             access == "read") -> "true";
Signature: "sig-rsa-md5-hex:f00f5673"
```

Fig. 4. Sample KeyNote assertion authorizing either of the two keys appearing in the Licensees field to read the file "/etc/passwd".

assertions for lightweight operation (compared to AWK, used by PolicyMaker), safety, and readability. As we shall see in Section 4, the simplicity of the language has not unduly impacted its usefulness in a variety of different applications, although there are several improvements we intend to make in a future release, as we discuss in Section 5.

In PolicyMaker, compliance proofs are constructed via repeated evaluation of assertions, along with an arbitrated "blackboard" for storage of intermediate results and inter-assertion communication. In contrast, KeyNote uses an algorithm that attempts (recursively) to satisfy at least one policy assertion. Referring again to Figure 3, KeyNote treats keys as vertices in the graph, with (directed) edges representing assertions delegating authority. In the prototype implementation, we used a Depth First Search algorithm, starting from the set of trusted ("POLICY") assertions and trying to construct a path to the key of the user making the request. An edge between two vertices in the graph exists only if *(a)* there exists an assertion where the *Authorizer* and the *Licensees* are the keys corresponding to the two vertices, and *(b)* the predicate encoded in the *Conditions* field of that KeyNote assertion authorizes the request.

Thus, satisfying an assertion entails satisfying both the *Conditions* field and the *Licensees* key expression. Note that there is no explicit inter-assertion communication as in PolicyMaker; the *acceptance records* returned by program evaluation are used internally by the KeyNote evaluator and are never seen directly by other assertions. Because KeyNote's evaluation model is a subset of PolicyMaker's, the latter's compliance-checking guarantees are applicable to KeyNote. Whether the more restrictive nature of KeyNote allows for stronger guarantees to be made is an open research question.

Ultimately, for a request to be approved, an assertion graph must be constructed between one or more policy assertions and one or more keys that signed the request. Because of the evaluation model [3], an assertion located somewhere in a delegation graph can effectively only refine (or pass on) the authorizations conferred on it by the previous assertions in the graph. (This principle also holds for PolicyMaker.)

It should be noted that PolicyMaker's restrictions regarding "negative credentials" also apply to KeyNote. Certificate revocation lists (CRLs) are not built into the KeyNote (or the PolicyMaker) system; these can be provided at a higher (or lower) level, perhaps even transparently to KeyNote. The problem of credential discovery is also not explicitly addressed in KeyNote, but we discuss possible solutions in Section 5.

Finally, note that KeyNote, like other trust-management engines, does not directly *enforce* policy; it only provides "advice" to the applications that call it. KeyNote assumes that the application itself is trusted and that the policy assertions are correct. Nothing prevents an application from submitting misleading assertions to KeyNote or from ignoring KeyNote altogether.

4   Applications of KeyNote

In this section we briefly describe the use of KeyNote is systems we and others have built. Although the ability to use KeyNote in such a wide range of applications validates its generality, we discovered several shortcomings to the system that we intend to fix in the next version. We discuss these future directions in the next section.

Network-layer Access Control. One of the first applications of KeyNote was providing access control services for the IPsec [8] architecture. The IPsec protocol suite, which provides network-layer security for the Internet, has been standardized in the IETF and is beginning to make its way into commercial implementations of desktop, server, and router operating systems. IPsec does not itself address the problem of managing the *policies* governing the handling of traffic entering or leaving a node running the protocol. By itself, the IPsec protocol can protect packets from external tampering and eavesdropping, but does nothing to control which nodes are authorized for particular kinds of sessions or for exchanging particular kinds of traffic. In many configurations, especially when network-layer security is used to build firewalls and virtual private networks, such policies may necessarily be quite complex.

In [9,10] we introduced a new policy management architecture for IPsec. A *compliance check* was added to the IPsec architecture that tests packet filters proposed when new security associations are created for conformance with the local security policy, based on credentials presented by the peer node. Security policies and credentials can be quite sophisticated (and specified in KeyNote), while still allowing very efficient packet-filtering for the actual IPsec traffic. The resulting implementation [11] has been in use in the OpenBSD [12] operating system for several years.

Distributed Firewalls. Conventional firewalls rely on topology restrictions and controlled network entry points to enforce traffic filtering. The fundamental limitation of the firewall approach to network security is that a firewall cannot filter traffic it does not see; by implication, everyone on the protected side has to be considered trusted. While this model has worked well for small to medium size networks, networking trends such as increased connectivity, higher line speeds, extranets, and telecommuting threaten to make it obsolete. To address the shortcomings of traditional firewalls, the concept of a *distributed firewall* has been proposed [13]. In this scheme, security policy is still centrally defined, but enforcement is left up to the individual endpoints. Credentials distributed to every node express parts of the overall network policy. The use of KeyNote for access control at the network layer enabled us to develop a prototype distributed firewall [14]. Under certain circumstances, our prototype exhibited better performance than the traditional-firewall approach, as well as handle the increasing protocol complexity and the use of end-to-end encryption.

This functionality has been used in other projects where dynamic access control was necessary. In [15], the ability to effectively control a large number of firewalls, any of which can be contacted by any of a large number of potentially users was allowed to build a distributed denial of service (DDoS) resistant architecture for allowing authorized users to contact sites that are under attack.

The STRONGMAN Architecture. The distributed firewall concept was later generalized in the STRONGMAN architecture, which allowed coordinated and decentralized management of a large number of nodes and services throughout the network stack [16, 17]. STRONGMAN offers three new approaches to scalability, applying the principle of local policy enforcement complying with global security policies. First is the use of a compliance checker to provide great local autonomy within the constraints of a global security policy. Second is a mechanism to compose policy rules into a coherent enforceable set, *e.g.,* at the boundaries of two locally autonomous application domains. Third is the lazy instantiation of policies to reduce the amount of state that enforcement points need to maintain. STRONGMAN is capable of managing such diverse resources and protocols as firewalls, web access control (discussed later), filesystem accesses, and process sandboxing. Work on STRONGMAN is continuing, focusing on the ease of management and correctness components of the system.

Web Access Control. Another use of KeyNote has been in web access control, where it is used to mediate requests for pages or access to CGI scripts. To that end, we built a module for the Apache web server, *mod_keynote*, which performs the compliance checking functions on a per-request basis. This module has also been distributed with the OpenBSD operating system for several years, and the functionality has been folded into the STRONGMAN architecture.

Micropayments: Microchecks and Fileteller. One of the more esoteric uses of KeyNote has been as a micropayment scheme that requires neither online transactions nor trusted hardware for either the payer or payee. Each payer is periodically issued certified credentials that encode the type of transactions and circumstances under which payment can be guaranteed. A risk management strategy, taking into account the payer's history, and other factors, can be used to generate these credentials in a way that limits the aggregated risk of uncollectible or fraudulent transactions to an acceptable level. [18] showed a practical architecture for such a system that used KeyNote to encode the credentials and policies, and described a prototype implementation of the system in which vending machine purchases were made using off-the-shelf consumer PDAs.

[19] uses this micropayment architecture to build a credential-based network file storage system with provisions for paying for file storage and getting paid when others access files. Users get access to arbitrary amounts of storage anywhere in the network, and use a micropayments system to pay for both the initial creation of the file and any subsequent accesses. Wide-scale information sharing requires that a number of issues be addressed; these include distributed access, access control, payment, accounting, and delegation (so that information owners may allow others to access their stored content). Utilizing the same mechanism for both access control and payment results in an elegant

and scalable architecture. Ongoing work in this area is examining distributed peer-to-peer filesystems and pay-per-use access to 802.11 networks [20].

Active Networking. Finally, STRONGMAN has been used in the context of active networks [21] to provide access control services to programmable elements [22,23,24]. An active network is a network infrastructure that is programmable on a per-user or even per-packet basis. Increasing the flexibility of such network infrastructures invites new security risks. Coping with these security risks represents the most fundamental contribution of active network research. The security concerns can be divided into those which affect the network as a whole and those which affect individual elements. It is clear that the element problems must be solved first, as the integrity of network-level solutions will be based on trust of the network elements. In the SANE architecture, KeyNote was used to limit the privileges of network users and their mobile code, by specifying the operations such code was allowed to perform on any particular active node. KeyNote was used in a similar manner in the FLAME architecture [25,26,27], and to provide an economy for resources in an active network [28].

Grid Computing. KeyNote is used to manage the authorization relationships in the Secure WebCom Metacomputer [29,30]. WebCom [31] is a client/server based system that may be used to schedule mobile application components for execution across a network. In Secure WebCom, KeyNote credentials are used to determine the authorization of x509-authenticated SSL connections between WebCom masters and clients. Client credentials are used by WebCom masters to determine what operations the client is authorized to execute; WebCom master credentials are used by clients to determine if the master has the authorization to schedule the (trusted) mobile computation that the client is about to execute.

Transferable Micropayments. WebCom is a network of systems that work together to solve large problems. Systems that provide access to their resources can be paid using hash-chain based micropayments [32]. KeyNote credentials are used to codify hash-chain micropayment contracts; determining whether a particular micropayment should be accepted amounts to a KeyNote compliance check that the micropayment is authorized. This scheme is generalized in [33] to support the efficient transfer of micropayment contracts whereby a transfer amounts to delegation of authorization for the contract. Characterizing a payment scheme as a trust management problem means that trust policies that are based on both monetary and conventional authorization concerns can be formulated.

Case-based Reasoning Systems. It is considered in [34] how similarity techniques that are used by case-based reasoning systems might be adapted to support degrees of imprecision when delegating authority based on KeyNote credentials. A key is considered authorized for some action if it authorized for another similar action, within some degree of similarity. [34] demonstrates how to codify similarity measures within KeyNote credentials such that a test for authorization amounts to a compliance check.

5   Future Directions

We now discuss the various improvements we plan on making to the next version of KeyNote, based on our experiences with several applications as well as comments from the user community. These improvements include changes to the language and assertion format as well as enhancements to our distribution implementation. We focus on changes that will allow us to use KeyNote in new contexts and classes of applications.

Bit Operations. A regrettable omission that became almost immediately obvious was KeyNote's lack of support for bit-level operations (bit-wise AND, OR, XOR, NOT, *etc.*). Lack of bit operations made it especially awkward to apply KeyNote to network-layer access control, as discussed in Section 4. In this application, we needed to test IP addresses against network subnets (*e.g.*, "does the address 128.59.19.32 belong to the 128.59.23.255/21 subnet ?"). In pseudo-code, this comparison would be expressed as "128.59.19.32 & 255.255.248.0 = = 128.59.23.255 & 255.255.248.0". Since KeyNote does not support bit-wise operations, we had to resort to tricks such as the string-wise comparisons "128.59.19.32 >= 128.59.16.0 && 128.59.19.32 <= 128.59.23.255". This is both visually unappealing and non-intuitive; IPv6, with its longer addresses, will only exacerbate this problem. These comparisons can be performed more concisely by breaking up the address into individual octets and performing numerical operations/comparisons, but the end-result is even less comprehensible to a human reader. We intend to extend KeyNote to natively support bit-wise operations, similar to string and numeric operations.

Sets and Arrays. By modern programming language standards, KeyNote does not seem to support an especially rich collection of data types or data structures. This was a deliberate design decision, of course, in line with our minimalist philosophy, but, as with the lack of bit operations, experience has suggested some obvious potential enhancements. In particular, in access control systems and other security schemes, it is often natural to reason about sets, arrays, and lists. In the current KeyNote system, such operations must be simulated with simple strings and regular expression operations, but this often leads to rather opaque (and inefficient) constructions. A future version of the language may benefit from a richer collection of set data structures, along with operations for testing membership, *etc.*

Function Calls. Currently, the action environment must be populated by the invoking application prior to performing the compliance check. In the prototype, it is possible to populate the action environment on-demand (*i.e.*, as each action attribute is accessed by an assertion). However, it is not possible to use *parameterized* action attributes, *i.e.*, populate an action attribute based on the content of some other variable or a parameter contained in the assertion itself. For example, consider a policy that allows any user access to a file as long as there is a particular entry for that user in a system database. In principle, the action environment could be populated with the complete database — however, the assertion writer would have to know *a priori* the names of all users (if they are used as the lookup key in the database), and these names would then be used as action attributes (containing that user's information), in order to access them from inside an assertion. This will result in considerable initialization costs as well as semantic confusion (since new variable will have to appear in the action environment)t as new users are added. To solve this problem, we intend to add application-specific function calls. These will take as argument a string, and return a string.

Naming and Scoping. One of the earliest architectural goals of KeyNote (and, indeed, of the original PolicyMaker system) was to minimize the distinction between a local "policy" and a remote "credential." In our philosophy, the only difference between a policy and a credential is that the latter is signed; a corollary of this should be that one can convert a local policy into a remotely-distributable and usable credential simply by signing it. In practice, however, this is only true for the simplest of policies. Policies might refer to principal identifies in assertions that are meaningful only locally and that are not expected to be visible outside the context of the policy itself.

To make it truly possible to treat a policy as a single construct that can be signed and used remotely, KeyNote would need a scope system that would allow an entire group of assertions to share a single, private principal naming context and be signed and exported as a group. "Internal" principal names would not be visible outside their scope. This should be a straightforward change to the language, entailing the introduction of syntactic scope grouping operation and the obvious semantics for resolving names.

Exception Handling. The algorithm currently used for determining the acceptance record of an assertion uses the highest value returned from all the clauses in the Conditions field. For example, the following pair of clauses will return "true" if the AES or 3DES is used as the encryption algorithm, regardless of the authentication algorithm.

```
Conditions:
  app_domain == "IPsec policy" -> {
    encryption_algorithm == "AES" ||
        encryption_algorithm == "3DES" -> "true";
    authentication_algorithm == "SHA1" -> "false";
  }
```

This approach has made rule specification very easy and flexible. One disadvantage, however, has been the difficulty of concisely disallowing one particular request from among a large set of acceptable requests. To address this, we intend to extend the KeyNote language to contain an "except" construct that can be used to wrap classes of clauses. Once all the classes in the wrapped class have been evaluated, another set of clauses associated with the construct are evaluated to handle any exceptions. If any of these clauses match, the acceptance record of the wrapped class is modified accordingly. Syntactically, the construct might look like:

```
Conditions:
  app_domain == "IPsec policy" && {
    encryption_algorithm == "3DES" ||
        encryption_algorithm == "AES" -> "true";
  } except {
      authentication_algorithm == "none" -> "false";
  }
```

Credential Attributes. It is sometimes useful in the process of evaluating a KeyNote assertion to change the action attribute set that subsequent assertions will see. For example, if a KeyNote assertion would evaluate to true if a particular set of conditions is met, it may want to communicate this fact to subsequent assertions by adding an action attribute to the action attribute set that they will see. This tries to recapture some of PolicyMaker's blackboard functionality.

Syntactically, such a feature would be implemented as a new KeyNote field, the `Attributes:` field. The syntax is similar to the `Local-Constants:` field; just a list of name/value pairs. However, unlike the local-constants field which causes just lexical substitution in the current credential, the Attributes field affects the action attributes set of all subsequent evaluations.

Multiple Assertion Representations. Some environments, *e.g.,* the WWW DAV system [35], use specific languages and representation medium in all aspects of the system (in the case of DAV, XML is used). When using KeyNote in such environments, it would be useful to have alternate, semantically equivalent representations for assertions. Our work in web access control (Section 4) has prompted us to investigate an XML schema for KeyNote assertions. One challenge is the integration of assertions, represented in different formats, in the same compliance check, *e.g.,* using policies in the currently-used format and credentials in an XML-based encoding.

Revocation. Perhaps the most common request for a new feature is support for some form of revocation. As we discussed in Section 2, KeyNote (and monotonic trust-management systems in general) do not support the notion of "negative credentials", as these make it difficult to reason about the correctness of the system and the evaluation logic. Revocation can be built independent of the compliance checker, at a different level. However, this makes use of KeyNote less natural for applications that have an explicit notion of revocation; such applications must parse KeyNote credentials and perform the necessary revocation checks in the application code instead of leaving it to the trust management engine. The KeyNote language itself natively supports only time-based revocation (*i.e.,* credential expiration), by encoding the appropriate rules in the Conditions field of an assertion, *e.g.,* the following expression:

```
Authorizer: SOME_KEY
Licensees: SOME_OTHER_KEY
Conditions: app_domain == "IPsec" &&
  (encryption == "3DES" || encryption == "AES") &&
  current_time <= "20031215052500" -> "true";
Signature: ...
```

would cause the credential to return "false" after 5:25am, December 15, 2003.

Revocation is a difficult problem in general, and is especially so for monotonic trust management. One possible approach for a future version of KeyNote is to treat revocation as another principal in the Licensees field. To encode an revocation rule under a particular scheme, *e.g.,* the OCSP protocol, we would simply use a conjunctive expression in the Licensees field:

```
Authorizer: SOME_KEY
Licensees: SOME_OTHER_KEY &&
 "OCSP:revocation.cs.columbia.edu:3232:REVOCATION_KEY"
Conditions: app_domain == "IPsec" &&
  (encryption == "3DES" || encryption == "AES") &&
  current_time <= "20031215052500" -> "true";
Signature: ...
```

In this example, the assertion would allow a request to proceed if the conditions were fulfilled (the encryption algorithm was 3DES or AES), it had not expired, and the OCSP revocation server found at revocation.cs.columbia.edu, port 3232, did not indicate to us that the credential had been marked as invalid. The REVOCATION_KEY can be used to protect the communication between the compliance checker and the revocation server. Other revocation schemes such as Certificate Revocation Lists (CRLs), Delta-CRLs, refresher certificates, *etc.* can be used in the same manner.

Bytecode Interpreter. The KeyNote prototype was built using the *lex* and *yacc* tools to parse the assertion format. As a result, the prototype contains a lot of code that depends on the standard *C* library, for doing string operations and memory allocation. Furthermore, because these tools are meant to support a large class of grammars, the generated parsers are fairly general and, consequently, more inefficient than a hand-crafted parser would be. While these constrains are not particularly restrictive, they make it practically impossible to use KeyNote inside an operating system kernel. To allow for easy integration of KeyNote inside an operating system kernel (or resource-limited embedded devices), we intend to create a bytecode interpreter. A front-end compiler will parse the credentials and convert them from the respective format (*e.g.,* the current format, or an XML-based one) to a bytecode program that can be uploaded to the kernel-resident compliance checker. In this manner, it will be similar to the BPF packet-filtering system [36]. Another advantage of this approach is the ability to use credentials of different formats in the context of the same policy evaluation. We are currently investigating the appropriate bytecode instruction format and semantics to use. Note that this improvement need not entail changes to the KeyNote language *per se.*

Debugging Tools. Since we released KeyNote, we frequently receive requests for help in debugging some problem with KeyNote. In practically all cases, the users are not setting the correct values in the action environment (that is, values corresponding to what their policies check for). Similar problems arise from typos or using the wrong key as an Authorizer or Licensee in a credential. A good interactive debugging tool (*e.g.,* a GUI-based trial-and-error system) would save both KeyNote users and implementors considerable time and frustration, and, again, need not entail changes to the language.

6   Concluding Remarks

We reported our experience using the KeyNote trust-management system, on satisfying the needs of authorization and access control for a number of different applications. As a result, we have determined a set of features and improvements that we intend to integrate into a future version of KeyNote. Despite these omissions from the initial release, KeyNote has proven remarkably flexible and useful in a variety of contexts. We believe that we have thus validated our original hypothesis from 5 years ago, that a simple trust-management system can address the needs of most applications that have authorization and access control requirements. Our future work will focus on solving specific problems, easing the use of KeyNote in new environments, and exploring new directions for trust management, without diverting from our goal of simplicity and compactness.

Acknowledgments. We would like to thank Simon Foley for contributing some of the text in Section 4.

References

1. Blaze, M., Feigenbaum, J., Lacy, J.: Decentralized Trust Management. In: Proceedings of the 17th Symposium on Security and Privacy. (1996) 164–173
2. Blaze, M., Feigenbaum, J., Ioannidis, J., Keromytis, A.: The Role of Trust Management in Distributed Systems Security. In: Secure Internet Programming. Volume 1603 of Lecture Notes in Computer Science. Springer-Verlag Inc., New York, NY, USA (1999) 185–210
3. Blaze, M., Feigenbaum, J., Ioannidis, J., Keromytis, A.D.: The KeyNote Trust Management System Version 2. Internet RFC 2704 (1999)
4. Blaze, M., Feigenbaum, J., Strauss, M.: Compliance Checking in the PolicyMaker Trust-Management System. In: Proceedings of the Financial Cryptography '98, Lecture Notes in Computer Science, vol. 1465. (1998) 254–274
5. Blaze, M., Feigenbaum, J., Resnick, P., Strauss, M.: Managing Trust in an Information Labeling System. In: European Transactions on Telecommunications, 8. (1997) 491–501
6. Lacy, J., Snyder, J., Maher, D.: Music on the Internet and the Intellectual Property Protection Problem. In: Proceedings of the International Symposium on Industrial Electronics, IEEE Press (1997) SS77–83
7. Levien, R., McCarthy, L., Blaze, M.: Transparent Internet E-mail Security. http://www.cs.-umass.edu/~lmccarth/crypto/papers/email.ps (1996)
8. Kent, S., Atkinson, R.: Security Architecture for the Internet Protocol. RFC 2401 (1998)
9. Blaze, M., Ioannidis, J., Keromytis, A.: Trust Management for IPsec. In: Proceedings of Network and Distributed System Security Symposium (NDSS). (2001) 139–151
10. Blaze, M., Ioannidis, J., Keromytis, A.: Trust Management for IPsec. ACM Transactions on Information and System Security (TISSEC) **32** (2002) 1–24
11. Hallqvist, N., Keromytis, A.D.: Implementing Internet Key Exchange (IKE). In: Proceedings of the Annual USENIX Technical Conference, Freenix Track. (2000) 201–214
12. de Raadt, T., Hallqvist, N., Grabowski, A., Keromytis, A.D., Provos, N.: Cryptography in OpenBSD: An Overview. In: Proceedings of the 1999 USENIX Annual Technical Conference, Freenix Track. (1999) 93–101
13. Bellovin, S.M.: Distributed Firewalls. *;login:* magazine, issue on security (1999) 37–39
14. Ioannidis, S., Keromytis, A., Bellovin, S., Smith, J.: Implementing a Distributed Firewall. In: Proceedings of Computer and Communications Security (CCS). (2000) 190–199
15. Keromytis, A.D., Misra, V., Rubenstein, D.: SOS: Secure Overlay Services. In: Proceedings of ACM SIGCOMM. (2002) 61–72
16. Keromytis, A., Ioannidis, S., Greenwald, M., Smith, J.: The STRONGMAN Architecture. In: Proceedings of DISCEX III. (2003)

17. Keromytis, A.D.: STRONGMAN: A Scalable Solution To Trust Management In Networks. PhD thesis, University of Pennsylvania, Philadelphia (2001)
18. Blaze, M., Ioannidis, J., Keromytis, A.D.: Offline Micropayments without Trusted Hardware. In: Proceedings of the 5h International Conference on Financial Cr yptography. (2001) 21–40
19. Ioannidis, J., Ioannidis, S., Keromytis, A., Prevelakis, V.: Fileteller: Paying and Getting Paid for File Storage. In: Proceedings of the 6th International Conference on Financial Cryptography. (2002)
20. Miltchev, S., Prevelakis, V., Ioannidis, S., Ioannidis, J., Keromytis, A.D., Smith, J.M.: Secure and Flexible Global File Sharing. In: Proceedings of the USENIX Technical Annual Conference, Freenix Track. (2003)
21. Alexander, D.S., Arbaugh, W.A., Hicks, M., Kakkar, P., Keromytis, A.D., Moore, J.T., Gunter, C.A., Nettles, S.M., Smith, J.M.: The SwitchWare Active Network Architecture. IEEE Network, special issue on Active and Programmable Networks 12 (1998) 29–36
22. Alexander, D.S., Arbaugh, W.A., Keromytis, A.D., Smith, J.M.: A Secure Active Network Environment Architecture: Realization in SwitchWare. IEEE Network, special issue on Active and Programmable Networks 12 (1998) 37–45
23. Alexander, D.S., Arbaugh, W.A., Keromytis, A.D., Muir, S., Smith, J.M.: Secure Quality of Service Handling (SQoSH). IEEE Communications 38 (2000) 106–112
24. Alexander, D., Menage, P., Keromytis, A., Arbaugh, W., Anagnostakis, K., Smith, J.: The Price of Safety in an Active Network. Journal of Communications (JCN), special issue on programmable switches and routers 3 (2001) 4–18
25. Anagnostakis, K.G., Ioannidis, S., Miltchev, S., Smith, J.M.: Practical network applications on a lightweight active management environment. In: Proceedings of the 3rd International Working Conference on Active Networks (IWAN). (2001)
26. Anagnostakis, K.G., Ioannidis, S., Miltchev, S., Ioannidis, J., Greenwald, M.B., Smith, J.M.: Efficient packet monitoring for network management. In: Proceedings of IFIP/IEEE Network Operations and Management Symposium (NOMS) 2002. (2002)
27. Anagnostakis, K.G., Greenwald, M.B., Ioannidis, S., Miltchev, S.: Open Packet Monitoring on FLAME: Safety, Performance and Applications. In: Proceedings of the 4rd International Working Conference on Active Networks (IWAN). (2002)
28. Anagnostakis, K.G., Hicks, M.W., Ioannidis, S., Keromytis, A.D., Smith, J.M.: Scalable Resource Control in Active Networks. In: Proceedings of the Second International Working Conference on Active Networks (IWAN). (2000) 343–357
29. Foley, S., Quillinan, T., Morrison, J., Power, D., Kennedy, J.: Exploiting KeyNote in WebCom: Architecture Neutral Glue for Trust Management. In: Fifth Nordic Workshop on Secure IT Systems. (2001)
30. Foley, S., Quillinan, T., Morrison, J.: Secure Component Distribution Using WebCom. In: Proceedings of the 17th International Conference on Information Security (IFIP/SEC). (2002)
31. Morrison, J., Power, D., Kennedy, J.: WebCom: A Web Based Distributed Computation Platform. In: Proceedings of Distributed computing on the Web. (1999)
32. Foley, S., Quillinan, T.: Using Trust Management to Support MicroPayments. In: Proceedings of the Annual Conference on Information Technology and Telecommunications. (2002)
33. Foley, S.: Using Trust Management to Support Transferable Hash-Based Micropayments. In: Proceedings of the International Financial Cryptography Conference. (2003)
34. Foley, S.: Supporting Imprecise Delegation in KeyNote. In: Proceedings of 10th International Security Protocols Workshop. (2002)
35. Whitehead, E.: World Wide Web Distributed Authoring and Versioning (WebDAV): An Introduction. ACM StandardView 5 (1997) 3–8
36. McCanne, S., Jacobson, V.: A BSD Packet Filter: A New Architecture for User-level Packet Capture. In: Proceedings of USENIX Winter Technical Conference, Usenix (1993) 259–269

Fidelis: A Policy-Driven Trust Management Framework

Walt Teh-Ming Yao

Computer Laboratory, University of Cambridge
William Gates Building, Cambridge CB3 0FD
wtmy2@cl.cam.ac.uk

Abstract. We describe *Fidelis*, a policy-driven trust management framework, designed for highly decentralized distributed applications, with many interoperating, collaborative but potentially distrusting principals. To address the trust management needs for such applications, Fidelis is designed to support the principle of separation of *policies* and *credentials*, and the notion of full domain autonomy. Based on these, credentials are considered simply as static data structures, much like membership cards in real life. Policies, which are autonomously specified, administered and managed, interpret and provide the semantics for these credentials. In this paper, we describe the Fidelis policy framework which serves as the abstract, conceptual foundation. We also describe a specific implementation of the policy framework, in the form of the Fidelis policy language. Both the syntax and the semantics of the language are described. A discussion is given to show that the Fidelis approach is attractive for many applications.

1 Introduction

In recent years, we have witnessed the evolutionary development of a new breed of distributed applications that are highly decentralized, of Internet-grade scalability, and locally autonomous. Most importantly, they often require to work collaboratively, with either previously known or unknown parties. These characteristics prompt an ongoing research on new techniques for addressing the new authorization needs.

One approach is based on the notion of *delegation of authorization*. The origin of this notion can be traced back to distributed capability systems [1,2]. However, it has recently been more widely studied in the work on *trust management systems*, e.g. PolicyMaker [3], KeyNote [4], RT [5] and SDSI/SPKI[1] [6,7]. The underlying idea is to distribute authorities and security policies through *delegation*. Delegation is expressed by means of *credentials*, and a *chain of credentials* represents a delegated authorization from the issuer of the first credential to the subject of the last credential. A credential chain is effectively treated a capability.

---

[1] Also known as *key-oriented access control* for that they build upon public key cryptography.

P. Nixon and S. Terzis (Eds.): Trust Management 2003, LNCS 2692, pp. 301–317, 2003.

While delegation of authorization encourages decentralization, it does not fully address the open nature of decentralized environment with highly autonomous but collaborative domains. For example, consider a joint air miles scheme: several airlines form a coalition to enable earnings of air miles across all partner airlines. Each airline would have already had its own air miles scheme. The coalition requires all partners to recognize each other's members. Ideally, an airline would only need to recognize valid membership cards from partner airlines. Nevertheless, delegation of authorization cannot express such policies directly; instead, each airline would need to delegate the "earn air miles" authorization to every other partner airlines' keys. Each airline would then in turn delegate all these authorizations to its members. When a customer buys a ticket from an airline, he/she would then be authorized to earn air miles on the account. Such approach has a serious weakness that the airline who delegates the authorization would rely on others to make sane and honest use of their keys. Additionally, the administrative cost of this style of delegation is exponential. For example, if a new airline joins the scheme, every member must produce a new delegation. The main reason behind these weaknesses is due to the artificial use of delegation of authorization to model the policies.

This paper introduces a policy-driven trust management framework, *Fidelis*. Its development originates from our prior work on OASIS (Open Architecture for Secure, Interworking Services) [8,9,10], which is a role-based architecture for distributed authorization management. The design of the Fidelis framework focuses on two principles, aiming at supporting large-scale, decentralized and collaborative applications:

- separation of policies and credentials.
- full support for domain autonomy.

Unlike most other trust management systems where the notions of policy and credential are somewhat orthogonal, the design of Fidelis advocates a different approach. Credentials are simply assertions that have no processing semantics. Policies interpret credentials with locally-defined semantics. They are specified independently and separately from the principal which specifies and issues credentials. Policies are considered purely "local", i.e. only meaningful to the principal who specifies and manages them. This property of policies forms the basis of domain autonomy in Fidelis.

The work on Fidelis [11] consists of the policy framework, the design and implementation for web services, and several demonstration applications. In this paper, however, we will focus on the policy framework. The paper is organized as follows. In the next section, concepts of the Fidelis policy framework are described. Built on these concepts, Sect. 3 describes Fidelis Policy Language (FPL) – a language for expressing distributed authorization and trust-based policies. Both the syntax and the semantics will be presented. We then provide a qualitative discussion of the policy framework in Sect. 4. In Sect. 5, we relate and compare this work with other notable work. A description of the current status and pointers for future work will be provided in Sect. 6.

2   Fidelis Policy Framework

This section describes the key concepts in the Fidelis policy framework.

2.1   Principals

A *principal* in the Fidelis framework represents a uniquely identifiable unit of individuals or processes. Principals in Fidelis are public keys, i.e. a principal must *control* (i.e. speak for) its public key pair. There exists three types of principal: *simple*, *group* and *threshold* principals. A simple principal is a plain individual; the latter two are called *composite principals*, which consist of one or more simple principals, and are considered as a logical unit by the policy framework. A group principal represents a conjunction of simple principals, whereas a threshold principal is a group principal with a *threshold value*. Threshold principals enable the specification of threshold schemes. An example is given in Sect. 3.3. In this paper, we use A, B, and C to denote principals.

2.2   Trust Statements

The main building block of the policy framework is the notion of *trust statements*. Trust in Fidelis is defined as *a set of assertions that a principal held with regard to another principal*. A trust statement declares a set of assertions, defining semantics to each assertion. It may be instantiated to create *trust instances*. Trust instances in Fidelis equate to assertion credentials in other trust management systems.

A trust instance has four parts: the *truster*, the *subject*, the *validity condition* and a set of values. The truster is the issuer of the trust instance; the subject is the principal to who the trust instance is issued. The assertions may be viewed as a set of name-value pairs. However, since the names are declared in the corresponding trust statement, only values are required to represent assertions in trust instances.

A validity condition specifies the condition under which a trust instance is valid. A variety of mechanisms [12,13,14,15,8] may be employed for this purpose. The framework requires the adherence to the *determinism principle*, whereby the validity of a trust instance cannot be negated once it is *guaranteed*. A consequence of this is that the processing behaviour will be deterministic, with no "sudden surprises".

In the framework, every principal may issue trust instances. There is no distinction between "servers" and "clients". A trust instance is signed with the private key of its truster. The authenticity of a trust instance can therefore be verified by checking the signature with the truster's principal identifier (i.e. a public key).

2.3   Trust Networks and Trust Conveyance

A majority of the current work on trust management systems are based on the notion of delegation of authorization as described in Sect. 1. Fidelis framework

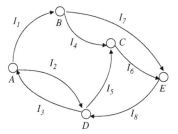

Fig. 1. A trust network

attempts to model a more general notion – the notion of *trust networks*. Technically, a trust network is a collection of trust instances. More formally, a trust network, T, is a labelled, directed graph. Suppose the basic components in the framework are:

- **U**: the set of all principals.
- **I**: the set of all trust instances.

A trust network can then be defined as:

$$T = (V, E)$$

where $V \subseteq \mathbf{U}$ is the set of vertices and $E \subseteq \mathbf{U} \times \mathbf{U} \times \mathbf{I}$ is the set of edges. An edge $(A, B, I_1) \in E$, written as $A \xrightarrow{I_1} B$, represents a trust instance I_1, issued by principal A (truster) for principal B (subject). Figure 1 shows an illustration of a trust network.

Construction of a trust network is primarily through *trust conveyance*. Trust conveyance is to model the act of *knowledge-passing*, which is very often found, either explicitly or implicitly, in daily life. For example, word-of-mouth is a form of knowledge-passing, and so is advertisement and/or recommendation. Trust is said to be *conveyed* if one principal passes a trust instance to another. The former principal is called the *conveyance source* or the *source* and the latter is called the *conveyance target* or the *target*. The source is not required to be the truster of the trust instance being conveyed. Similarly, the target need not be the subject of the trust instance it is receiving. Figure 2 illustrates an instance of conveyance, in the context of public key certification. A public key certificate is a form of trust instances: the truster, in this case Bob, asserts that the key of the subject is given in the assertion. Another principal, Cindy, may somehow obtain this trust instance and decide to propagate it to David, the conveyance target.

While the act of trust conveyance expands one's trust network, it does not introduce nor destroy trust globally – considering a global trust network consisting of all principals and trust instances, acts of trust conveyance will not alter the trust network.

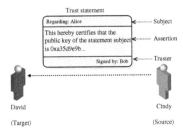

Fig. 2. Conveying trust

The concept of trust networks forms the foundation of the Fidelis policy framework. In essence, policies define "patterns" which are searched in a trust network during policy computation. More discussion is given in Sect. 2.5.

2.4   Actions

An action is an application operation, which may be subject to the outcome of policy computation. There are two *modes* for actions. An action can be either *authorization* or *obligation*. An authorization means that the action *may* be performed if the policy computation grants it; an obligation means that the action *must* be performed if the policy computation demands it. Action is represented as a set of name-value pairs. The interpretation however is application-dependent. An action may directly correspond to an access mode (e.g. `read`, `write` for a file system) in an operating system; it may also be a high-level task, such as `withdraw_money` in an ATM machine, which consists of several low-level operations.

2.5   Policies

Policies in the framework are sets of rules. There are two types of policy: *trust policies* govern the issuance of trust instances, and *action policies* determines the invocation of actions. Policies are local properties and hence may be expressed using any local mechanism. The framework however defines a *policy evaluation model* based on trust networks in Sect. 2.3. In the model, a policy is considered as a predicate for trust networks. A policy P is satisfied by a trust network T, written as,

$$T \vdash P$$

if and only if P yields **true** on input of T as a parameter. Any computation may be encapsulated in P. In Sect. 3, we describe the Fidelis policy language (FPL), which considers P as a pattern filter and returns **true** if at least one pattern is found in a given trust network.

The framework assumes that every principal can specify, manage and amend its own policies in an autonomous fashion. There exists no formal structures between principals globally. Effectively, the system consists of a flat space of principals who may freely interact with one another. Some local structures may however exist to increase administrative convenience. For example, a university may impose a local hierarchy of faculties, departments, laboratories and other units – each of which under its own administration, with a central University authority overseeing their operations.

3   Fidelis Policy Language

The Fidelis policy framework is intentionally abstract, omitting details such as policy specification. This section describes the Fidelis policy language (FPL), which provides a concrete instantiation of the framework. The syntax of the language is first described, and followed by the description of its semantics.

3.1   Principal

There are three types of principals: simple, group and threshold principals, as described in Sect. 2.1. For a simple principal, it is written as a literal public key, as follows:

```
rsa-1024: 30fa890281faba01dac25a935af9...
```

The string left to the colon identifies the public key cryptosystem, in this case, 1024-bit RSA; the string after the colon gives the actual public key in hexadecimal. A group principal may be specified either as a literal list of public keys separated by commas or as a variable. When given as a variable, the variable will be bound to a set of public keys during execution – useful when the group is dynamically constructed, e.g. from a database query. An example group principal is shown below:

```
{ rsa-512: e8cf79116c538d3b0694c1af5d6ad6ec,
  dsa-1024: d75684c66242815a23d2c4dad4b3bdbb,
  rsa-512: 30165913753649c30bc4f9b6fc06d04f }
```

A threshold principal is written as a group principal with a threshold value, using the keyword -of. The threshold value is either an integer or a variable whose value will be dynamically bound. An example threshold principal, requiring at least two principals from the group would be:

```
2-of {rsa-512: 023296de..., rsa-512: ca91f513...,
      rsa-512: f6994a9b..., }
```

The language provides keywords for special principals, **self** and **any-key**. The keyword **self** refers to the public key of the policy owner, which can be bound at deployment time. The keyword **any-key** is provided as a wildcard for public keys. It is intended for policies that need not consider a specific truster or subject, e.g. *any principal certified by the local authentication server may log onto the workstations.*

3.2 Representation of Trust Statements and Actions

In FPL, both trust statements and actions are represented as typed predicates.
For example, suppose C defines the `credit_rating` statement. A trust instance
of `credit_rating` issued by A to B would be:

```
C.credit_rating("companyA", 4): A -> B
```

Trust statements and actions must be declared prior to use in policies. The
declaration of the `credit_rating` statement may be:

```
statement credit_rating (string company, int rating)
```

The name is scoped locally within a principal. Global uniqueness is unnecessary, and SDSI/SPKI-style linked names [6,7] may be constructed when referencing trust statements or actions defined by other principals. For the purpose
of this paper, a simple type system is used, consisting of primitive types: `int`,
`float`, `string`, principal identifiers (`pubkey`) and principal groups (`group`).

3.3 Trust Policies

A trust policy specifies conditions and rules for constructing new trust instances.
A trust policy in FPL has the following structure:

[⟨*trust statement*⟩, ...]	(1)
[**without** ⟨*trust statement*⟩, ...]	(2)
asserts ⟨*trust statement*⟩	(3)
[**where** ⟨*expression*⟩] [**set** ⟨*expression*⟩]	
[**grants** ⟨*action*⟩ , ...] [**valid** ⟨*validity expression*⟩]	

The heart of a trust policy is the `asserts` clause (3), which defines the goal
of the trust policy. When a trust policy is evaluated against a trust network, the
basic conditions for the goal are that:

– all the specified trust statements in (1) are present in the trust network, and
  are *valid*;
– none of the specified trust statements in the `without` clause (2) is present
  in the trust network;

The matching of trust statements follows a parameter binding rule similar
to Prolog-style unification. Suppose the following trust statements are given as
conditions in (1) for a trust policy:

```
A.t1(p1, p2): A->p, A.t2(p2, p3): A->p, ...
```

Suppose the trust network, TN, is given to evaluate the policy,

```
TN = { A.t1(10, 20):A->B,
        A.t1(10, 30):A->B,
        A.t2(20, 30):A->B }
```

then trust instances `A.t1(10, 20):A->B` and `A.t2(20, 30):A->B` would satisfy the conditions, as the values bound to p2 and p (i.e. 20 and B) would be consistent across all trust instances. `A.t1(10, 30):A->B` and `A.t2(20, 30):A->B` will not satisfy due to the disagreement of the binding for p2.

The expression in the **where** clause provides an instrument for constraining parameters in trust statements. For example, one may add the following clause to the example above to constrain the value of p1:

```
where p1 > 5 && p1 < 15
```

The **set** clause is intended for creating *contextual variables*. Contextual variables are created during the evaluation and are scoped to that particular evaluation run. For example, given the following clause:

```
set q1 = p1 * 1.15;
```

the variable q1 will be created with a value computed at evaluation time. It may then be used, for example, in the trust statement in the **asserts** clause to initialize parameters for new trust instances.

The other two clauses, **grants** and **valid**, are for implementing capability-style trust instances and specifying the validity mechanism for new trust instances respectively, and will be discussed more fully later.

Example 1: Recommendation. The Hong Kong Jockey Club has a membership rule whereby a candidate member must be endorsed by two voting members. A voting member has the right to propose and second for membership and there are currently around 200 voting members in the club.

One approach to represent this policy would be modelling both roles and endorsements as trust statements. We identify two roles, club member and voting member, and trust statements may be declared as:

```
statement as_member(), as_voting_member();
statement endorsement();
```

With this design, the Jockey Club issues an instance of `as_member()` for every member, and additionally `as_voting_member()` for every voting member. Furthermore, the act of endorsement is embodied as the issuance of the `endorsement()` trust statements. With the definition of these trust statements, the membership policy could then be written as:

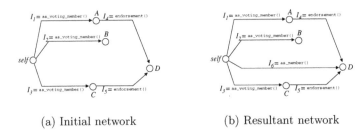

(a) Initial network   (b) Resultant network

Fig. 3. Example: Hong Kong Jockey Club

```
endorsement(): 2-of { voters } -> p
as_voting_member(): self -> voters,
asserts as_member(): self -> p
```

In essence, this policy defines the rule of granting instances of `as_member()`. To satisfy this policy, two conditions that must be met when provided with a trust network:

1. `endorsement(): 2-of { voters } -> p`, which matches an instance of endorsement in the trust network whose truster is any two principals from the group given in the variable `voters` and binds the subject of that trust instance to the variable `p`.
2. `as_voting_member(): self -> voters`, which matches instances of `as_voting_member` in the trust network which are issued by the policy owner (`self`), and adds their subjects to the group `voters`.

Suppose the trust network in Fig. 3(a) is given to obtain a new trust instance of `as_member` for the principal D. The variable `voters` will be bound to $\{A, B, C\}$ and the edges $A \xrightarrow{I_4} D$ and $C \xrightarrow{I_5} D$ will satisfy the conditions, and therefore an instance of `as_member` may be issued, resulting in a new trust network shown in Fig. 3(b).

Example 2: Authorization trust. FPL provides a special mechanism that extends the use of trust instances to model *authorization certificates* in key-oriented access control such as PolicyMaker/KeyNote [3,4] and SPKI [6,7]. An authorization certificate in key-oriented access control can be considered as a special kind of trust instance, whereby the subject is delegated with authorizations by the truster.

Consider a banking service. Suppose the bank has defined the following trust statements:

- `owner(string ac_num)`: issued to every customer, asserting their ownership of the account `ac_num`.

- `capabilities()`: a special "capability-style" trust statement embodying authorized actions. Such instances may be, for example, contained in a smart card.
- `suspended(string ac_num)`: issued to the bank itself, indicating operations on the account `ac_num` have been suspended.

Suppose the banking operations include: querying the account balance, depositing money into the account and withdrawing money from the account. Suppose also the issuing of a `capabilities()` trust statement to a principal is subject to:

1. the principal owns an account with the bank, and
2. the account is not explicitly suspended.

Furthermore, the validity of the `capabilities()` instance must be linked to the lifetime of the account. The policy may then be written as:

```
1    owner(account_no): self -> p validity as v1
2    without suspended(account_no): self -> self
3    asserts capabilities(): self -> p
4    grants balance(account_no): p, withdraw(account_no): p,
5            deposit(account_no): p
6    valid v1
```

Line 1 and 2 expresses the two conditions respectively. In Line 1,

```
... validity as v1
```

provides a symbolic name, v1, for the validity condition in the `owner()` instance. This is then used in Line 6, the `valid` clause, which sets the validity condition for the new `capabilities()` instance to be v1. This effectively links the validity conditions of the `owner()` and `capabilities()` instances. The `grants` clause (Line 4 and 5) specifies the actions that will be included in the new trust instance. As the trust policy includes the `without` clause, the conditions in the `without` clause (i.e. `suspended()`) will also be included in the trust instance.

A principal possessing an instance of `capabilities()` may present it to an access point for services. On access, the access point would only need to:

1. search the requested action in the `capabilities()` instance.
2. ensure the `capabilities()` instance is valid.
3. ensure that the included `suspend()` instance does not exist.

This key-oriented style of access control simplifies the access control monitor – authorization decisions depend on straightforward checks rather than complex policy evaluation. The decision process is therefore speedy. However, as will be discussed in Sect. 3.4, key-oriented access control is not always appropriate.

3.4   Action Policies

In the previous section, the use of **grants** clause tightly couples trust instances and actions. This coupling is often inflexible in real-world applications. Firstly, the use of trust instances may not always be known in advance. Conceptually, they represent *beliefs* that are subject to the interpretation of the recipient principals. Secondly, especially in distributed environments, as the recipient of a trust instance is taking the risk of breached access, the recipient should specify the policies for its services rather than relying on the truster. Similar view is shared with Herzberg et al. [16]. FPL supports the notion of *action policies* which relate actions with trust instances.

The syntax for action policies is a subset of trust policies. It has the following structure:

```
[ ⟨trust statement⟩, ... ] [ without ⟨trust statement⟩, ... ]
[ where ⟨expression⟩ ] [ set ⟨expression⟩ ]
grants ⟨action⟩, ...
```

An action policy includes a mandatory **grants** clause and does not include **asserts** and **valid** clauses as in trust policies. Other syntactical aspects are identical to the ones for trust policies. The evaluation semantics for action policies is also consistent with trust policies, except for the meaning of the **grants** clause.

Recall from Sect. 2.4 that there are two modes for actions. If the mode is authorization, the **grants** clause provides a list of authorized actions if the conditions are met; if the mode is obligation, the list of actions in the **grants** clause must be carried out if the conditions are met. There is no specific support in the language to specify the modal behaviour of actions. The mode of an action depends on the application context.

Example 3: distributed authorization. Suppose a distributed computing environment consists of an authentication service and a file service. Suppose the file service protects files using access control lists (ACL) based on the identity authenticated by the authentication service. Suppose the authentication service defines a trust statement to represent an authenticated user:

```
statement auth_user(string username);
```

Suppose file access is represented as actions, defined by the file service:

```
action access (string obj, string access_mode);
```

The authorization policy at the file service may then be written as:

```
AS.auth_user (user_id): AS -> p
where acl_lookup(obj, mode, user_id)
grants access(obj, mode): p
```

where the conditional predicate `acl_lookup` determines whether a user is in the ACL of a file with a specified access mode, and `AS` refers to the principal identifier of the authentication service. Note that `AS.auth_user()` is a linked name, referencing `auth_user()` defined by `AS`.

When access to a file is requested, `p` is bound to the identifier of the requester, `obj` and `mode` are bound respectively to the name of the requested file and the access mode. The action policy grants access to the file, if and only if:

- an `AS.auth_user()` trust instance issued by `AS` with `p` as the subject exists, and
- the user `user_id` is authorized for the requested access mode on the file, i.e. `acl_lookup` returns **true**.

3.5   Inference Semantics

Here we describe the semantics for processing queries against both trust and action policies. A query is composed of:

- a trust network, which represents the assertions known and willing to disclose by the requester. We shall assume all trust instances in the trust network have been cryptographically verified for their integrity.
- a *query template*. A query template may be considered as a trust instance or an action request with wildcards on some or all parameters. The former type is called a *trust template* and the latter type is called an *action template*.

The processing of a query results in a trust instance or an action request depending on the query template, and optionally a *trace* of execution. The resulting trust instance or action request is an instance that *matches* the query template. An action request and an action template match if and only if their names, values of parameters and requesters (if specified in the template) match. Similarly, a trust instance and a trust template match if and only if their names, values of parameters, trusters and subjects match.

Let the set of all policies (both trust policies and action policies) defined by a principal be **P**. The execution of a query consists of a sequence of *evaluations* of policies in **P**. Each evaluation works in the context of a single policy, and takes as input a trust network, a query template and an environment, and a trust or action instance is returned as output. Let **N** be the set of all trust networks, where each trust network is a set of trust instances. We can represent the execution of a query as a directed, labelled graph,

$$D = (L, M)$$

where $L \subseteq \mathbf{N}$ is the set of vertices and $M \subseteq \mathbf{N} \times \mathbf{N} \times \mathbf{P}$ is the set of edges. The goal of a query execution is to find a path in D,

$$l_1 \xrightarrow{m_1} l_2 \xrightarrow{m_2} \ldots \xrightarrow{m_{n-1}} l_n$$

such that there exists a trust instance or action request $t_n \in l_n$ that matches the query template, where l_1 is the initial trust network. An edge $(l_j, l_{j+1}, p_j) \in M$

means that the evaluation of the policy p_j transforms the trust network l_j into l_{j+1}, where $l_{j+1} = l_j \cup \{t_{j+1}\}$. The evaluation of p_j finds a minimal subset $l'_j \subseteq l_j$ such that if p_j takes input l'_j and some environment (i.e. a set of contextual bindings to variables), t_{j+1} will be produced as output. The evaluation needs to satisfy the following rules:

1. for each prerequisite ⟨*trust statement*⟩ in p_j (i.e. those not in the without clause), there exists exactly one corresponding trust instance in l'_j. Correspondence means the trust instance must be an instance of the trust use, *and* its parameters must agree with their binding, as defined below.
2. every variable must be bound to a value. For every ⟨*trust statement*⟩ (including the without clause) in p_j, a variable for a parameter, the truster or the subject must be bound to the value provided by the corresponding parameter, truster or subject in the matching trust instance.
   For a trust template or action template, a parameter variable is bound to a value provided either by a previous binding, the query template or a name-value pair from the environment. Where multiple bindings are possible for the same variable, all bindings must agree to the same value.
3. for each ⟨*trust statement*⟩ in the without clause in p_j, there must not exist a corresponding trust instance in l_j and in any other mandatory repository.
4. all parameter bindings must satisfy the conditions in the where clause in p_j if it exists.
5. if the optional set clause exists in p_j, it must be evaluated after all variables are bound. Since the evaluation of the assignment expressions may create or modify variable bindings, this requirement guarantees the evaluation of the set clause will not cause an unexpected side-effect.
6. all trust instances in l'_j must be valid according to their validity conditions.

The resulting trust instance or action request is constructed by instantiating the query template, filling variables with their appropriate bindings. For a trust instance, its validity condition will be as specified in the valid clause if it exists. Otherwise, it will be default to the validity condition with the *shortest* guarantee period in the set of trust instances used to satisfy the policy. For the complete rules for computing default validity condition, please see [11].

Let $m_j = (l_j, l_{j+1}, p_j)$ and suppose l'_j satisfies p_j, then a pair (m_j, l'_j) is called a *realization* of the policy p_j. The chain of realizations

$$((m_1, l'_1), (m_2, l'_2), ..., (m_{n-1}, l'_{n-1}))$$

is called the *execution trace* for a query. The execution trace provides detailed information of the query evaluation, and may be used as a proof of the correctness of the answer or for audit purposes.

4   Discussion

Rich credentials v.s. rich policies. The key difference between Fidelis and most other trust management frameworks (e.g. PolicyMaker, KeyNote, and the RT framework) is the role of credentials. In this discussion, we refer credentials in PolicyMaker, KeyNote and the RT framework as *rich credentials* since credentials in these systems contain a rich body of information, including encoded policies. On the other hand, in Fidelis, trust instances are *simple credentials* that carry static attributes of subjects. Policies are separately specified from the credentials, and the interpretation of the attributes in a credential is purely determined by the principal who specifies the policies.

The Fidelis approach cleanly separates credentials and policies. Some advantages of this separation have been briefly described in Sect. 1. Additionally, as policies are local entities, evolution of policies does not affect other principals. This simplifies the tasks of policy management. In contrast, if policies are distributed in the form of rich credentials, change of policies would mean revocation of all issued credentials. The approach of rich credentials therefore poses a scalability concern. Furthermore, the interoperability of rich credentials is more problematic, as the semantics of the rich credentials has to be universally supported by all principals in the system. On the contrary, the design of Fidelis ensures interoperability with existing systems. Trust instances may be coded as X.509, SAML or SPKI certificates, and policies may be written to conform to the semantics of these systems. Fidelis thus provides an integration path with established systems.

Expressiveness. The Fidelis policy framework does not define the mechanisms how policies are specified. The expressiveness of Fidelis discussed in this section applies to the policy language described in Sect. 3. Fidelis Policy Language is designed to express two kinds of policies: trust policies and action policies. Aside from the syntactic sugar, the essence of the language is first-order logic. Each prerequisite ⟨*trust statement*⟩ is similar to a positive predicate in a first-order formula, and each ⟨*trust statement*⟩ in the **without** clause equates to a negated predicate. Based on this foundation, the expressiveness of the FPL is similar to that of first-order logic.

Some additional features contribute to this expressive power: the support for group and threshold principals, fine-grained filtering of parameters in the **where** clause, and the extensibility to support application-defined languages for the conditional and assignment expressions. These combined features achieve a high degree of expressive power, supporting prerequisite-based, recommendation/reputation, and delegation-based policy types.

5   Related Work

There exists several notable trust management systems in the literature. One of the earliest such systems, PolicyMaker [3], builds on top of the notion of *programmable credentials*, where credentials are essentially predicate filters. The successor, KeyNote [4], standardizes several aspects of PolicyMaker. Its credentials feature a highly structured program in the form of conditional expressions. Simple Public Key Infrastructure (SPKI) [7] is designed as an access control architecture, featuring *delegation certificates*. These systems attempt to capture policies through the notion of *delegation of authorization*. They share a similar processing strategy, which attempts to find a *delegation path* from presented credentials to the local, trusted policies. The Fidelis policy language defines a more powerful processing model, which allows multiple paths in a trust network to be identified.

PolicyMaker/KeyNote and the more recent RT framework [5] feature *rich credentials*. Policies in these systems are specification of chains of credentials. The semantics of their credentials play an important role in defining the policies. On the contrary, Fidelis features a clean separation of policies and credentials. It features simple credentials with *rich policies*, which are locally defined by every principal.

OASIS [8,9,10] is designed for distributed role-based access control, with an extensive support for policy-driven role activation. Role activation may be subject to prerequisite roles, *appointments* and *environmental predicates*. An appointment can be considered as a special kind of trust instances, whose intention is to allow role activation. These components allow the specification of complex real-world policies relating to roles. Many ideas in Fidelis originate from the research on OASIS. While OASIS has extensive policy support, it is not designed for general trust policies, for example, recommendation-based policies are awkward in OASIS.

Trust Policy Language (TPL) [16] is similar to OASIS in that policies are used to direct role assignments. It supports recommendation-based policies, which map a collection of recommendation certificates into a role. It has filter mechanisms based on simple conditions and certificate types. It also has a mechanism for negative credentials to be verified. However, it lacks in the support for general prerequisite and application-defined conditions. Moreover, its support for non-monotonic policies does not allow for fine-grained specification, given that it is simply based on a revocation list approach. While conditions on fields can be specified, it does not allow inter-certificate correlation as provided by Fidelis. This poses some limitations on its expressiveness.

6 Conclusion and Future Work

This paper introduces *Fidelis*, a policy-driven trust management framework designed to facilitate interworking between distributed applications. The most distinctive feature of Fidelis is the notion of separation of policies and credentials. Policies may be defined for the issuance of trust instances and for governing action decisions based on trust instances. In this paper, we have presented the Fidelis policy framework and describe the Fidelis policy language, which implements the policy framework.

Other aspects of the Fidelis framework have been described in [11]. Some highlights include:

- the design and implementation of the Fidelis framework on the web services platform, based on SOAP and XML.
- the design and analysis of an algorithm that implements the semantics of Fidelis Policy Language.
- a trust negotiation framework built on top of the Fidelis policy framework.

Future work of Fidelis includes integration with computational trust models. These models attempt to compute the trustworthiness of principals for certain actions, with regard to the cost and risks. Additionally, the trust negotiation framework described in [11] presents a starting point of a flexible framework for incremental disclosure of trust instances. Enhancement work on the negotiation framework is also currently underway.

Acknowledgement. The author would like to thank Jean Bacon for many helpful comments and interesting discussions on the design of Fidelis. The author acknowledges the support of the Engineering and Physical Sciences Research Council (EPSRC) under the grant *OASIS Access Control: Implementation and Evaluation* (GR/M75686/01), which is the predecessor of Fidelis.

References

1. Needham, R.M., Herbert, A.H.: The Cambridge Distributed Computing System. Addison Wesley (1982) ISBN 0-20114-092-6.
2. Wulf, W.A., Cohen, E.S., Corwin, W.M., Jones, A.K., Levin, R., Pierson, C., Pollack, F.J.: HYDRA: The kernel of a multiprocessor operating system. Communications of the ACM **17** (1974) 337–345
3. Blaze, M., Feigenbaum, J., Lacy, J.: Decentralized trust management. In: Proceedings of the IEEE Symposium on Research in Security and Privacy, Oakland, CA, IEEE Computer Society, Technical Committee on Security and Privacy, IEEE Computer Society Press (1996) 164–173
4. Blaze, M., Feigenbaum, J., Ioannidis, J., Keromytis, A.D.: The KeyNote trust management system. Internet Request for Comment RFC 2704, Internet Engineering Task Force (1999) Version 2.
5. Li, N., Mitchell, J.C., Winsborough, W.H.: Design of a role-based trust-management framework. In: IEEE Symposium on Security and Privacy, Los Angeles, CA, IEEE Computer Society Press (2002) 114–130
6. Rivest, R.L., Lampson, B.: SDSI–A simple distributed security infrastructure. See http://theory.lcs.mit.edu/~rivest/sdsi10.ps (1996)
7. Ellison, C.M., Frantz, B., Lampson, B., Rivest, R., Thomas, B., Ylonen, T.: SPKI certificate theory. RFC 2693, Internet Engineering Task Force (1999) See http://www.ietf.org/rfc/rfc2693.txt.
8. Hayton, R., Bacon, J., Moody, K.: OASIS: Access control in an open, distributed environment. In: Proceedings of IEEE Symposium on Security and Privacy (Oakland, CA, May 3–6), Los Alamitos, CA, IEEE Computer Society Press (1998)
9. Yao, W., Moody, K., Bacon, J.: A model of OASIS role-based access control and its support for active security. In: Sixth ACM Symposium on Access Control Models and Technologies (SACMAT 2001, Chantilly, VA, May 3–4), New York, NY, ACM Press (2001) 171–181
10. Bacon, J., Moody, K., Yao, W.: A model of OASIS role-based access control and its support for active security. ACM Transactions on Information and System Security **5** (2002) To appear.
11. Yao, W.T.M.: Trust Management For Widely Distributed Systems. PhD thesis, Computer Laboratory, University of Cambridge (2002)

12. ITU-T (Telecommunication Standardization Sector, International Telecommunication Union) Geneva, Switzerland: ITU-T Recommendation X.509: The Directory – Public-Key and Attribute Certificate Frameworks. (2000)
13. Naor, M., Nissim, K.: Certificate revocation and certificate update. In: Proceedings of the 7th USENIX Security Symposium (SECURITY-98), Berkeley, Usenix Association (1998) 217–228
14. Wright, R., Lincoln, P.D., Millen, J.K.: Efficient fault-tolerant certificate revocation. In: Proceedings of the 7th ACM Conference on Computer and Communications Security (CCS-00), New York, NY, ACM Press (2000) 19–24
15. Hayton, R.: OASIS: An Open Architecture for Secure Interworking Services. PhD thesis, Univeristy of Cambridge Computer Laboratory (1996) Technical Report No. 399.
16. Herzberg, Mass, Mihaeli, Naor, Ravid: Access control meets public key infrastructure, or: Assigning roles to strangers. In: RSP: 21th IEEE Computer Society Symposium on Research in Security and Privacy. (2000)

Implementation of an Agent-Oriented Trust Management Infrastructure Based on a Hybrid PKI Model

Yücel Karabulut

Department of Computer Science, University of Dortmund,
August-Schmid-Strasse 12, D-44221 Dortmund, Germany
yuecel.karabulut@udo.edu

Abstract. Access control in modern computing environments is different from access control in the traditional setting of operating systems. For distributed computing systems, specification and enforcement of permissions can be based on a public key infrastructure which deals with public keys for asymmetric cryptography. Previous approaches and their implementations for applying a public key infrastructure are classified as based either on trusted authorities with licencing or on owners with delegations. We present the architecture and main features of a trust management infrastructure based on a hybrid model which unifies and extends the previous public key infrastructure approaches. The trust management infrastructure constitutes a flexible framework for experimenting with the applications of different trust models.

1 Introduction

In the Internet most interactions including business transactions occur between strangers, due to billions of spontaneous users and the fact that most of them do not share a common security domain. Thus, Internet constitutes a global computing infrastructure in which entities need to reason about the trustworthiness of other entities in order to make autonomous security decisions.

More specifically, spontaneous users wish to find information and several heterogeneous and autonomous sources wish to share their resources and aim at supporting potential clients. While requesting accesses to the resources, clients may be unwilling to reveal their identities for private reasons and thus prefer to remain anonymous. Additionally for a resource owner, it may be necessary to see evidences of a client's eligibility rather than to know *who* they are. According to these trends, a client proves her eligibility to see a piece of information by a collection of her characterizing properties (e.g. profession, organizational membership, security clearance, academic title) and each autonomous source follows a security policy that is expressed in terms of characterizing properties.

In the modern computing environments emerging from these trends, some basic assumptions of traditional access control approaches are not longer valid. Traditional access control mechanisms operate under a closed world assumption,

P. Nixon and S. Terzis (Eds.): Trust Management 2003, LNCS 2692, pp. 318–331, 2003.

in which all of the entities are registered and locally known. When the server and the client are unknown to one another and when resources are to be shared across administrative boundaries, the conventional authorization scheme fails. The conventional approach to authorization involves authenticating the client to a local, administratively-defined user identity, then authorizing that user according to an access control list (ACL) for the resource. Given that the identities of clients cannot be known in advance to the servers, these identities cannot be put on the access control lists and other identity-based authorizations of the servers to decide who can do what.

In order to overcome these and related difficulties we need to employ new access control mechanisms [20] matching the characteristic properties of modern computing environments. Accordingly, we can specify and enforce permissions of clients on remote servers by employing modern access control approaches which are based on asymmetric cryptography. In order to employ asymmetric cryptography in open computing environments we need appropriate trust management infrastructures that enable entities to establish mutual trust. Accordingly, we have designed a hybrid PKI model to be used for specifying and enforcing permission in open computing systems. The hybrid PKI model, as reported in [7, 8], unifies and extends previous PKI approaches [2,19,13,14,11].

We have used the hybrid PKI model to implement an extended version of our design of secure mediation [5] basing the enforcement of confidentiality and authenticity on certified personal authorization attributes rather than on identification. In order to prove the key ideas and to implement the general design of the hybrid PKI model, a specific approach has to be taken into account. For this purpose, we have implemented an agent oriented and KQML[1]-based trust management infrastructure [18,20,8]. In this paper we present the structure and key features of the components of our trust management infrastructure which constitutes a flexible framework for experimenting with the applications of different trust models.

This paper is structured as follows. Section 2 gives a brief introduction to the use of asymmetric cryptography for specifying and enforcing permissions and outlines the hybrid PKI model underlying to the implemented trust management infrastructure. Section 3 presents the implementation objectives. Section 4 then exhibits the main features and components of the trust management infrastructure (section 4.1) and presents a control flow among the functional and security components for a selected operation (section 4.2). Finally, section 5 reviews related work and presents conclusions.

2   Outline of the Hybrid PKI Model

The use of asymmetric cryptography in conjuntion with access control lists (ACL) is considered as the state-of-art for access control systems. Asymmetric cryptography needs to be founded in an appropriate management of trust.

---

[1] KQML stands for Knowledge Query and Manipulation Language.

In various forms, trust has to be assigned to public keys and to the pertinent properties that are claimed to be true for a public key or the holder of the corresponding private key, respectively. Management of trust is organized within a *public key infrastructure*, PKI for short.

In its simplest form, a PKI is a system for publishing the public keys used in asymmetric cryptography. *Property assignment* and *trust evaluation* are two basic functionalities common to all PKI approaches. Property assignment is the process of binding a computer or other entity, or even some other piece of information, such as a capability, to a public key. Property assignment is captured by a *digitally signed document* which might be a *certificate* or a *credential*. Trust evaluation is the process of determining whether a certificate/credential captures a "real" property assignment.

A typical scenario exploiting the use of certificates/credentials for access control runs as follows. A client is represented by (one of) his public key(s) and characterized by the assigned properties. The client proves his eligibility to see a piece of information by a collection of his characterizing properties. Assignments of characterizing properties including identities to public keys are done by signing issuers. A resource owner follows a security policy that is expressed in terms of characterizing properties. Any agent as resource owner receives a signed request together with a set of certificates/credentials stemming from the pertinent client. The agent firstly ensures the authenticity with respect to the bound public keys and with respect to the actual holder of the corresponding private key by applying appropriate challenge-response protocols and secondly evaluates his trust in the issuer. Then the agent decides on the permission of the request by evaluating the properties extracted from submitted certificates/credentials with respect to his confidentiality policy.

Depending on the application and the underlying trust relationships between the involved entities, such scenarios can be realized by employing different PKI models. At the coarsest level of generalization, PKI models are distinguished into two categories: hierarchical (traditional) PKIs, e.g. X.509 [2,19], and non-hierarchical PKIs (i.e. trust networks), e.g. SPKI/SDSI [13,14,11]. There is a wide variety of circumstances in which both models can be applied.

Most of the works investigating the application of certificate/credential-based access control treat both PKI models as competing technologies [24,17,28,31,10, 23], even as dueling theologies [3]. We see arguments of the style this-model-is-better-than-another-model. We take a different position. PKI trust relationships must be built on real-world[2] trust relationships. In many real-world scenarios, trust relationships consist of hierarchies, trust networks, and combinations of two. Therefore, we argue that a trust management infrastructure, as required by dynamic computing environments, has to use and to link both kinds of PKI models.

---

[2] It is also important to observe that in some cases, such as the use of PKI to support anonymity, it can be important to make sure that PKI trust relationships don't follow real world trust relationships.

In [7], we classified previous PKI approaches as based on trusted authorities with licencing and dealing with free properties (characterizing attributes including identities), e.g. X.509, or based on owners with delegation dealing with bound properties (including capabilities), e.g. SPKI/SDSI. We extended and integrated these approaches into a hybrid PKI model which uses protocols to convert *free properties* into *bound properties*. Furthermore, we unified licencing and delegation by introducing *administrative properties*. Figure 1 visualizes an instance of the hybrid PKI model linking previous PKI models.

Following and extending the basic approach of X.509 [2,19], free properties and the corresponding certificates[3] are handled by trusted authorities using licencing (as shown on the left side of the upper part of Figure 1). Again, following and extending the basic approach of SPKI/SDSI [13,14,11], bound properties and the corresponding credentials[4] are handled by owners of services using delegation (as shown on the right side of the lower part of Figure 1).

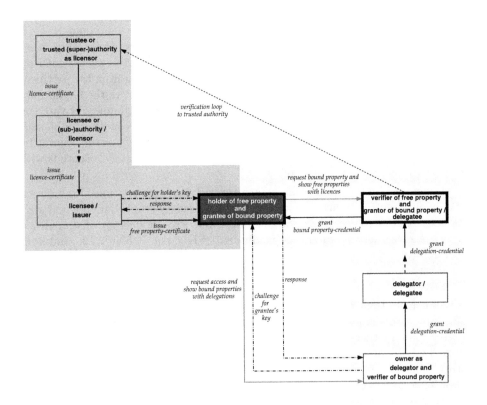

Fig. 1. Outline of an instance of the hybrid model for a PKI

---

[3] X.509 uses the terms *public-key certificate* and *attribute certificate*.
[4] SPKI/SDSI uses the term *authorization certificate*.

An instance of the full hybrid PKI model consists of overlapping components of three kinds: a) trusted authorities (also called trustees) and licensees for and a holder of a free property together with a verifier of this free property, b) an owner and delegatees for and a grantee of a bound property, and c) a holder of free properties and a grantor of a bound property.

The grantor follows a *property conversion policy* that maps free properties on bound properties, where the property conversion policy is a part of grantor's whole security policy. More precisely, the property conversion policy specifies *which set of free properties an entity has to enjoy in order to obtain a bound property assignment*. The middle part of Figure 1 visualizes the situation. The entity on the right is the grantor following a property conversion policy. The entity in the center requests a promise for a permission, i.e., a bound property. The grantor, after verifying the submitted free property-certificates with the supporting licences, applies his conversion policy on the free properties extracted from the submitted certificates, and finally, if all checks have been successfully completed, grants a bound property-credential where the subject (grantee) is the same as in the submitted free property-certificates.

3   Implementation Objectives

The motivation to elaborate the hybrid PKI model has not only originated from the conceptual challenge arising due to the incompatible security domains of mediation participants [5], but also due to a corresponding implementation task. Both the challenge and the implementation task are related to our view that all entities are highly autonomously cooperating, and accordingly all entities are implemented as software agents which base their communication on KQML [15, 16,30] and their data exchanges on CORBA [25].

Figure 1 visualizes the interactions between the involved entities in an instance of the hybrid PKI model. Based on these interactions and on our view that all entities are highly autonomously cooperating software agents we primarily need to focus on two aspects in order to implement the intended trust management infrastructure[5].

The first aspect is related to the KQML-based communication between the involved agents. The agents communicate by sending certain kinds of messages, called *performatives*, to each other. Considering the interactions involving among agents in an instance of the hybrid model, we need to implement new KQML performatives. For this purpose, we extended the works presented in [16,30] which propose secure-communiation related and PKI-related extensions to KQML. The new extensions to KQML, as reported in [18,8], are used by the agent interactions that are involved in an instance of the hybrid PKI model.

The second aspect, which is the focus of this paper, deals with the implementation task with respect to software agents involved. In order to simulate a

---

[5] [18] uses the term *hybrid PKI demonstrator* instead of trust management infrastructure.

hybrid PKI scenario we need to implement software agents of four kinds according to the roles and corresponding responsibilities of the entities involved in an instance of the hybrid PKI model:

- Agents representing issuers of administrative properties and free properties as trusted authorities and licencees;
- Agents representing verifiers of free properties and grantors of bound properties as delegatees;
- Agents representing holders of free properties and grantees of bound properties;
- Agents representing grantors and verifiers of bound properties as delegators and owners.

In general, however, all agents should be able to act in any of these roles during their lifetime. In particular, all agents should be enabled to deal with free and bound properties and to convert the former into the latter.

4   The Overall Architecture

In order to fulfill the requirements with respect to the second aspect discussed in section 3 we need a *core functionality* to be made available for all agents. The required core functionality is provided by our *agent core* which constitutes a base software library serving for the construction of the specific agents involved in an instance of the hybrid PKI model. Figure 2 visualizes the structure of the agent core and the data flow among the components of the agent core.

4.1   The Agent Core

The agent core is implemented in Java and on a Solaris platform. The agent core uses the agent library *libAgent*, which has been developed within the framework of MultiMediaMediator project [6] in our working group. With the help of the libAgent's development stage, we could focus on the application specific details of our agents, since the libAgent smoothly hides the CORBA related development complexity.

The agent core consists of five main modules: agent security module, agent functional module, agent human interface, agent communication interface and the agent PKI framework. In the following we present the main features and components of each module.

Agent Security Module. The *agent security module* has four components, the agent security knowledge base, ASECKNOB, the agent credential manager ACR-EMA, the agent property manager APROMA, and the agent trust manager ATRUMA.

The agent security knowledge base ASECKNOB maintains the following parts:

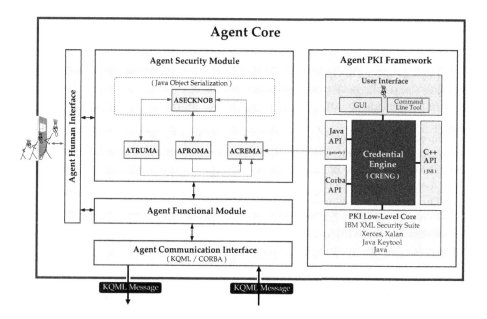

Fig. 2. Structure of the agent core

- The *property database* that is generated from the property definitions which are either locally defined by the administrator of an agent or imported from other agents.
- A *trust relationships database* that contains entries, each of which is related to a (trusted) agent and consists of the name, the public encryption key and the public verification key of the trusted agent. The entry also specifies the kind of the trust relationship (e.g. trusted authority, trusted delegatee) regarding the agent named in the entry.
- The *certificates* and *credentials* including licence-certificates, free property-certificates, delegation-credentials, and bound property-credentials.
- A (Horn clause) *rule base* that specify implications among properties which are invoked when free properties are converted to bound properties.

The agent credential manager ACREMA is programmed to perform the following tasks:

- Issuing the licence-certificates, free property-certificates and granting bound property-credentials and delegation-credentials;
- Inserting the certificates and the credentials and the corresponding chains into ASECKNOB;
- Retrieving the certificates and the credentials and the corresponding chains from ASECKNOB;
- Evaluating the chains of certificates and credentials;
- Verifying the authenticity and validity of submitted certificates and credentials;

- Implementing the content management operations for certificates and credentials including extracting the free properties and bound properties from certificates and credentials, respectively;
- Implementing the operations needed to manage the keystore including fetching the public keys from the Java's keystore;
- Implementing the utilized challenge-response method for authentication.

In order to evaluate and to build the chains of certificates and credentials as well as to sign and to verify the individual certificates and credentials, the ACREMA makes use of the simple service calls of the credential engine module that belongs to the agent PKI framework.

The agent property manager APROMA implements the classes and functions which are responsible for the management and storage of property definitions. Furthermore, APROMA implements the property conversion policy used by corresponding agents in order to determine whether a given set of free properties qualifies for some bound properties. APROMA also provides methods for importing and exporting property definitions between agents.

The agent trust manager ATRUMA implements the operations needed to store and to retrieve the information (e.g. public keys) about the trusted agents.

Agent Functional Module. The *agent functional module* implements classes and functions to process and evaluate the content of the KQML performatives. The functional module is a kind of scheduler analysing the incoming KQML performatives and scheduling the protocol steps to be executed. For this purpose the task control unit of the functional module coordinates the required function calls relating to the different components of the security module. What the content of a KQML performative expresses depends on the specific agent in which the performative is implemented.

Agent Human Interface. The *agent human interface* is designed as an interface for the administrators of the agents to use and set up the corresponding agents. Depending on the kind of agent, the respective administrator is provided to perform a selected set of tasks through an agent specific graphical user interface. Below we list the main tasks which can be performed using the graphical user interfaces of the implemented agents. More precisely, through these interfaces the administrators can:

- maintain the property definitions including the insertion, deletion and update of property definitions;
- maintain the trust relationships database by inserting new entries, and deleting and updating the existing entries;
- import property definitions from other agents;
- issue licence-certificates and free property-certificates;
- grant delegation-credentials and bound property-credentials;
- visualize the received certificates and credentials in XML format.

Agent Communication Interface. The *agent communication interface* implements classes and functions for sending and the reception of CORBA messages which are used to communicate performatives.

Agent PKI Framework. The *agent PKI framework* is a collection of tools which can be used to experiment with the basic PKI models and the hybrid PKI model [7,20]. The agent PKI framework provides basic PKI services such as encoding, issuing, and verifying certificates and credentials. The main particularity of the agent PKI framework is that it supports a broad spectrum of PKI-enabled applications by providing a variety of programming interfaces. Furthermore, the agent PKI framework is designed and implemented to hide the complexity of the underlying security mechanisms, while facilitating service requests through simple service calls.

The details of the implementation are reported in two master's thesis [18, 22]. The implementation is partially based on investigations which resulted in a credential model (i.e. unifying the existing certificate and credential models [2, 19,9,13,14]) which can be found in the master's thesis [21].

The credential engine, CRENG for short, is the core module of the agent PKI framework. CRENG is implemented in Java on a Solaris platform. The PKI framework is universal, since it provides an application programming interface (i.e. implemented by using Java Native Interface) for arbitrary C++ applications and agents (e.g. our MultiMediaMediator agent [5]). The framework also provides a CORBA interface for CORBA-enabled applications. Our implementation of the agent PKI framework is broad enough to allow the conduction of experiments with different PKI approaches and a hybrid PKI model. We proved the applicability of the agent PKI framework by employing it for the credential manager of the agent security module and the credential manager of the MultiMediaMediator agent [5]. Figure 2 visualizes the high-level architecture of the agent PKI framework.

In the following we outline the main features of the implemented PKI framework:

- Generating public/private key pairs, keystore and self-signed X.509 certificates. We use the X.509 certificates created by Java *keytool* [29], to obtain the public key stored in the digital certificate which is physically stored within the keystore.
- XML-encoding of certificates and credentials.
- Issuing of XML-encoded certificates and credentials.
- Verifying the signatures of certificates and credentials.
- Validity checking for certificates and credentials.
- Building chains of certificates and credentials, including licence-certificates and delegation-credentials, respectively.
- Evaluating chains of certificates and credentials (except of dealing with revocations so far).

The agent PKI framework also provides content management operations for certificates and credentials, including extracting the free properties and the bound properties. A GUI and command-line interface provided by this PKI framework facilitate the administration of certificates and credentials.

We opted for an approach to certificates and credentials based on digitally signed XML documents [12,27,26,4] in order to have freedom of experimenting and researching, and not to be constrained by any of the existing certificate and credential formats. Additionally, XML has the advantages of presenting self-describing documents and being widely used by various scientific disciplines. However, our approach is compatible with both X.509 and SPKI/SDSI philosophies. We have used IBM's *XML Security Suite* [4] for signing and verifying XML documents. XML Security Suite supports both DSA and RSA for digital signatures. Our implementation uses DSA for signing and SHA-1 for hashing. The XML Security Suite employs the XML parser *Xerces* and XSLT[6] stylesheet processor *Xalan* for the manipulation of XML documents [1].

We decided to design a common format for representing certificates and credentials. By using this format, it is possible to represent the certificates (except X.509-like attribute-certificates) and credentials presented in [20]. In order to represent the attribute-certificates, the *subject* field must be extended to include a reference to an identity-certificate. Moreover, for the sake of simplicity, the *type* field indicates only the kind of the underlying document. This field could also be extended to encode the cryptographic algorithm used to generate the digital signature. Apart from these differences, the structure of a signed XML document is heavily based on the format presented in [7] and compires the following fields:

- a *subject* field which contains two public keys used for verification and encryption, respectively.
- a *content* field which textually describes the assigned properties. A property has a property name and a corresponding value, e.g., [name=FBIAgent, value=TRUE] or [name=age, value≥18], etc.
- a field for a *responsible agent*: this field contains the public verification key of the agent which visibly represents the entity that is responsible for the property assignment and that has generated and digitally signed the XML document.
- a *type* field which indicates whether the signed XML document is a certificate or a credential.
- a *delegation* field[7] which is used only for credentials to indicate whether the credential under consideration is a bound property-credential or a delegation-credential.
- a *validity* field which encodes a certain time period during which the property assignment is valid.
- a *signature* field which contains a digital signature generated by using DSA and SHA-1.

---

[6] XSLT is a language for transforming XML documents into other XML documents.

[7] In the current implementation of the agent PKI framework, the *delegation* field of an XML document has the same semantic as the delegation bit used in the SPKI/SDSI approach in which a delegatee might use the encoded properties of a document for his own service requests.

As discussed in [7], a collection of digital documents could form a *directed acyclic graph (dag)*. In order to focus on the major PKI services and to keep the PKI framework manageable, we employed *chains* instead of dags. A chain is also represented as an unsigned XML document which contains a set of signed XML documents. For the verification of certificate chains and credential chains, we have implemented algorithms which we have adopted from [2,19] and [13,14], respectively.

4.2   A Selected Operating Sequence: Acquiring Credentials

In this section we present the operation seqence of a performative which is used by an agent in the role of a holder of free property to apply for bound property-credentials. We assume that the holder of free property has already collected his free-property certificates from some trusted authority agents and received the bound properties for inspection from an agent in the role of a grantor of bound property before applying for a bound property-credential. After the task control unit of the functional module has received the performative and conducted a challenge-response procedure successfully, basically the following steps are performed for the case that all security checks are positively evaluated (otherwise appropriate exceptions are executed):

1. The task control unit extracts the contents of the parameters from the performative and inserts them into ASECKNOB by calling the appropriate persistence functions of APROMA and ATRUMA.
2. The task control unit sends the signed request to ACREMA.
3. ACREMA verifies the authenticity of the signed request included in the received performative. For this purpose ACREMA employs the appropriate function calls of CRENG.
4. ACREMA extracts the requested bound properties and the public verification key of the user agent from the signed request.
5. ACREMA asks APROMA whether the requested bound properties are locally known.
6. After verifying the authenticity and the validity of the free property-certificates and the corresponding licence-certificates, ACREMA extracts the free properties from the verified certificates. The set of free properties are forwarded to APROMA.
7. APROMA checks whether the included set of free properties "qualifies for" bound properties requested.
8. The result of checks are forwarded to the agent human interface and shown by this interface to the administrator as grantor of bound property.
9. After inspecting the shown values, the administrator generates a bound property-credential encoded in XML. The encoded XML document is forwarded to ACREMA.
10. ACREMA signs the generated XML document by using CRENG. The signed document now constitutes the issued bound property-credential. ACREMA adds the corresponding delegation credentials to the issued bound property-credential.

11. Finally, the task control unit prepares a new performative in which the issued bound property-credential and delegation credentials are encoded. The performative is sent in a KQML message to the requesting user agent.

5   Related Work, Conclusions, and Further Work

Most of the works investigating the application of certificate/credential-based access control treat both PKI models discussed in Section 2 as competing approaches and base their work on a single PKI model. Even some of these works abstract from any particular PKI model.

In [32] the authors propose to use credentials in a Web-based client/server architecture. They present the tasks needed for credential management both on the client side and server side. [33] investigates trust negotiation strategies and discusses credential disclosure policies. These works do not make any assumptions on the underlying PKI model. [31] uses X.509 based identity/attribute certificates and use-condition certificates (policy assertions) for access control. [17] presents a credential framework for relying applications. The credential framework converts credentials with different formats to a common interface which is to be used by credential relying applications. This work focuses on X.509 certificates and concentrates on unifying different credential formats. [24] presents an agent-oriented security architecture which has been implemented using SPKI-like authorization certificates. They focus on authorization and delegation in distributed agent systems. [10] introduces a credential-based formal framework and a model to regulate access and information release over the Internet. An exciting work of Li et al. [23] presents a formal framework (i.e. called RT framework) extending the approach of SPKI/SDSI. This work combines the strengths of RBAC and the strengths of SDSI part of SPKI/SDSI. The future extensions of our work with respect to integrating distributed RBAC into our approach could profit from the proposal presented in this work.

We presented a trust management infrastructure based on a hybrid PKI model which unifies and extends the previous approaches. The trust management infrastructure constitutes a flexible framework for experimenting with the applications of different trust models. There are various topics for future research and development. The prototype implementation for the core functionality should be converted into a more mature state. Such an advanced implementation would open to experience various applications besides secure mediation. An advanced implementation would also allow to evaluate the actual performance of our approach in terms of effectiveness and efficiency.

References

1. The Apache XML project. http://xml.apache.org/.
2. ITU-T recommendation X.509: The directory - public-key and attribute certificate frameworks, 2000.

3. Dueling theologies. In *1st Annual PKI Research Workshop*, Gaithersburg, Maryland, USA, Apr. 2002.
4. IBM XML Security Suite.
   `http://alphaworks.ibm.com/tech/xmlsecuritysuite/`, Apr. 2002.
5. C. Altenschmidt, J. Biskup, U. Flegel, and Y. Karabulut. Secure mediation: Requirements, design and architecture. *Journal of Computer Security*. To appear.
6. C. Altenschmidt, J. Biskup, J. Freitag, and B. Sprick. Weakly constraining multimedia types based on a type embedding ordering. In *Proceedings of the 4th International Workshop on Multimedia Information Systems*, pages 121–129, Istanbul, Turkey, Sept. 1998.
7. J. Biskup and Y. Karabulut. A hybrid PKI model with an application for secure mediation. In *16th Annual IFIP WG 11.3 Working Conference on Data and Application Security*, Cambridge, England, July 2002. To appear.
8. J. Biskup and Y. Karabulut. Mediating between strangers: A trust management based approach. In *2nd Annual PKI Research Workshop*, Gaithersburg, USA, Apr. 2003. To appear.
9. M. Blaze, J. Feigenbaum, and A. Keromytis. The KeyNote trust management system version 2. RFC 2704, IETF, Sept. 1999.
10. P. Bonatti and P. Samarati. Regulating service access and information release on the web. In *Proceedings of the 7th ACM Conference on Computer and Communication Security*, pages 134–143, Athens, Greece, Nov. 2000.
11. D. Clarke, J.-E. Elien, C. Ellison, M. Fredette, A. Morcos, and R. L. Rivest. Certificate chain discovery in SPKI/SDSI. *Journal of Computer Security*, 9(4):285–322, 2001.
12. D. Eastlake, J. Reagle, and D. Solo. XML signature core syntax and processing. `http://www.ietf.org/rfc/rfc3275.txt`, work in progress, RFC 3275, Internet Engineering Task Force, Mar. 2002.
13. C. Ellison. SPKI/SDSI certificates.
   `http://world.std.com/~cme/html/spki.html`, Aug. 2001.
14. C. M. Ellison, B. Frantz, B. Lampson, R. Rivest, B. M. Thomas, and T. Ylonen. Simple public key certification. Internet draft, work in progress. `http://www.ietf.org/ids.by.wg/spki.html`, June 1999.
15. T. Finin, Y. Labrou, and J. Mayfield. KQML as an agent communication language. In J. M. Bradshaw, editor, *Software Agents*. MIT Press, Cambridge, 1997. `http://www.cs.umbc.edu/kqml/papers/`.
16. Q. He, K. P. Sycara, and T. Finin. Personal Security Agent: KQML-Based PKI. In *Proceedings of the 2nd International Conference on Autonomous Agents*, pages 377–384. ACM Press, 1998.
17. A. Herzberg and Y. Mass. Relying party credentials framework. In D. Naccache, editor, *Topics in Cryptology - CT-RSA 2001, The Cryptographer's Track at RSA Conference*, LNCS 2020, pages 328–343, San Francisco, CA, 2001.
18. P. Hildebrand. Design and implementation of a KQML-based hybrid PKI for secure mediation. Master's thesis, Department of Computer Science, University of Dortmund, Apr. 2002.
19. IETF X.509 Working Group. Public-key infrastructure (X.509). `http://www.ietf.org/html.charters/pkix-charter.html`, 1998.
20. Y. Karabulut. *Secure Mediation Between Strangers in Cyberspace*. PhD thesis, University of Dortmund, 2002.
21. C. Kröger. Integration of access control systems into a credential-based security environment. Master's thesis, Department of Computer Science, University of Dortmund, Sept. 2000.

22. P. Lehmann. Design and implementation of a credential manager. Master's thesis, Department of Computer Science, University of Dortmund, Apr. 2002.
23. N. Li, J. C. Mitchell, and W. H. Winsborough. Design of a role-based trust-management framework. In *IEEE Symposium on Security and Privacy*, pages 114–130, Berkeley, California, USA, May 2002.
24. P. Nikander. *An architecture for authorization and delegation in distributed Object-Oriented Agent Systems*. PhD thesis, Helsinki University of Technology, Mar. 1999.
25. Object Management Group. The common object request broker, architecture and specification. CORBA 2.3.1/IIOP specification. http://www.omg.org/library/c2indx.html, Dec. 1998.
26. X. Orri and J. M. Mas. SPKI-XML certificate structure. Internet Draft draft-orri-spki-xml-cert-struc-00.txt, work in progress, Internet Engineering Task Force, Nov. 2001.
27. J. Reagle. XML signature requirements. http://www.ietf.org/rfc/, work in progress, RFC 2807, Internet Engineering Task Force, July 2000.
28. K. Seamons, M. Winslett, T. Yu, B. Smith, E. Child, and J. Jacobsen. Protecting privacy during on-line trust negotiation. In *2nd Workshop on Privacy Enhancing Technologies*, San Francisco, CA, Apr. 2002. To appear.
29. Sun Microsystems. Keytool - Key and Certificate Management Tool. http://java.sun.com/j2se/1.3/docs/tooldocs/win32/keytool.html.
30. C. Thirunavukkarasu, T. Finin, and J. Mayfield. Secret agents - a security architecture for the KQML agent communication language. In *4th International Conference on Information and Knowledge Management - Workshop on Intelligent Information Agents*, Baltimore, Maryland, USA, Dec. 1995.
31. W. Thompson, W. Johnston, S. Mudumbai, G. Hoo, K. Jackson, and A. Essiari. Certificate-based access control for widely distributed resources. In *Proceedings of the 8th USENIX Security Symposium*, Washington D.C., Aug. 1999.
32. M. Winslett, N. Ching, V. Jones, and I. Slepchin. Assuring security and privacy for digital library transactions on the web: Client and server security policies. In *Proceedings of Forum on Research and Technical Advances in Digital Libraries (ADL'97)*, pages 140–152, Washington, DC, May 1997.
33. T. Yu, M. Winslett, and K. Seamons. Interoperable strategies in automated trust negotiation. In *Proceedings of 8th ACM Computer Conference on Computer and Communication Security*, pages 146–155, Philedelphia, Pennsylvania, Nov. 2001.

Authenticated Dictionaries for Fresh Attribute Credentials[*]

Michael T. Goodrich[1], Michael Shin[2,3], Roberto Tamassia[3], and
William H. Winsborough[4]

[1] Dept. Info. & Comp. Sci., University of California, Irvine
Irvine, CA 92697 USA
goodrich@acm.org
[2] Department of Computer Science, Johns Hopkins University
Baltimore, MD 21218 USA
mys@cs.jhu.edu
[3] Department of Computer Science, Brown University
Providence, RI 02912 USA
{mys,rt}@cs.brown.edu
[4] Network Associates Laboratories
Rockville, MD 20850 USA
willian_winsborough@nai.com

Abstract. We describe several schemes for efficiently populating an
authenticated dictionary with fresh credentials. The thrust of this
effort is directed at allowing for many data authors, called sources, to
collectively publish information to a common repository, which is then
distributed throughout a network to allow for authenticated queries on
this information. Authors are assured of their contributions being added
to the repository based on cryptographic receipts that the repository
returns after performing the updates sent by an author. While our
motivation here is the dissemination of credential status data from
multiple credential issuers, applications of this technology also include
time stamping of documents, document version integrity control, and
multiple-CA certificate revocation management, to name just a few.

Keywords: authenticated dictionary, certificate revocation, third-party
data publication, authentication of cached data, dynamic data structures, digital credential, trust management

1 Introduction

Many problems in distributed systems require that content from various authors be validated for authenticity and integrity. One of these problems is authorization in decentralized systems. Traditional authorization systems assume

[*] Work supported in part by DARPA through AFRL agreement F30602-00-2-0509
and SPAWAR contract N66001-01-C-8005 and by NSF under grants CCR-0098068
and CDA-9703080.

P. Nixon and S. Terzis (Eds.): Trust Management 2003, LNCS 2692, pp. 332-347, 2003.

organizations have a hierarchical structure in which authority emanates from a single entity. However, this assumption breaks down when independent organizations engage in collaboration or commerce, particularly in large numbers. In this case, authority emanates from many entities. Blaze, Feigenbaum, and Lacy [3] introduced *trust management* (TM) as a collection of principles for supporting authorization in such a decentralized environment. TM systems such as KeyNote [2] use credentials or chains of credentials to represent capabilities, that is, rights with respect to specific resources. Others, such as SPKI/SDSI [7] and *RT* [15], enable entities to manage and combine their judgments about one another's authority based on more general entity attributes. What these systems have in common is that authority is distributed among a potentially large number of entities, each of which may issue credentials. Additionally, credentials from several entities may need to be combined to form a proof that a particular resource request is authorized.

In the authorization systems mentioned above, an entity is typically represented by a public/private cryptographic key pair. Using its private key, an entity signs the credentials it issues, enabling authenticity and integrity to be verified. The assertions carried in credentials may be subject to changing circumstances. A credential's validity ends when it expires or is revoked. Updates concerning a credential's validity status can be disseminated by the issuer either as positive revalidations, or as negative revocations.

For convenience here, we assume that Alice is a typical credential issuer. For example, Alice may be a certification authority[1] who has the ability and responsibility of authenticating various entities. Presumably Alice is motivated to make her assertions verifiable, since she issues signed certificates. To accept such a certificate, Bob, a typical agent relying on a certificate issued by Alice, may require proof that as of a certain time in the recent past, Alice had not revoked the certificate. Yet Alice's strengths may not include the ability to answer a large volume of online certificate-status queries. Thus, Alice and Bob are both motivated to utilize a third-party, Charles, who will maintain certificate status information for Alice and provide verifiable answers to queries from users, such as Bob, as quickly and efficiently as possible.

In practice, of course, it is impossible to disseminate credential status updates instantaneously, particularly when invoking a third-party, Charles, to process updates and queries. The longer it takes, the greater the risk of basing decisions on stale information. The rate at which risk accumulates depends on the nature of the information, as well as on the application for which credentials are accepted. Ultimately, Bob must determine what level of risk is tolerable. Yet whatever that level may be, we desire a system that will quickly communicate any updates from Alice to Bob with minimal overhead and minimal additional trust required in Charles.

---

[1] For our purposes, the terms "certificate" and "credential" are essentially interchangeable. Historically, a "certificate" has typically carried a binding of a name to a public key, while "credential" has often been used more broadly for associations with keys.

1.1   Considering Many Credential Issuers

Prior work in the area of distributed data authentication (see, e.g., [1,4,5,6,10,11, 12,13,18]) has focused primarily on disseminating updates from a single, trusted source (merging the roles of Alice and Charles). Providing a high degree of availability through these previous solutions, a small-scale credential issuer would incur significant start-up cost. Economies of scale would suggest that credential issuers could contain their costs by using a shared infrastructure to disseminate credential status data. If we consider credential issuers to be the authors of credential status data, then several authors may use the same publisher, Charles. In this case, the authors entrust to the publisher the dissemination of credential status data to its consumers, the authorization agents. In the current paper, we present algorithms that can be used for this purpose. Our design goals are as follows:

- Authors must be able to determine whether their updates are being published in a timely manner.
- Determination that updates are occurring should be done efficiently and without requiring trust in the responders.
- The repository should provide cryptographic *receipts* verifying that updates are occurring.
- Update receipts should be small, so as to minimize network traffic, and should be easy to verify.

In addition, the following client user-interface design goals are shared with prior work:

- Answers to client queries must be highly available, meaning that it should be possible to obtain answers at any time without prior arrangement.
- Answers must be validated efficiently for authenticity and integrity.
- Client users must be able to reliably determine the time at which data they receive in answers was certified by its authors.
- Clients need not trust responders.

1.2   Our Contributions

In this paper, we describe how to extend prior authenticated dictionary techniques [1,4,5,6,10,11,12,13,18] to show how a publication service can make highly available the current, authenticatable validity status of each credential issued by one of a large number of credential authors. Our techniques for supporting many authors involve the novel use of efficient authenticated data structures. Moreover, we offer an author, Alice, a trade-off between how much state she wishes to maintain for her data and the size of the receipts that the publication repository, Charles, provides to prove he is processing her updates correctly. An important feature of our solutions is they allow Alice to delegate computations and data archiving to Charles without delegating large degrees of trust to him. Indeed, the protection of trust in a distributed environment is an important principle in our work.

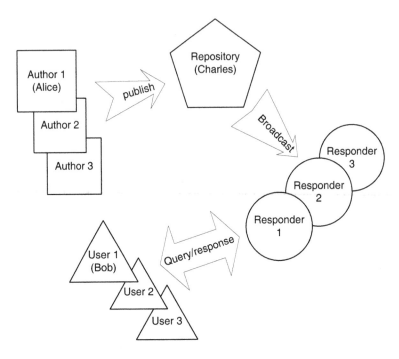

Fig. 1. Entities in a multi-authored authenticated dictionary

The paper is organized as follows. We begin with a general discussion of background and motivation for multi-authored authenticated data repositories. We follow this discussion, in Section 3, with a presentation of two simple-minded schemes for providing for multiple authors in an authenticated setting, showing that both of these schemes have serious drawbacks. We then present, in Section 4, three variations on a novel intermediate scheme, showing its efficiency with respect to several measures. Finally, in Section 5, we describe a number of extensions to our scheme.

2 Background and Motivation

As mentioned above, the framework we are addressing in this paper involves several groups of entities operating in a distributed environment, as illustrated in Figure 1.

- An *author* (Alice). The authors are the issuers of credentials and/or credential status information. They are assumed to be online only during their interaction with the data repository. They may have limited storage and processing abilities; hence, they do not wish to process queries for users.
- A *user* (Bob). The users are consumers of credential and/or credential status information. They desire quick response for a query requesting a credential or

the revocation status of an existing credential. They have trust in the issuer of a credential or credential status information, but they do not necessarily trust the publishing system that is archiving and providing query responses for this information.

- The *publication repository* (Charles). The publication repository stores the credential and/or credential status information for the authors. Charles processes updates for authors, providing them with receipts that confirm his acceptance of these updates. He also broadcasts these updates out to the responders, who perform the actual processing of user requests.
- The *responders*. The responders accept updates from the publication repository, Charles, and answer queries on this data for users. In addition to the answers that responders provide, they also provide cryptographic proofs, derived from *basis* information provided by Alice and Charles, that their answers are as accurate as if they had come directly from Alice and Charles.

We assume Alice has some recourse in the event that Charles fails to fulfill his publishing obligations correctly. It may satisfy Alice's purposes to presume that should Charles fail, Alice would make this known, thus damaging Charles's reputation to such a degree as to act as a sufficient deterrent. However, if Alice's ability to conduct her operations would be significantly compromised, stronger assumptions may be required. For instance, Alice could maintain a minimal online presence, operating a site, referred to in the credentials she issues, that gives instructions about how to contact responders operated by her current publisher. This level of indirection would enable Alice to replace Charles should he fail to meet his publishing obligations. Depending on the contract Alice and Charles enter into, Alice may also have legal recourse. Thus, we have a spectrum of possible recourses.

So as to better motivate this framework, let us briefly discuss some applications.

2.1   Archiving and Time Stamping

An important service in a distributed collaborative environment is that of archiving and time stamping. Such a service stores documents and other data ordered by creation time, and allows users to retrieve these documents and verify their creation times. In our framework, the document and data creators are the authors, the publication repository is the archive, the responders provide answers to queries, and the users request documents and their time stamp verification. For efficiency, Alice may wish to sign only a cryptographic digest (hash) of her documents, and it may actually be this digest that is archived for time stamping purposes. In addition, note that in this application Alice will never delete anything from the archive, since that would violate the principle of time stamping. Her updates in this case are limited to insertions.

Charles's signature is useful for corroborating the date at which Alice makes her assertion. It proves that Alice had signed the assertion by the date Charles signs it. It prevents Alice signing something later than the date shown, or anyone else claiming that she did so. Note that this is not inherently related to Charles's function as a distribution channel in any way more fundamental than convenience.

2.2   Certificate Validity Status

Digital certificates are a central part of any public-key infrastructure (PKI), in that they bind identification information to a public key. Such mappings could be for individuals, groups, or even roles and permissions within a dynamic coalition. But certificates may need to be revoked before they expire, due to changes in roles, system compromises, or lost private keys. Once a certificate is revoked, it is no longer valid. Thus, an important, but often neglected, step in any protocol involving digital certificates is the verification of the revocation status of a digital certificate. Putting this application into our framework, we see that the authors are the certification authorities (CA's) that issue and revoke certificates. Likewise, the publication repository and its responders provide a certificate status querying service, with verifiable responses to queries. The client users in this case are any entities that wish to verify the status of a given digital certificate. Clients may also need to be able to prove that status to others.

Validity status data can be represented as a collection of certificates valid at a certain time, or as a similarly dated collection of certificate revocations, each giving, say, the serial number of the certificate. Clearly in either case, the representation must support insertion. In the former case, the (verified) presence of the certificate in the collection establishes its validity as of the associated time. Authors must be able to delete a credential to revoke it, thus rendering it invalid after the next time quantum. The acceptor of a credential determines how recently validity must be proven and therefore what amount of latency (introduced by publication or by caching of validity proofs) is acceptable. Verification of negative query responses may be needed in some applications, for instance, to justify (to a third party) denial of access.

When status data is represented by a collection of revocations, the (verified) absence of an unexpired credential's serial number in the collection establishes the credential's validity as of the associated time. Thus, it is essential that the representation of this collection support verifiable negative answers to user queries. Verifiable positive answers may also be necessary in some applications to enable acceptors to justify credential rejection.

The essential functionality of either representation is to enable the acceptor to verify that the issuer has revalidated a certificate at some point in the recent past. Normal operation need not allow authors to "unrevoke" or reinstate a revoked credential; if required, a new certificate carrying the same assertion can be issued instead. However, to maintain efficiency it may be important to be able remove revocations from the data structure, for instance, after the corresponding credentials have expired. After that time, the revocation is no longer needed to invalidate the credential. Yet removal of revocations must be undertaken cautiously, particularly as the revocation time approaches the expiration time.

In many applications it is important to ensure that revocations are not removed before they have been published, as doing so could defeat auditing and the detection of fraudulent transactions [14].

For a certificate to be accepted by Bob, he must have adequate proof of its validity as an assertion made by Alice as of a given time. It may contribute to this proof if the publisher, Charles, signs the association of credential validity status and the publication time. (This reduces the need for Bob to trust Alice not to replace her credential validity status data at a later time while lying about the time of the changed assertion. Again, this might be significant if Bob must justify to third parties decisions he takes based on certificates.) Depending on Bob's purposes, he may require that validity status information be signed by Alice herself rather than accepting it solely on Charles's authority. At minimum, to accept any revocation information on Charles's authority, we would expect Bob to require that Alice identify Charles as her publisher. This could effectively be done, for instance, if Alice maintains a minimal online presence, as suggested above. This would enable Alice to publish a single credential, signed by herself, positively identifying Charles (by his public key) as Alice's current publisher. If Alice should have to replace Charles, the credential would be replaced by one issued to Alice's new publisher and the revocation of the credential previously issued to Charles would be published by Alice's new publisher.

2.3   Data Integrity Verification

Whenever coalition data is hosted in untrusted locations, there is a possibility that it may be tampered with. Thus, in these contexts, there is a need for documents, web sites, and other content to be validated. But if this validation has a large overhead, there will be a temptation to circumvent the validation step. Therefore, we feel that data integrity verification is an ideal application for a distributed multi-author authenticated dictionary. In this case, the authors are the document or web site producers, who, in addition to distributing their content to various sites also publish digital digests of their content to the authentication system run by the publication repository. Whenever a client, Bob, accesses a document of web site, an authorization agent for Bob quickly verifies that the content of that document or web site has not been modified by anyone other than the author. The authorization agent for Bob makes a judgment about how fresh verification data must be to sufficiently limit the risk associated with relying on the credential. For example, the author of the status data, may provide a suggested "shelf life" for updates, which Bob may take into account in his determination. This expiration time data would be contained in the signed basis returned with the query response from a responder for Charles.

2.4   Credential Discovery in Permission Systems

In another application related to distributed authorization, the data structures discussed here can be used to support the discovery of credentials issued by a given author [16]. In this case, the credentials themselves are stored in the multi-author authenticated dictionary, and their (verified) presence is a testimony to their validity. Should Alice require that a credential be revoked, she can remove it from the authenticated dictionary, thereby preventing its validity being verified after that time. Thus, status updates and discovery can be supported through the same structure.

The authorizer makes the final determination as to how recently valid a credential must be for its purposes. However, Alice may also provide a recommended "shelf life" for credentials she issues. When credential shelf life is sufficiently long in relation to the rate at which credentials are issued and expire, it may reduce Alice's cost to publish credentials for the purpose of supporting discovery in the archival structure discussed in Section 4.2 and to publish revocations separately in one of the structures that support validation of negative answers. In this case, after using the first structure to discover a credential, Bob would check the revocation structure to verify the credential's validity, as discussed in Section 2.2 above.

3   Some Simple-Minded Schemes

We begin our algorithmic discussion by pointing out two simple schemes, which provide two opposite ends of a spectrum of how much trust the authors place in the publication repository. Throughout our discussion of these simple schemes, as well as our improved schemes, we will refer to a typical data author as "Alice," we will refer to a typical client user as "Bob," and we will refer to the publication repository as "Charles." The first such solution we review is one in which a typical author, Alice, places little trust in the publication repository, Charles.

3.1   Independent Authentication

One possible solution for the many-author authenticated dictionary problem is for each author, Alice, to implement her own authenticated dictionary, e.g., using the scheme of Goodrich, Tamassia, and Schwerin [11]. In this case, Alice would maintain a hashed data structure, such as a tree or skip list, would make the updates in this data structure, and would sign and time-stamp a new "root" for this structure at every time quantum; this set of information is called the *basis*. But rather than distributing the updates and newly-signed basis to her own collection of responders, Alice would in this case simply forward the updates and basis to the repository, Charles. Charles would then maintain the same data structure as Alice, and would distribute the updates and new basis to the responders. In other words, Charles is in this case little more than a distribution channel to the responders. He does not sign anything—instead, he just passes the authors' signatures on. Authors, such as Alice, must maintain their own copies of the data structures they publish. On the positive side, this solution supports each user, Bob, to be able to verify the validity status, as of a given update date, of each credential issued by the author.

An author, Alice, signs the root hash of her data structure, together with the date, forming a sub-basis. The date and root hash of Alice's data structure are provided in the clear to the query issuer, Bob (the update consumer), together with the sub-basis and the rest of the authenticated dictionary proof. Bob checks that the signed root hash of the data structure is indeed the computed digest of the hash chain. Finally, Bob can decide whether the date is fresh enough for his purposes. Note that Bob does not have to trust the publisher, Charles, nor the responder, in this case.

The fact that Alice's data structure is incorporated into Charles's larger repository enables the author to verify through an efficient query to an untrusted responder whether all application data (such as credential status information) as of a given update time is being published, and when. For this the author, Alice, poses one query to a responder and compares the hash value at the root in the response to her own root hash. As soon as she finds a responder that answers queries using this root hash as the basis, Alice can verify that her entire update has been published.

There are unfortunately several disadvantages to this simple scheme:

- Each data author, Alice, must be sophisticated enough to implement a complete authenticated dictionary.
- There is a high likelihood that the publication repository, Charles, and his responders, will have to maintain many different kinds and versions of authenticated dictionaries, which makes for a cumbersome software maintenance plan.
- The time quanta for the different authenticated dictionaries are likely to be out of phase, which complicates the authentication guarantees provided by the system when many data authors are involved.

Let us therefore consider the other extreme.

3.2   Fully-Trusted Central Repository

At the other end of the trust spectrum is a scheme in which Alice and Bob fully trust the publication repository, Charles, to publish Alice's update accurately and promptly. In this case, it is sufficient for Charles to implement a single authenticated dictionary for all authors, which he then distributes out to the responders. Alice forwards updates to Charles and fully trusts him to perform those updates (be they insertions or deletions) on the published database. Data and trust is therefore aggregated at the publication repository, Charles. He implements a single authenticated dictionary for all the authors, and his responders answer queries using a proof basis that is signed only by him. The advantage of this scheme is that it has a simple software maintenance plan of keeping everything at the publication repository. This approach has several disadvantages, however, including the following:

- Having authors fully trust the publication repository may be unrealistic. In many applications, authors will at minimum require support for auditing

to detect incorrect omissions or additions to the repository that Charles maintains on Alice's behalf.
- Each user, Bob, must also fully trust Charles, since Charles's basis is the only cryptographic verification for a query's accuracy.
- The publication repository, Charles, becomes a single point of failure of trust, for compromising him compromises the security of the entire system.

Thus, there are significant drawbacks at both extremes of the spectrum of trust regarding the publication repository, Charles. Let us, therefore, consider some novel approaches that place only moderate trust in him.

4 A Multiply-Authored Authenticated Dictionary

In this section, we consider an intermediate solution, which maintains efficiency while requiring only moderate trust in the publication repository, Charles. We offer three versions of this intermediate solution, depending on the needs and abilities of Alice's repository.

In each solution, Charles stores a separate authenticated dictionary for each author, Alice, using a hierarchical hashing scheme (tree-based or skip-list-based) or an accumulator scheme. In each case a response is returned together with a validity *basis* that is signed by Alice and Charles. This basis contains the root hash value together with a time stamp indicating the most recent time quantum(s) in which this hash was considered by Alice and Charles (either together or separately) as the digest for all of Alice's data.

4.1 Minimally Compliant Authors

The first version we consider is the case of an author, Alice, who is minimally compliant with our approach. That is, Alice has minimal additional resources that she wishes to deploy for repository archiving. She may wish, for example, to maintain very little state. Indeed, Alice may not directly participate in the protocol at all, but instead indirectly participate by having a third-party agent pull her updates and transfer them to the publication repository.

In this case, the only state Alice needs to maintain is the current "root" hash of the authenticated dictionary for her data. Let $U = \{u_1, u_2 \ldots, u_k\}$ be a set of updates, that is, insertions and deletions, for Alice's data. The publication repository, Charles, upon receiving this sequence of updates, processes them in order one at a time. Each update, u_i, involves Charles searching a path in the authenticated data structure for Alice, updating that path to do the insertion or deletion, and updating the hash values along the path from the updated element to the "root" (possibly with local structural changes to maintain balance in the structure). Let P_i denote the search path prior to the update and let P_i' denote the search path after, including the hash values of nodes immediately adjacent to these paths. Then, as a receipt of this transaction, Charles returns to Alice the sequence $\mathcal{P} = \{P_1, P_1', P_2, P_2', \ldots, P_k, P_k'\}$. Alice (or her agent) can then verify inductively that all the updates were performed correctly by starting with her cached hash value for the root (which should correspond to the root hash of P_1), and iteratively checking the computed hash value of P_1', P_2, P_2', and so on. Moreover, we require that path siblings be identical in P_i and P_i', and that path roots be identical in P_i' and P_{i+1}. If all the hashes check out as being computed correctly, then Alice accepts that the updates have occurred, and she caches the root hash of P_k' as the new root hash. Note, in addition, that she can query a responder at any time to verify that this is also the root hash that is being used as the basis to her database for authenticated queries.

Charles and Alice will then mutually sign the new root hash, together with the current date, and this mutually-signed value will serve as the basis. Additionally, Charles can re-sign this root hash with each time quantum if there are no updates during that quantum, provided Alice has the ability to contact other authors in the case of her discovering that an update has been ignored by Charles. Otherwise, Alice will have to re-sign the root hash, along with Charles, in each time quantum.

In terms of the analysis of this scheme, there is a natural trade-off between the state that Alice is willing to maintain and the efficiency of the repository's receipt. For, in this minimal scheme, Alice need only maintain a cache of $O(1)$ size: namely, the root hash value. But, in order to validate a batch of k updates in this scheme, Charles needs to send Alice a receipt of size $O(k \log n)$, where n is the total size of Alice's database. We can design a scheme that is more efficient than this, however, if Alice's updates are all of a certain form.

4.2   Authors with Archive Data

A simplifying case of the multi-authored authenticated dictionary is when all updates involve only insertions and only positive answers to queries (i.e., the query element is present in the dictionary) need to be authenticated. Such a situation could arise, for example, in applications where authors wish to archive the digests of their documents, say, for time-stamping purposes. In the credentialing context, this case arises when credentials are valid for a fixed period and cannot be revoked.

In this case, Charles can store Alice's data in an authenticated tree or skip-list structure ordered by insertion time. Since such a tree is inefficient for searching, he should require that each responder maintain an alternative search structure, ordered by item keys, that maps an item in the key-ordered dictionary to its version in the authenticated data structure. This is needed because the hash values that produce the root digest signed by Charles and Alice are in the authenticated data structure ordered by insertion time.

Moreover, if Charles is operating a general time-stamping service for a whole collection of authors, he can store in a separate "super" data structure the sequence of all historical values of authors' authenticated data structures.

Let $U = \{u_1, u_2 \ldots, u_k\}$ be a set of updates, that is, a sequence of k insertions for Alice's data. Given such a sequence, the publication repository, Charles, adds the elements from this set of updates in the given order to the authenticated data structure he is maintaining for Alice. Since this data structure is ordered by insertion time, these elements comprise a contiguous sequence of elements at the "end" of the data structure. Thus, the union of all that paths from these elements to the root consists of at most $O(k + \log n)$ nodes. Therefore, Charles can present to Alice a receipt that consists of the union of these paths, together with the hash values of adjacent nodes. This receipt can be checked as in the scheme described in the previous subsection, but it is much smaller in size. In particular, the insertion by Alice of k items requires a receipt of size only $O(k + \log n)$, rather than $O(k \log n)$, where n is the total size of Alice's database. If Charles is additionally maintaining a global archive of updates for m different authors, then there would be an additional portion of size $O(\log m)$ that would be added to the receipt Charles gives to Alice to verify that he has added her changes to the global archive.

Therefore, we are able to achieve an efficient receipt size for the case when all of Alice's updates are insertions, while keeping the state Alice must maintain to be constant. If Alice is willing to maintain state equal to the size of her database, however, we can achieve an efficient receipt size even in the case where updates consist of insertions and deletions.

4.3   Maintaining Limited State at an Author

Suppose that Alice is willing to maintain state equal to the size of her database. In this case, Charles can maintain Alice's authenticated dictionary as a hashed red-black tree (e.g., see [9]). The reason we choose a red-black tree, in this case, is that it has the property that updates and searches can be done in $O(\log n)$ time, but any update, be it an insertion or deletion, requires only $O(1)$ structural changes to the underlying binary search tree.

Let $U = \{u_1, u_2 \ldots, u_k\}$ be a set of updates, that is, a sequence of k insertions and deletions for Alice's data. In this case, Charles performs all of the updates in U on the authenticated red-black tree he is maintaining for Alice. He then sends back to her a receipt R that consists of all the *structural* changes he made to this tree, that is, the sequence of node insertions, removals, and tree rotations. They then both sign the final hash value of the root as the new basis. The total size of the receipt is $O(k)$. The reason this is sufficient is that, given the node changes dictated by Charles, Alice can recompute the hash value at the root of the tree in $O(k + \log n)$ time. Moreover, Alice doesn't even need to know that the binary tree is the underlying structure for a red-black tree. To her, it is simply a binary search tree with hash values stored at the internal nodes, much like a classic Merkle hash tree [17].

4.4   Common Themes

Thus, we have described three variations on an intermediate solution, where the publication repository, Charles, performs some computations on behalf of each data author, Alice, but does not fall in either extreme of taking complete control from Alice nor simply acting as a mere publication channel for Alice. Each of our schemes have the basis derived from something signed by both Alice and Charles. Moreover, Alice's need only place minimal trust in Charles, for she can always pose as a user, Bob, and request an authenticated query from one of Charles's responders. If that response does not use the correct, up-to-date basis, Alice is free to reveal this breach of trust to the other users. Moreover, she can prove that Charles in error if he does not use the basis derived from her most recent updates, for she will have a signed receipt from Bob that can be used to show what the basis should be. Indeed, if Alice combines all the receipts she has received from Charles, she can prove the entire contents of what her database contains.

The three scenarios presented in this section are summarized in Table 1.

Table 1. Comparison of three scenarios for multi-authored authenticated dictionaries. All bounds are asymptotic, with the "big-Oh" omitted to simplify the notation

Scenario	Operations	State	Receipt Size	Verification Time
Min. Compliant Authors	ins. and del.	1	$k \log n$	$k \log n$
Authors w/ Archive Data	ins.	1	$k + \log n$	$k + \log n$
Authors w/ Limited State	ins. and del.	n	k	$k \log n$

5   Discussion, Conclusions, and Additional Issues

There are several additional issues that surround the publishing of authenticated data by many authors. We investigate several of these issues in this section.

5.1   Push versus Pull for Author Updates

When many authors have the ability to push updates to a publication repository, Charles, this site becomes potentially vulnerable to denial-of-service attacks. This danger is avoided in single-author version of an authenticated data structure by taking off-line the generation of the structure.

In the multiple-author context, we can reduce the risk of denial-of-service attacks against Charles by adding a subscription requirement to the model. That is, the authors who wish to publish information to Charles's repository must subscribe to the service, for which Charles could, for example, charge a fee based on usage. This economic model could reduce overwhelming numbers of updates sent to Charles in an attempt to deny other authors their right to publish.

Because we assume that the time quantum is defined by the publisher, we can strengthen the model further by switching author updates from a push approach to a pull approach. That is, each subscribed author, Alice, could be polled by

Charles (or an agent for Charles) in each time quantum for her updates. The net effect of using a pull approach would be that the freshness of a batch of updates per time quantum would be maintained, but now it would be impossible to flood Charles with a simultaneous stream of updates from many authors. Even a clearly frivolous sequence of updates from a subscribed author could be cutoff mid-stream by Charles in this pull setting.

5.2   User Subscription

In the system we have described, users pull validity proofs from responders. An alternative approach is to enable users to subscribe to updates on specific queries, which would be pushed out to them as they are published. In open systems, the field of potential users is so vast that pushing validity proofs is feasible only based on subscription. While a subscription may permit the consumer to avoid initiating a per-use check for freshness, it requires the user to trust the publisher to provide timely updates on changes in revocation status. This trust can be limited by requiring the publisher to provide a "heartbeat" (see [8]) at regular intervals to indicate that the subscribed-to credential remains valid. In our setting, where the user's trust in the publisher must be minimal, the heartbeat's content could be the validity proof itself. The heartbeat approach is optimized for prolonged user-resource interactions such as login sessions or continuous data feeds. However, the heartbeat approach builds in the limitation on freshness given by the heartbeat period, so the period must be relatively short. As such, it is not well suited to applications where authorization decisions are more sporadic. Moreover, the use of heartbeats begs the question, What does the user do when a fresh validity proof does not arrive or the proof received is not fresh enough to meet the user's needs? In these cases users should have the option of contacting different responders to obtain adequately fresh validity proofs.

5.3   Offline versus Online

The authenticatable data structures we have presented are constructed off-line at periodic intervals defined by the publisher and then pushed out to untrusted responders. While the modest delay this introduces may slightly increase the user's vulnerability to an attack employing recently revoked credentials, it promises defenses against denial of service attacks that are far simpler than are available for on-line issuance and revocation services, where Byzantine failure and secure group communication must be addressed (see for instance [19]). As we have discussed, the time-quantum assumption allows the user protocol to employ untrusted, highly available responders and allows author updates to be pulled rather than pushed.

5.4   Credential Sensitivity

Credentials may be sensitive and therefore protected. In this case, authors should not have to entrust protection to publishers. Instead, the update should not contain potentially sensitive credential content, but rather should contain only credential identifiers, such as a serial number. Thus, given a credential, the publication can be consulted to determine its validity status, while information content of the credential cannot be obtained from the publication.

5.5   Locating Responders

There are two parts to the issue of locating an appropriate responder: locating the publisher of the validity status of a given credential, and locating a responder for that publisher. In addition, a user would naturally desire a responder that is close in the network and lightly loaded with query requests being processed.

5.6   Conclusion

In this paper, we have studied the problem of disseminating an authenticated dictionary through an untrusted or partially trusted publisher. We have considered several architectural issues involved with such publication, including the necessity of receipts, the efficiency of receipts, and methods for pushing updates. In this context, we have presented efficient algorithmic solutions for a variety of levels of trust in the publisher. We have additionally provided an extremely efficient solution for the case when data removal need not be supported.

References

1. A. Anagnostopoulos, M. T. Goodrich, and R. Tamassia. Persistent authenticated dictionaries and their applications. In *Proc. Information Security Conference (ISC 2001)*, volume 2200 of *LNCS*, pages 379–393. Springer-Verlag, 2001.
2. M. Blaze, J. Feigenbaum, J. Ioannidis, and A. D. Keromytis. The KeyNote trust-management system, version 2. IETF RFC 2704, Sept. 1999.
3. M. Blaze, J. Feigenbaum, and J. Lacy. Decentralized trust management. In *Proceedings of the 1996 IEEE Symposium on Security and Privacy*, pages 164–173. IEEE Computer Society Press, May 1996.
4. A. Buldas, P. Laud, and H. Lipmaa. Accountable certificate management using undeniable attestations. In *ACM Conference on Computer and Communications Security*, pages 9–18. ACM Press, 2000.
5. P. Devanbu, M. Gertz, A. Kwong, C. Martel, G. Nuckolls, and S. Stubblebine. Flexible authentication of XML documents. In *Proc. ACM Conference on Computer and Communications Security*, 2001.
6. P. Devanbu, M. Gertz, C. Martel, and S. Stubblebine. Authentic third-party data publication. In *Fourteenth IFIP 11.3 Conference on Database Security*, 2000.
7. C. Ellison, B. Frantz, B. Lampson, R. Rivest, B. Thomas, and T. Ylonen. SPKI certificate theory. IETF RFC 2693, Sept. 1999.

8. E. Freudenthal, T. Pesin, L. Port, E. Keenan, and V. Karamcheti. dRBAC: Distributed role-based access control for dynamic coalition environments. In *Proceedings of the 22nd International Conference on Distributed Computing Systems (ICDCS'02)*. IEEE Computer Society, July 2002.

9. M. T. Goodrich and R. Tamassia. *Algorithm Design: Foundations, Analysis and Internet Examples*. John Wiley & Sons, New York, NY, 2002.

10. M. T. Goodrich, R. Tamassia, and J. Hasic. An efficient dynamic and distributed cryptographic accumulator. In *Proc. Int. Security Conference (ISC 2002)*, volume 2433 of *LNCS*, pages 372–388. Springer-Verlag, 2002.

11. M. T. Goodrich, R. Tamassia, and A. Schwerin. Implementation of an authenticated dictionary with skip lists and commutative hashing. In *Proc. 2001 DARPA Information Survivability Conference and Exposition*, volume 2, pages 68–82, 2001.

12. M. T. Goodrich, R. Tamassia, N. Triandopoulos, and R. Cohen. Authenticated data structures for graph and geometric searching. In *Proc. RSA Conference, Cryptographers Track (RSA-CT)*, volume 2612 of *LNCS*, pages 295–313. Springer-Verlag, 2003.

13. P. Kocher. A quick introduction to certificate revocation trees (CRTs), 1998. http://www.valicert.com/resources/whitepaper/bodyIntroRevocation.html.

14. N. Li and J. Feigenbaum. Nonmonotonicity, user interfaces, and risk assessment in certificate revocation. In *Proceedings of the 5th Internation Conference on Financial Cryptography (FC'01)*, volume 2339 of *Lecture Notes in Computer Science*, pages 166–177. Springer-Verlag, 2001.

15. N. Li, J. C. Mitchell, and W. H. Winsborough. Design of a role-based trust management framework. In *Proceedings of the 2002 IEEE Symposium on Security and Privacy*. IEEE Computer Society Press, May 2002.

16. N. Li, W. H. Winsborough, and J. C. Mitchell. Distributed credential chain discovery in trust management. *Journal of Computer Security*, 11(1):35–86, Feb. 2003.

17. R. C. Merkle. A certified digital signature. In G. Brassard, editor, *Proc. CRYPTO '89*, volume 435 of *LNCS*, pages 218–238. Springer-Verlag, 1990.

18. M. Naor and K. Nissim. Certificate revocation and certificate update. In *Proc. 7th USENIX Security Symposium*, pages 217–228, Berkeley, 1998.

19. L. Zhou, F. B. Schneider, and R. van Renesse. COCA: A secure distributed online certification authority. *ACM Transactions on Computer Systems (TOCS)*, 20(4):329–368, Nov. 2002.

Author Index